KU-522-352

Henry Roseveare

THE TREASURY

The Evolution of a British Institution

Allen Lane The Penguin Press

First published in 1969

Allen Lane The Penguin Press
Vigo Street, London, W.1

SBN 7139 0111 X

Printed in Great Britain by
Cox & Wyman Ltd., London, Fakenham and Reading

Contents

FOR MY MOTHER AND FATHER

Introduction

Let the books of the Treasury lie closed as religiously as the Sibyl's.
W. S. LANDOR, Pericles and Aspasia

When Thomas Madox published his classic *History and Antiquities of the Exchequer* in 1711, he wrote crushingly of his precursors, whose work – mere 'general lines or sketches' – fell 'infinitely Below the Dignity of the Subject'. In writing this book I have kept that indictment gloomily in mind. The Treasury has not yet found its Madox: this is not a *History of the Treasury*. As the first book to attempt a general outline of the Treasury's evolution it almost certainly fails to do justice to the complexity of its subject.

Properly conceived, a history of the Treasury could hardly fall short of being, at the same time, a social, an economic and a political history of Britain. Few departments of state have had interests more deeply or broadly vested in the development of British society, and no departmental function has had a longer continuous history. The specialized responsibilities of a Treasurer were the first to emerge distinctly from the amorphous royal household which governed post-Conquest England. The emergence of the Treasury as a department, with its own office, personnel and records, is another matter – as I shall shortly explain. But for most of their long history, Treasurer or Treasury have stood near or have actually been the centre of government – which will surprise no one who believes that, in any organized community, the direction of finance must occupy the centre with the compelling logic of a gravitational force.

However, the structure of English government has rarely been founded on logic. It was not until 1919 that the Haldane Committee on the *Machinery of Government* (which included some passionate critics of 'Treasury control') came to the reluctant conclusion that financial administration was an irreducible, indivisible function, and also a dominant one which must necessarily govern others. As a result, history was compelled to catch up with logic, and after 1919 the Treasury was invested with considerably more effective authority than it had exercised before.

The point is worth stressing. Although the purpose of this book is to underline the importance of the Treasury's role in English history I am not afraid that its significance is underrated: rather the reverse.

In modern times we have grown accustomed to the image of a uniquely powerful department – monolithic, mysterious, and sometimes a little menacing, looming behind the more unpopular decisions of government. But, as later chapters will show, the Treasury's economic responsibilities, like its control of the Civil Service, are – or were – relatively novel aspects of its work, dating respectively from 1947 and 1920. It is largely in our own time that the Treasury has acquired that preponderance of authority which has made it such a controversial ingredient in the structure of government. In contrast, for much of the nineteenth century, when the Treasury is popularly supposed to have enjoyed a Gladstonian summer of power and prestige, the department was acutely self-conscious of weakness. In the eighteenth century, although it was at the centre of the political world, it suffered the erosion of much of that administrative authority which it had exercised vigorously between the reigns of Charles II and Queen Anne. As for the five hundred years between the Conquest and the accession of Elizabeth I, the Treasurer was invariably eclipsed by other sources of initiative, and this embarrassingly negative point is the main burden of Chapter 1.

The power of the historic Treasury is therefore not to be taken for granted. As an institution it has been plastic, even passive, in the hands of other forces of national development. Parliament, above all, has dictated its character, not just in the formal sense of legislating for it, but in the real sense of shaping its duties after a distinct conception of parsimony and propriety. Indeed, the back-bench critics of the modern Treasury could be fairly reminded that some of its worst aspects – notably the narrow conception of 'candle-ends' Treasury control and the clumsy forms of public accounting – are very much the legacy of their predecessors. Just as the baronial critics of the medieval Crown had seen in the archaic disciplines of the Exchequer a serviceable curb on misgovernment, so in the early nineteenth century, when back-benchers exerted unusual influence on administrative reform, similar motives turned the Treasury into an austere and unimaginative agency of parliamentary control. Some of the consequences are still with us.

In this aspect of its development, then, the history of the Treasury could be said to be the history of Parliament. Other influences shaping the department are likely to seem equally impersonal, ranging as they do from the fiscal inadequacies of Stuart government and the eighteenth-century ideal of a 'balanced constitution', to the Keynesian economics of full employment and percentage targets of growth in the National Product. To that extent some chapters embody a degree of constitutional and economic background history which risks seeming elementary to a specialist and tedious to any layman who simply wants to know 'what did the Treasury really *do*?'

I have tried to answer that important question, but there is this difficulty – that at all times the Treasury has *done* an extraordinary variety of things which, in their sheer multiplicity and pettiness, are likely to prove just as tedious as my interpretative generalizations. Some of the Treasury's rulers have found it so. For example, when Sir Stafford Northcote became Financial Secretary in 1859 he was appalled by the miscellaneous character of the items on his desk (they ranged from the establishment of a money-order system with the colonies, and new regulations for the pre-payment of letters, to the extension of Carlton House Terrace and the removal of pictures from Marlborough House)[1] and before long was wondering, like Financial Secretaries before and since, just how long he could stick it. In the eighteenth century, likewise, the range of business was sufficient to require just one of a dozen permanent officials to cope with routine relations with the Army, the Navy, the Ordnance, the American customs, the garrisons at Gibraltar and Minorca, two revenue departments and the Treasurer of the Royal Household. Even to extract a 'typical day's business' from the teeming Minute Books of the late seventeenth century would be a difficult and ultimately meaningless exercise.

Of course, there are colourful stories to be culled from the records. Here (at random) one may find Charles II's hard-pressed Treasury lords wondering if they can really spare £300 to buy 'a little house near St James's Park' for one of the King's mistresses. Here, in 1739, are Walpole and his colleagues, authorizing the payment of the £250 reward for the capture of Dick Turpin. Here, in 1792, is Captain Nelson writing to 'My Lords' from the West Indies about the remittance to England of his crew's prize money.... And so one might go on, readily staging a sensational, picture-hatted pageant from the manuscripts.

But the result would be quite unfaithful to the humdrum nature of Treasury business. It was hardly exciting; it was not always important. Again, it was a Victorian Financial Secretary who shrewdly observed in 1869: 'This is a useful department to be in; it gives you the clue to most others'. But 'it does not of course compare in interest with Education and Poor law . . .'.[2] Indeed, if anything characterized the common experience of Treasury officials in the eighteenth and early nineteenth centuries it was a genteel boredom. This was a small department and they had relatively little to do, notwithstanding the apparently broad range of their nominal responsibilities. To a very large extent their duties consisted of hack-work – the mere copying, according to set forms, in a graceful hand, of certain routine documents of the utmost aridity. Little wonder that there were problems of discipline and recruitment. Little wonder that the department seemed quite incapable of meeting the challenge of the nineteenth-century 'revolution in government'. The measures which transformed this institution into the relatively formidable instrument of Gladstonian economy are, therefore, the most important in its history and they have a correspondingly large place in this narrative. They reformed a rather dreary luncheon club for superannuated gentlemen into the hard-working Victorian *élite* of first-class minds. Not that it ceased to have the character of a club, and a very exclusive one at that.* But at least hours which had once been little more than 11 A.M. to 3 P.M. came to overflow the boundaries of a normal working week, and apathy gave way to self-confidence – not to say conceit.

However, there are considerable difficulties in the way of recovering this kind of institutional life at second- or third-hand. The memoirs and reminiscences of Treasury men are rare (though never more so than today) and most of those that survive belong to the unusually literate generation which entered the department in the second half of the nineteenth century. One cannot claim, therefore, to have brought to life the 'inwardness' of the Treasury over the whole of its existence. The attempt would be pretentious, and the results superficial. But this is not to say that I regard the personalities of Treasury men, or the corporate personality of the department, as irrelevant to its formal history. Far from it. Administrative history has already suffered enough from being treated (in the way A. N. Whitehead once characterized the Lockeian view of Nature) as 'a dull affair, soundless, scentless, colourless; merely the hurrying of material, endlessly, meaninglessly'. The truth is, rather, that the seemingly inert materials of administrative history – seals, writs, minute books, files, even furnishings – are often extraordinarily eloquent of corporate personality and individual neuroses, and they deserve some attention.

One gains a sense of this from one of the welcome instances where Sir Thomas Heath's description of the Treasury in the 1920s warms into life. It is in his account of developments in the format of Treasury files – a subject banal enough, one might suppose, yet for Heath clearly charged with a significance transcending considerations of utility. Evidently anyone with doubts about the working of an intelligent principle behind the administrative universe is expected to be reassured by the Treasury's discovery in the course of nearly

* Writing of his entry into the Treasury in 1910 – when top hat and tails were still office uniform – Sir Andrew MacFadyean has recalled 'the relationship of colleagues was very much that of a rather select club'. *Recollected in Tranquillity* (1964), p. 45. Like the tails, this probably did not survive the First World War.

forty years – 1868 to 1904 – that papers filed consecutively from front to back were more efficiently viewed than those filed from back to front![3]

Seven hundred and fifty years before, in by far the best account of the machinery of English finance ever written, Richard Fitz Nigel had similarly hinted at profound mysteries underlying the 'ancient course' of the Norman Exchequer.[4] He never explained what they were, but it is easy to detect that the material appurtenances of Exchequer audit – the checkered cloth, the counters, the tally-sticks and, above all, the reverently inscribed Pipe Rolls – were instruments in an esoteric cult of exactness which mesmerized its devotees for nearly eight hundred years.

A final example of the way in which the, apparently neutral, apparatus of Treasury procedures could become highly charged with significance has more serious implications. It is provided by Pepys, who was peculiarly fitted to observe the Restoration origins of the Treasury as a department of state, with its distinct location, personnel and records. Not only was he a spending official in frequent touch with the Treasury and the Exchequer, but he was temperamentally attuned to the finer points of administrative techniques. He himself was a skilled practitioner of what would now be called 'Organization and Methods', and he looked keenly for this expertise in others. Thus, when an Exchequer official, Sir George Downing, buttonholed Pepys and the Earl of Oxford to come and admire the elegance of his book-keeping, Pepys could authoritatively commend it as 'very pretty' – which was high praise.[5] A year later, Downing was Secretary to the Treasury, one of the earliest and most creative administrators to fill that post. Thanks to his passion for order, system and remorseless book-keeping, the new Treasury department acquired the invaluable foundations of its official records.

At the same time it enjoyed the direction of a singularly competent board of Treasury lords, appointed in 1667, and it was the most efficient of their number, Sir William Coventry, who similarly invited Pepys to come and admire one of *his* innovations. It was a writing-desk-cum-filing-cabinet, with neatly labelled drawers and partitions. Furthermore, it was circular and, as Coventry demonstrated, he could swivel around inside it, reaching his papers at will. Pepys was interested; nothing could be neater.[6]

Unfortunately, the device – of which the Treasury lord was inordinately proud – came to the knowledge of the Duke of Buckingham and Sir Robert Howard, two politician-poetasters who lost no opportunity of mischief-making at the Restoration court. They hit on the idea of staging a knock-about Whitehall farce in which Coventry and a Treasury colleague would appear, each swivelling away behind his desk, arguing 'about the disposing of their books and papers, very foolish'.[7] It was, perhaps, a harmless piece of fun at the expense of men who took themselves too seriously, but the infuriated Coventry challenged the Duke to a duel, and the King, who had found Coventry far too strict for comfort, sacked him and put him in the Tower to cool. The stratagem had proved elegantly successful in the best traditions of Restoration comedy. Before long the Treasury Board was dissolved and Howard was Secretary to the Treasury.

I do not want to labour the significance of this story, but there are aspects of it which are suggestive. In the context of Charles II's financial plight it certainly mattered that an unusually conscientious Treasury leadership had been undermined by unscrupulous triflers. It mattered also that the episode had class overtones. For what had marked out the 1667 Treasury Board to the point of scandal was that they were of lower social and official status than was customary in that office – 'rougher hands' as Charles called them, who would be left unmoved by the civil importunities of an aristocratic court. As for Downing, his attributes might have been fashionable in another three hundred years. Left-wing rebel (a Cromwellian of impoverished puritan family), new-frontiersman (brought up in New England), from a red-brick university (educated at Harvard), he had a genuine enthusiasm for technological innovation and, like others who have left their mark on the Treasury – Sir Charles Trevelyan, Ralph Lingen, Warren Fisher, even Keynes – he was thought insufferable by at least some of his colleagues. Indeed, it has been seriously argued that Downing's humble origins (unlike those of Howard – who was a son of the Earl of Berkshire) disqualified him from real influence in the courtly milieu proper to a Secretary to the Treasury,[8] and although I disagree with much else in this author's analysis I am glad to take his word for that. Indeed, the undermining of the 1667 Treasury Commission could be said to mark a significant triumph for gentlemanly amateurism over real professionalism. The future, for much of the Treasury's history, was to lie with gentlemanly amateurism.

The point has a topical significance and seems calculated to appeal to those critics of the modern Treasury who see amateurism – gentlemanly or otherwise – as its major institutional failing. But the effect is quite incidental. This book was not designed as a contribution to the 'What's-wrong-with-Britain' genre. Yet, merely to describe the Treasury's later evolution is to criticize it, and for the argument on amateurism critics will find plenty of ammunition in Chapters 6, 7 and 8. The well-bred *élite* which governed the late-nineteenth-century Treasury was certainly the designed product of a social and political philosophy which saw the gentleman-administrator as a vital bulwark against democratic barbarism in the public service. Capable of moving familiarly in the social world of the governing community, the old-Etonian Treasury official was arguably more efficient than his inferiors, and for Gladstone – whose passion for equity should never be mistaken for a belief in equality – he was probably more intelligent as well. Upon these confident assumptions the Treasury embarked on the hazards of competitive Civil Service entry, with results described in Chapters 6 and 7.

However, there is nothing novel about this conspiracy theory which sees the Treasury official – at best – as an instrument of inspired incompetence, or – at worst – as the vehicle of a malign political purpose. It has been current for over a century. Similarly, the reformer's cry for 'sound business principles' in the administration of government finance will fall with dreary familiarity on the ears of anyone who has read their way through the critical periodicals of the nineteenth century. In fact, a rather one-sided debate between the Treasury and its critics has been going on since the eighteenth century, reaching high points of intensity in the 1780s, the 1820s, the 1850s, 1900 and 1942. Some sort of awareness of this has obviously contributed to the conventional image of the Treasury as an institutional bogy, fair game for journalistic pejoratives. But the awareness is of the most rudimentary kind. Every generation seems to discover for itself the peculiar iniquities of 'Treasury control' and each generation launches itself afresh upon the monster. In the process, the arguments for and against the unique theology of 'Treasury control' have acquired a monotony which may well have affected my account. But any reader who cares to follow up my summaries of successive parliamentary inquiries, notably since 1870, will probably emerge better informed about this concept than those who have been responsible in recent times for reassessments of the Treasury's historic functions. We could have been spared much well-intentioned humbug from the Treasury about the 'liberalization' of Treasury control if it had remained alive to principles of departmental responsibility enunciated in Gladstone's heyday. At the same time, critics of the Treasury could not have got away with the tendentious nonsense that has disfigured some recent attacks on its twentieth-century record.

That underlines the point with which this introduction began. The Treasury has not yet found its Madox. But the lack of an authoritative and comprehensive *History of the Treasury* is neither surprising nor particularly significant. The short explanation of the failure is that no one has been foolhardy enough to try. More surprising is the dearth of those monographs on aspects of Treasury history which clearly must precede a full-scale study. A handful exists, but – at the risk of having my motives misinterpreted – it must be said that most published monographs, however scholarly, suffer from errors of fact and interpretation which arise from their limited horizons. The common failing is to attribute uniqueness to developments within their orbit which actually have their roots outside. This is some justification for my attempt to put the cart before the horse and provide a broad sketch of the whole course of Treasury development. Sections of it, notably the account of the internal growth of the department, are based on the original records of the Treasury and reflect research which I hope to publish in more detail. I have drawn widely upon the manuscript collections of Treasury ministers and officials and upon the sources of parliamentary proceedings. The rest leans on secondary works and therefore vulgarizes intricate studies of abstruse subjects. Unfortunately it has not been possible in a book of this scale to do justice to all the dimensions of the Treasury's work – to fiscal history, parliamentary management, control of the Civil Service, overseas finance, etc. These aspects, which have a continuous history, figure only where I have thought them relevant to the main movements of the Treasury's evolution as an institution. I have had to impose my own interpretation on that, and in this respect lack of any pattern to follow has been as much of a help as a hindrance.

As it is, the plan of this book could hardly be more pedestrian. I have begun plodding forward from 1066 in order to trace the evolution of the Treasury's parent institution, the Exchequer, from its Norman origins to those reforms of the mid-sixteenth century which at last gave England a unitary financial administration. The Treasury itself does not emerge as an institution until Chapter 3, and discriminating readers may choose to begin there. But these early years do illustrate the continuity of problems which have been remarkably long-lived – administrative inertia, fiscal conservatism and the ease with which government finance can become prostituted to political expediency. They also illustrate the debts which England has sometimes incurred to individuals of outstanding vigour or exceptional vision – a de Rivaux, a Stapledon, a Cromwell or a Downing. Later centuries have been less well-endowed, but I have been careful to draw attention to men like Edmund Burke and Joseph Hume who, as critics outside the administrative system, did so much to shape the character of the nineteenth-century Treasury. Indeed, the technical developments to which they contributed are sufficiently important to deserve separate treatment, and, for that reason, Chapter 5 stands rather to one side of the main narrative of internal Treasury evolution. Similarly, the growing complexity of the Treasury's role in the twentieth century has compelled the separate treatment of its administrative, and of its economic, functions. But although reflected, in 1962, by the Treasury's functional division into two 'Sides', Pay and Management and Finance and

Economic, the separation is rather artificial and ultimately dangerous, as critics of the 1968 Fulton Report on the Civil Service would be ready to demonstrate.

On this latter document, the latest landmark in the Treasury's history, the few remarks which close the book are necessarily those of a layman and make no special claim to attention. The same apology has to be made for the whole of Chapter 9. I can boast of no inside knowledge or personal experience. I have made comparatively few demands upon Treasury officials and have badgered no Cabinet ministers. I made a point of writing this last chapter on the same basis as all the others – from published or manuscript sources accessible to the public. If this is grossly inadequate or misleading then the authorities have only themselves to blame, but, in fact, the amount of material available among official (particularly parliamentary) publications is rather greater and more revealing than the man in the street might first suppose, and I have tried to make full use of it.

Unfortunately, it is less easy to come by economic enlightenment. It would have been as much beyond my powers, as my purpose, to attempt any kind of original critique of the Treasury's economic management, but on this theme also the volume of evidence is rather too great than too small and I have confined myself to reflecting some of its features. The range and penetration of the contemporary debate upon economic management has created a critical climate quite unequalled in the Treasury's history and must be counted as a major factor in its current evolution. In purveying this material, second-hand, I will inevitably disappoint just those readers who have learnt to deplore the amateurism implicit in the post-war Treasury's faith in its educated 'laymen'. They may be the only readers to feel that in this sense, and no other, the Treasury is now getting the kind of historian it deserves.

I am equally afraid that, in traversing nine hundred years of English history by a comparatively neglected route, I have made numerous blunders – of fact and interpretation. There would have been many more but for the kindness of friends who have purged much of the grosser nonsense in my manuscript. For this, and much more, I am particularly indebted to Valerie Cromwell (and her husband, Professor John Kingman), to Henry Parris, to James Ogilvy-Webb, to Peter Marshall and to Alan Smith. Maurice Wright kindly allowed me to see the first two chapters of his important study, *Treasury Control of the Civil Service, 1854–1874* (Oxford, 1969) which has been published since this book was completed. For permission to read other material in advance of publication I am greatly indebted to Roy Macleod, Henry Parris, P. G. M. Dickson and John Sainty. Sir Roy Harrod has kindly allowed me to cite some interesting material from his biography of Keynes. Mr Shelton, of Glyn, Mills & Co., has added to my long-standing debt to him with material on A. S. Harvey. Sir Ralph Hawtrey and Sir Otto Niemeyer were good enough to answer my queries about the character of the Treasury when they entered it in 1904 and 1906 respectively, but they are in no way responsible for anything I have said about their careers or their contemporaries. My material has been drawn entirely from sources accessible to the public. That from the Public Record Office and the Treasury is Crown copyright and is cited with the permission of the Controller of Her Majesty's Stationery Office. My debts to the staffs of the British Museum and the Public Record Office are almost beyond adequate acknowledgement, and I am particularly grateful to Mr Ford of the Treasury Registrary for the helpfulness with which he put material at my disposal. Lastly, I must thank my wife for the encouragement and forbearance which has allowed this book to be completed.

SOURCE NOTES

1. A. Lang, *Life, Letters, and Diaries of Sir Stafford Northcote, First Earl of Iddesleigh* (1890), vol. I, pp. 155–6.
2. J. L. B. Hammond and L. B. Hammond, *James Stansfeld* (1932), pp. 91–2.
3. Sir Thomas L. Heath, *The Treasury* (1927), pp. 142–7. For a modern example of these taboos see D. L. Munby's evidence to the Fulton Committee on the Civil Service, *Evidence*, vol. 5(2), p. 990, para. 32.
4. Richard Fitz Nigel, *Dialogus de Scaccario* (1959), ed. C. Johnson, p. 126.
5. *The Diary of Samuel Pepys,* 14 May 1666.
6. *ibid.,* 4 July 1668.
7. *ibid.,* 6 March 1669. It is possible to supplement this account with details from British Museum manuscripts, in particular Add. MSS, 36, 916, f. 128 and Egerton MSS, 2, 539, f. 327b.
8. S. B. Baxter, *The Development of the Treasury, 1660–1702* (1957), p. 181.

CHAPTER 1

The Medieval Origins: 1066-1554

Scriptum quippe est: 'ubi est thesaurus tuus ibi est et cor tuum'.
RICHARD FITZ NIGEL, Dialogus de Scaccario, *c.* 1178

THE KING'S TREASURE

'For it is written, *where your treasure is, there will your heart be also.*'[1] Nothing could be more trite than that. And yet, if one must somehow justify the primacy of finance in the history of English government, nothing could seem more apt. Edward the Confessor would have demurred, no doubt. Sleepless one night, he is alleged to have watched tolerantly while an enterprising thief pilfered the treasure, kept – naturally enough – under the royal bed. Edward's heart was set on better things. But for the ordinary succession of post-Conquest kings, who had few claims on canonization, treasure mattered in a way which would have made that kind of restraint rather unlikely. For, even in a feudal society held together by obligations of service and payment in kind, royal administration centred necessarily upon the efficient management of monetary resources which were the sinews of government, in peace as in war. For a Richard upon his Crusades, an Edward upon his Borders, a Henry in France – indeed, for any of these warring, peripatetic kings – St Matthew and the author of the *Dialogus* knew what they were talking about.

Yet, even when one has made the elementary distinction between the custody of treasure and the administration of finance, it would be wrong to suppose that something called 'the Treasury' was at the heart of medieval English government. The king was that heart, sole and unfettered, and for the five hundred years between the Conquest and the reign of Queen Elizabeth I he could, and generally did, manage his finances through such agencies as he chose. Chancery, Chamber, Wardrobe, Treasury and Exchequer played complementary and sometimes interchangeable roles in the guardianship of the king's profit. The inconvenient essence of financial administration in medieval England was flexibility carried to the point of fluidity.

THE TREASURER AND THE EXCHEQUER

Fluidity certainly characterizes the earliest history of the Treasury. As if in some dimly lit aquarium, where the personnel of the Norman royal household loom and disappear, ambiguous, enigmatic, historians have peered about in search of the origins of the great departments of state. Fortunately, a shadowy figure seen flitting through Domesday Book appears to have been styled *thesaurarius*, and upon a consensus of learned opinion this 'Henry the Treasurer', serving William the Conqueror and perhaps his successor, takes his place as the first identifiable officer with that title.[2] Thereafter it becomes rather easier to name the lengthening succession of Treasurers than to explain their status or their functions. The origins of the office still remain as mysterious as the migration of eels.

Thus there are no signs of a distinct Anglo-Saxon office of 'Treasurer' although pre-Conquest governments were clearly highly skilled in the collecting, auditing and assaying of their cash revenues. Alfred the Great is credited with sufficient command of his annual resources to have planned a budget, and none of this expertise was lost in the Conquest. Norman financial administration followed smoothly in the wake of its predecessor and had everything to gain by doing so. As in Anglo-Saxon times, the royal treasure was located principally at Winchester, and the simple fact of the Treasurer's frequent physical separation from the markedly restless Norman court is almost enough to explain why, in advance of any departmental specialization, the Treasurer's gradually emerged as a fairly distinct office. It was not a post of the greatest importance. Although he supervised two other senior officials, the chamberlains of the Treasury, and – at 5*s*. a day – received one of the highest public salaries, the Treasurer was himself subject to the check of the King's acting deputy, the Justiciar, and also of occasional commissions composed of barons and leading members of the household. It was out of this relationship that a far more important institution, the Exchequer, gradually emerged.

For, however it might be handled, the collection, custody and disbursement of the King's revenue regularly posed problems which were judicial rather than administrative. As the author of the *Dialogus* put it in a phrase which would be serviceable at almost any time in the Treasury's later history, 'the highest skill at the Exchequer does not lie in calculations, but in judgments of all kinds'. And the judgements were crucial ones in which the King's profit had to be most scrupulously guarded against the persistent corrosion of deceit, default and neglect. This was solemn work which could be neither casual nor continuous, and for the earliest stages of its evolution the Exchequer is usually described as 'an occasion rather than a place'. The occasion settled down to the half-yearly cycle of Easter and Michaelmas. The place eventually acquired a fixed location at Westminster. Meanwhile it was in no way absurd to leave the central treasury, with its records and relics, in safekeeping at Winchester. The King's court assembled there for some of the great festivals of the year, and it was in easy reach of Porchester, the principal military staging post for France. Other strategic treasuries were scattered about England at the service of these itinerant Kings. But even before the loss of Normandy by King John had robbed Winchester of this significance, it was found convenient to bring the main treasury and its expert staff to Westminster to stay as a permanent and subordinate part of the Exchequer. There they were absorbed, and not until the late seventeenth century is it plausible to speak of 'the Treasury' as an institution distinct from the Exchequer.

By then, as we shall see, the identity of Lord Treasurers as responsible and authoritative ministers with clerks of their own had become sufficiently well established to set them notionally and physically apart from the executive routines of the Exchequer. What we now call 'the Treasury' must therefore find its parentage in the private office of the Treasurer rather than the 'treasury of the receipt' which was an intrinsic part of the ancient Exchequer. The thread of financial expertise which links the one to the other is somewhat tenuous – often tangled, often frayed. The incursions of other departments of the royal household cut across and obscure the line of advance. Initiative in financial administration remained in practice as in theory with the King.

Yet the medieval Exchequer was the vehicle of a remarkably sustained tradition in English government. Sometimes eclipsed, often ignored, the Exchequer was never quite moribund. Its lethargic rituals concealed a curiously sluggish vitality which was preserved by officials no less professional and a good deal more tenacious than their colleagues in the royal household. As an institution the Exchequer had the qualities of some great pachyderm. Ponderous, dignified, it was elephantine in its movements but elephantine in its memory. Its methods armoured it against subversion, its mystique held innovation at bay. It was, in an intricate, shuffling way, highly reliable and 'as sure as Exchequer' was an old English proverb. In the late seventeenth century one of the architects of a newly powerful Treasury, Sir George Downing, was to rhapsodize: 'the Exchequer is one of the fundamental pillars of monarchy, the easiest and the cheapest'. 'Death,' said Burke, in barbed compliment, 'domineers over every thing but the forms of the Exchequer.'

This was almost true. Held together by the reversionary interests of generations of sinecurists the eighteenth-century Exchequer still stood, the central prop of the financial system. But the prop was now rotten. Inefficiency and absenteeism had helped to drain it of strength, and even its institutional virtues were as irrelevant as some Norman castle-keep in a tranquil age. But, as we shall see, it took over fifty years for Parliament and the Treasury to supplant this obstacle, and, when they did eventually destroy it, in 1834, it had its curious revenge. Even now, the Comptroller and Auditor-General, who is the real heir of the ancient Exchequer, is far too robust to be called its ghost. With his functions of authorization, record and audit he performs some of the fundamental tasks of the institution which took shape in twelfth-century England.

THE 'ANCIENT COURSE OF THE EXCHEQUER'

Like the Treasury, the ancient Exchequer has rather mysterious origins, and its complex structure in early maturity would probably remain obscure if it was not illumined by that remarkable treatise, the 'Dialogue of the Exchequer'.[3] Its author, Richard Fitz Nigel (or Fitz Neal), the son of a distinguished Treasurer, was himself Treasurer between about 1160 and 1195 and was therefore equipped with an unrivalled knowledge of the machinery of finance. The Exchequer of which he gives such a reverently detailed account was already by the reign of Henry II a sophisticated administrative institution, already the centre of an elaborate legal mystique and already old enough for Fitz Nigel to have only a hazy and inaccurate knowledge of its origins. Yet the main structure told its own story. Divided into two parts, the so-called 'Upper' and 'Lower' Exchequers, it exactly reflected the gradual union between, respectively, the court of the Justiciar with its great clerical and baronial members and the relatively humdrum executive functions of the Treasury. With its strongroom, its watchman and its halfpenny nightlight guarding the treasure – which included Domesday Book, the King's Seal and the great account rolls of the realm as well as chests of coin and treasure – the Lower Exchequer is recognizably the central safe-deposit of the Crown. It was also the centre for the receipt and issue of revenue, served by weighers and melters skilled in their craft, by four tellers to count and record, and by the deputies of the Treasurer and the chamberlains to supervise the accounting, seal up the money bags and have custody of the keys. It was here that the routine work of the Exchequer was done, remarkably well-spaced by holy-days and vacations but growing increasingly heavy by the thirteenth century.

It is in the Upper Exchequer, at the half-yearly audits, that we shall now find the Treasurer seated, watched by his superiors, the Justiciar and the Chancellor, and even, on occasion, by the King himself. Before the assembled dignitaries, on a table five feet by ten, lay the checkered cloth like the chess-board from which the institution took its name. Just as wooden 'tally-sticks' served the Exchequer as receipts for money, with notches carefully graded from thousands of pounds – a handsbreadth – down to the merest scratch for a penny, so the cloth with its columns drawn for thousands, hundreds, scores and tens of pounds, for shillings and for pence, was a simple but foolproof accounting device in a largely illiterate society. Using counters, the amounts which, according to the record, were owing by the summoned accountant would be laid out in the upper row of columns. Below these were represented the sums which he could actually account for in either cash or tallies. Removing counter for counter a balance left in one row or the other concretely witnessed to a surplus or deficiency. Happily the accountant might find himself exactly cleared at the final, Michaelmas audit and his *quietus*, or discharge, could be carefully inscribed on the Great Roll of the Pipe. This record, so nicknamed simply because of its cylindrical shape when rolled up, lay at the heart of the seemingly primitive ritualism of the audit. It was the ultimate legal record of Exchequer proceedings, dictated by the Treasurer to a panel of scribes – with whom sat the Chancellor's clerk, the future 'chancellor of the exchequer' – and virtually unalterable except by the solemn consent of the court. The Pipe Rolls still survive, the oldest consecutive series of English public records, almost unbroken from 1156 to 1830; but as statements of the King's exact financial position they have limited value. Their entries conform to no system of balanced book-keeping; the revenue they recorded became decreasingly significant and their issues represented a fraction of the royal expenditure. Yet already by Henry II's reign they had acquired a sanctity which forbade reform. Indeed, this is true for much of the Exchequer's personnel and practice. Some of the major posts had become hereditary at an early date, and the mysteries of the King's accounts – more complex than can be briefly conveyed – had acquired a life of their own which the officials made it their business to perpetuate. It is greatly to Fitz Nigel's credit that he allows us a sly glimpse of the bored Treasurer nodding sleepily over the audit proceedings, but he himself was clearly captivated by the 'ancient course of the Exchequer' and was passive before its anomalies. With alarm one seems to discern in the 1170s already the glacial features of an administrative traditionalism which was to inch its way through several hundred years of English history.

ROYAL REVENUE

Fortunately, not all the tributaries of royal revenue flowed into this one, deeply-scored channel, which is primarily concerned with 'ordinary' revenues – regular, annual and conventional. Fiscal ingenuity and administrative enterprise tended rather to collaborate in the raising of 'extra-ordinary' revenue – occasional, often levied in emergency and sometimes unorthodox in its character. And in the course of the Middle Ages the more bountiful of these tended to flourish outside the purview of the Exchequer.

The Exchequer's jurisdiction reposed primarily upon those ancient rights and revenues arising directly or indirectly from the King's territorial sovereignty. The physical dimensions of that sovereignty had been charted in the earliest and still the most remarkable of Exchequer documents, the Domesday Book. Drawn up, it has been argued, by a single, very senior official of the Winchester Treasury, the book was essentially a summary of the great volume of reports collected by the Domesday survey of 1086 – a survey into nothing less than 'the whole wealth of England, actual and potential'.[4] Under the massive weight of its authoritative detail the land and its occupants lay pinioned in a great net of recorded obligations.

For, as supreme landlord, the King was entitled to much more than the rents of the vast Crown lands scattered throughout the counties of England. Services and dues arose from *all* the land in the possession of tenants-in-chief, lay or ecclesiastical, and many of these services could be commuted for cash. Thus the basic military obligation of knight's service in the feudal levy soon gave way to a monetary payment or *scutage* which, called for at the King's discretion, was in effect an emergency tax. Then there was *danegeld*, an Anglo-Saxon land tax unique in Western Europe which the Normans cheerfully perpetuated. Upon his own possessions, the royal demesne, the King might freely levy a *tallage*, and useful sums called *dona* or *auxilia* could be extracted from privileged communities, such as prelates, religious houses or Jews. On three clearly defined occasions the King could raise a special contribution: for the knighting of his eldest son, the first marriage of his eldest daughter or for the ransom of his own person. But on any occasion confiscations or the default of heirs might augment the royal demesne with the estates of tenants-in-chief. Bishoprics were frequently left vacant to yield up their rents, and those estates which escaped the calamity of escheat, or return to the Crown, might easily be caught up by reliefs, i.e. payments, on the succession of an heir or the marriage of a daughter. Windfalls of a pettier kind also fell into the royal lap. Wrecks, treasure trove, loot dropped by fugitive thieves and the property of felons were mingled with such dubious tribute as royal fish (whales, sturgeons), and the custody of waifs, strays and idiots.

However, far more important in a society seemingly ravaged by homicide, robbery, wounding and rape were the profits of justice, for the revenue potential of fines, fees and forfeitures was fully exploited. Unquestionably, the great elaboration of legal resources made available to the subject under Henry I and Henry II was of permanent value to the community, but looming over it one may detect the Janus-face of medieval justice, gazing one way at equity, another way at profit. By 1215 the enormous volume of financial business arising from the legal activity of the last fifty years had overwhelmed the Exchequer and induced its first administrative breakdown.

ADMINISTRATIVE PROBLEMS

Underlying this breakdown, and others which followed, were fundamental problems which face almost any system of government finance. They were an inelasticity of revenue, the incompetence of local administration and the inadequacy of central direction.

As for the first, it will be obvious from the foregoing description that too many sources of royal income were accidental, casual or customary to be capable of flexible exploitation or expansion in emergency. Those that were exploited – the profits of justice and the feudal aids and reliefs – proved very costly in terms of social and political discontent. Much of the significance of the Magna Carta of 1215 lies in its rejection of attempts, dating at least from the reign of Henry I, to make royal revenue, fixed in principle, actually elastic enough to meet unusually large royal needs. War emergencies created most of those needs, and it has been suggested that 'the whole history of the development of Anglo-Norman administration is intelligible only in terms of the scale and pressing needs of war finance'.[5] But in the face of this strain the principles of royal finance were supposed to be unyielding and Magna Carta restated them. The 'reliefs' paid on the inheritance of heirs were to be fixed – £100 for an earl, £5 for a knight; the estates of royal wards were to be responsibly administered and no widow was to be bartered into a dishonourable marriage (Clauses 2–7). 'To no one will we sell justice' (Clause 40), and 'A free man shall not be amerced for a trivial offence, except in accordance with the degree of the offence' (Clause 20). Above all, 'No scutage or aid is to be levied in our realm except by the common counsel of our realm, unless it is for the ransom of our person, the knighting of our eldest son, or the first marriage of our eldest daughter' (Clause 12).

Traditionally, a good deal more has often been read into Magna Carta than is actually there, but at least it has never been supposed to mark a financial settlement with the Crown. That the King can and must 'live of his own' was implicit in a document which so carefully circumscribed what was his own.

Concern for the King's cash solvency or realistic provision for his permanent financial needs measurable in the exact arithmetical terms of annual receipts and expenditure was incomprehensible in a society where even the Exchequer rarely produced anything so ambitious as a balance sheet or annual estimate.[6] Indeed, Exchequer machinery which continued to use roman rather than arabic numerals until its demise in the nineteenth century was not equipped for that task. Nor, for that matter, was the community really prepared before the eighteenth century to guarantee the Crown anything more than a grudging and often unrealistic provision for its permanent financial needs. The age of accurate, national finance accounts was the age of the steam engine. Instead, Magna Carta deliberately blocked some of the Crown's efforts to keep its legitimate resources in step with the times. For example, for some years King John had tried to reform the local administration of his dues by wholesale purges among those baronial maids-of-all-work, the sheriffs, and by the exaction of bigger sums from their successors.[7] Hitherto, the sheriff's relationship with the Exchequer had been based on the half-yearly payment of (i) the 'farm' of the county – a precise, customarily fixed sum for receipts from Crown estates – together with (ii) the casual, elastic receipts from justice and the yield of feudal taxes. The fixed element, based on Domesday Book valuations and unresponsive to price rises and increased costs, had permitted profits to the sheriff which may have been enormous.[8] But John's attempt to change the status of baronial sheriffs from well-to-do farmers to paid officials, yielding up all increments to the Crown, was profoundly resented, and Clause 25 of the Magna Carta required all shires to be at the ancient 'farm' without any increments. Fortunately for the Crown this ultimately proved an ineffectual obstacle to future reforms but it is an early indication of the sort of political difficulties which medieval government faced whenever it tried to exact realistic returns of its dues from an unsalaried local officialdom. Indeed, throughout a large part of English history, the burden of fiscal government was to lie heavily across the shoulders of officials who, whatever they might be called – sheriff, justice of the peace, receiver or commissioner of taxes, were essentially amateurs and local men caught up in the pressures and loyalties of local communities. At best their interests were tangential to the interests of central government, and central government invariably had to make sacrifices to them. In the eighteenth century, as we shall see, local revenue administration mattered as much as a vehicle for political influence as a fiscal resource.*

THE REFORMS OF THE THIRTEENTH CENTURY

At the centre amateurism was less of a problem, although standards sometimes wavered. It was, rather, a rigid and unimaginative professionalism which allowed twelfth-century methods to fall behind thirteenth-century problems. By King John's reign the Pipe Rolls, pedantically recording every item of arrears and current obligations, had become choked with a vast body of small debts arising largely from the Crown's novel judicial exactions. It required something special in the nature of vigour and inventiveness to break through the problem.

Fortunately, this was forthcoming. The thirteenth century witnessed some of those rare spasms of reforming initiative which have occasionally lifted English government, by its boot-straps, to a higher plane of competence. The strong man in this case was Peter de Rivaux, a specially trusted Poitevin adviser of young Henry III. The fact that between 1232 and 1233 he was appointed simultaneously to every important financial office in England and Ireland, including twenty-one shrievalties, was less a manifestation of autocratic favouritism than a confession that only in this extraordinary way could the Crown now control the 'commanding heights' of the financial system. Nothing less could ensure that effective reforms of the central and local organization would march in step. The results were seen in a drastic overhaul of Exchequer business. Arrears were strictly reviewed, sheriffs displaced. Their office ceased to be lucrative. The Exchequer's own type of incompetence and corruption was purged and a more versatile system of records came to the rescue of the overburdened Pipe Rolls. In several of its aspects the thirteenth-century Exchequer acquired standards of professionalism which outlived de Rivaux's fall in 1234.

Simultaneously, however, one may discern a line of development in English government which was to deprive the Exchequer or the Treasurer of any chance of monopolizing the direction of financial policy. Not that they had ever done so. The King, it has already been emphasized, was the effective centre of the system and all agencies of

* Even in the late nineteenth century, sub-postmasterships were the local perquisites of the governing political party, and collectors of income tax in Ireland remained so until 1912.

government were manifestations of his household and his will. Thus the logistics of an itinerant royal court ensured that it was the more mobile 'Chamber' of the King's household, attendant on his person, which was the agency of day-to-day, and hand-to-mouth, finance. Furthermore, by one of those obscure processes of refinement which make medieval English government seem like a set of Chinese boxes, an inner department of the Chamber, called the Wardrobe, came to be the specialist accounting and financial department of the household. Associated with de Rivaux's ascendancy, this development also outlasted him, and the subsequent alternation of Wardrobe and Chamber as the directing organs of medieval government is the main burden of its administrative history.

The Treasurer's status in a reformed Exchequer was therefore reduced 'to a position of purely administrative importance . . . a process which greatly increased the dignity and administrative independence of the Treasurer but reduced his sphere to that of routine finance and removed him from the centre of politics'.[9] Some of de Rivaux's successors were of very inferior quality and at least one was disgraced for taking bribes. Occasionally, it is true, the Treasurer's office was to be held by men of considerable stature. Walter Langton (1295–1307) has been described as 'the first treasurer to attain the position of virtually principal minister'[10] and Walter Stapledon (1320–21, 1322–5) was to achieve even more as a reformer than de Rivaux. But this should not conceal a fundamental deficiency in the department which endured until the late sixteenth century: 'the medieval exchequer . . . had not, and could not have, any financial policy. The king lived from day to day.'[11]

This makes it all the more interesting that spasmodic baronial reform movements should have seen the regeneration of the Treasurer and the Exchequer as one of their most important objectives. For example, the so-called Provisions of Oxford of 1258, and Provisions of Westminster of 1259, were baronial schemes which sought to reverse recent trends and oblige all revenues to pass through the Exchequer under the eyes of a responsible Treasurer. They failed, and between 1263 and 1268 the Exchequer actually collapsed again under the weight of its existing business. Once again the Pipe Roll procedures had to be relieved by clerical innovation in the accounting and recording methods, some of which were embodied in the Statute of Rhuddlan of 1284. But the years 1309–11 saw a fresh attempt to reinstate the Exchequer's sole jurisdiction over all receipts of the realm, and the culmination of the process arrived between 1321 and 1325 when Walter Stapledon took the whole system in hand, modernized the Exchequer's book-keeping, diversified the records, increased the staff and strictly defined their functions. It was a major spring-clean and the mark it left endured until the important reforms of the sixteenth century.

This concern of the baronial leaders of the community with the methods and forms of financial administration has suggested to historians that they saw in the Exchequer and its rituals something 'more constitutional' than Wardrobe or Chamber finance. Even Richard Fitz Nigel, who, in his prefatory remarks to the *Dialogus*, had presented the King's financial claims in the exalted terms of Divine Right, had gone on to say:

> The Exchequer has its own rules. They are not arbitrary, but rest on the decisions of great men; and if they are observed scrupulously, individuals will get their rights, and your majesty will receive in full the revenue due to the Treasury.

This is a classic statement of faith in the capacity of an institution to embody the rule of law and, indeed, there is plenty of evidence to show that the 'ancient course of the Exchequer' was for long regarded as a major constitutional guarantee of responsibility and propriety in the financial dealings of the Crown. It fell short of providing anything resembling independent 'Treasury control', for there could be no regulating will independent of the absolute and potentially extravagant will of the King. Not until after the Revolution of 1688 was the dilemma posed by the administrative conscience of the Treasury and the arbitrary will of the Crown solved in favour of departmental authority. But the aspiration to keep the financial initiative of the Crown within conventional and approved bounds was made evident from an early date.

THE BEGINNINGS OF PARLIAMENTARY CONSENT

This aspiration emerges most clearly in the sphere of extra-ordinary revenue. Since the middle of the twelfth century the rigidity of traditional revenues and the abandonment of danegeld after 1162 had been offset by some quite striking changes in the system of taxation. Experiments were made in the taxation of income and chattels, in attempts to re-assess taxation on land and in the development of an effective customs system. All three are important, but particularly the first for it led not only to a fairly regular system of direct taxation on personal wealth but gradually nourished one of the vital relationships of national development – the practice of representative parliamentary consent to extra-ordinary supply.

The principle of consent to special monetary contributions was not novel. However fearsome and implacable the twelfth-century Crown might sometimes appear in its ordinary financial prerogatives, the posture of baronial subjects had never resembled that of toads under the harrow, and to the requests of the King for a 'gracious' aid in some alleged necessity the great magnates of the realm might, or even might not, give their consent. They did so as individuals; it was not always clear that the majority could bind the minority, and the rates of contribution to which they agreed might vary between them. Before each one of them lay the problem of passing the tax obligation on to their tenants by a process of negotiation. Even on the royal demesne, where the formalities of consent did not arise, an emergency tallage was a matter for piecemeal settlement with the boroughs and individual communities. However, in the course of the thirteenth century this feudal individualism gave way to agreements of a more corporate nature. The 'great council' of the magnates still dominated the bargaining. After 1237, when there was a first-class row with the King, they collectively refused nine successive requests, for they were determined that these emergency aids should not degenerate into a regular tax. As it was, they conceded occasional grants only in return for concessions from the King – the confirmation of charters, the redress of grievances, and the promise that the demand for aid would not be repeated. Nevertheless, it was in the interests of both parties that the wider community should be implicated in these agreements. Contributions were levied on all men but the very poorest, and the assessment and collection depended largely on the assistance of the local communities. There could be no better way of securing their collaboration than by involving them in the grant. Thus in the second half of the thirteenth century the practice gradually developed of summoning representatives of the boroughs and the shires with full powers to negotiate the details of the grant. The formalities of their consent did not imply their right of refusal. Their 'full powers' were a guarantee of submission rather than of independence. Indeed, the whole development by which representatives of the nation were drawn upon to bind the community in Parliament to a comprehensive tax has been represented as a triumph for a far-sighted monarchy. In the process a non-feudal collective unity had emerged.[12]

At the same time there were gains for the community. In the crisis year of 1297 Edward I conceded, at the point of the baronial sword, the regular principle of representative consent to extra-ordinary taxation, and by 1340 any remaining ambiguities about the taxation of the royal demesne or the levying of customs duties were cleared in favour of parliamentary consent. 'Modern parliamentary control over the purse,' it has been said, 'dates effectively from the Statute of 1340',[13] and although this may seem to antedate by five hundred years the establishment of truly effective, *modern* parliamentary control of the purse (in the Exchequer and Audit Departments Act of 1866), the later Middle Ages unquestionably witnessed some precocious experiments in the regulation of royal finance. Extra-ordinary parliamentary grants were often appropriated to specific purposes and machinery was sometimes set up for retrospective audits. Estimates of expenditure were demanded and misappropriation searched out for punishment by parliamentary commissions not very dissimilar in powers from the modern Parliamentary Accounts Committee.

All this will seem a little less surprising if it is appreciated that the principle of 'appropriation' was implicit in the feudal foundations of royal revenue. As we have seen, aids were given for specific purposes or in recognized circumstances, and it was always axiomatic that customs tolls were designated for the protection of English commerce on the high seas. Indeed, it was arguable that the same concept of obligation and trust extended to the use of the King's ordinary revenues for the good of the commonweal. To make that trust explicit was therefore no profound constitutional innovation in the Parliaments of the fourteenth and fifteenth centuries and any attempts to exploit it against the Crown were strongly resisted.

Nevertheless, the main point stands: the community, represented with increasing effectiveness by the Commons in Parliament, was capable of a lively concern for the efficiency of the Crown's financial administration. 'Throughout the fifteenth century,' writes Professor Jacob, 'the commons took the greatest interest in public finance' – 'not only because they saw in the King's fiscal difficulties the opportunity to increase their own authority', but because 'they were also concerned to ensure that the King should have the fullest possible revenue from, and make the best possible use of, his own resources'.[14] The latter passage has more than immediate significance. It holds the clue to a major ambiguity in parliamentary attitudes towards Crown finance which was to survive in theory until the late eighteenth century and in practice until the early nineteenth. Put simply – the parliamentary aspiration for an effective administration of public finance invariably fell short of a determination to *control* that administration. It is therefore no use imagining that the House of Commons was always heading remorselessly towards some Gladstonian apotheosis of 'the public purse'. The ideal was, rather, a competent, solvent and essentially autonomous Crown which did not need to be curbed by hazardous exercises in parliamentary opposition. Until the nineteenth century the House of Commons was conceptually and institutionally unequipped for anything more strenuous, and, as we shall see, this had an important, if negative, influence on the development of the Treasury.

BORROWING AND DEBT MANAGEMENT

Meanwhile, there seems to be little evidence that the concern of fifteenth-century Parliaments had any influence on the development of the Exchequer. Their anxiety about royal solvency, expressed in legislation to restore extravagantly distributed land to the Crown's possession, hardly offset chronic deficiencies in an aspect of Exchequer administration which has not yet been mentioned – that is, the raising of loans. Yet there was nothing new about the problem. From the earliest times kings had had to borrow to cover deficits, meet emergencies and, above all, bridge the gap between needing and actually receiving the laboriously collected fruits of their revenue. They had turned to wealthy merchants like William Cade of St Omer, indispensable to Henry II for the breadth of his commercial contacts as well as for his riches. Aaron of Lincoln, on the other hand, was the greatest of that small and vulnerable community of Jews whose whole business it was to lend at interest. At his death in 1185 Aaron's assets were so large that the Crown, to whom all usurers' estates were conveniently forfeit, had to set up special Exchequer machinery to administer them. But by 1290 the Jewish community, frequently mulcted, maltreated and occasionally murdered, was sufficiently dispensable to be expelled by Edward I. Italian business houses – the Riccardi, Frescobaldi, Bardi, Peruzzi – took over their role, and they did so on the credit of a revenue which since 1275 had been healthily reinforced by permanent customs duties. For centuries to come royal credit was to be directly vested in the conditions of trade, thus ensuring – if nothing else did – that the profit and power of the merchant would go hand-in-hand with the profit and power of the King. For the fourteenth-century de la Pole family of Kingston-upon-Hull, the first merchant–financier dynasty to be ennobled (as Earls, later Dukes, of Suffolk) it manifestly did.

Unfortunately, the price of royal borrowing ran to more than the distribution of honours. It proved more costly than a rate of interest which, in defiance of the Church's prohibition of usury, might rise to 33 per cent. At best, it told heavily on Exchequer machinery, and, at worst, jeopardized the stability of the throne.

The fault, such as it was, lay partly in the incapacity of the ancient course of the Exchequer to cope, over prolonged periods, with large-scale debt management. In a narrow sense, loan transactions were 'irregular' and fitted awkwardly into the neat routines of receipt and issue. They led to confusion, cancellations and all kinds of fictions in Exchequer records. In the broader context of financial administration they strained the system of revenue collection to the point of collapse. For example, it was the common practice for the Exchequer to send off creditors as well as spending officials to collect their money at source – from the local revenue agents. In this manner quite a high proportion of revenue never passed through the Lower Exchequer, although recorded and audited in the Upper Exchequer as if it had. Unhappily it was also rather common for the creditor to find the revenue collector in arrears or heavily overdrawn. Sometimes the King might abrogate the liabilities assigned on a particular revenue and insist on the cash receipts being transmitted to him without diversion. The liabilities were postponed and the disappointed creditor sent off on some fresh goose-chase, while the Exchequer and the revenue collector adjusted their records to the new state of affairs. In the reign of Henry IV (1399–1413), for example, the volume of such valueless assignments issued by the Exchequer rose to about £10,000 per annum against a revenue which averaged £90,000 per annum, and there was worse to come as royal revenue slumped below £50,000 to a mere £33,000 per annum during the 1450s.[15] The political effect of these bad debts upon the precarious Lancastrian dynasty can be imagined.

But the full responsibility for this lay in theory and in practice with the Crown. There were no enforceable obligations upon a debtor King. He could, and sometimes did, break his word with impunity. Indeed, underlying a large area of royal borrowing there was a constitutional theory of obligation which made the credit relationship quite unreal. The well-to-do subject could be summoned to lend money in proportion to his wealth without any option of refusal, for it was his duty and he could count himself lucky to be repaid, let alone receive interest. 'Forced loans' of this kind were to enjoy an Indian summer in the reign of Charles I. Meanwhile, on loans based on more businesslike negotiations with merchants and magnates, realism demanded an interest rate above 25 per cent, for repayment might take years. There was very little the Exchequer could do to redeem this state of affairs. In the hands of a thriftless King it was passive if not impotent. Reduced to a mere accounting agency for transactions which largely took place beyond its control, it was rarely in step with events, and the preparation of a balance sheet of the King's position in 1433 was a rather unusual measure of initiative in a newly-appointed Treasurer. It revealed to Parliament a debt of £165,000 – which was to double before mid century.

DEVELOPMENTS IN THE EXCHEQUER

The failure, although rooted in the Exchequer's character, is the more egregious in the light of circumstances which were potentially favourable to its influence. For during the reign of Richard II (1377–99) the Chamber and Wardrobe had fallen back from their earlier pre-eminence and were no longer major administrative departments. In theory at least, the financial field was clear if the officials of the Exchequer were capable of asserting themselves. But they were not. 'The late fifteenth-century Exchequer was not like the modern treasury. It was entirely governed by routine: there was no elasticity of any kind.'[16] And, in case the authority of this opinion should seem undermined by its naïve faith in the modern Treasury, one can add another verdict, that the fifteenth-century Exchequer 'had reached a point of development which made changes not only unnecessary but even difficult'.[17]

Yet there were *some* significant internal developments in the department which helped to differentiate its functions and prepare the ground for the emergence of a purely administrative department, the Treasury, from the very mixed character of the medieval institution. For instance, the reforms of de Rivaux and Stapledon had greatly reinforced the judicial activities of the Upper Exchequer. It was, in fact, a revenue court, a court of common law and a court of equity, and in all these roles must be distinguished from the several distinct appeal tribunals which were called the Court of Exchequer Chamber.[18] Not surprisingly, the Barons of the Exchequer, who carried the main burden of this judicial work, became increasingly drawn from the legal profession by the fourteenth century and had to be kept in touch with the administrative technicalities of finance by a 'cursitor Baron' who was skilled in the 'cursus' or 'ancient course' of the Exchequer. But professionalism was less evident elsewhere in the department. On the one hand, the lay element in the Exchequer remained associated with certain hereditary posts, like the two Chamberlainships, and laymen being, almost by definition, unlettered, they were usually found in relatively undemanding posts doing the rougher work.[19] The more responsible tasks of recording and auditing had always been in the hands of clerics – the tonsured, although not necessarily ordained, mainstays of the medieval civil service. They had the advantage, as celibates, of being unlikely to found hereditary dynasties of office-holders, and they were also highly mobile, passing through various branches of the King's service into the ultimate haven of a benefice. But this convenient division of labour began to break down in the fourteenth century and by the fifteenth the entry of laymen into government was sufficiently marked to look like a stampede of 'rising civil servants on the make'.[20] The first lay Treasurer had been appointed in 1340 and in 1410 the Chancellorship of the Exchequer passed finally into the hands of laymen. The latter, however, was still a minor official with duties confined to the Upper Exchequer. He kept the Exchequer seal, supervised some of the records, and appointed a few underlings but he had no administrative or judicial responsibilities and he was certainly not the Treasurer's right-hand man. The Treasurer, whose authority spanned Upper and Lower Exchequers, began to appoint a deputy or under-treasurer in the fifteenth century who before long had become an important officer of state, usually of the knightly class and often a lawyer by training.[21] The ultimate authority of the Chancellor of the Exchequer began its growth from his union with the office of under-treasurer in the mid sixteenth century.

The rise of the laymen, however, is associated in the Exchequer with two divergent but equally dangerous tendencies. On the one hand, the under-treasurer became a 'political' appointment in the sense that he came and went with his master, the Treasurer – and there were many Treasurers in the troubled years of the fifteenth century. On the other hand, the new lay incumbents of Exchequer offices began to put down roots, hold their appointments for life and procure the privilege of appointing deputies and successors.[22] In fact, the seeds of sinecurism were quite rapidly planted, and although the fruits were not rotten until the eighteenth century there may have been some immediate loss of efficiency. Certainly it was not from the Exchequer that the Crown's financial redemption was to come. It came, as was appropriate, from the sources of all medieval government – from the King, from his household and from the Crown lands.

THE RECOVERY OF ROYAL SOLVENCY

The paradox of the Lancastrians' plight, which did more than anything to permit their defeat in the Wars of the Roses, lies in the fact that when Henry Bolingbroke seized the Crown in 1399 'he most probably became the greatest landowner that England had seen since the days of the Conqueror'.[23] Heir to the vast estates of the Duchy of Lancaster, vested in the huge possessions of his wife and ruler now of the great Crown estates, his capacity to 'live of his own' – however narrowly 'his own' might be interpreted – was assured if he acted with vigour. Notwithstanding the rapid erosion of these resources during the next fifty years the same was still true for his successors, and the triumphant Edward IV's promise in Parliament to 'lyve uppon my nowne, and not to charge my Subgettes but in grete and urgent causes' held real hope of fulfilment. Nothing original was required of financial administration. The material and the pattern lay to hand. Thus, while Edward's energy was outstanding, his methods were conventional. They were a natural and un-self-conscious revival of the Chamber administration that had characterized English government since the twelfth century. The Chamber, with its coffers directly under the King's eyes, again became the main treasury, yet supplementing rather than supplanting the Lower Exchequer. The Upper Exchequer continued to be the ultimate court of record, although it was found convenient to audit many revenues simply and directly in the King's Chamber and to exempt certain trusted officials from its jurisdiction. Later, after 1485, as Henry VII found his feet, the Exchequer briefly resumed its traditional authority over cash receipts and accounting as if nothing had happened.[24]

THE TUDOR 'REVOLUTION IN GOVERNMENT'

Yet something had happened which, before very long, modified the Exchequer's structure and significantly adjusted its place in English government. The revival of Chamber finance by the Yorkist Kings was initially based on a system of Crown land administration which borrowed heavily from the personnel and practices of ordinary baronial estate management. Both commodities, personnel and practices, were highly professional – direct, flexible and efficient. The injection of these qualities and these men markedly influenced the 'civil service' of the day. However, everything in the system still depended on the King, upon his vigour, watchfulness and direction. In this respect the Tudor dynasty joined rather than initiated a tradition which had been worthily sustained by Edward IV and Richard III. Henry VII is marked out more by success and single-mindedness than by any originality. Forever hoarding, personally auditing, signing, or even drafting his Chamber treasury accounts, Henry VII was an outstanding exponent of medieval government at its most thrifty and conscientious.

But what might happen under a less attentive King? The character of Henry VIII raised the question, although not in an acute form for he was no sluggard. Nevertheless, his reign experienced a conjunction of circumstances which helped to shape this direct and flexible system into a sturdier, self-sufficient mould. Apart from an inherent tendency towards formalization in any type of improvisation there were good practical reasons for putting *ad hoc* estate management on a sounder footing. A perfectly respectable example already existed in the Court of the Duchy of Lancaster – a formal department administering those vast estates with a high degree of efficiency. Furthermore, there was the problem raised by the fruits of the break with Rome – the monastic lands and the revenues of the Church. These revenues were new, distinct and problematical and required careful attention. Finally, there was the man – Thomas Cromwell – in whom has been seen the imaginative architect of a reformed financial system.[25]

The case for Cromwell as a revolutionary innovator has been challenged, but the main argument in his favour manifestly stands. Between 1532 and 1540, through a plurality of offices (the King's principal secretary, Lord Privy Seal, Master of the Rolls, Master of the Jewels and Chancellor of the Exchequer) this protégé of Wolsey dominated the organs of English government more effectively and more creatively than any minister since de Rivaux's day. From his vantage points he was able to impose system, if not shape, upon the now bountiful revenues of the Crown. Thus in 1536 a Court of Augmentations, modelled closely on the Court of the Duchy of Lancaster, was set up to administer all the lands, notably monastic, newly added to the Crown's possessions. The older Crown lands remained in the hands of General Surveyors who were not institutionalized as a Court until 1542. But years earlier Cromwell's work in this field had indicated the route of developments which were to be completed after his fall. In a similar manner, a Court of First Fruits and Tenths (dealing with ecclesiastical revenue), and a Court of Wards (handling the King's feudal claims upon tenants-in-chief) emerged in 1540 as distinct, statutorily-based institutions.

The essence of this achievement lay in the replacement of the fugitive improvisations of Chamber finance with institutions far more stable, if more bureaucratic. Organs of the King's government no less than their precursors, these novel departments managed to embody a qualitative advance which made them truly national institutions as well. With their statutory foundations and expert staffs they promised to have a permanence and professionalism which would transcend the passing whims of the King and render his personal supervision unnecessary. In addition they had solid technical merits which outmatched those of older national institutions such as the Exchequer. They combined, in fact, all the best elements of household government – directness of method, simplicity of accounting – with the orderliness and judicial authority which had been the traditional monopoly of the 'ancient course'. Ultimately, when their amalgamation with the Exchequer took place in 1554, this directness and simplicity was to be their greatest contribution to the machinery of English finance.

THE LEGACY OF THE MIDDLE AGES

However, that consummation belongs to the next chapter. The transmission of the virtues of Henry VIII's revenue courts to a reinvigorated Exchequer marks the beginning of a new era but not necessarily the death of the old. The Exchequer, as I have indicated, was not prepared to be reformed, let alone die, without a struggle, and the 'ancient course' was to prove a sturdy vehicle of medievalism well into the nineteenth century. There were, in addition, several other medieval legacies to late-sixteenth-century government which were of questionable value and stubborn vitality. The problem of an incompetent in local revenue administration was to produce renewed difficulties in Elizabeth's reign, and the handing over of the Customs collection to syndicates of merchant-financiers was a singular confession of administrative failure in one of the most promising areas of royal revenue. Crown borrowing, likewise, was to lurch through the catastrophic expedients of Henry VIII's reign – which incidentally saw the debasement of the coinage – into the tortuous experiments of Elizabeth in the continental money market. Bearing in mind the immature character of financial institutions in sixteenth-century England it must be doubted whether royal credit could have been more sensitively handled, but as it was, the constitutional theory, which justified forced loans and those extortionate mulcts which were laughingly known as 'benevolences' and 'free gifts', rendered finesse in the courtship of the moneyed community rather superfluous. The only drawback was that the relative success of Henry VIII's recourse to compulsion tended to undermine the goodwill of those Parliaments which were called upon for emergency supply. The docility of the sixteenth-century House of Commons was never to be taken for granted and there were stormy passages in supply debates which contrast oddly with the fulsome language of most finance bills. Indeed, the Tudors were rather lucky to acquire from Parliament a new fiscal resource called the 'subsidy', which was a considerable improvement on their other medieval tax legacies. Since 1334 the principal form of extra-ordinary aid, called the 'Fifteenth and Tenth',* had ceased to be a realistic tax, freshly assessed on the growing wealth of the community, but had become fixed at no more, and usually less, than the

* A tax on the assessed capital value of movable goods, one fifteenth in the counties, one tenth in the cities and towns. By the sixteenth century, exemptions granted for impoverished areas had reduced the value to about £33,000 but it was common for Parliament to grant it in multiples of the 1334 valuation. Thus the four Fifteenths and Tenths granted for defence against the Armada were theoretically worth over £120,000.

sum yielded in 1334 – that is, about £39,000. But the subsidy, which evolved between 1512 and 1515, was a remarkably complex tax on the income, wages and movable possessions of every person in the country, and although its effectiveness declined in the course of the century it began life as an unusually realistic levy.[26] Together with the decrepit Fifteenth and Tenth it did service until the Civil War.

It was, therefore, a very mixed inheritance of the medieval and the modern which Henry VIII passed on to his successors. The fluidity which had characterized English government for so long had certainly gone – and this was not the least of the Tudor achievements – but such flexibility as remained in the Cromwellian system left it doubtful from which direction administrative initiative in financial matters was likely to come. From the King? From the new 'Privy Council'? The major drawback of Cromwell's ascendancy was that it left only one possible answer, which was to be invalidated by his fall.

Could it then be the Treasurer's turn? The question, artificial as it is, seems more than a little absurd if it is addressed to the Treasurers of the fifteenth century. Too many were sinecurists and nonentities – and if they were rich nonentities so much the better for it became common by mid-century to appoint only Treasurers wealthy enough to keep the Exchequer oiled with loans from their own resources. Even in the early sixteenth century it would be unwise to read too much into the Gilbertian title of 'Lord High Treasurer'. Peers they often were – Henry VII and Henry VIII were served by the Dukes of Norfolk – and they ranked very high among the dignified officers of state. But as Treasurers they were not yet the arbiters of national finance, and there was, as yet, no sign of any commanding institution called 'the Treasury'.

SOURCE NOTES

1. The text is from St Matthew, 6, v. 21.
2. See H. G. Richardson and G. O. Sayles, *The Governance of Medieval England from the Conquest to Magna Carta* (1963), p. 220. However, S. B. Chrimes in *An Introduction to the Administrative History of Medieval England* (1966), prefers William de Pont de l'Arche (*c.* 1130) 'as being the first identifiable holder of the office' – p. 28.
3. *Dialogus de Scaccario* (1950), ed. C. Johnson.
4. V. H. Galbraith, *The Making of Domesday Book* (1961), pp. 53, 202–3.
5. J. O. Prestwich, 'War and Finance in the Anglo-Norman State', in *Transactions of the Royal Historical Society*, 5th Series, vol. 4, 1954, p. 36.
6. H. Jenkinson and D. M. Broome, 'An Exchequer Statement of Receipts and Issues, 1339–1340', *English Historical Review,* vol. 58, 1943.
7. B. E. Harris, 'King John and the Sheriffs' Farms', *English Historical Review,* vol. 79, 1964, p. 532.

8. M. Mills, 'The Reforms at the Exchequer, 1232–42', *Transactions of the Royal Historical Society*, 4th Series, vol. 10, 1927.
9. R. F. Treharne, *The Baronial Plan of Reform, 1258–63* (1932), p. 16.
10. S. B. Chrimes, *An Introduction to the Administrative History of Medieval England* (2nd edn, 1966, p. 134).
11. F. M. Powicke, *King Henry III and the Lord Edward* (1947), p. 120.
12. R. S. Hoyt, 'Royal Taxation and the Growth of the Realm in Medieval England', *Speculum,* vol. 25, 1950; J. G. Edwards, 'The *Plena Potestas* of English Parliamentary Representation', in *Oxford Essays . . . to H. E. Salter* (1934).
13. B. Wilkinson, *Constitutional History of Medieval England, 1216–1399* (1958), vol. 3, p. 338.
14. E. F. Jacob, *The Fifteenth Century, 1399–1485* (1961), p. 78.
15. A. Steel, *The Receipt of the Exchequer, 1377–1485* (1954), pp. 105, 107, 114, 323.
16. Jacob, *op. cit.,* p. 446.
17. G. R. Elton, *The Tudor Revolution in Government* (1953), p. 13.
18. Sir William Holdsworth, *A History of English Law* (7th edn, 1956), vol. I, pp. 238, 242.
19. *The Collected Papers of T. F. Tout* (1934), vol. 3, 'The Civil Service in the Fourteenth Century', p. 201.
20. Steel, *op. cit.*, p. 122.
21. J. L. Kirby, 'The Rise of the Under-Treasurer of the Exchequer', in *English Historical Review,* vol. 72, 1957, pp. 674–5.
22. J. C. Sainty, 'The Tenure of Offices in the Exchequer', in *English Historical Review,* vol. 80, 1965, pp. 453–4.
23. B. P. Wolffe, 'Acts of Resumption in the Lancastrian Parliaments, 1399–1456', in *English Historical Review,* vol. 73, 1958, p. 584.
24. B. P. Wolffe, 'The Management of English Royal Estates under the Yorkist Kings', in *English Historical Review,* vol. 71, 1956, pp. 11–15.
25. The classic exposition of Cromwell's claims is Professor G. R. Elton's *Tudor Revolution in Government* (1953).
26. R. S. Schofield, 'The Geographical Distribution of Wealth in England, 1334–1649', in *Economic History Review,* 2nd Series, vol. 18, 1965.

CHAPTER 2

The Lord Treasurer: 1554-1667

All Treasurers, if they do good service to their masters, must be generally hated.
KING JAMES I

THE REINVIGORATED EXCHEQUER

While Thomas Cromwell lived – a superb administrative juggler – the expensive anomalies of the system of parallel revenue courts were obscured by his sheer dexterity in making them work. But within a few years of his disgrace and execution in 1540 a process of consolidation began. In 1547 the Court of General Surveyors and the Court of Augmentations were amalgamated in a greater Court of Augmentations, and in 1554, after two years of deliberation, Exchequer jurisdiction was restored over all but two financial agencies – the Court of Wards, which was to survive until the Civil War, and the Court of the Duchy of Lancaster, which has remained intact to our own day.

Those who took part in the formal ceremonies of 25 and 26 January 1554, when the Exchequer was invested with its powers, believed them to mark a restoration of the 'ancient course' to its pristine authority and purity. This over-simplified view of the Exchequer's traditional role is interesting in itself; it reflects the professional confidence of Exchequer officials in the all-sufficiency of their court, and this confidence was to play an important part in its future. But 1554 is more significant for marking a new departure. The restored Exchequer of 1554 was greatly the richer for its Cromwellian inheritance. In its amalgamation with the Court of Augmentations it had absorbed, not demolished, the techniques of audit and control practised in the new revenue courts. Its seven auditors of land revenues now combined the functions of the fourteenth-century Exchequer auditors of 'foreign accounts' with those of the modern Court of Augmentations. They dealt with a wide range of revenue accounts 'augmentation-wise' – that is more simply and directly than those still heard by the twelfth-century rituals of the Pipe Office. A few years later, in 1560, Elizabeth permanently revived the two 'auditors of imprests' who had also been members of the Court of Augmentations. They were to deal with the accounts of Ireland, the Mint, loans, war expenditure, the Navy, the Ordnance, the Works, etc., 'prestwise', which also meant simplicity and dispatch. By the early seventeenth century, it has been calculated, over ninety per cent of government revenue was being audited by machinery which the Exchequer had not possessed before 1554.[1]

Pastured upon this rich crop of new, fee-paying business it was now high summer for the officials of the Exchequer and they should have been happy. The Exchequer was, for the first time, a truly national treasury. All but a fraction of the Crown's revenue now passed under its purview if not actually through its hands and the four tellers and, indeed, all the old officers of the department now assumed a new importance. But new opportunities stimulated new greeds, and along the boundaries between 'the ancient course' and the newly incorporated methods they fought each other like ferrets to mark out their profits and jurisdictions. For the next few decades the Exchequer was shaken by a conflict fought almost entirely in terms of ancient and questionable precedents.[2] And the result, a triumph for antiquarianism which gave the 'Clerk of the Pells' the right to keep his expensive duplicate Issue Roll and the Pipe Office some claim on the imprest accounts, added nothing to efficiency. Rather, it left the Exchequer deeply and enduringly marked by a rigidly self-centred conservatism. The entrenched positions consolidated during this 'war in the Exchequer' were to prove invulnerable to all reform for another two hundred years.

THE LORD TREASURER AND HIS AUTHORITY

But while ossification had set in within fifty years of the Exchequer's reconstruction, the Treasurer took on a new lease of life, full of vigour and authority. The contrast itself serves to give forewarning of the approaching separation between the two departments, although for the moment no significant organic change accompanied this shift of vitality. Like his fellow-officials, the Treasurer was believed to possess powers hallowed by antiquity and guaranteed by utility. To meddle with them for the sake of reform or aggrandizement would have been a kind of sacrilege, unthinkable to a bureaucracy of *dévots*. As it was, in formal dignity as opposed to real power, the Lord Treasurer now ranked high enough, second only to the Lord Chancellor among the lay officers of state. His authority rested formally on two appointments theoretically distinct and separately made. As Treasurer of the Exchequer he was appointed by humdrum Letters Patent and sworn in before the Barons of the Exchequer. As Lord Treasurer of England he received the tall willow wand of office, the white staff – to lean on when he was weary, suggested Chief Justice Coke, or to beat off importunate suitors. His duties, as defined by the oath he took before the Lord Chancellor, were to serve the King and people, do right by rich and poor, counsel the King, keep his treasure, and do everything in his power to secure the King's due profit. For his pains he received (officially) £1 a day and a small allowance for robes. His tenure was none too secure, and much inferior to that of the Chancellor of the Exchequer who until 1672 was thought to be unimportant enough to appoint for life. To dismiss a Lord Treasurer out of hand it was sufficient to break his wand. In practice, of course, these exalted officers were allowed to die peacefully in office, although in the stress of the early Stuart crises at least two were bundled off in disgrace and in 1628 there were no less than four men living who had held the white staff.

Nevertheless, the unification of 1554 had been wholly and profoundly beneficial for the Lord Treasurer. This is hardly surprising: William Paulet, Marquis of Winchester and Lord Treasurer since 1550, had been its principal architect. Too little is known about Winchester, but his long training in government service had clearly given him formidable administrative equipment, and his scrupulous conservatism perfectly complemented Cromwell's inventiveness. He seems to have put his enhanced position at the service of strict economy, and before his death in 1572, in his late eighties, he had taught Elizabeth those habits of frugality which stuck to her for the rest of her life.[3]

But Winchester was no first minister, and it is still fair to observe of the Treasurership that the dignity of the office and the stature of the incumbent were separable conceptions. Winchester was a great royal servant in a newly powerful post, but even on revenue matters he deferred to William Cecil who, as principal Secretary of State, had made something like a premiership out of his highly elastic duties. And when, as Lord Burghley, Cecil himself became Lord Treasurer in 1572, one may agree with his contemporary biographer – 'This place he honoured as much as the place honoured him'. But, the biographer goes on, 'He grew now to some greatness . . .' and, like his son Robert Cecil (Earl of Salisbury and Lord Treasurer, 1608–12), he was to demonstrate that the vantage point of the Treasury, with its command of patronage and the purse, could add significantly to ministerial stature. It did nothing for mediocrities like the Earl of Marlborough, Lord Treasurer 1624–8. Nor, as we shall see, did the professional competence of Cranfield, businessman turned administrator, save him from subordination and destruction by more powerful courtiers. Much depended on variables: the competence of the Treasurer, his standing in the Council, his relations with the sovereign. Thus, although the history of the Treasury between 1554 and 1667 is still essentially the history of English monarchy, it is, to an extent much greater than before, the history of its Lord Treasurers.

The twenty-six years of Burghley's treasurership amply demonstrate the sort of close association that could exist, and should always have existed, between the Crown and its finance minister. Elizabeth's attentiveness to profit and economy matched that of her grandfather. The young Queen whom Winchester scolded for being 'too liberal' had become, in Bacon's polite phrase, 'sparing in gifts' long before her death, and the womanly eyes which gazed blandly on Leicester and Essex probably hardened when she looked into their military expenditure. 'I never was any greedy, scraping grasper,' she told her Commons in 1601, 'nor a strait, fast-holding Prince, nor yet a waster.' Quite true; she was just an excellent business-woman and an ideal mistress to Burghley, 'counting him both her Treasurer, and her principal treasure', and 'never resolving anie private suit or grant from herself that was not first referred to his consideration and had his approbation before it passed'.

Upon this ideal footing it is not surprising that for a time Burghley came near to achieving the deceptively simple object of his financial policy. It differed in no way from the advice he gave his son and made up in common sense what it lacked in sophistication: 'Beware thou spend not above three of four parts of thy revenue.' In fact, by 1584 Burghley had accumulated a treasure of nearly £300,000, more than a whole year's ordinary revenue. It was shortlived. Wars with Spain and in Ireland dissipated it, and although it was based on a real administrative effort to economize it would not have been possible without large parliamentary supplies.

Nevertheless, the quality of Burghley's treasurership, with its comprehensive attention to questions of trade, industry, labour and consumption, tempts one to call in question the belief that the formulation by the Treasury of anything so ambitious as a policy had to wait until the end of the seventeenth century. Burghley was perhaps not the economic 'mastermind' that he was once called, and it may well be that Elizabethan government was 'more planned against than planning'.[4] But the unique collaboration of Queen and Treasurer ensured that an unrivalled concentration of authority was directed at getting away from hand-to-mouth expedients and at putting the revenue on a sounder footing. The yields from Customs and Crown lands made some response to Burghley's efforts and Elizabeth's prudence kept household expenditure within decent bounds. Unfortunately, the scale of the problems facing the Treasury by the end of the sixteenth century dwarfed even Burghley's stature and rendered his labours futile. War, Inflation and Corruption were three monsters which threatened the state. The accession of James I was to add a fourth – Extravagance.

THE EARLY STUARTS AND THEIR PROBLEMS

Yet it would be quite unfair to blame James for all the crises which followed. In the last months of her reign Elizabeth had 'raged exceedingly' against a complicated state of affairs which had its proximate cause in the Spanish and Irish wars and its deeper roots in fifty years of price inflation. The depreciation of the coinage, the sale of Crown lands, a new Book of Rates, revenue farming and the painful courtship of a tight-fisted House of Commons were inadequate answers, and seen to be so.

Here was the real danger to the Crown. The exhaustion of the more conventional techniques of financial management had left the Treasury with few remedies which were not worse than the disease. Expedients full of ill-omen, such as 'forced loans', had already been tried, and a Parliament which had produced £1½ million in taxation between 1585 and 1603 was rightly indignant with the Crown's selfish misuse of its profitable prerogatives. Worse still, the Queen's very parsimony was among the factors which were sapping the administrative vitality of the state. A courtier indicated two aspects of this when he recalled, 'We have not many precedents of her liberality.' 'Her rewards consisted chiefly in grants of leases, of offices, places of judicature....'

Now, the gift of offices, properly bestowed, was an entirely wholesome prerogative, but their distribution wholesale among the Crown's creditors in lieu of monetary payment was a disastrously false economy, for a bureaucracy denied its proper recompense was quick to find its own rewards. Extortionate fees, obligatory gratuities, and the downright sale of favour became commonplaces of Elizabethan government. To call all of it 'corruption' prejudges something which, like tipping, had become a social and economic necessity, but the Queen's last years were certainly marred by a demonstrable decline in public morality.

It was left to James I and his court to turn this decline into a Gadarene stampede. But for the first ten years of his reign he was protected from the worst consequences of his folly by the excellence of his Elizabethan inheritance. To speak only of the Treasury, Thomas Sackville, Earl of Dorset, was a not unworthy successor to Burghley, who had died in 1598, and he was followed by Burghley's son, Robert Cecil, Earl of Salisbury, whose appointment in 1608 instantly disposes of any idea that Kings get the sort of Treasurers they deserve. James, in Professor Tawney's blunt phrase, was 'a financial moron' and Cecil's tenure became a painful kind of martyrdom.

In terms of personal authority and ascendancy within the Council, Salisbury lacked few of his father's advantages. Combining his old post as principal Secretary of State with that of Lord Treasurer, he enjoyed an unusual concentration of power. But in terms of collaboration with the Crown he could look for nothing from James but frivolous condescension. When he took charge he found debts of nearly £1 million. By 1610 he had reduced this to £300,000 but upon an annual ordinary revenue of £460,000 James was still running up a deficit of £50,000 per annum. A few excuses can be made for James; the induction of a new reign was expensive, and he was a married man with a large household. His insistence on a peaceful foreign policy was, financially, a positive virtue. More important, the obsolescent foundations of royal revenue, eroded by inflation and corruption, required that sooner or later the King's capacity to 'live of his own' should be called in question. James's liberality to his hangers-on simply brought that day nearer and forced on Salisbury the premature necessity of a radical solution.

But a radical solution required parliamentary collaboration, for the problem had now passed, or at least seemed to have passed, the bounds of ordinary administrative resources. If the burden of the Crown's support was to be more broadly based it could only be by consent to new and permanent taxation. That was the rub. In the forty-four years of Elizabeth's reign Parliament had actually yielded up subsidies totalling some £3 million but it had done so only in emergency, grudgingly and with a good deal of fuss. Its attitude to any request for a quite unprecedented *permanent* levy on its purse could be predicted. As it was, Salisbury – in exploiting the Crown's special financial prerogatives – had already prejudiced the Crown's case. In 1606, a judicial decision in the Court of Exchequer (*Bate's Case*), had opened the way for new Customs duties imposed by the Treasurer without parliamentary consent. Salisbury began to extract from this opportunity an extra £70,000 per annum, but legal opinion, which was strongly represented in the House of Commons, began to move against the validity of the judgement. In addition, there was mounting political discontent with less questionable, but more onerous, sources of royal income such as Wardship – the feudal right of the Crown to manage, very lucratively, the estates of minors inheriting crown tenures, and to dispose of female heirs in marriage – and Purveyance – the right of the Crown to purchase victuals and services at its own valuation, which, by a process of composition, had now turned into a form of direct taxation on the counties.

In this unpromising situation Salisbury outlined to the Parliament of 1610 the scheme for the so-called 'Great Contract': £600,000 down to pay the King's debts and leave him a nest-egg; and £200,000 per annum to support his annual revenue. In return the King might agree to yield up the more burdensome of his anachronistic incomes. It took ten months and two sessions of Parliament for this horse-trading to run its course, and the outcome was not simply failure but disaster. Influential courtiers such as Sir Francis Bacon and the able, if improbably named Chancellor of the Exchequer, Sir Julius Caesar, had correctly predicted that no good could come of this barter. The Commons had felt their strength, the Crown had displayed its weakness, and the breakdown of negotiations permanently soured relations between them. Salisbury died within two years in some disgrace, with the dubious merit of having turned a financial crisis into a political crisis.

This was soon well on its way to becoming a constitutional crisis. For the ugly thing about the Treasury's predicament was that it could not pursue solvency without running into extremely deep waters. Within the ramshackle empires of the great departments nothing could be done without bringing down the whole frightful debris of medievalism. The notion of reconstructing efficient, salaried departments was quite unthinkable. As it was, the widespread sale of official posts meant that the existing structure was held together by a web of property rights whose vested interest in conservation was virtually unassailable. Even in the few areas where this was not so the Treasury could do nothing unless it was supported by King and Council. Efforts were made in the 1620s and 30s to reform the fees and practices of several great departments – Navy, household, law courts – but the work was curiously sterile.

Meanwhile, rebuffed by Parliament, the Crown was thrown back upon the exploitation of some of its archaic, fiscal privileges. On the fringe of the main revenues – Customs, Crown lands, Wardship, the profits of justice – there were opportunities for feudal exactions which, although legitimate, were to prove extraordinarily costly in social and political disorder. For they fell almost entirely upon the backbone of society, that land-owning, parliamentary class of gentry which, if not necessarily 'rising' or 'declining', was almost universally precarious in its fortunes, and politically most powerful.

There is no question of seeing in this situation the inevitability of civil war. That crisis lay far ahead in the contingencies of 1642, but the failure of the Great Contract and the expedients which ultimately followed helped to open up a fissure within the governing community already undermined by religious dissensions and economic grievances. The sale of honours, the revival of the Forest Laws, the forced loans, were successive steps on the path which led by way of the Ship Money taxes of the 1630s to the radical Parliament of 1640.

Meanwhile, upon the rather unequal footing of great necessity and small profit, the Crown's relations with the City were more fruitful than those with Parliament, but the contrast is more apparent than real. Loans to the Crown were a hazardous adventure for which the City was ill-equipped and ill-inclined. It was barely a generation since the destruction of Antwerp had thrown the Crown back upon the domestic money market, and its institutions and techniques had not matured. For its own part, the Treasury had not yet learned the subtler arts of businesslike inducements. A few wealthy merchants, some of the great trading companies, the syndicates of revenue farmers, the Corporation of the City, were sometimes cajoled into making loans. Too often they were bullied. As a marketable commodity the King's credit was a non-starter and it was totally unrealistic for the Treasury to insist on paying no more than the legal maximum rate of ten per cent interest. Its alternative inducements – grants of offices, patents of monopoly, Crown lands – tended to prove ruinously costly in the long run. A sloppy reliance on the enforced prolongation of reluctant loans had ruined the King's credit long before the parliamentary armies foreclosed on the royal bankrupt.

'TREASURY CONTROL' UNDER CRANFIELD

The Treasury's role in all this could not fail to be important but it was not paramount. The Privy Council was the principal agency of fiscal enforcement, backed up by the cooperative law courts. Lawyers were the most fertile source of fiscal innovation, and clergy its most ardent apologists. It should not be surprising, therefore, that after Salisbury's death in 1612, no Lord Treasurer can be described (even with apologies for the anachronism), as a 'prime minister'. The strongest candidate, Richard Weston, Earl of Portland and Treasurer, 1628–35, was briefly the first among equals in a faction-ridden court, but his ascendancy was hardly constructive. He was 'Lady Mora', the embodiment of delay and inefficiency to more purposeful ministers such as the Earl of Strafford and Archbishop Laud.

The decline in standards at the Treasury was, perhaps, rather overdramatized by Salisbury's immediate successor. Thomas Howard, Earl of Suffolk, after four years in office, was exposed by a committee of inquiry and found guilty of bribery and peculation. To clear the air a little the Treasury had to be put into the hands of a Commission headed by the Archbishop of Canterbury.

But the Treasurer whose tenure most strikingly demonstrates all that was worst, and all that was best, in early Stuart government was Lionel Cranfield, Earl of Middlesex. Beginning his career as a merchant's apprentice, he displayed a dismal lack of originality in marrying his master's daughter and making a fortune in commerce. But it was a fortune partly based on a skilful exploitation of the Crown's administrative weakness, and his appointment in 1613 as Surveyor General of the Customs was an instance, not unusual in this age, of poacher turned gamekeeper. Sheer merit and a modicum of patronage took him further. Master of the Great Wardrobe in September 1618, he was appointed Master of the Court of Wards in January 1619, a Privy Councillor in 1620 and Lord Treasurer on 13 October 1621.

Cranfield was unique not only in the humbleness of his origins but in his determination to put normal business standards at the service of the Crown rather than his own pocket. 'The King,' he announced, 'shall pay no more than other men do, and he shall pay ready money, and if we cannot have it in one place we shall have it in another.' It was a bold manifesto. In this spirit Cranfield had already cut swathes through the criminal profusion of the royal household. But, confronted with the total situation, even he quailed. 'The more I look into the King's estate, the more cause I have to be troubled,' he wrote.[5]

Yet the remedy was simple enough. It was simple because the Crown had no alternatives. There was no question of parliamentary help; there was little hope of fiscal innovation. The court must simply accept stringent economies under strict Treasury control. But what was 'Treasury control'? Early seventeenth-century Treasurers were no more assured of exclusive control over Exchequer issues than their predecessors. Theoretically they gave orders to the Exchequer only upon authorization received from the King under the Privy Seal. In practice they could get that authorization upon their own discretionary recommendation, and this gave them a similitude of ministerial initiative. But the chain of command was very vulnerable. With easy access to the King's compliant ear, there was little to stop other ministers, such as the two Secretaries of State or powerful royal favourites, from securing the King's authority for Exchequer issues. And, of course, there was nothing to curb the King. Thus, in the last analysis, 'Treasury control' added up to little more than the moral authority a Lord Treasurer could command against the will of the King. It was all very well for Bacon to say that a Treasurer's duty was 'to stop suits, put back pensions, check allowances, question merits ... and in short to be a screen to your Majesty', but which Treasurer was going to be foolhardy enough to try? Cranfield evidently was.

By October 1622 he had persuaded the King to declare that no grants from the main revenues of England and Ireland were to be legally valid unless specifically approved by the Treasurer.[6] This was a great but precarious personal triumph and the subsequent uproar paid tribute to Cranfield's audacity. It seemed as if he had actually succeeded in binding James to the disciplines of the Treasury. This could not last. Within a year the rodent courtiers had nibbled their way through the King's resolve, and Cranfield's fall soon followed.

The terms of Cranfield's impeachment in 1624 are irrelevant. They bore little relation to his real offence, which was to have slammed the till shut on too many aristocratic fingers. He was accused of corruption, of course, but by later standards no Lord Treasurer was free of that taint. Suffolk was exposed, as we have noted, and Audley End (which, as James wittily remarked, was too grand for a King but good enough for a Lord Treasurer) still remains as a fragmentary monument to his great wealth. But the great houses of the Cecils – Theobalds, Burghley, Exeter, Hatfield, Cranborne and others – were not paid for by the Lord Treasurer's stipend of £368 per annum. Nor were they paid for wholly by anything so unsubtle as embezzlement or bribery.[7] There was (and still is), a nice distinction between bribes and gifts, and Stuart officialdom was skilled at drawing it in its own favour. There were, likewise, many legitimate opportunities – thanks to the dilatoriness of Exchequer audit – of profiting privately from the prolonged custody of public money. Until the end of the eighteenth century these opportunities were the recognized basis of official fortunes. Nor was it thought dishonourable in Lord Treasurers if they took shares in those contracts over which they adjudicated. Dorset, Salisbury and Cranfield all dabbled in the contracts by which the Customs and other revenues were 'farmed' out for fixed rents to syndicates of courtiers and businessmen. Some of their huge profits derived from their being simultaneously, although not *ex officio*, Masters of the extremely lucrative Court of Wards. And Salisbury's private enterprises barely stopped short of piracy.

But the white staff alone was thought to be worth £7,000 per annum to an honest man; much more if he was prepared to risk damnation.* Lord Montagu, Viscount Mandeville, paid the King £20,000 to be Treasurer in 1620 and he was probably not the loser when he was transferred to the post of Lord President of the Council less than a year later. In this company Cranfield had nothing to be ashamed of. As Lord Keeper Bacon had learned in 1621, to be accused of corruption was to be accused of having enemies. Indeed, the sight of the

*A moderate estimate of what the office was worth is indicated by the £8,000 per annum salary conferred on the Lord Treasurer after 1660. A Treasury Commission had to share the same sum.

bourgeois Lord Treasurer, warming his backside by the Privy Council fire while he roundly told some favourite what he could do with his expense accounts, was not calculated to make friends in a court of aristocratic spendthrifts. Cranfield's conviction in the House of Lords marked little more than the triumph of the all-powerful favourite, the Duke of Buckingham, over a servile court and a servile King. 'All Treasurers, if they do good service to their masters, must be generally hated', was the King's futile tribute to the best financier he had ever had.

THE TREASURY IN COMMISSION

The fate of successive Lord Treasurers, grappling hopelessly with the politics and personalities of an unstable court, raises the question – 'Would the Treasury have been better managed by a Commission?' With an eye on future developments this is worth considering. In fact, of the years between 1612 and 1620 the Treasury had been in the hands of Commissioners for nearly five, so the means of comparison were there. Yet the verdict of the times seems to have gone against corporate management. Bacon was among the Commissioners of 1618, and in an interesting memorandum he told the King that he thought a single Lord Treasurer infinitely preferable to a Commission because 'it is not possible that a body of many should meet in time, meet in place, meet in mind, answerable to the assiduous care, constant pursuit and peremptory commandment of one man'. The 'invention and stirring, and assiduity and pursuit' needed for the conduct of the Treasury could only be found in an autocratic Lord Treasurer, not a committee.

Commissioners, then, were regarded as temporary expedients which left little impression on the character of the early-seventeenth-century Treasury. However, it has been suggested that the heavier demands they made on clerical labour, for the duplication of memoranda, the keeping of minutes perhaps, may have fostered the origins of the Treasury secretariat.[8] This cannot be readily proved but it is plausible. Sole Lord Treasurers tended to draw on their own households for clerical assistance, and some of Burghley's private secretaries, men such as Sir Michael Hickes and Vincent Skinner, had a prestige in public life not greatly inferior to that of the future grandeur of a Parliamentary Secretary to the Treasury. Yet they remained essentially personal servants with no independent claims on the government. In any case, the Exchequer, though staffed by an increasing number of sinecurists, still had the competence to meet most of the Treasurer's administrative requirements. The key figure here was the Auditor of the Receipt, an important official since 1554, through whose hands passed the records of receipt and the authorizations for issue. It is most likely that the early secretaries to the Treasury developed their informal records in performing the relatively humble task of communicating with the Exchequer officials on their master's behalf. They had no independent power of initiative.

Furthermore, to draw too sharp a distinction between the Commission, with several heads, and the Lord Treasurer, with only one, obscures the value to the latter of other financial officials, not least the Chancellor of the Exchequer. Increasingly important since his post had been combined with that of under-treasurer, he was now effectively the Treasurer's second-in-command and theoretically his successor, although between 1560 and 1640 only one, Richard Weston, moved on to become Lord Treasurer. But Chancellors like Sir Walter Mildmay (1566–89), Sir John Fortescue (1589–1603) and Sir Julius Caesar (1606–14) were extremely able men, capable of forming policies and expounding them convincingly in the House of Commons.

This last activity would have been of greater importance to the Treasury if Parliament had played any constructive part in the support and management of government finance, but it did not. It was one thing for the Commons to protest the unlawfulness of extra-ordinary taxation without parliamentary consent; it was quite another for them to claim any responsibility for superintending royal expenditure. On occasions, it is true, the criticisms of the Commons had led to legislation against revenue maladministration. But Parliament was too rarely in being – averaging about three weeks per annum in the reign of Queen Elizabeth and less than seven weeks per annum between 1603 and 1640. When it did meet, after the failure of the Great Contract, it was rarely in the mood to give the Crown's necessities a sympathetic hearing.

If there must be blame for this state of affairs it can only be shared between the Crown, which disdained to take Parliament into its confidence, and the Commons, who refused to regard the Crown's financial problems as their own. Shielding their purse behind the threadbare maxim that the King must 'live of his own', and throwing an endless series of grievances in the path of debate, they consistently evaded appeals to their sense of loyalty and recoiled angrily from the argument that they *owed* some due maintenance to the Crown. Only in 1624, when the shift in James's foreign policy at last matched their own militant protestantism, did they make a constructive response. Their vote of 1624 for some £280,000 temporarily revived the medieval principle of appropriation: the money was to be handled by nominated Treasurers accountable to Parliament for its expenditure upon the military campaign against the Habsburgs. But although, as a device for asserting parliamentary control over supply and expenditure, appropriation had an interesting past and a great future, it had little place in early Stuart government. The Crown would not permit, nor did the Commons yet aspire to, the sort of responsibility it entailed.

THE INTERREGNUM

Nevertheless, to pass too hopefully from the squalid incompetence of early Stuart government to the vigorous new order of the Puritan revolution is to risk disappointment. In narrowly administrative terms the Parliamentarian and Cromwellian régimes added little to the central organization of government finance. The old, Exchequer-based system was not swept away; it was not even reformed. It was ignored. In the first months of crisis in 1642, as the two sides aligned themselves, a few of the Exchequer's senior personnel took themselves off to the King's camp, but the majority of the department's active officials remained behind as neutrals or parliamentarians. Even so, there was really nothing for them to do. The Exchequer was soon at a standstill. Even in the royalist camp, the new Chancellor of the Exchequer, Sir Edward Hyde (later Earl of Clarendon), found his authority superseded by the more urgent demands of the Treasurer at War. De-centralization, *ad hoc* expedients, 'a multiplicity of Treasuries', these were to be the characteristics of Civil War financial administration. On both sides the traditional machinery collapsed.

In its place, on the parliamentary side, there was created a series of special organizations, collecting and disbursing revenue from particular sources to particular ends. The Committee for the Advance of Money was appointed in November 1642 to co-ordinate funds and borrowing from the parliamentary camp, and the Committee for Compounding, the Committee for Sequestrations, the Committee for Plundered Ministers, and the Committee for the Sale of Crown Lands extracted funds from the defeated Royalists. Some degree of central control was ensured by the comprehensive requirements of the Army Committee, and the Committee of Accounts, with its local sub-committees, attempted to impose some regularity of audit, but from an early stage in the conflict the whole business of recruiting, equipping and paying the troops was being administered at local level by County Committees. There are few possible alternatives to the verdict that 'The Civil War was won by Committees'.[9]

It was not until June 1649 that the Council of State appointed yet another committee to 'consider how the treasury of the Commonwealth could be run in one channel', and it was not until 1654 that Cromwell at last re-established a central institution of finance. It was not a committee this time, it was the Exchequer – the whole traditional apparatus, unaltered and – with the exception of the provision that tallies should be inscribed and recorded in English – unreformed. Exactly a century after its last restoration the resilience of the 'ancient course' had triumphed again. Direction of the Exchequer was vested in a body of Treasury Commissioners who were, in reality, a subcommittee of the Council of State and very much subordinate to the direction of Lord Protector Cromwell. It marked therefore no innovation, no advance towards administrative emancipation. The path was cleared for a quite painless transition to Restoration government when, after a brief tenure by a Commission, the control of the Exchequer was once again bestowed upon a conventional Lord Treasurer, the pious Earl of Southampton.

THE RESTORATION: PORTENTS OF CHANGE

The conservatism of these decisions makes it easier to take stock, for the ordinance of June 1654 and the settlement of 1660 seem to bring the Treasury back full circle to 1554. There should be nothing very surprising in this. Cromwell was an Elizabethan at heart, as was Clarendon, the architect of the Restoration. Bitter enemies, they shared a nostalgia for the orderly government of that golden age when authority and liberty had been reconciled by the conscientious professionalism of the Queen and Council. This was the pattern they sought to restore and there could be no room in it for self-sufficient departmentalism, answerable to Parliament rather than the Crown. In his diagnosis of the breakdown of that traditional order, Clarendon showed himself well aware of its financial aspects. He saw on the one side 'the excess of the court in the greatest want, and the parsimony and retention of the country in the greatest plenty'. Maladministration had produced 'projects of all kinds, many ridiculous, many scandalous . . . the envy and reproach of which came to the King, the profit to other men'. But he saw nothing in these 'distempers' to invalidate the traditional structure of government. If the King could be induced to do his duty with the help of a competent Council, then Clarendon could see no grounds for innovation and was to resist it at every turn. The development of the Treasury after 1660 cannot be taken for granted.

Nevertheless, the Restoration settlement did embody some distinct, if precarious, changes. It explicitly recognized that Parliament had a permanent place in government, and although the repeal of the

Triennial Act in 1664* left Charles II much freer to manage without it, convenience and financial necessity effectively ensured its regular summons. In any case, Parliament had now assumed a degree of financial responsibility which was quite welcome to Charles. It had agreed in principle that he should have an annual income of £1·2 million and it made some efforts to see that he got it. In doing this it transmitted the most important financial legacies of the Civil War, the highly unpopular innovations of Excise and Assessments. The latter were essentially extra-ordinary taxes levied in emergency and consisted of lump sums payable monthly, assessed upon the counties and raised by them among their ratepayers. Levied repeatedly between 1660 and 1663 to meet the debts of the state, they effectively supplanted the obsolete medieval and Tudor subsidies, and were to prove the backbone of war finance. The Excise was still more important. First levied by Parliament in 1643 and reluctantly retained in 1660, it went some way to achieving the objectives of the 1610 Great Contract. In recompense for the abolition of the Court of Wards and the right of purveyance, half the Excise duties were granted to the Crown in perpetuity and half to Charles for his life. Directly linked to the nation's economy or, at least, to its consumption of alcohol, it doubled the elasticity of royal revenue and was the best bargain Charles ever made.

At the same time, in calling into being a large body of skilled officials, the Excise greatly enlarged the administrative responsibilities of the Treasury, and was a major source of that professionalism which is the least tangible legacy of Interregnum government. It is probably more important as a myth than a reality, but Pepys, who was in a good position to judge, firmly believed that the civil service of the Commonwealth, supplanting the aristocratic sinecurists of the royal court, had produced a particularly worthy type of administrator – painstaking, methodical, disinterested. The gifts so praised seem hardly more than those of any sedulous clerk, but these, in Stuart government, were far too rare to be taken for granted. In a century when several Lord Treasurers display an endearing incapacity to add up correctly the simpler routines of clear thinking were peculiarly precious. The man of 'method', the man of 'business' who could attend to public affairs with dispatch and accuracy, was a man worthy of the age of Newton. Hobbes, after all, was proud to have taught the Cavendishes how to keep their household accounts, Locke condescended to publish 'A New Method of Making Commonplace Books', and Defoe was to insist that 'Matters of Accounts are my particular Element, what I have Alwayes been master of'. The scientific revolu-

*The Triennial Act of 1641 had provided revolutionary machinery for automatically convening a parliament once in three years, should the King fail to do so. After 1664 the obligation was only a moral one.

tion of the seventeenth century had made numeracy respectable, even in government.

Pepys was therefore profoundly flattered to be praised as 'a man of the old way, for taking pains'. This was in 1668 when Restoration government seemed to be falling to pieces. That same day (January 31), he had noted with satisfaction that an important Parliamentary Accounts Commission had been 'fain to find out an old fashioned man of Cromwell's to do their business for them [as Secretary]'. It would be wrong to generalize too freely from this sort of evidence. Although Clarendon admitted that despair and idleness in exile had rendered many Cavaliers unfit for public service, not all of them were drunken incompetents. Pepys had an axe to grind, and the Cromwellian régime had produced its own brand of incompetence, corruption and humbug.

But the Puritan Revolution had unquestionably fostered a useful spirit of public service to the state. With deep roots in social and economic crisis, it had nourished aspirations far broader than any embodied in the revolutionary constitutions of the Interregnum. An anxiety to see the economic destinies of the country backed by a thrifty, conscientious government and an equable, comprehensive fiscal policy was one of the most powerful forces to come out of mid-seventeenth-century England. In so far as a handful of men sustained and applied that ideal, it was to be vital in shaping the future development of the Treasury, for it was through this institution that it was soon to find its most effective expression.

SOURCE NOTES

1. G. E. Aylmer, *The King's Servants* (1961), p. 35.
2. G. R. Elton, 'The Elizabethan Exchequer: War in the Receipt', in *Elizabethan Government and Society: Essays presented to Sir John Neale* (1961), ed. S. T. Bindoff, J. Hurstfield and C. H. Williams.
3. Ironically, Winchester's personal extravagance left him heavily in debt to the Queen and others at his death. See L. Stone, *The Crisis of the Aristocracy, 1558–1641* (abridged edn, 1967), p. 245.
4. J. Hurstfield, *The Queen's Wards* (1958).
5. R. H. Tawney, *Business and Politics under James I: Lionel Cranfield as Merchant and Minister* (1958), p. 198.
6. *ibid.*, pp. 217–18.
7. L. Stone, 'The Fruits of Office: The case of Robert Cecil, First Earl of Salisbury, 1596–1612', in *Essays in the Economic and Social History of Tudor and Stuart England* (1961), ed. F. J. Fisher.
8. Aylmer, *op. cit.*, p. 38.
9. D. H. Pennington, 'The Accounts of the Kingdom, 1642–49', in *Essays in the Economic and Social History of Tudor and Stuart England* (1961), ed. F. J. Fisher, p. 182.

CHAPTER 3

The Rise of the Treasury: 1667-1714

You shal see this business go on to that height
that Holland shal not outgoe us in point of Credite.
This is a great vow but by God's assistance you shal see it.
SIR GEORGE DOWNING TO PEPYS, 1666

THE END OF AN ERA

The fourth Earl of Southampton, Lord Treasurer of England, died on 16 May 1667. 'There is a good man gone,' lamented Pepys. Since he was neither sententious nor clairvoyant he did not add – 'We shall not see his like again' – but in fact Southampton was to prove the last of his kind. Although a few other men were to hold the white staff as Lord Treasurer before the office finally passed into the hands of Commissioners in 1714, they were heirs to a new order in the Treasury which marks out 1667 as a turning point in its history.

Southampton was not wholly to blame for the fact that a minor revolution followed his death: he was a thoroughly blameless sort of man. Painstaking, pious, he had been a good servant of the Crown for most of his sixty years, with an independence and decency of spirit which had recently made him stand out against the further persecution of nonconformity. Indeed, it was the excellence of his character rather than the modest breadth of his administrative experience that had made him seem an acceptable choice as Lord Treasurer in August 1660. Unfortunately, Southampton had his very human faults. 'For my Lord Treasurer,' remarked a caustic official, 'he minds his ease, and lets things go how they will: if he can have his £8,000 per annum, and a game at l'ombre* he is well.' To be quite fair, the Treasurer was tired and disillusioned and the state of the Exchequer gave him ample excuse to indulge that melancholia for which he was notorious. Intent on his pleasures, the King ignored him and by 1665 his indifference had nearly broken the Treasurer's heart. Time and time again Southampton brought the figures before the King, begging him 'please to cast your eye upon them and to spend upon this subject but one hour',

*A Spanish card-game fashionable in the late seventeenth century.

but Charles never did. Instead, sickened by the importunities of indigent Royalists, unable to extract from his revenues the full £1,200,000 per annum which Parliament had promised him, the King had drifted moodily into deeper debt, selling Dunkirk (a Cromwellian conquest) to the French for some £200,000 and entering into a disastrous Dutch war in the shabby hope that some of the parliamentary supplies would stick to his fingers. Of course, he was no stranger to poverty. A threadbare exile since his teens, he had returned to large debts which Parliament had only partially and grudgingly honoured. He could never quite recapture the euphoric promise of those first days of Restoration when he had thrust delighted hands into more gold than he had ever seen. By 1667 he had had enough. It was really Charles II who made the revolution possible.

THE TREASURY COMMISSION OF 1667

Without consulting his ministers Charles decided to put the Treasury into commission. As we have seen, this was not unprecedented, but it was unusual, and his choice of Commissioners marked a radical departure from tradition. Tradition demanded dignitaries of the Privy Council, mature, sober men in the conventional mould of the uninspired Southampton. But Charles wanted new blood. He wanted, he said 'rougher hands', 'ill-natured men, not to be moved with civilities', and his choice fell on three men of his own generation, all experienced in certain aspects of financial administration yet well below the normal dignity of the office. Sir William Coventry, Sir Thomas Clifford, Sir John Duncombe were in their thirties, marked out by their competence, vigour and impatience with courtly conservatism. To them were reluctantly added the existing Chancellor of the Exchequer, Sir Anthony Ashley Cooper (later Earl of Shaftesbury), and the Duke of Albemarle, better known to history as the General Monck whose army had made the Restoration possible. As the First Lord of the new Treasury Commission Albemarle was little more than a figurehead and, in Pepys's crisp opinion, a blockhead too. Neither he nor the Chancellor was to exercise the political or administrative dominance later associated with their positions. Effectively, and legally as a quorum of three, the power of the Treasury could lie with the 'rougher hands', and in the course of rather less than five years they were to reward that trust. But it is arguable that no decision they ever made was more momentous than their first – their choice of Secretary.

SIR GEORGE DOWNING

Sir George Downing has one over-riding claim to fame which tends to obscure his real significance: he gave his name to that street in which, some time after 1682, he began building four large houses 'fit for persons of good quality to inhabit in'. With this claim has gone an extremely unsavoury reputation for greed and treachery which even the closest study of his career does not wholly dispel, although it does suggest that the qualities which earned him this reputation are the counterpart of those which made him such a forceful administrator. Pepys, whose dislike of Downing was mixed with a certain amount of admiration, wrote of his former employer that 'he values himself upon having of things do well under his hand'. Very little was allowed to stand in his way. By 1667 Downing was in his forty-fourth year with an impressive, if chequered, career behind him. Linked by birth with the college- and colony-founding puritan families of Mildmay and Winthrop, he had been taken to New England as a child where he acquired the incidental distinction of being the second student to graduate from the newly-founded College at Harvard. He returned to England during the Civil War and quickly rose from a regimental chaplaincy to be a chief of intelligence in one of Cromwell's armies at the age of twenty-six. Marriage into the aristocracy, a seat in Parliament, a post in the Exchequer and diplomatic missions rapidly followed. By 1660 Downing had made himself valuable enough to be knighted by Charles and retained in his diplomatic post at The Hague.

In an understandable effort to modify his substantial reputation it has been asked if Downing would have been such an important financial figure if his diplomatic career had taken place in Poland rather than Holland.[1] Unfortunately, this under-estimates both Downing and the Poles. Seventeenth-century Poland possessed quite sophisticated techniques for controlling public expenditure from which England might well have benefited, and Downing's restless intelligence would have made the best of its opportunities anywhere in Europe. But, undeniably, the young Dutch republic offered him unique lessons in the management of public finance. Its credit structure, public and private, was securely founded on one of the oldest national banks in Europe, set up in 1609. Dutch capital, Dutch credit dominated European trade no less surely than her fleets and her cosmopolitan merchants. England's economy, in contrast, seemed as sluggish and unwieldy as her ships – 'rather tubs than ships' in Downing's scornful opinion.

As a Member of Parliament before and after the Restoration

Downing had done more than most to put this right. The comprehensiveness of his programme for England's economic regeneration was quite unrivalled. In a single speech in 1660, 'Sir George Downing moved to revive the Committee for the Woollen Manufacture of this Kingdom; and desired they might also consider the state of the Pilchard or Herring fishery; and the settlement of the East India Company; which was ordered'. Currency and tariff reform, technological innovation and industrial development, Downing promoted them all. But his principal achievement was to have been the architect of the Navigation Acts of the 1660s, the cornerstone of that part of the protective mercantile system for which even Adam Smith had nothing but praise. 'I find,' wrote Downing, expressing the essence of his philosophy, 'that a Gardener doth not more contribute to the growing of his herbs and trees than doth the Government of any country to the growth of its trade.'

There was not much originality in Downing's ideas; one may find their antecedents in earlier writers and their common inspiration was Dutch; but he was surely unique in the energy and practicality with which he applied them. A significant example of this occurred in 1665 in the first stages of the Dutch war which, as Envoy at The Hague, Downing had done much to foment. Seventeenth-century diplomats did not necessarily pack their bags on the outbreak of hostilities, and from his heavily guarded house he was in a good position to witness Dutch preparations. He had been sceptical of their ability to keep interest rates down *and* sustain a large public war loan, but within a single week he was staggered to see the Dutch raise a substantial sum at no more than 4 per cent. The loan was actually oversubscribed.

As an Exchequer official, one of the four tellers through whose offices the public revenue passed, Downing knew just how poorly royal credit compared with that of the resilient Dutch republic. The current rate of interest in England was 6 per cent. This was a ceiling fixed by the usury laws. It did not inhibit borrowing at less than that rate – much City investment was at 4 or 5 per cent – but it set the norm for public borrowing, and, indeed, so suspect was the King's credit that a realistic rate was 10 or 12 per cent, which the King often paid. Little had happened since the early seventeenth century to improve the terms of government borrowing except, perhaps, the emergence of the goldsmith-bankers as middlemen in the mobilization of funds. Early in 1665, one of the largest – Edward Backwell – had over £500,000 on deposit from nearly eleven hundred clients, but until war loans got under way barely 10 per cent of this was directly re-invested in government loans. The principal source of funds still remained those syndicates of businessmen who 'farmed' the revenues of Customs and Excise. Downing was unhappy with this situation, partly because he suspected the bankers of exploiting a monopoly and partly because the system of revenue farming lent itself to practices which, since the Middle Ages, had been the bane of the Exchequer. Not only was there the danger of excessive borrowing on the credit of the incoming revenue, but the habit of deputing the farmers to make payments direct to government creditors was, in Downing's opinion, a shameful abdication of responsibility. The Exchequer was reduced to a mere accounting agency and while the credit for prompt payments seemed to accrue to the farmers the odium for delayed ones fell upon the Treasury. This was the negation of government finance.

Downing formulated and promoted his remedies with remarkable speed. Returning to England by September 1665 he had, after stormy scenes with the gouty Lord Chancellor, convinced the King in time to carry them through the October session of Parliament. They were embodied in the 1665 Act granting the King an additional Aid of £1,250,000. Normally such extra grants were made without strings attached. As with his ordinary revenue the King was trusted to spend it wisely. But, as we have seen, there were medieval and more recent precedents for making it statutorily explicit that the money should be spent for the purpose intended, and the Act revived this principle of 'appropriation'. The Exchequer alone was to receive and disburse the money and its records were to be open to public inspection. More important were the provisions for borrowing which embody Downing's unique contribution. The Act declared that if ordinary citizens were prepared to advance money on the credit of this fund they were to receive in return from the Treasury Lords, signed Orders, numbered chronologically, authorizing their repayment in sequence with half-yearly instalments of 6 per cent interest. These foolscap-size, printed Treasury Orders were to be legally assignable by endorsement and they could be expected to mature for repayment during the eighteen to twenty-four months it would take to collect the tax.

The political and constitutional implications of Downing's measure have always been fully appreciated. This parliamentary appropriation of extra-ordinary additions to the royal revenue soon became, as some courtiers had feared, an habitual device for curbing Charles and a displeasing invasion of the royal prerogative. Parliamentary credit had, for at least a portion of the government's resources, supplanted the unreliable personal credit of the King. But from the point of view of financial history it was important that public investment had been encouraged and a new form of government security created to enlarge the rather narrow range of existing negotiable instruments. Its administrative significance is that it threw new responsibilities on the

Treasury and Exchequer. Higher standards of accuracy and punctuality would be needed from these institutions if public confidence was to be maintained. In one small sector at least the Treasury was obliged to stand on its own feet, accountable to the public rather than the King.

As an Exchequer official, Downing did more than his fair share to make his scheme a success, but he was contending against great odds. The Plague had emptied London, business capital was tied up in naval contracts, and private coffers were disappearing into innumerable back gardens. There was a run on the banks. In the event, Downing did well to raise nearly £200,000 in individual loans in the teeth of the Treasurer's indifference, and Pepys was happy to concede 'I do really take it to be a very considerable thing done by him; for the beginning, end and every part of it, is to be imputed to him'.

THE ESTABLISHMENT OF TREASURY CONTROL

Thus, by 1667, Downing's reputation was sufficiently formidable for the new Treasury lords to declare 'that they did not intend to be ruled by their Secretary, but do the business themselves'. This back-handed testimony to his competence seems more remarkable when it is remembered how novel the position of the secretaryship still was. At best it was a semi-official appointment, with certain functions but no powers, no security and no salary. Its scope was to remain elastic for another generation, but Downing was the first to demonstrate its full potential. This caused no friction. The Commissioners and their Secretary worked well together and it is hardly possible to disentangle the source of Treasury initiatives. Some measures were distinctly Downing's, for he was a fertile legislator. In particular he was the promoter of the 1667 Act which extended the principles of the Additional Aid to the King's ordinary revenue. In future, Treasury Orders registered numerically on any one of the King's principal revenues – Customs, Excise, Hearth Tax – were to be legally assignable and payable 'in course' – a tremendous step forward in establishing Treasury control of government borrowing and expenditure. No less significant for the establishment of control was the great blossoming of Treasury records into systematic series – Order Books, Warrant Books, Letter Books and, above all, the Minute Books which stretch in an almost unbroken series until their cessation in the mid nineteenth century. Bold 'No. 1s' upon the covers of the 1667 volumes still testify to this novel initiative. Even the pettiest details reflect the impact of new brooms. Treasury business now migrated to quarters in the ramshackle range of the King's chambers at Whitehall, adjoining the royal laboratory, where it was carried on like some cottage industry. But this was rather better than its old quarters in the Exchequer rooms at Westminster, and its removal from Palace Yard is of historic significance in marking the physical separation of the two departments. At first, its equipment hardly matched the occasion. The Commissioners remedied this with the wholesale acquisition of furnishings – chairs, hangings, carpets, candlesticks, a couch and a handbell. Even the arrival of two close-stools, red leather, brass-studded, looks deeply purposeful. It was unfortunate that Pepys should glimpse Duncombe lolling with his feet on a chair, and the purchase of yet another couch looks ominous. But a watchful, wondering public was soon impressed. 'The Commissioners of the Treasury,' noted an Under-Secretary of State, 'meet every day and begin very smartly in their business.'

Enough has been said about the inadequacies of Stuart finance to indicate the directions in which the Treasury had to act. It was not enough that a demoralized Lord Treasurer had been replaced by vigorous young Commissioners. The King must be curbed. Within a few months of their appointment they had formally warned him against making extravagant verbal promises, against careless 'secret service' expenditure, and against granting away posts and privileges. In the course of 1668 they were to collaborate with a committee of the Privy Council in preparing a strict retrenchment of the royal expenditure, but it was an uphill task. When Sir William Coventry roundly told his flippant King, 'I see your Majesty do not remember the old English proverb, "He that will not stoop for a pin will never be worth a pound",' Charles must have realized what it meant to place himself in 'rougher hands'. The 'Treasury attitude' had come of age!

The same tough line was taken with the Treasury's main rivals, the two Secretaries of State. With their control of the Signet seal they stood astride that vulnerable chain of command along which authorization for Exchequer issues must pass. Too often they had initiated such authorizations without the Treasury's prior knowledge. After a brief tussle, an historic Order in Council of 31 January 1668 restated the extent of exclusive Treasury control over the revenue and departmental expenditure. All orders and most appointments relating to the collection and disbursement of the revenue must first pass the Treasury's scrutiny; grants, pensions and other royal bounty were to be checked, and 'secret service' expenditure, over which the Secretaries had some jurisdiction, was to be strictly confined. The Order was triumphantly inscribed on a board and hung up in the Treasury chambers. Soon after, a reorganization of Privy Council committees recognized the full administrative responsibility of the Treasury for all financial questions, and from this moment dates the continuous history of effective Treasury control.*

After that it was easier to bring lesser departments to heel. The Navy Board gave trouble and it was necessary to show some finesse in dealing with the revenue farmers who were, after all, the major source of credit, but the defaulting Hearth Tax farmers were placed under arrest and the powerful syndicate of Customs farmers found the Treasury lords extremely hard bargainers. Indeed, the whole revenue-collecting hierarchy was submitted to searching, and recurring, review. Working their way through thickets of incompetence, the 'rougher hands' gradually laid down the routines of control, chivvying the Exchequer, coaxing the bankers and handing out inadequate but neatly parcelled funds to a clamorous Navy and a greedy household. Soon, Charles could boast to his sister, the Duchess of Orleans, 'you are very ill-informed if you do not know that my Treasury, and indeed all my other affairs, are in as good a method as our understandings can put them into'.

Yet by 1672 all this work seemed in ruins. The Commission itself had crumbled – Albemarle dead, Coventry dismissed, Downing transferred – and a declaration of royal bankruptcy, the 'Stop of the Exchequer', had shattered the King's credit. What then had they achieved? In what sense had the Commission of 1667 marked a turning point in Treasury history?

To appeal to the contrast between the melancholic Treasurer and the masterful Commissioners seems too facile an answer to be wholly convincing – but it was certainly the impact of personalities, the *qualitative* change in the Treasury's administration as much as any gain in powers, which led a Member of Parliament to remark in 1679 that 'the Treasury is better managed by Commissioners than by a Lord Treasurer'. In their largely successful efforts to restore order to the King's finances the 1667 Commission had set standards of competence which could not be betrayed with impunity. However, although its techniques and routines were to remain lasting parts of the Treasury's equipment, its legacy was vulnerable. The Commission was succeeded by a Lord Treasurer, and then another; management by a Board had not yet become the rule, and the incompetence of Downing's immediate successors seriously threatened his achievement. It needed genius and determination among the Treasury's future rulers to guide it to the heights it commanded by 1714, and it could not have attained them if it had not been carried there on the shoulders of economic and constitutional change.

*The texts of these historic statements of 'Treasury control' are given in the Appendix at the end of this chapter.

PROSPERITY AND POLITICS

In 1669, a Select Committee of the House of Lords on Trade and Rents heard the sort of evidence on Dutch commercial superiority that had been familiar for the last forty years. Their low interest rate, their banks, their mercantile law, religious toleration, education – the whole commercial orientation of Dutch society – were for the umpteenth time sadly contrasted with English deficiencies. Yet in 1669 there were already signs that the stagnation of the late 1650s and the dislocation of the 1660s were giving way to growth. Of those giving evidence, the East India Company merchant, Josiah Child, at least was prepared to say that the Navigation Laws were taking effect, and the rather speculative trade statistics for the next quarter-century certainly suggest that considerable growth was taking place in just those sectors where Downing had hoped to see it – in the import and re-export by English shipping of colonial produce, sugar, tobacco, calico; in that school of English seamanship, the Newfoundland fishing industry, and in the important bulk-carrying Baltic trade.[2] If at the same time there was an irreducible boom in luxury imports from France it was simply one of the few regrettable symptoms of the new prosperity.

The responsiveness of the revenue to this growing prosperity was a belated justification of the Restoration fiscal settlement. For the first dozen years of Charles II's reign, despite the addition in 1663 of the vastly unpopular 'Hearth Tax', the ordinary revenue had not yielded the £1·2 million per annum demanded of it. But in the 1670s, particularly when England's withdrawal from the Franco-Dutch war of 1672–8 left her the run of north European commerce, Customs and Excise were producing healthy returns. Significant changes in revenue administration accompanied this development. The oscillation between depression and boom had weakened the traditional arguments justifying 'farming'. The necessity, in bad times, of indemnifying the revenue farmers for the dislocation of trade, and the certainty, in good times, that they were making a handsome profit, had rather weakened the attraction of getting a fixed rent from them. Why couldn't the Treasury manage the revenue itself? There were several reasons behind the decision to break off the new Customs farm contract of 1671. The successful bidders, already in control of the Excise, showed signs of exploiting a thoroughly dangerous monopoly, and there may even be some truth in the story that the hot-tempered Treasury lord, Sir Thomas Clifford, caught the principal farmer eavesdropping on the King and flung him downstairs.[3] Whatever the case, in September 1671 the Customs revenue was hastily placed under government management by a Commission headed, appropriately enough, by Sir George Downing. The Excise remained under a compromise between farming and management until 1683, but during the Treasurership of Sir Thomas Osborne, Earl of Danby (1673–9), the main revenue was more completely under central control than ever before.

Politically, this was important. The Customs revenue had always been the most reliable fund from which to meet salaries and pensions, and since the Restoration the nature of those pensions had become increasingly political. The continuous existence of the Parliament elected in 1661 ensured this, for although Charles had complete freedom to summon, prorogue and dissolve, the subtler art of managing the House of Commons eluded him until, by the dexterous use of 'influence' or corruption, something like an organized 'court party' had been formed. By 19 February 1670, when eighty ordinary M.P.s rose from their seats and walked out in disgust at the slavish way the courtiers were voting, that process had gone far, and by 1674, when the control of this party had passed from the Secretaries of State to the Treasurer, the pattern of future parliamentary politics had begun to take shape. Danby, as head of the Treasury and organizer of the court party, had more in common with the age of Walpole than the age of the Cecils.

The uncommitted M.P.s, led by a small 'country party', were not slow to respond. In 1675, Danby and the whole financial administration came under heavy attack. As Lord Treasurer he was impeached for perverting the 'ancient course of the Exchequer', a Bill was introduced to purge all pensioners and office-holders from the Commons, and the grant of additional supplies was accompanied not only by strict appropriation clauses but by the suggestion that the money should be handled by the City of London rather than the Exchequer. Behind this last proposal lay disgust at the continuing 'Stop of the Exchequer' of January 1672, when Charles had postponed repayment of bankers' loans and Treasury Orders registered under Downing's Act of 1667. The House of Commons had little sympathy for the small circle of goldsmith–bankers who, ground between their angry creditors and an empty Exchequer, tottered on into bankruptcies during the late 1670s and 80s. But the discredit of the Exchequer was a matter of public concern. He was not a jealous man, said a mischievous M.P., but if he met someone leaving his wife's room in his underwear he would be forced to suspect her; the Exchequer likewise had betrayed a trust. Downing, who had no sense of humour at the best of times, was deeply upset by all this and made a rather moving speech, defending the professional integrity of the Exchequer and pointing out, quite correctly, that the decision to impose the 'stop' had been made in the Privy Council, not in the Exchequer. But in trying to draw a distinction between a political and an administrative decision he was ahead of his times. There was no remedy against a defaulting King, and upon that hard fact the professionalism of the Restoration Treasury broke down.

In the event, the Treasury and Exchequer retained their responsibility for the new parliamentary supplies, but the debates of 1675 are worth attention because they foreshadow the sort of principles which were to govern early-eighteenth-century parliamentary finance. Sitting quite regularly between 1660 and 1681, Charles II's House of Commons had ample opportunity to develop techniques of control over the successive parliamentary additions to the Crown's ordinary revenue. Already in 1666 they had forced Charles to accept a retrospective appropriation audit of the very large sums – over £5 million – that had been voted for the Dutch war. Lost in the morass of departmental book-keeping, the Commission of Accounts could produce little except the well-founded suspicion that considerable sums had been wastefully borrowed and wastefully spent. Thus between 1670 and 1679 additional supplies were not only strictly appropriated to clearly defined purposes but accompanied by parliamentary guarantees of borrowing at specified rates of interest. 'We give public money,' said the oldest M.P. in the House, 'and must see that it goes to public use. Tell [count] your money, fix it to public ends. . . .'[3]

There was to be an unfortunate hiatus in the development of these principles. The party conflicts arising from the 'Popish Plot' of 1678–81 and the efforts to exclude the Roman Catholic James, Duke of York, from the throne had by 1681 produced a strong Tory reaction in favour of the Crown. It survived long enough to allow James II a financial settlement of unparalleled generosity in 1685. Fuddled by loyalty, bemused by his threatening injunction to 'use me well', the House of Commons voted him an unconditional revenue little short of £2 million per annum. It was a piece of craven irresponsibility which the revolutionary Parliament of William's reign was determined not to repeat. As a result the arrangements made between Parliament and the Crown after 1688 were the reverse of a settlement. William III was never put in possession of distinct, permanent revenues which could have ensured his ability to 'live of his own' – although the House of Commons still refused to part with that convenient ideal. £1·2 million per annum, they decided, was still adequate for the ordinary peace-time expenses of government, and half this sum, they ordered, should be appropriated to the costs of civil government. But, with rather more deliberation than the Parliaments of Charles, they saw to it that William could not rely on receiving such a sum in perpetuity. At best he could rely on the Excise and a few of the minor, hereditary Crown revenues during his lifetime, but the major item of the Customs was granted him for only four years in the first instance, and heavily mortgaged. The intention to hobble the Crown by these means was quite explicit and deeply resented by William. Why, he asked his friend Bishop Burnet, should they suspect him, who had come to save their religion and liberties, when they had trusted James so much, who had sought to destroy both?

However, the restraints on William's financial independence had their constructive aspect. Additional parliamentary supplies, without which government could not have been carried on, were now habitually appropriated, regular departmental estimates were called for and closely scrutinized, and from 1691 until 1697 a series of Accounts Commissions imposed a searching audit of government expenditure. These were revolutionary encroachments on the royal prerogative, but they seemed fully justified by a rate of war expenditure that reached the unprecedented level of £5 million per annum. Indeed, it was war rather than revolution that fostered the main financial innovations of this period. The Bank of England, the Exchequer Bill, the Land Tax were the by-products of an expensive conflict fought in Ireland, Flanders and upon the high seas of Europe, West Africa and the Caribbean. It lasted for nine years and cost nearly £45 million. It sired the National Debt.

THE FINANCIAL REVOLUTION

These developments transformed the character of English government finance. New techniques of administration, new concepts of responsibility, supported by an intense public interest in the mobilization of credit give a special significance to the financial history of the reigns of William and of Anne. In few periods has there been such a fertility of fiscal invention. In no period have the politics of finance been more fiercely fought. One must think now in terms of 'public revenue', of which the Crown's income was an incidental and diminishing portion, and of 'public expenditure' upon ends sanctioned less by the dynastic interests of the Crown than by a parliamentary assessment of national needs. From the deliberate failure to make a proper revenue settlement had emerged, unplanned, what was to become a cardinal principle of modern finance – the annuality of supply – the provision, that is, of only such funds as were needed for the carefully estimated services of a single year. Not until the nineteenth century was the enforcement of that principle made watertight, but its beginnings are here. Finally, in apparent contrast to this short-term financing, there was the creation of a long-term, public debt. Unintentionally, something of this nature had come into being with the 'Stop of the Exchequer'; since 1672 a sum of £1·3 million had festered away, unpaid but unforgotten. In pledging the Excise to the payment of 6 per cent per annum on this debt from 1677, Charles II and Danby had undertaken the first, though shortlived, 'funding' operation in English history.* Payments ceased in 1683 and it needed a judicial verdict in the classic *Bankers' Case* before interest resumed in 1705 at the reduced rate of 3 per cent. Meanwhile some less constrained experiments in long-term debt formation had taken place. The 'Million Loan' of 1692–3 offered 14 per cent annuities or a 'Tontine' – a gamble on survival, assuring 10 per cent until 1700 and then £70,000 per annum shared among the survivors or their nominees, the last of whom actually lived until 1783. This was followed by the 'Million Lottery Loan' of 1694, offering £10 tickets carrying 10 per cent for fourteen years, with one ticket in every forty earning prizes worth up to £1,000. The third of these curious experiments, designed to raise £1·5 million was the 'Tonnage Act' which brought into being the Bank of England.

The significance of this is well understood. The parliamentary revolution had relieved the City of the anxieties it had traditionally felt about making large loans to the government, and the moneyed community, headed by the King and Queen, had no hesitation in subscribing the £1·2 million capital required to qualify them for incorporation. By December 1694 the newly chartered Bank had lent £1·2 million to the Exchequer, largely in Bank-notes, in return for 8 per cent per annum plus expenses. It was a great, but a very precarious, success, and the Bank's unique importance in English financial history should not be taken for granted. Selected by the Chancellor of the Exchequer from over seventy proposals, William Paterson's scheme was neither the most ambitious nor the least impracticable. It fell rather short of being the monopolistic 'central bank', issuing legal tender through numerous provincial branches, that some had hoped for. Its charter was temporary, the £1·2 million loan was redeemable after 1705, and its privileges were not yet exclusive. True, a government-backed 'Land Bank' failed ignominiously in 1696, but despite the privileges granted to it by a 1697 charter the Bank of England still had to face serious rivals in two associated finance companies, the Sword Blade Company and the South Sea Company.[4] Rather, the Bank of England *earned* its unique position by an outstanding record of collaboration with the Treasury – a reciprocal

*By 'funding' (the essence of the financial revolution) is meant the appropriation of a specific tax-revenue for the provision of interest payments on a consolidated body of debts; a long-term mortgage, as it were, guaranteed by an assured fund or income.

relationship in which sometimes the one, sometimes the other, held the initiative. From the outset, the Bank of England had to undertake rescue operations quite unforeseen by its founders – 1696, for example, was a crisis year. The war was going badly, huge revenue deficiencies were building up and on top of all this the Treasury was forced to undertake a full-scale recoinage. The Bank did the government two great services that year, by taking over a large proportion of these deficiencies and by agreeing to circulate Exchequer Bills.

These were interest-bearing, transferable paper notes, in direct line of descent from Downing's Treasury Orders, but being issued in convenient multiples of £10, payable on demand at the Exchequer, they were rather more attractive. Even so, the Treasury's unaided efforts would not have ensured their acceptability and the Bank was invaluable in lending the Bills some of the respectability which its own paper notes already enjoyed. In all these operations, and particularly in manipulating the foreign exchanges for the remittance of military expenditure, the Bank displayed a mastery to which the Treasury could only submit. Both were the gainers, the Bank securing new privileges, profitable business and successive renewals of its charter, the Treasury having at its disposal the wealth and talents of the City's ablest financiers. Their collaboration was to be at its best during the War of the Spanish Succession which broke out in 1702.

Meanwhile, the creation of a long-term public debt – over £5 million had been funded by 1698 – had not occurred in a fiscal vacuum. An avalanche of new Customs duties buried the 1660 Book of Rates and blurred the simple outlines of Downing's Mercantile System. More duties were added under Queen Anne than in the three reigns preceding. Excise duties were increased, and new ones created. Malt and sea-coal, pipe-clay and leather, bachelors, widows, houses and hawkers all fell under contribution in this 'war to the last guinea'. A Stamp Tax, a Salt Tax, and a tax on hackney coaches were to have a long life ahead of them. But the most substantial and significant of the government's new revenues was the so-called Land Tax. Apart from some ill-fated Poll Taxes, this step-child of the Civil War and Caroline Assessments was the nearest thing to an income tax that the seventeenth century could contrive. Levied upon income arising from public appointments (other than posts in the Forces), from investments, from merchandise, and above all from land, it was essentially a property tax which, by gradual degeneration came to mean a tax only on land. By 1698 it had ceased to pretend to be a real assessment related to growing wealth and had settled down as a fixed quota distributed among the counties to raise from their landed rate-payers. At the maximum rate of 4*s*. in the £ it was expected to yield £1·9 million per annum, and in fact it produced a total of some £19 million in William III's reign compared with £13 million each from the Customs and the Excise. Like the Income Tax in the nineteenth century it was to be the principal fiscal resource of eighteenth-century governments in emergency.

The administration of all these taxes necessarily called into being a greatly enlarged revenue-collecting bureaucracy. The Commissioners of Stamps (1694), the Commissioners of Hackney Coaches (1694), the Commissioners of Hawkers and Pedlars (1697), and the Commissioners of Salt (1702) joined the Commissioners of Customs (1671) and of Excise (1683), and the Office of Taxes (1665) as professional revenue boards subordinate to the Treasury. By the accession of Queen Anne the Treasury's was by far the largest departmental empire yet seen in English government.

THE PERMANENT STAFF OF THE TREASURY

Compared with this proliferation around it, the internal development of the Treasury looks meagre. But striking administrative innovation mattered less now that the main principles of control had been so firmly laid down. The essential task was to maintain them, and on the whole this was done. Although Treasurers and Treasury lords like Danby, Rochester and Godolphin were exposed to the fiercest cross-currents of late-seventeenth-century politics, they were able to keep their footing on a solid substratum of departmental competence.

In 1690, the Chancellor of the Exchequer, Richard Hampden, seemed to pay tribute to this when he presented some rather complicated figures to the House of Commons. Apparently not wishing to seem to be showing off, he remarked apologetically – 'A man of better understanding than I may not understand my trade, but it may be explained to him by the officers'. If indeed this was the first parliamentary tribute to the professional competence of the Treasury staff it was hardly premature. For some years now the clerical establishment had been taking shape round the Secretary to the Treasury and by 1690 there was a distinct hierarchy of senior clerks (five at first, then four), under-clerks and a few 'supernumeraries'. In this matter, as in others, Downing's secretaryship was vital. The multiplication of records under him called for exacting clerical standards, and his principal clerk, Roger Charnock (whom Pepys once met at Hampton Court, roaring drunk), was given some sobering responsibilities. 'Charnock to mind me of it', 'Charnock to do it', read Downing's endorsements to his memoranda. But the process by which two or three overworked assistants developed into a small department with tenures independent of its master, the Secretary, remains clouded. In any case, for some time to come it was to Exchequer officials, in particular the Auditor of the Receipt, that the government and Parliament still looked for authoritative reports on revenue and expenditure. While the post of Auditor was held by that pushful intriguer and dramatist, Sir Robert Howard, M.P., this was understandable. But with his death in 1698 the Auditor was soon displaced by the Secretary to the Treasury as the regular channel of information and while Exchequer posts generally drifted back into sinecurism, the Treasury establishment advanced to new levels of competence. Indeed, as the volume of Treasury business grew it was likely to be the senior clerks rather than the Secretary who were masters of financial detail. Upon this basis they could be trusted to prepare reports for the Board and handle such confidential matters as the 'secret service' funds. They were well rewarded. Their share of Treasury fees might exceed £400 per annum each, and they tended to collect other valuable perquisites. One or two found seats in Parliament, and they were often well-connected, by marriage if not by birth. But very rarely do they seem to have sacrificed their professionalism to their social pretensions; it was by a slow, painstaking progression through this small community of second-rank public servants that the most distinguished Treasury Secretary of the eighteenth century was to climb – William Lowndes.

More will be said of him in his turn. Between Downing's departure and the appointment of Lowndes there were at least two other able Secretaries, Henry Guy and William Jephson. Jephson was particularly well liked by the House of Commons for his helpfulness on matters of financial detail and they deplored his premature death. But Guy was unquestionably the most important political figure of them all. Well-bred, well-educated, wealthy and witty, Guy was a polished figure, thoroughly acceptable at court in a way in which Downing never was. By virtue of his intimacy with Charles, James and, to a lesser extent, William, he was able to carry the secretaryship to a high point of confidential influence. But his fourteen years at the Treasury came to a bad end; in 1694 he was proved to have accepted a bribe and was sent to the Tower. Even so, his influence survived, and Lowndes, who succeeded him, was really his nominee and curate. A rather bashful Lowndes was forced to admit to a Commission of Accounts in 1702 that as long as Guy lived he had to pay him half his earnings; and there was nothing to be done about it. It was a debt of honour. When Guy died in 1710 the position was regularized, for a second, or joint, secretaryship was created for Thomas Harley with whom the unfortunate Lowndes had to go on sharing his fees. Henceforth there were always to be two Secretaries at the head of the Treasury establishment.

Later eighteenth-century developments were to produce a division of labour between the administrative and political sides of their work, and even in 1710, the exploitation of Lowndes – the painstaking 'civil servant' – by more 'political' figures such as Guy and Harley, suggests a distinction between them which, strictly speaking, is quite unwarranted. The insulation of public servants from public politics was not to be given proper definition until the nineteenth century, and Lowndes, like his predecessors, had his feet in both camps. He was a Member of Parliament from 1695 until his death in 1724.

Nevertheless, there was a strong aspiration, of which Guy's disgrace was a symptom, to purge the House of Commons of all office-holders and create a real divorce between the legislature and the executive. The intention was to serve the ideal of a 'balance of the constitution' between a 'pure' and independent Parliament and a powerful Crown (as well as to promote the age-old conflict between the 'ins' and the 'outs'). Furthermore, the vast growth of the Treasury's authority over an expanding and manifestly subordinate revenue-collecting bureaucracy had helped to strengthen that intention. Earlier in the seventeenth century no one would have taken it for granted that a minor official, entrenched in some begged, purchased or inherited place, was the political dependent of his nominal superiors. Office, however petty, had often conferred independence. But a deliberate Treasury campaign, beginning in 1667, to make most revenue appointments tenable 'at pleasure', instead of 'during good behaviour' or for 'life', had served to change all that, and the extent of court party patronage under Danby and his successors had helped to make its political implications alarmingly clear. It was now reasonable to distinguish between the responsible chiefs of old departments of state and a new class of well-paid dependents who manned the numerous new Boards. Thus, although the 1690s saw several attempts at total exclusion, and although the great Act of Settlement in 1701 actually embodied a clause which would have displaced *all* office-holders from the House of Commons, it was fortunate for the character of modern British government that a formula of piecemeal and conditional exclusion was finally reached. By the terms of Acts of 1705 and 1707 it was provided that occupants of any office created after 1705, together with a few which had earned the specific displeasure of the House, were to be totally disqualified from election; while any Member of Parliament accepting an 'old' office, existing before 1705, automatically forfeited his seat but might seek re-election. This last provision was to remain an embarrassment to British politicians until 1926, and other provisions of the 1707 Act have hampered modern governments. However, it was not until an Act of 1741 that clerks of the Treasury and other government departments were made totally incapable of holding seats, thereby creating one of the basic conditions of an independent, non-political civil service.

THE TREASURY UNDER ATTACK

Meanwhile, the Treasury and its dependent Revenue Boards came under considerable parliamentary pressure from the succession of Accounts Commissions which sat between 1691 and 1713. Although run by Members of Parliament (with one exception), they should not be confused with the modern Public Accounts Committee of the House of Commons which has different origins and a very different character. These were highly partisan bodies, and it has been shrewdly observed that 'the criterion of party strength between 1690 and 1701 was not nearly so much the composition of the Cabinet as that of the Committees [Commissions] of Accounts'.[5] Their administrative value was almost always minimal, and it was hardly worth their considerable salary bill to learn that the Commissioners of Sick and Wounded had been paying 25*s.* per pound for bruised rhubarb when its real value was 9*d.* But this was not their purpose. They were hunting big political game and Henry Guy was one of their first victims and Robert Walpole one of their last. In 1702 they set on the Paymaster General of the Forces, the Earl of Ranelagh, and in 1711 they felled the great Duke of Marlborough.

Both these attacks have some administrative interest. For example, Ranelagh, a revenue farmer in the reign of Charles II, enriched London with his gardens but impoverished Ireland with his exactions. Between 1689 and 1702 he handled huge sums as Paymaster General and the confusion of his accounts, as well as his opulence, laid him open to charges of misappropriation. But that same confusion made it difficult to prove anything against him and the Accounts Commission's report is largely significant because it lays bare the inadequacy of departmental responsibility to either Parliament or the Treasury. But there were great difficulties in the way of enforcing accountability among the enormous number of officials who now handled public money: and the root of those difficulties lay in the Exchequer. Most Exchequer posts were held for life, some were hereditary, and the incumbents could not be dispossessed for anything as innocuous as inefficiency. Immune to dismissal for anything short of treason, it took proved dishonesty to justify their suspension, and that was none too easy as some late-seventeenth-century scandals were to prove. Thus, snug in their sinecures (for the real work was done by modestly paid deputies) the patent officers of the Exchequer could safely ignore the Treasury's pleas for the expeditious performance of their duties. Where those duties were the auditing and declaration of public accounts the consequences of delay, let alone malpractice, were extremely grave, and the 1696 Act 'for the better observation of the course anciently used in the receipt of the Exchequer' was a response to a situation little short of crisis.

It has been noticed by Professor Baxter that 'the regulations of 8 & 9 W. III. c. 28, para. 12 bear a close, almost a suspicious, resemblance to the Lowndes report of October 1686'.[6] Of course they do. Lowndes was the draftsman. His rather fine portrait shows him with the Act firmly held under his hand.[7] This was not inappropriate, for although the Act was primarily declaratory of the traditional duties of the Exchequer it was brilliantly original in establishing Treasury control over the men who actually performed those duties – the deputies to the patent officers. Henceforth they were to be appointed only with Treasury approval during 'good behaviour', a formula which cleverly satisfied both parties. While the patentees remained secure in their emoluments the Treasury had some small guarantee of competence. It seemed a workable compromise. Yet in January 1703 Lowndes still took a discreetly pessimistic view of Exchequer failings. Giving evidence before the Parliamentary Accounts Commission he declared 'he knows nothing of their corruptions, but apprehends favour may have been unduly shewn to the Accountants in not making out process as they ought to have done', and, hinting broadly that key officials in the Exchequer had been bribed not to pursue the government's debtors, went on to admit that the Exchequer had been better run in the past by men like Duncombe and Rochester. Not surprisingly, the Commons' Address to the Queen on 11 February concluded a scathing commentary upon Exchequer deceits with the indictment that 'there appears to have been a general mismanagement of the public revenue, which was principally owing to some of those great officers of the Treasury, who being more intent on their own private profit than the due execution of their public trusts, did neither discharge the duty of their own places, nor take care that the subordinate officers should discharge theirs'. However, with its remark that 'we cannot, in justice, omit to acknowledge the present good management of the Treasury' it becomes clear that the Address, the Accounts Commission and even Lowndes's evidence, were all part of the campaign to discredit the late Chancellor of the Exchequer, Charles Montagu, whose nickname – 'The Filcher' – was not wholly undeserved.

Nevertheless, the temptation to turn the administration of national finance to party advantage was rather out of keeping with the general conduct of the Treasury. In 1689, it is true, there had been some purging of Catholic and Jacobite officials, but subsequent attempts to make office-holding dependent on party ascendancies met with firm resistance. In 1695, when William III seemed to be contemplating some political dismissals from the Boards of Customs and Excise, the First Lord of the Treasury, Godolphin, fiercely expostulated – 'I cannot think it for your service to make changes in the management of your revenue to gratify party or animosity . . .'. If there was a case to answer, the Treasury and the Treasury alone should hear it and report upon it. 'I may be partial in this case, but I confess I think a commissioner of the Treasury has an employment uneasy enough in this kingdom without adding any mortification to it . . .'!

It is ironic therefore that Godolphin should have been the principal ministerial victim of the 1710 purges. A compulsive gambler, deceptively lethargic, the plump Godolphin had been the most reassuring guarantee of competence at the Treasury since 1679. From 1690 to 1696, and 1700 to 1701 he had been First Lord, and from 1702 to 1710 he held the white staff alone. These were critical years, and his competence and authority combined to earn him the title of 'premier'. There was no question of this being a party premiership. As a moderate Tory Godolphin was content to serve with moderate Whigs, with his first loyalties pledged to the Crown. That was his mistake. By 1710 party conflict had reached fever heat and the October elections were a Tory landslide. For many happy months Godolphin and the Whigs were tossed in the Tory blanket, Swift and Defoe holding the corners. . . .

In his *History of the Last Four Years of the Queen*, not published until 1758 but written in 1713, Swift set out a forceful condemnation of Godolphin and the whole system of 'Dutch Finance' – that is 'the pernicious Counsels of borrowing Money upon publick Funds of Interest' – and in doing so betrayed the rather old-fashioned assumptions of backwoods-Tory finance. In any case, he struck wide of the mark. Less brilliantly fertile than his Chancellor of the Exchequer, Montagu, with whom most of the great financial innovations originated, Godolphin had solid talents for administration, and between 1702 and 1710, during the most costly war England had yet fought, he had remarkable success in controlling the terms of government borrowing. Dexterous funding operations raised the National Debt from £4½ million to nearly £7½ million, yet the rate of interest never rose to the crisis levels of the 1690s.

A number of virtues lay behind this achievement: clerical competence at the Treasury, renewed vigour in the Exchequer, accurate estimates of tax yields, careful manipulation of the foreign exchanges and – above all – a relationship of confidence between Godolphin and

Marlborough, and Godolphin and the City. It was for these last that rabid Tories could not forgive him. Godolphin was dismissed and Marlborough disgraced. But the predominantly Whig City was a different kind of problem. However large its majority in the House of Commons, no administration could now afford to brush aside lightly a moneyed community believed capable of raising £6 million 'in a trice'. As Chancellor of the Exchequer, Robert Harley – the real leader of the new Tories – approached the City with some trepidation, and the Bank of England (not for the last time) seemed to recoil from an embrace which it found politically distasteful.

That, also, was a mistake. Although the Bank's petulant refusal to discount the government's foreign bills of exchange was short-lived it was enough to set the Tories in search of a new credit agency, and by May 1711 Harley was able to unveil it to the public. His scheme was to secure the very considerable amount of floating government debt, now over £9 million, by authorizing its subscription into the capital of a chartered trading company – the South Sea Company. The transfer would be compulsory, but those holding government bills, most of them at a considerable discount, would get stock at par in a company with exclusive privileges in the, supposedly, booming South Atlantic trade. This monopoly, plus 6 per cent interest from the Exchequer, plus management expenses, were the foundations of the Company's hopes.

For Harley, made Lord Treasurer and Earl of Oxford in May 1711, the successful flotation was an auspicious beginning to what was intended to be a triumphant régime of retrenchment. The achievement fell rather short of this. True, the war, which had added nearly £30 million to the nation's debts, was hurried to an economical conclusion; the £9·5 million of floating debt was duly funded in the South Sea Company stock at 6 per cent; but even with Bank of England cooperation, Harley's lottery loans were extremely expensive, and the high promise of Tory finance was not fulfilled.

It might be argued that Harley was not allowed to succeed, for he was dismissed on 27 July 1714. It was certainly not for incompetence that he fell; it was not even, as the dying Queen asserted, that he was habitually drunk. Harley had made a profounder miscalculation. A quasi-Jacobite intriguer, gambling on Stuart restoration, Harley had missed the tide which was bringing the Hanoverians to the throne. Thus it was a political, rather than an administrative revolution which marked the close of a distinctive phase of Treasury history, for although the Earl of Shrewsbury took the white staff the night before Queen Anne died he held it in trust for barely two months. For all practical purposes, Harley was the last Lord High Treasurer of England.

THE ASCENDANCY OF THE TREASURY

Late-seventeenth-century England had seen a surge of administrative vitality which it would be colourless to describe as 'evolution'. It had a vigour, an urgency, an inventiveness, quite unlike any earlier phase in English history.

Yet it would be wrong to take too insular a view of this. Most of the major European states had experienced crises in government by the mid-century and several of them had emerged, like England, purged and purposeful. Wherever found, whether in France under Colbert, Prussia under the Great Elector, or even the Russia of Peter the Great, the aspirations of European 'mercantilism' had manifested much the same forms: in commercial protection and fiscal innovation, in the founding of banks and trading companies, the issue of negotiable paper and the funding of public loans. Of course, measured by the standards valued by these absolutist states – discipline, professionalism, the coercive logic of strong, central government – England lagged behind. But measured in terms of spontaneity and skilful adaptation, the reconciliation of economic individualism with the fiscal needs of the state, England had nothing to be ashamed of. The commercial fruits of this alliance were soon to make her the envy of enlightened Europe.

The Treasury had been the principal beneficiary of this resurgence. No other department of state had interests so deeply vested in the social and economic evolution of England. No other department responded so skilfully. The Secretaries of State were close rivals, it is true. They too had benefited from the decline of the old Privy Council as the effective centre of government, and they too had created efficient, modern departments. Within the Cabinet system that had evolved by the reign of Queen Anne they were major contenders for supremacy. Advising Harley in 1704, Defoe had no doubt at all that 'the Secretaryes Office, well discharged makes a man Prime Minister of course'. He was not grossly mistaken, although, as we have seen, it was as Lord Treasurer that Godolphin and then Harley had sustained that role. After all, the decisive attribute of the premier was not the possession of the white staff or the seals but the sovereign's confidence, and, as Lord Salisbury was to show in the 1890s, there was no iron law binding the premiership to the Treasury.

But by the end of the seventeenth century there were compelling reasons why the chief contender for power should make his home in the Treasury. Danby's administration had made them clear and subsequent developments reinforced them, for, with every extension of the financial basis of government, the Treasury's access to the roots of power grew more secure. At best, ambition to control the largest departmental empire – at worst, a desire to have some fingers in the till – ensured the attractiveness of 'the place where the money groweth'. It was plausibly rumoured in 1690 that two members of the Treasury Commission had paid £200,000 'upon the nayle' for their places.

If so, they may have been disillusioned. The First Lord of the same Commission, the extremely wealthy Sir John Lowther, who had paid nothing, could not wait to get out. 'I agree I am not fit for my place in the Treasury,' he told a baffled House of Commons in 1691; 'I shall be much easier out of it, and I hope I shall leave it', which he shortly did. Godolphin likewise had groaned under the rigours of responsibility – 'the life of a slave in the galleys is a paradise in comparison of mine'. Indeed, it is only necessary to glance at the Treasury Minute Books to appreciate that the Treasury's chiefs were extremely hard worked, meeting morning and afternoon for an average of four days a week. Seven o'clock starts were not unusual and it was said of Rochester in 1680 that he was 'up every morning at five and at the Treasury an hour before the rest'.[8]

Here, in the sheer pressure of work, was one good reason why the Treasury might be better run by a Commission than a Lord Treasurer. In addition, by 1714 there was no reason why a First Lord of the Treasury sharing £8,000 per annum with three or four junior lords should be any less important than a Lord Treasurer keeping all this to himself. Given the Crown's confidence, given the *entrée* to the Cabinet (which the Chancellor of the Exchequer rarely had), then a First Lord might be premier as readily as a Lord Treasurer. Indeed, with shared responsibility, he would be a good deal less vulnerable to attack, as Harley should have appreciated. The anonymous author of the pamphlet *Munus Thesaurii* (1713) had tried to make just this point, depicting for Harley 'on what a slippery Precipice he stands that has the Administration of this Great Office' and the sticky fate that had befallen so many of his predecessors.

But the decisive influence in this question, as in so many others affecting the Treasury, was parliamentary. In a manner already described, the Revolution settlement had drawn the Treasury into a responsible relationship with the House of Commons that made it highly desirable that there should be as many articulate Treasury Lords there as possible. It was now regularly called upon to explain itself, to justify its estimates, to defend its accounts. 'The Accounts are amazing things,' mocked a critical M.P. in the House, after a ministerial débâcle in 1691: 'we were told last session "Country gentlemen understood not Accounts", and now it seems, the Commissioners of the Treasury do not.' That sort of thing could not be allowed to happen again, and it rarely did. Thanks largely to Lowndes the presentation of figures by the Treasury became more and more authoritative, and it was greatly helped by procedural developments in the House. On 11 December 1706, in order to prevent irresponsible pressure for public expenditure, it was resolved in the Commons 'That this House will receive no Petition for any sum of Money relating to public Service, but what is recommended from the Crown'. A few years later, on 11 June 1713, this became a Standing Order which, in substance, survives today. In endowing the Executive with the sole power of financial initiative in Parliament this measure has been of profound importance. To a degree which could not otherwise be taken for granted it rooted the Treasury in the leadership of the House.

Although the future lay with the Chancellor of the Exchequer, it is the great glory of William Lowndes that he was the first to assume that leadership on the Treasury's behalf. It was Lowndes who drew up the annual schemes of financial legislation, which were Budgets in all but name, and it was Lowndes who carried them through the Committee of Ways and Means. (Indeed, 'Ways and Means' became the Lowndes family motto!) True, Lowndes was a much less creative commercial legislator than Downing, and it was partly his fault that the tariff became clogged with indiscriminate, unprotective burdens. But with a career in the Treasury which spanned nearly fifty years (from 1675 to 1724) he was by far the most professional of its servants, and unlike Downing he was universally respected. It must have been Lowndes that Trevelyan had in mind when he wrote that 'in the Treasury of the first twenty years after the Revolution we see the emergence of the best modern traditions of the permanent Civil Service'.[9]

Yet Lowndes was only the most prominent of a new caste of men serving public administration which was numerically and qualitatively superior to any seen in England before. 'Caste' is perhaps the wrong word to apply to men so diverse in their social status and so readily cross-fertilized by other callings. Indeed, the healthiest feature of late-seventeenth, and early-eighteenth-century English government is the readiness with which it called upon the finest minds of the age wherever they might be found. John Locke, Isaac Newton and Lowndes were the protagonists in the great recoinage controversy of 1695–6.[10] Locke and Lowndes clashed directly, while Newton (Master of the Mint) backed Lowndes, but it was Locke's views which carried the day, although not necessarily with the best results. Locke had for long been something like an unofficial economic adviser to the Treasury. In 1668 he had written an important memorandum on the rate of interest for Shaftesbury, the Chancellor of the Exchequer. In 1696 he became a Commissioner of the Board of Trade. Earlier still,

Sir William Petty (1623–87), one of the founders of English statistical science, had directly influenced fiscal policy with his *Treatise of Taxes and Contributions* (1662). Gregory King (1648–1712), engraver, surveyor, and herald, who produced the best statistical analysis of the late-seventeenth-century English population that we have, was also Secretary to the Parliamentary Accounts Commission and made several tax studies for the Treasury. The most professional of these advisers was Charles Davenant (1656–1714). Son of the Poet Laureate, William Davenant, a Commissioner of Excise and a Tory Member of Parliament, he survived political vicissitudes to become Inspector General of Imports and Exports in 1703. The post itself, created by the Treasury on the recommendation of the Board of Trade in 1696, is expressive of the new administrative climate and its search for more orderly, rational, scientific techniques of government. Davenant's writings, his *Discourses on the Publick Revenue and Trade of England*, his *Memorials* on Coin, on Credit, on Ways and Means, constituted a superb body of advice for an administration which was still groping its way through the technicalities of continuous, large-scale, national finance.

The fact that the Treasury was now the recipient, rather than the dispenser, of advice, subtly reflects its changed relation with the Crown, and it is this which is the conclusive aspect of its development in the late seventeenth century. For it was by no means inevitable that the Treasury should gain its administrative independence. The responsibility and attention which Charles II abdicated to his 'rougher hands' had been largely resumed by William III. He was extremely alert to the problems of the Treasury and actively directed the financing of the war. He kept an interested eye upon the distribution of Treasury patronage. But the relationship was short-lived. Queen Anne attended the earliest of her Treasury Boards, showing a decent interest in the payment of her debts; but she rarely returned. The royal chair of state which waited at the head of the Treasury boardroom table was almost always empty. For all practical purposes the Treasury was now autonomous, free to construct its own future in English government.

APPENDIX

'Order in Council as to the manner of procuring the King's signature to warrants relating to his Majesty's revenue', 31 January 1668 (from *Calendar of State Papers, Domestic, 1667–1668*, pp. 197–8).

1. That all revenue offices pass by recommendation of the Treasury Commissioners, and that offices passed by the Secretaries of State pass with proviso of not increasing the ancient fee in King James's time.

2. That all warrants for money be imprested to the several Treasurers of the Navy, Household, Guards &c, and be countersigned by the Treasury Commissioners.
3. That warrants for regulation of revenue pass by the Treasury Commissioners.
4. That no free gifts or pensions be granted till the petitioner has set forth the value of the thing sued for, and the Treasury Commissioners have reported thereon.
5. That warrants for secret service pass by the Secretaries of State, but be restrained to those that are really such, and not other payments made under that name, which may be paid again under their proper name.
6. That the Secretaries of State draw no warrants for release of forfeitures nor anything relating to revenue, without a report from the Treasury Commissioners.
7. That the Secretaries draw no warrants on the Navy or other Treasurers for pensions, gifts &c whereby necessary money is diverted. The like caution to be used as to plate in the Jewel house, unless delivered to ambassadors and to the King's officers, on account to be returned.
8. That no patents pass by immediate warrant except such as really require it. That all revenue warrants for Ireland, not comprised in the civil and military lists, be first communicated to the Treasury Commissioners.

'Order for regulation and establishment of the Committees of the Privy Council', 12 February 1668 (from *Privy Council Minutes*).[11]
'All things relating to the Treasury in England or Ireland to be immediately referred to the Lords Commissioners of the Treasury, from whence it may come again to the Council Board, in case the matter be of such a nature as they cannot or would not willingly give their determination therein.'

SOURCE NOTES

1. S. B. Baxter, *The Development of the Treasury, 1660–1702* (1957), p. 179.
2. R. Davis, 'English Foreign Trade, 1660–1700', in *The Economic History Review*, 1954–5, pp. 150–66.
3. *Memoirs of the Life of Mr Ambrose Barnes* (1867), Surtees Society, vol. 50, p. 223.
4. For details of these schemes see J. P. Carswell, *The South Sea Bubble* (1960); J. K. Horsefield, *British Monetary Experiments, 1650–1710* (1960); or P. G. M. Dickson, *The Financial Revolution in England* (1967).
5. K. Feiling, *A History of the Tory Party, 1640-1714* (1950), p. 287.
6. Baxter, *op. cit.*, p. 129.
7. Sir J. Clapham, *The Bank of England: A History* (1944), vol. I, contains a reproduction of the portrait as its frontispiece in which the inscription of the Act may just be discerned.

8. Cited in Feiling, *op. cit.*, p. 191.
9. G. M. Trevelyan, *England under Queen Anne*, vol. 2, *Ramillies* (1932), p. 163.
10. For the best technical account of this controversy see Horsefield, *op. cit.*
11. The full text of the Order is printed in J. P. Kenyon, *The Stuart Constitution: 1603–1688: Documents and Commentary* (1966), pp. 482–4.

CHAPTER 4

The Eighteenth-Century Treasury: 1714-80

Everybody must be managed. Queens must be managed: kings must be managed; for men want managing almost as much as women, and that's saying a good deal.
THOMAS HARDY, Under the Greenwood Tree

THE PARADOX OF POWER

By modern standards, now that 'the public sector employs directly nearly 25 per cent of the nation's manpower',[1] the scale of eighteenth-century government looks rather puny. Exact comparison is quite impossible of course, and even approximation is hazardous. We have no reliable figures for the population – although estimates coincide at around 6·7 million for England and Wales by 1760. And in the circumstances of eighteenth-century society and government, where the working force was elastic and where substantial areas of administration were unsalaried if not unpaid, concepts like 'employed' and 'manpower' are not easy to define. However, with figures taken from the second half of the century, we may deduce that there were nearly 17,000 men 'employed' in government departments, some 14,000 of these in the revenue-collecting boards. The royal households, with their dependents might total less than 1,000, but throw in the armed forces – which rose to over 200,000 at the height of the Seven Years' War (1756–63) but averaged 68,000 over the period 1720–60 – add to this the work force of the naval dockyards, which approached 10,000 by mid-century, and one can concoct a fairly respectable figure, between four and five per cent of the adult male population.

Indeed, if – say, upon the accession of George III in 1760 – an aspiring politician had allowed himself to be taken up into a high place by some devil of ambition, the panorama of government spread before him would have seemed exciting enough. Through innumerable channels, public money and, with it, power, now flowed out to remote horizons – to America, to the Caribbean, to Africa, to India and to the continent of Europe. Everywhere, governors, garrisons, contractors, customs officials, colonial agents and the assiduous riff-raff of an expanding empire, took their turn in fingering the government's guineas. Nearer home the scene was thronged and was described in 1761 by a future bishop of Salisbury –

> when we consider the vast body of persons employed in the collection of the revenue in every part of the kingdom; the inconceivable number of placemen, and candidates for places in the *customs*, in the *excise*, in the *post office*, in the *ordnance*, in the *salt office*, in the *stamps*, in the *navy* and *victualling* offices, and in the variety of other departments; when we consider again the extensive influence of the *money corporations*, *subscription jobbers*, and *contractors*, the endless dependence created by the obligations conferred on the bulk of the gentlemen's families throughout the kingdom, who have relations preferred, or waiting to be preferred, in our *navy*, and numerous *standing army*; . . .[2]

When we consider all this, he was saying, there need remain no fear of government becoming *democratical*; the immense resources of the Crown would always ensure the dominance of the governing oligarchy. . . . And control of this elaborate empire might well seem an intoxicating vision. Yet it would have been an imaginative devil who could have indicated the Treasury as the seat of such control and a naïve politician who believed him. 'Treasury influence', 'Treasury boroughs', even 'the Treasury party' – these are familiar terms in the vocabulary of eighteenth-century politics; 'Treasury control' was not.

There is a paradox here which has got to be explained. On the one hand we have the Treasury, master-manipulator of the political world, deploying unrivalled resources of patronage in Parliament and the electorate at large. The effectiveness of its manipulation was an indispensable guarantee of political stability. The Treasury was the known *locus* of power, the fulcrum upon which relations between the Crown and the political community were understood to turn. Lord Chancellor Hardwicke defined this role when he reminded George II in 1755 –

> That the Head of his Treasury was indeed an Employment of great Business; very extensive, which allways went beyond the bare management of the Revenue. That is extended thro' both Houses of Parliamt. the Members of which were naturally to look thither. That there must be some principal Person to receive applications; to hear the wants & wishes & the Requests of Mankind with the Reasons of them; in order to lay the same before His Majesty for his determination.[3]

This is an aspect of the Treasury so well known, so skilfully analysed and portrayed by historians of eighteenth-century England, that I shall have little to add to it here.

But on the other hand there is the Treasury as the administrative centre of government, head of a large revenue-collecting bureaucracy, initiating financial programmes in the House of Commons, and holding the public purse of the state. How effectively did it exercise these responsibilities? This chapter will try to deal with that question, but a short, provisional answer might reasonably be – 'Poorly'. The

Treasury's management of the revenue left a great deal to be desired, its control over the spending of the other great departments was nominal, and its concern for the efficiency and probity of the public service was slight. Characteristics of eighteenth-century government which are, perhaps too readily, taken for granted – 'corruption', peculation, sinecurism, pluralism – are reflections of this state of affairs, and the intractability of the problems they posed will become clearer when we trace their elimination in the course of Chapter 5.

This may seem a rather abrupt decline from the high point of Treasury development which was reached in the reign of Queen Anne. Is it an illusion? Certainly by the standards of the early seventeenth century the administrative machinery of the eighteenth century was large and impressively competent. But a marked decline in the professionalism of the revenue administration following the political purges of 1714 was real enough.[4] Godolphin had done his best to protect the Treasury's empire from spoliation, but the triumph of the Tories in 1710 and their abasement in 1714 had come near to introducing a political spoils system, with dismissals following each turn in the parliamentary wheel. Fortunately there were strong prejudices against such a system and the long, stable ascendancy of the Whig oligarchy after 1714 fended it off. But some damage had been done. A tradition of professionalism had been broken, and the Treasury's management of its own family of subordinate departments fell away into an easy-going, tolerant compromise between fiscal needs and political expediency.

But this alone does not explain the survival of such a relationship until the 1780s. It does not account for the paralysis of the House of Commons which for nearly seventy years made no effective attempt to enforce the responsibility of the Executive for efficient, economical government. There are several possible lines of explanation – a persistently low level of administrative expertise, a vested interest in 'corruption' – but these are implausible. The inadequacies of the Treasury as a centre of administrative control have causes more complex than incompetence, more interesting than immorality. They derive largely from the abstract, but fundamental, sphere of constitutional theory. Indeed, it is reasonable to suggest that eighteenth-century government was in some sense the victim of an ideal of the constitution quite at odds with logic and reality.

THE TREASURY AND THE CONSTITUTION

Briefly stated, the ideal of the constitution which had shaped the aftermath of the Revolution of 1688 was that of 'balance' – a balance in government between the pure and independent entities of the Law, in the care of the Judiciary, of the Legislature, in the hands of Parliament, and of the Executive, at the command of the Crown. And within the Legislature there was another balanced relationship. Since the Middle Ages, constitutional theorists had believed the excellence of English government to repose in a working harmony between the Aristotelian elements of Monarchy, Aristocracy and Democracy. Reconciled by patriotism, protestantism and common utilitarian interest it had seemed reasonable that this watchful relationship should issue in effective government.

But of course, even in theory, it was obvious that there could be no true 'separation of powers'. The Crown, undisputed master of the Executive, freely appointing, if not freely dismissing, the judges, was also an essential part of the Legislature. Within set limits it held the initiative over the summons and duration of parliamentary sessions. Its assent was indispensable to any Act of Parliament, and, most alarmingly, it had always been powerfully represented in the House of Commons. It was the presence there of so many dependent courtiers in late-seventeenth-century Parliaments that had fostered this aspiration for some effective separation of powers. It was in pursuit of this ideal that such strenuous efforts had been made in the reigns of William and Anne to purge the House of Commons of office-holders. But, as we have seen, the efforts had failed and at any time in the eighteenth century there were nearly two hundred government 'placemen' present.

Thus, if there was a balance in reality it was because Legislature and Executive were interlaced, interdependent. Harmonious relations between the Crown and the Commons were secured by sanctions more effective than either patriotism or protestantism. Ties as gross as bribery or as subtle as flattery helped to bind a 'court party' of 'King's Friends' and dependents to the policies of the government; and what was not achieved by dependence could sometimes be won by persuasion. It was Sir Robert Walpole's great achievement to have manipulated both arts with equal dexterity. Ruthless in management, he was compelling in debate; with one foot in the King's closet, the other in the Commons, he was the colossus who bestrode this constitutional divide.

It was in the course of Walpole's long ascendancy that theory gradually caught up with practice. While critics like Lord Bolingbroke still preached the pure, archaic ideal of the 'separation of powers', writers like David Hume, and later Blackstone, taught the excellence of their mixture.

> Herein consists the true excellence of the English government, that all parts form a mutual check upon each other. In the legislature the people are a check upon the nobility, the nobility a check upon the people . . . while the king is a check upon

both, which preserves the executive power from encroachment. And this very executive power is again checked and kept within due bounds by the two houses. . . .[5]

The relevance of all this to the Treasury is twofold. In the first place it gave a degree of constitutional propriety to the Treasury's manipulation of patronage. As a guarantee of stability and collaboration in government the Treasury's cornucopia of places and pensions acquired a kind of legitimacy which transcended dreary considerations of competence and probity. From this flowed the positive role of the Treasury in eighteenth-century government. But the second point is less obvious, for it is negative. Notwithstanding the House of Commons' control of the purse, its respect for the administrative autonomy of the Crown seemed to inhibit it from insisting with any seriousness or regularity upon the Crown's detailed responsibility for its financial stewardship. The Treasury, quite simply, was not called to account.

THE DEFICIENCIES OF PARLIAMENTARY CONTROL

What this meant in practice is best demonstrated by the Civil List, for this was the practical expression of the 'separation of powers', a guarantee of the residual belief that the King could, and must, 'live of his own'. To meet increased costs the original £600,000 per annum pledged to William III's administrative expenses had been raised to £700,000 per annum in 1698 and was renewed at this figure for the reigns of Anne and George I. Designed to cover the expenses of the royal household and all the costs of civil government – the salaries and gratuities of government departments, the diplomatic service, public buildings, and numerous other pensions and charges – it was voted by Parliament as a once-and-for-all provision at the beginning of each reign, and what the Crown did with it thereafter was its own responsibility. There was no question of annual estimates or annual account to the House of Commons. However, large deficiencies tended to build up and the House was called upon to reconsider the problem in 1712, 1721 and 1725. Walpole skilfully secured his position with George II in 1727 by procuring for him a Civil List of £800,000 per annum and debts were again settled in 1747. Unfortunately the basis of the List was changed on the accession of George III. Hitherto it had been derived from allocated taxes yielding sometimes more, often less, than the stipulated sum; now it was to be a fixed stipend, not a revenue, guaranteed by Parliament from such annual funds that it chose to appropriate. This in itself did not destroy the independence of the Crown's expenditure, for as the Duke of Newcastle asserted in

1760, 'It is Your Majesty's own Money; You may do with it what you please.' But it was a poor bargain. If George had retained his grandfather's revenues they would have yielded well over £1 million by 1777. Instead he was heavily overdrawn and 1777, when he was grudgingly granted £900,000 per annum, saw a decisive step towards securing the accountability of the Treasury for the details of Civil List expenditure. Shortly, in 1782, Parliament was to establish its full right to scrutinize and reform any civil expenditure – and when it did so a new era had begun.

Meanwhile, the attacks on aspects of the Civil List, particularly that overrated bogy the 'secret service' money, should not be mistaken for any real parliamentary interest in civil administration. Their real purpose, as always, was to curb the 'corrupting influence of the Crown' believed to lurk in places and pensions. In pursuit of that end, Members of Parliament were either indifferent to considerations of efficiency or even hostile to it, for implicit in the political conflicts of the late seventeenth and early eighteenth centuries was a real fear of strong, authoritative government. Not for nothing had the House of Commons thrashed such over-mighty subjects as Marlborough, Montagu and Godolphin, riddling Queen Anne's executive with a cross-fire of inquiries, impeachments and discriminatory legislation. By 1714 ministers of all ranks had learned to keep their heads well down – snug, like hermit-crabs, in the strange, archaic bolt-holes of the royal household, or submerged, like the First Lord of the Treasury himself, in the corporate responsibility of a Board. The storm over the 'premiership' of Walpole is only the most notable symptom of this fear.

But indifference did not stop short with the civil administration. It is much more surprising that Parliament should have been equally compliant towards naval and military expenditure. While the Civil List was usually debated only at the beginning of a new reign, expenditure on the armed forces had been, since the Revolution, a matter for annual supply. Whether in peace or war, each year brought a new opportunity to challenge the government's estimates. And yet, for the most part, early eighteenth-century Estimates were accepted uncritically. Perhaps one should make a distinction here between the Estimates for the Navy and those for the Army. The latter were viewed rather less sympathetically, for a standing army was a traditional bogy in a way that 'England's wooden walls' were not. As a result the Estimates for the land forces were presented in greater detail to a more or less routine accompaniment of growls about tyranny and military oppression. The much larger Navy Estimates, on the other hand, usually passed with ease. Voted under only three heads they were hardly ever challenged in detail. In 1740 considerable embarrassment was caused when an independent M.P. (later bought off with a place on the Admiralty Board) treated the House to an expert break-down of naval expenditure. It was 'not from vanity or ostentation of greater knowledge and sagacity than other gentlemen are possessed of' that he spoke; country gentlemen, he suggested lightly, were too shy of seeming unpatriotic or ignorant of naval matters to query the Admiralty's estimates. As a result they were being allowed to get away with gross extravagance.... He concluded with an abstruse point about mooring charges. This was the sort of detailed challenge which the Estimates very rarely received.

Of course, less well-informed criticism was not so rare. Its intensity was a significant barometer, marking the changes in the political climate. Thus, from 1725 onwards, the opposition to Walpole invariably made the presentation of Estimates an opportunity for fierce but wildly generalized attacks. Likewise, after 1774, unease and disgust at the nature of the conflict with America heightened the sensitivity of the Commons to mounting expenditure. But in the middle years of the century, as England fought Spain and France for the possession of a world empire, the House of Commons accepted unprecedented Estimates without a murmur. In February 1759 Lord Chesterfield told his son, 'Near twelve millions have been granted this year, not only *nemine contradicente* but *nemine quicquid dicente*. The proper officers bring in the estimates; it is taken for granted that they are necessary, and frugal; the members go to dinner, and leave Mr West and Mr Martin [the Joint Parliamentary Secretaries to the Treasury] to do the rest'!

This situation might not have survived if the House of Commons had kept in being the kind of Public Accounts Commissions that had been common in the reigns of William and Anne, but after 1713 they had fallen into abeyance. Sir Robert Walpole, whose indiscretions as Secretary at War had put him in the Tower for a spell in 1712, had every reason to hope that such committees were dead and buried. William Pulteney's motion of February 1726 for a Select Committee of inquiry into all public debts incurred since 1714 was easily defeated. But in 1735 there was a more serious challenge when another distinguished opposition leader, Sir William Wyndham, moved for a Select Committee on the Navy Estimates and a revival of the Accounts Commissions of the 1690s –

> I cannot comprehend how it was possible, in every year of this long term of peace, to find pretences for putting the nation to such a vast expence: and I must think, if our parliaments, for these twenty years past, had followed the example in the precedents now read to you, and had always appointed a select committee to examine the estimates yearly laid before them, it would not have been possible to prevail with them to agree that such an expence was necessary.

Walpole reacted with rather more restraint than a scalded cat, but there is no mistaking his emotion: 'the naming of a select committee, to inquire into accounts and estimates, is a very extraordinary method of proceeding, a method which has not been practised for many years, and never was often practised; we must suppose it will give a general alarm.' The motion was defeated by a none too healthy margin of 198 to 168, but it proved decisive. The following year, William Pulteney's excellently argued case for a proper scrutiny of estimates was rejected without a division and this seems to have killed the idea for another fifty years. The prevailing philosophy on accountability was roundly stated in 1775:

> Could any ministers carry on the business of the public if any gentleman in this House had a right to call for such an account? It would be impossible . . .; the public service can never be advanced by calling for accounts which destroy your confidence in them.

TREASURY CONTROL OF EXPENDITURE

The success of mid-eighteenth-century governments in stifling the faint aspirations of the House of Commons for a responsible relationship holds the key to the inadequacy of Treasury control over eighteenth-century government expenditure. It need be no secret, reserved for the next chapter, that the mature formulation of Treasury control was in direct response to the formulation of parliamentary control. Between 1714 and 1780 that incentive was almost totally lacking.

This is not to say that the Treasury failed to exercise any restraint over demands for military expenditure. Intermittently, it did. Over the Estimates for the Ordnance department it had traditionally exercised a close supervision. And, although the basic strength of the armed forces for the coming year was a matter settled by the King and Cabinet, the Treasury was fully entitled to call upon the Secretary at War and the Treasurer of the Navy for an advance statement of their claims. It sometimes submitted these to revision. For example, on 14 January 1729, the Treasury Minute Book records –

> Mr Pelham, the Secretary at War, comes in and lays before my Lords the Several Estimates for the Forces, which are to be layd before the House in the next Session. My Lords discourse him thereupon and he with their Lordships agree to the alteration and amendment of some articles inserted therein which he is to see performed accordingly.

But this is sufficiently rare to be worth recording. Had it been more frequent it would still be naïve to believe that the Treasury was guided by a concept as hypothetical as economy or as sophisticated as efficiency. The motive was, at best, the prudent one of not straining the credulity of the House too far. Indeed, it was the customary and deliberate practice to pitch the Navy Estimates too low rather than at a level which would have secured efficiency.

Beyond this point – the cursory examination of Estimates – Treasury control was largely formal. After parliamentary approval and the voting and appropriation of a suitable supply, royal warrants under the Privy Seal were drawn up which authorized the issue of this money to the relevant spending department – the Treasurer of the Navy or the Paymaster of the Forces – in large, round sums up to the total granted. Under this general authority the Treasury later gave its specific orders to the Exchequer to issue convenient sums at stated times until the totals authorized under the Privy Seals and, ultimately, the Act of Parliament were exhausted. It gave these orders at times, and for amounts, requested by the spending department, but no money could be issued without its direction, and it was the Treasury's particular responsibility to see that the totals were not exceeded or the appropriation flouted. Theoretically, it had complete discretion to adjust the priorities of departmental spending, although here again it usually yielded to departmental prompting. After this, the propriety of the expenditure which followed was a matter for the departments concerned – which had their own financial machinery – and for the auditors of the Exchequer. The latter, in the fullness of time – perhaps twenty years later – would work round to checking the departmental account of expenditure against the record of authorization and then 'declaring' it as a fully audited account before the Chancellor of the Exchequer. If there were improprieties then the Exchequer would pursue its ponderous remedies and the Treasury might be called upon to enforce or mitigate them. But its attention to these wearisome procedures was forced and intermittent. It did not and could not break through the medieval anomalies of the audit system until Parliament came to its aid.

Meanwhile, one should not expect too much of the Treasury's control of military expenditure. To our own day this remains the largest area of expenditure least susceptible to ordinary considerations of economy, and the pressures were no different in the age of Chatham. Conversely, one should not assume completely unbridled waste and corruption in the departments. Most military expenditure was determined by traditional rates and fixed establishments. The largest single item in the Navy Votes, the 'Sea Service', was calculated at the rate of £4 per man per lunar month – a rate which remained unaltered between the days of Blake and Nelson. Furthermore the Treasury did exercise a direct control over contracts for two important items of expenditure – the remittance of money to troops abroad, and their victualling. Here, too, they calculated prices according to fixed formulae which, although they precluded shrewd economies, helped to prevent wild profiteering. The result seems to have been that, under the very difficult conditions of the American War of Independence, the Army – if not well led – was comparatively well fed.[6]

But there remains an aspect of military expenditure which completely defied the principle of parliamentary sanction and which was barely checked by Treasury restraint. It was the freedom of the Navy and the Army to incur debts far beyond the Estimates, the appropriated supply, or even Treasury authorization. In the case of the Army there was the simple practice of anticipating future parliamentary supply for unforeseen items not provided for in the Estimates by withholding Army pay for up to a year. The so-called 'Army Extraordinaries' were financed by the diverted pay, and the resulting deficit on the ordinary account was then presented to Parliament for retrospective sanction and supply. In this way, at times of crisis, the House of Commons was habitually faced with a *fait accompli* running into millions. The counterpart to the Army Extraordinaries was 'the Navy Debt', far more important in that it was larger, permanent and played a significant role in the money market. The Debt was the direct product of the practice of underestimating Naval supply and consisted of 'Navy Bills' – quite simply the unpaid receipts of the Navy for goods, services and victuals. Registered in chronological sequence for repayment 'in course' (which was an unpredictable period of one to two years), they carried interest and could be bought in the stock-market for discounts of up to 20 per cent, according to estimates of their date of redemption. They were a highly speculative commodity, suitable only for big investors. They were also a continuous defiance of parliamentary appropriation, since while Parliament was paying off one series of accumulated arrears a new series was forming at the expense of seamen's pay.

It seems remarkable that Parliament should have tolerated these practices, but it did. At the end of the century critics of Pitt were still fighting a convention 'which rendered all the votes of the House of Commons, or bills for appropriating the supplies, ridiculous and nugatory', but years of compliance testified against them. Parliament had not only paid up for the unappropriated arrears, it had acquiesced in occasional Votes of Credit to meet future excesses. Votes of Credit were nothing less than blank cheques handed to the Crown by Parliament upon which it might draw as it pleased to meet some presumed emergency. They were indeed opposed, but here too opposition followed the tides of political opportunism and there was no consistent attack upon them until the war of American Independence.

THE ADMINISTRATION OF REVENUE

Yet, if Parliament failed to breathe down the Treasury's neck about the way its money was spent, one might expect it to have shown some attentiveness to the way it was raised. And of course it did, though watchfulness of the House of Commons in everything relating to the Land Tax, its recurring indignation about Customs evasions and its hypersensitivity to the Excise should not be mistaken for a constructive or particularly penetrating interest in revenue administration. The Salt Tax debates of 1732, the Excise debates of 1733, the Cider Tax of 1763, the Stamp Duties of 1765, were at the centre of some of the biggest political storms of the century, but these paroxysms of financial rectitude were extremely partisan and usually negative. Nothing could have been more retrograde than their successful attack upon Walpole's far-sighted Excise scheme of 1733, which had proposed to transfer some of the weight of taxation on land and commerce to an efficiently administered tax on consumption.

But revenue administration, like other aspects of civil administration, was not their proper concern. Its expenses were met at source, by deductions and poundage rates on the revenue raised, or – like the Office for Taxes – its salaries were met from the Civil List. If there was to be supervision of this sphere it would be Treasury supervision, owing little or nothing to parliamentary prompting. But here again, the Treasury was the victim of haphazard, historic evolution. The Customs, the Excise, the Land Tax, the Salt Tax and all the other revenue branches were distinguished from each other by entrenched peculiarities against which the Treasury could bring no uniform technique of control. From one Board to another the effectiveness of Treasury control might vary considerably. It reached an unusually low ebb in the case of the Commissioners for Hawkers and Pedlars. When their habitual embezzlement over a period of years was exposed in 1727, the Treasury loftily excused itself to the House of Commons on the grounds that 'the multiplicity of arduous, important and intricate affairs... having so taken up the attention of the Managers of the Treasury, that it was no wonder if so inconsiderable a branch of the revenue had escaped their notice'.

It was much less supercilious about the major revenues. Two powerful incentives ensured its attentiveness to the efficiency and staffing of the Customs and Excise Boards: a natural anxiety to maximize revenue and an irrepressible itch to exploit their patronage. Fiscal and political motives are thoroughly intermingled in eighteenth-century Treasury control. The tension between the two was most marked in the administration of the Land Tax. Falling rather heavily upon that narrow community of land-owners best represented in Parliament – voted by them, assessed by them and paid by them – it was political dynamite and yet, at the same time, the most flexible and productive of the direct taxes. It required political and administrative artistry of a high order to reconcile the needs of the Exchequer with the tranquillity of the political nation, and it is here that Walpole's fiscal policy is seen to best advantage. He not only kept the tax down to the bearable rate of 2*s*. in the £ for the years 1722–38 but managed to sustain a good rate of yield. He even taught the Opposition to love the tax, if only as a lesser evil than increased Excise duties.

The credit for all this can hardly go to the country gentlemen who, as unpaid Commissioners appointed under Act of Parliament, supervised the assessment upon themselves and their neighbours. Adept at dodging their own full share they were disinclined to press others and generally tolerated an alarming laxity among the assessors and collectors who did the donkey-work. Likewise, the fifty-odd County Receivers were notoriously sluggish in transmitting the money to the Exchequer. Although appointed and controlled by the Treasury, the Receiverships were juicy prizes for rewarding or creating local electoral influence. Huge sums passed through their hands, large sums stuck there; and while they performed a useful role as country bankers, speculating with their balances, as tax collectors they were something of a liability. Nor can the credit go to the Office for Taxes which was immediately responsible for the direction of this and other assessed taxes. Falling a victim to the political purges of 1711 and 1714, it never fully recovered the professionalism that Godolphin had tried to nurture.[7] Throughout this period it remained lethargic and inefficient. The burden therefore fell upon the Treasury. It was Walpole's Treasury which scolded the Commissioners and threatened the Receivers, which scrutinized the returns and set the Exchequer in motion against defaulters. Under Walpole the Treasury distinctly reinvigorated the machinery of local tax administration. Yet at the same time it was the Treasury of Walpole and his successors which appointed political nominees and winked at large areas of incompetence. The paradox is expressive of the dilemma which faced an essentially political administration.

The pattern therefore repeats itself throughout the revenue-collecting departments. Everywhere, considerations of electoral influence compromised unhappily with considerations of administrative efficiency. The Customs service was particularly vulnerable, carrying as it did a medieval supercargo of redundant officials and expensive sinecurists. On the one hand there was the hierarchy of Customs collectors inherited from the seventeenth-century 'farmers' and appointed by the Treasury ever since 1671. They effectively did the work required of them. On the other hand there was the more ancient hierarchy of medieval customs officials, superseded by the farmers but retained to perform token duties of supervision and record. Securely entrenched under their patents of appointment, drawing handsome incomes from services performed by deputies, their posts were keenly sought after. Towards the end of the century the positions of 'Collector Inwards', 'Collector Outwards', and 'Controller In and Out' in the port of London were still held by an Earl and two Dukes. The Treasury's influence over most of these appointments, effective and non-effective, was quite considerable and in the course of the century increasingly exercised in the interests of political patronage.[8]

In varying degrees the same is true of the Excise, the Post Office and the Salt Tax department, for all of which Walpole and his successors might at any time have a substantial waiting list. One, surviving from the 1760s, records patrons and their clients, one wanting 'a sinecure of 80£ or 100£ p.ann.', another anxious 'to be a clerk in some Office', another, more discriminating, prepared to accept £70–100 for a sinecure but demanding £200–300 per annum if actually required to labour! Fortunately, there were a few areas in which some Revenue Boards could preserve an independent jurisdiction, areas quite often where the real work was done. A resolute Board might even fend off the Treasury and sustain a standard of professionalism by putting its foot down on the qualification of nominees. Thus in 1767 the Secretary to the Treasury, Charles Jenkinson, warned an influential borough patron seeking the disposal of a minor Salt Tax post –

> If you recommend a proper person I have no doubt that we shall succeed but the office is very strict in the Qualifications they require. I have known the whole power of the Treasury made use of to induce them to give way and they would not.

Indeed, the commissioners at the head of some revenue boards were fortunate in enjoying a reasonable security of tenure. This tended to preserve incompetence: the Commissioners of Appeals in Excise were said in 1763 to have heard only one appeal in thirty years, and the Commissioners for Hawkers and Pedlars left their token duties to their solicitor; but the price was just worth paying for the continuity of administrative expertise to be found elsewhere in the revenue service. Consequently, through no great merit of its own, the Treasury was the beneficiary of reasonably expert opinion in its formulation of fiscal policy. All revenue matters presenting any technical difficulty were referred, almost automatically, to the appropriate board. Decisions on petitions, appeals and, above all, legislation, might often originate in the subordinate department, even though couched in the humble language of a recommendation. Disguised in the authoritative tones of a Treasury Minute they would duly re-emerge as the signal for action. Through this channel, extremely able administrators like Henry Reade of the Tax Office, Charles Carkesse and John Tyton of the Customs, or John Pownall of the Board of Trade, were able to make valuable contributions to the course of eighteenth-century government.

THE TREASURY AND THE AMERICAN COLONIES

This rather ignoble contrast, between the Treasury's misuse of its authority over departmental personnel and its submissiveness to departmental advice, is a suitable context in which to consider the assertion that 'the Treasury, more than any other branch of the British Government, was responsible for the loss of the American colonies'.[9]

On the one hand it is true, particularly for the early eighteenth century, that 'the Treasury was more widely represented in America than were other administrative agencies of the Crown'.[10] The Customs service in the colonies was numerous, and it grew with each new acquisition. Along the eastern seaboard of America from the sugar islands of the Caribbean to the fishing settlements of Newfoundland, the pattern of trade was set within the code of the English Navigation Acts. However, central direction of what was essentially a system of commercial protection, not of revenue collection, never lay solely with the Treasury. The responsibility was shared in increasing measure with the Board of Trade, and the latter's direction in the 1750s under the vigorous Earl of Halifax contrasted sharply with the typically lax supervision of the Treasury. The same indifference to competence, the same inclination to divert administrative equipment to the mechanics of patronage, vitiated the American, as it did the English, revenue bureaucracy. Probably a much larger volume of effective directives passed from the Privy Council via the Secretary of State than from the Treasury.

However, with the Seven Years' War, which in the case of the bitter fighting in America with the French and their Indian allies was really a nine years' war beginning in 1754, the Treasury's responsibility for victualling and the remittance of pay involved it in America more deeply than ever before. By 1763 it had acquired a very lively sense of the financial deficiencies of British government in the colonies. A new impatience with the large-scale evasions of the Navigation Acts, a resentment against the failure of the colonies to make any significant contribution to their defence, mark a momentous shift in Treasury policy, and this was given enormous urgency by a National Debt which had risen from £70 million in 1754 to £130 million by 1763, and a rate of American defence expenditure which seemed likely to exceed £300,000 per annum. Under the resolute direction of George Grenville, a narrow- but tough-minded First Lord and Chancellor of the Exchequer (1763–5) it is not surprising that the Treasury began to look around for some means to offset this state of affairs, and by July 1763 the Treasury had elicited a three-point programme from the Customs Board. It was sensible and seemingly innocuous – i.e. that, since absenteeism was rife, the American customs collectors should be compelled to attend to their duties; that to prevent fraudulent oppression they should be remunerated with a poundage rate on what they collected and not by fees extracted from the colonists; and that certain customs duties should be lowered to an extent which would make smuggling unprofitable. By 28 September the Treasury had turned this into a detailed representation to the King in Council, 'to the end that those Defects which it is not in the power of this Department of Government alone to Remedy may in consequence of His Majesty's Commands be otherwise provided for in the most effectual manner...'' which strikingly demonstrates its dependence on the full machinery of British government (the Privy Council, the Secretaries of State, the Board of Trade, the Admiralty, the Army – to say nothing of Parliament and public opinion) for the enactment, administration and enforcement of a new fiscal policy.

However, it is precisely in the novelty of the Treasury's fiscal initiative that the case against the Treasury (and the colonists' case against Britain) lies. It was under the direction of the Joint Secretaries to the Treasury, Charles Jenkinson and Thomas Whateley, that the inflammatory 'Sugar Act' of 1764 and the Stamp Act of 1765 were prepared. They were shrewdly designed to maximize revenue at rates which, compared with English taxation, were moderate and equitable. Thereafter, supported by expert legal and fiscal opinion, the Treasury pursued its new revenue policy without qualms about the colonists' case for 'no taxation without representation'. There was nothing novel about that issue in the Treasury's view. It had been raised, and settled in Parliament's favour, decades before. The only difference was that token revenues were to be replaced with more substantial ones – a matter of scale, not of principle. Even when the Stamp Act was repealed by Grenville's successors as unworkable, the principle was re-affirmed by the Declaratory Act of 1766. Shortly, in 1767, it was the Chancellor of the Exchequer, the volatile and rather unscrupulous Charles Townshend, who introduced the tax legislation which was decisive in turning American resentment into rebellion. His Revenue Act not only imposed new customs duties, which were to lead ultimately to the celebrated 'Boston Tea Party' of 1773, but proposed changes in the financial basis of colonial governments which seriously threatened their practising self-sufficiency. Simultaneously, the creation by the Treasury of a separate American Board of Customs led to problems which were political, not fiscal. The Treasury, which had been careless in its appointments to the American Board, intervened to mitigate the violence and corruption of its activities, but it was too late. The Board was driven from Boston to take refuge in a neighbouring fortress and revenue administration thereafter became a matter of coercion under military force. The path led straight to the fighting at Lexington Green.[11]

There is irony in the fact that the Treasury which conceived these policies was more efficient and constructive than it had been for years. Under Grenville, and Lord North (who became Chancellor of the Exchequer in 1767 and First Lord in 1770), the Treasury was brought to a level of competence which compares with that of Godolphin's day. But even this does not quite justify hanging the loss of the American colonies round the neck of the Treasury alone. This can only be done by inflating the Treasury's importance at the expense of Parliament and all the other agencies of British government, and by crediting it with a much greater degree of autonomy than it really possessed. For all its technical equipment and for all its political weight, the mid-eighteenth-century Treasury was still too slight a vehicle to carry that heavy responsibility on its own.

THE TREASURY ESTABLISHMENT

The War of American Independence was to be decisive in exposing this weakness. It not only created an acute financial crisis, it called in question the whole structure of British government, revealing more clearly than ever before the constitutional anomalies on which it was based. Consequently, the peculiar paradox of the Treasury – the gap between its political pretensions and its administrative competence – was also brought into the open, and it was to solve this problem that the British constitution and its government made their next great move forward.

With this prospect in view it is time to consider some simple but fundamental questions about the Treasury as a department. How well equipped was the permanent Treasury to perform its routine duties? How efficiently was it organized? How adequately was it staffed? From what level in the hierarchy did expert initiatives emerge? One can ask these and other questions with some hope of getting an answer because by the mid eighteenth century the Treasury had emerged from its formative years and had become a community of identifiable individuals with ascertainable functions. It at last becomes possible to write the internal history of the Treasury.

KENT'S TREASURY BUILDING

Something should be said first about the physical setting. There had been nothing particularly impressive about the external trappings of the late-seventeenth-century Treasury. Some of the dependent revenue offices were better housed. Christopher Wren's great Customs House, built in 1671, burnt down in 1715 and rebuilt in 1718, was a London showpiece, and the Excise Commissioners and the General Post Office occupied fine mansions in the City. The Treasury meanwhile had remained in its sometimes malodorous quarters in the old palace of Whitehall. From the range of assorted buildings which ran west from the riverside (a point roughly opposite the R.A.F. Memorial on the Embankment) to the Holbein Gate (a site just outside the Scottish Office) its windows looked out on to the fine parterre of the Privy Gardens, with its great sundial and ordered walks (a site now submerged by the Ministry of Defence). One of the first things James II had done was to rebuild the whole motley range as a unified whole to designs by Wren. Completed in 1686, the Treasury moved back to chambers now panelled and marbled, hung with white damask, adorned with silver (some of which is said to survive). A great board-room table, new chairs and a chair of state for the King replaced the threadbare acquisitions of 1667. But the splendour was short-lived. On 4 January 1698 a fire destroyed much of the old palace, licking the very corners of Inigo Jones's Banqueting House. The palace was never rebuilt. The Treasury, with its records happily intact, took refuge first in the Westminster home of its Secretary, Lowndes, and from here it moved, together with the Privy Council and the Secretaries of State, into a part of the old palace that had remained unscathed. Between the Horse Guards' Parade ground and Downing Street, with Whitehall to the east and St James's Park to the west, a complex jumble of Tudor and Stuart buildings housed Henry VIII's Great Tennis Court, the Tiltyard and the Cockpit.

The Cockpit, originally a large octagonal building, had served its barbarous purpose until the early seventeenth century; it had then become a playhouse, much frequented by Pepys, but after 1670 it was replaced by new residential apartments, abutting on to those being erected in Downing Street. Here at the Cockpit the central offices of government made their home and for a century to come 'the Cockpit' had the same general connotations for government that 'Whitehall' or 'Downing Street' has today. However, in 1732 the Treasury's chambers were found to be in 'a ruinous and dangerous condition' and the staff was again put on the streets. They moved across the road into the Lottery Office, a small building crouching at the south end of the Banqueting House. Only now was the decision made to build a permanent home. In 1733 the commission was given to William Kent, the fashionable draughtsman and architect, and by the end of 1736 the building was ready. It cost £18,000.

The reader may judge it for himself. Despite a ruined skyline the south and east sides of Horse Guards' Parade have changed relatively little since the mid eighteenth century, and even Tudor fragments of old Whitehall have been carefully preserved by the Ministry of Works. However, looking at the rather abrupt statement which the Treasury building makes when seen from the parade ground, it is only fair to mention that Kent's original design envisaged a much longer frontage, flanked by wings which would have balanced the fortress-like solidity of the existing block, with its impressive pediment, severe Doric pillars and heavy rustication. As it is, the effect is what one might expect from a Yorkshire admirer of Palladio – a rather wintry classicism, full of strength but a little heavy-handed. The west elevation which overlooks St James's Park and the garden of No. 10 has a parsimony of detail which, however appropriate it may have been to its inmates, is extremely bleak.

The interior, however, does better justice to Kent's mastery of domestic detail. The main rooms were splendidly embellished – richly ornamented ceilings, fine mahogany doors, panelling and mantelpieces individually designed by Kent. At the heart of the building is the Board Room, a handsomely proportioned chamber which still retains some of its original furnishings – the great table, massive chairs and chair of state. However, the building is no museum; today it houses the Cabinet Office, and considerations of utility have obscured or destroyed certain historical features such as the original fitted cupboards in the old 'Revenue Room' above the Board Room. As its present occupants must be aware, Kent's Treasury has always been an inefficient building, with its lavish waste of space and with access to one main room only possible by transit through another. Perhaps the building reflects less credit on Kent than his work for private patrons, like Walpole at Houghton, or Lord Cobham at Stowe.

Yet Kent performed one other service in giving British government a fixed location. He undertook the conversion which equipped No. 10 Downing Street as the home of the First Lord of the Treasury. So far it had had only private occupants, but in 1732 George II offered the crown lease to Walpole who, in his son's words, 'would only accept it for his office of First Lord of the Treasury, to which post he got it annexed for ever'. A good deal of reconstruction had to be undertaken in these rambling premises, which were really two or more houses, and Kent performed it quite successfully. Most important of all, he linked up No. 10 with the Treasury by passage-ways, thus creating the physical axis round which central government still turns.

THE CLERKS OF THE TREASURY

But what of the staff which filled the new Treasury premises? Although numbering barely thirty-five, from Joint Secretary to letter carrier, the organization of the mid-eighteenth-century Treasury Establishment seems relatively complex until one brushes to one side the attendant fringe of messengers, doorkeepers, stokers, bag-carriers, office keeper and the so-called 'necessary woman'. These domestic posts were not to be despised. At £400 per annum, from which candles and fuel had to be found, the office keeper had one of the largest Treasury allowances and Walpole, returning to office in 1721, found it worth his while to dispossess the incumbent and put back his client and relative, Thomas Mann. The messengerships likewise, some held under patents and performed by deputies, were keenly sought after by dependents of the First Lord. As a parliamentary inquiry into Walpole's 'secret service' expenditure disclosed in 1742, even the deputy messengers were sometimes entrusted with highly confidential, and no doubt lucrative, duties.

But the main interest must centre upon the clerical staff which, after successive refinements, became the Administrative class of the modern Treasury. Its structure was extremely simple. Under the two Joint Secretaries, four chief clerks supervised the work of about a dozen under-clerks. Theoretically, the concept of the 'Treasury Establishment' was precise enough: it signified a specific number of officers carried upon the salary bill of the Civil List, and by this test there were a dozen under-clerks during most of the first half of the century. But it was common for the Lords of the Treasury to appoint one or two 'supernumerary' or 'extraordinary' clerks to supplement the main body or wait until a vacancy occurred. In addition there was a good deal of uncertainty whether the handful of clerks in the 'Revenue Room' were part of the Establishment or not. Known formally as 'the Clerks who make up the Accounts of the Public Revenue for Parliament', their duties were clear enough and very valuable, but as their salaries were registered on the Customs revenue they were not, by that test, a part of the Establishment. In practice it was common, by mid-century, for clerks to pass from one part of the department to the other, and in 1757 the Lords of the Treasury made the admirable decision to train all junior clerks by giving them some experience in the technical work of the Revenue Room. Unfortunately this was reversed in 1776 and until 1834 the Revenue Room was regarded for promotion and appointment purposes as a distinct and even inferior branch. There is some irony in the fact that after its incorporation in the main Establishment the financial responsibilities of the Revenue Room marked it out as the premier division of the nineteenth-century Treasury.

Meanwhile, the main Establishment proved rather elastic. The number of under-clerks rose steeply during the 1760s to over two dozen. This sudden and temporary inflation may reflect a deliberate misuse of patronage by the unsettled, acquisitive administrations of George III's early years, or a deliberate effort to swamp the clerical offspring of earlier, discredited governments. Certainly there can be no doubt that appointments to the Treasury staff were the coveted fruits of favouritism, political influence and kinship. Lowndes, excellent administrator that he was, had no shame in placing three of his large family in the Treasury, and it was to her 'frind' Mr Lowndes that Clara Burnaby wrote in 1722, begging a Treasury place for her son, her 'poor Boy, Ned' who 'as soon as ye Lottery is over will be idle'. In due course Edward Burnaby entered the department and rose to be a chief clerk. In 1721 Sir John Pratt was a caretaker Chancellor of the Exchequer for eight weeks, just long enough, it would seem, to get the promise of a Treasury salary for his son Thomas. Entering in January 1724, a seventeen-year-old schoolboy straight from Westminster, Pratt drew an income from the Treasury for the next eighty years! Walpole, with the same comprehensive generosity that found a Stamp Office post for the husband of his mistress's maid, saw to it that Peter Leheup, a relation of his sister-in-law, entered the Treasury as an under-clerk, while Charles Jenkinson, lodging with a Mr Brummell, took a liking to his son William and brought him into the department as his clerk. In due course Brummell became a confidential private secretary to Lord North, and brought in his brother Benjamin and his son William. Only his second son, George, the celebrated 'Beau' Brummell, declined to join his prosperous relatives on a Treasury stool. Yet the Treasury Board was quite happy to countenance this kind of nepotism. As late as 1846 an untried youth was appointed explicitly as a tribute to his long-serving father.

In other cases, the web of relationships that bound these clerks to politicians of the first and second rank is difficult to trace, but it can be safely assumed that it was always there. There was no damned nonsense about merit in gaining entry to the Treasury. The social origins of the clerks were usually respectable enough, in an exacting age, to justify the phrase 'the gentlemen of the Treasury'. Younger sons of good families, elder sons of lesser families, they were fairly entitled to endorse themselves 'gent.' or 'esquire'. At least four clerks inherited baronetcies while on the Establishment and a couple more were sons of peers. Underlying this phenomenon there was none of the calculated social exclusiveness of the mid-nineteenth-century Treasury; only the dubious assumption that good connections were the best ascertainable guarantee of a good education. Several can be traced to the best schools of the day, although, entering the office as youths of sixteen or seventeen, few had attended a university. Henry Kelsall's academic credentials – Westminster School, Scholar and Fellow of Trinity College, Cambridge, Fellow of the Royal Society – are something of an exception (although one should not read into them the distinction they later came to imply). Entering the Treasury in 1714, he was a chief clerk for most of his forty-eight years in the department.

He was also a Member of Parliament between 1719 and 1734. Indeed, Kelsall and his contemporary, Christopher Tilson, are the two Treasury clerks whom the Opposition had in mind in 1733 when they attacked the presence of such underlings in the House. Pulteney acknowledged his respect for them: 'they deserve it, they are gentlemen, and men of figure and fortune in their country' – but, he warned the House,

> we may in a little time see all the little under-clerks of the treasury, and other offices, members of this House; we may see them trudging down to this House in the morning, in order to give their votes for imposing taxes upon their fellow-subjects; and in the afternoon attending behind the chair of a chancellor of the exchequer . . .!

In 1741, when they eventually passed the Act disqualifying government clerks from election to Parliament, they may have had Tilson particularly in mind since the current investigations into Walpole's secret service expenditure found him deeply implicated in these questionable proceedings. Thereafter Treasury clerks had to resign if they wished to enter the Commons, and one or two did so. As if to confuse posterity, Henry Fane (I) and Henry Fane (II), both Treasury clerks but only remotely related, followed each other as Members of Parliament for Lyme Regis, between 1757 and 1802.

Background and status entitled the clerks of the Treasury to cut a figure in the world; their emoluments enabled them to sustain it. How much they earned is difficult to determine exactly, for there was no uniform system of remuneration and the opportunities for haphazard fringe benefits were numerous. The chief clerks shared between them one-third of the Treasury's fees, the rest being divided between the two Joint Secretaries. Surviving Fee Books show that this gave each chief clerk about £330 per annum in 1711, rising through the 1720s and 30s to over £550 per annum and reaching £700 per annum in the 1750s. By 1770 they were averaging £850 per annum, and at the height of the American War of Independence, when the volume of business was particularly heavy, they achieved £1,278 each. It was not long after this, in 1782, that Treasury fees were pooled to provide fixed salaries of £800 per annum for the chief clerks and £3,000 per annum for the Joint Secretaries. The under-clerks, meanwhile, had always been salaried, receiving a basic £100 per annum from the Civil List, regardless of seniority. But in addition they too enjoyed fees, levied on a different and lower scale than those of the chief clerks, and these were distributed in proportion to length of service. Sums of between £30 and £350 per annum supplemented their salaries, although it is unlikely that these figures account for their full profits. Several were pluralists, holding lucrative sinecures in subordinate departments, and – by a convention which will be described later – they may have benefited from the flotation of government loans. The 'gentlemen of the Treasury' were unquestionably well-to-do.

Indeed, they were probably far too comfortable. In 1761 and 1776 several senior under-clerks respectfully declined promotion to the more remunerative but far more onerous post of chief clerk. In 1759 and 1761 it was necessary to appoint complete outsiders to the vacant chief clerkships. Ambition was not simply lacking, it was provided against. A Treasury Minute of July 1757 recorded 'that the Under-Clerks rise according to seniority as has been usual in the office'. But the refusals of 1776 opened the Board's eyes. The recalcitrants were pensioned off, the remainder reorganized and an historic Minute of 22 February 1776 laid down that 'in all future regulations of this Office and distributions of the Business, they shall regard the ability, attention, care and diligence of the respective Clerks, and not their Seniority, and that in their opinion this Rule at all times hereafter ought to be attended to, and pursued, in order the better to conduct and carry on the public business'. The Minute of July 1757 was not wholly wrong-headed in an age when the alternative to promotion by seniority was almost certain to be promotion by favouritism. Nevertheless, in view of the fact that only two vacancies for a chief clerk arose between 1724 and 1752, the way in which the three vacancies of 1752–7 seemed to satisfy the ambitions of the department is rather surprising. The Lords of the Treasury had an ageing and thoroughly apathetic body of clerks on their hands and there was not much they could do about it. In theory they could dismiss clerks out of hand, but the remarkable unwritten convention of eighteenth-century administration gave them effective security of tenure. It needed some flagrant act of dishonesty to justify dismissal. A rare instance occurred in 1754 when the unscrupulous lottery dealings of Peter Leheup, now a chief clerk, were exposed by a parliamentary inquiry. The Board had to throw him out.

Thus the great enlargement of the under-clerk establishment in the 1760s probably reflects a desire to rejuvenate the department. It can hardly reflect a matching increase in business. The Treasury remained a rather leisurely place until the French Revolutionary and Napoleonic Wars. It was later estimated that in 1815, at the end of that great war, the Treasury was handling 'registered papers' – i.e. separate items of incoming business, great or small – at the rate of 19,761 a year, or sixty-three per day. This was, rather unfairly, compared with only 906 per annum or three daily in 1767, a period of peace, but it serves to give some idea of the modest scale of mid-eighteenth-century business. Nor was this business particularly exacting. Until the second half of the nineteenth century the young gentlemen of the Treasury spent much of their time copying out, in a graceful hand, the formal warrants, orders and letters that made up the bulk of the outgoing correspondence. There was no inferior grade of copyists or writers to perform these humdrum labours for them; this was their task, to execute largely clerical duties with the integrity and expertise guaranteed by their background and education. Some degree of specialization was possible, although it was not until 1782 that Treasury business was distributed among 'Divisions'. For example, in 1776 the February reorganization arranged that one under-clerk dealt with the routine relations with the Army, Navy, Ordnance, America, the Gibraltar and Minorca garrisons, the Stamp Office, etc. etc., while another concentrated on such responsibilities of the Civil List as the royal woods and forests, parks, the Crown land revenues, the salaries of the great officers of state, the judges and law officers, etc. . . . The absurdly wide range of items under their care is some indication of the superficiality of their responsibilities, which demanded little except familiarity with certain set forms of procedure by which issues from the Exchequer received their due authorization.

It was dull work from which there was little escape. No recognized avenue of promotion led to posts outside the Treasury. Not surprisingly, there was a problem of absenteeism among the under-clerks, and successive Treasury Minutes had to enjoin proper attendance during hours which, in 1752, were defined as 9 A.M. to 3 P.M. for a five-day week, and in 1757 as 10 A.M. to 4 P.M., including alternate Saturdays for two pairs of junior under-clerks in rotation. By 1780 it is clear that most clerks only looked in after 11 A.M.

There was something of a contrast – too sharp to be healthy – between the duties of the under-clerks, however senior, and those of the chief clerks. The four chief clerks alone were privileged with direct access to the Joint Secretaries and the Treasury lords, attending the meetings of the Board and performing duties described by a Treasury Minute of 31 July 1759 (which was cited in the 1780s in an account of 'The Business done in the Treasury by the Officers'):

The first is to read at the Board all Petitions, Memorials, &ca. The second to draw or examine and correct (when it may be necessary) all Warrants, Orders and Contracts, to be laid before the Lords of the Treasury for their Signature.
The third to enter the Minutes of the Treasury, and write the Letters for Issues to the Navy, Army and Ordnance, entering on the respective Memorials the sums issued, and the times when issued, and carefully laying up the Memorials when the Issues thereupon shall be completed; and to examine all stated Accounts and also to make up the Accounts of the Office Fees.
The fourth, to write all Letters (other than for the above mentioned Issues) and References according to the directions given by their Lordships Minutes, and to do all Parliamentary Business. And besides this general Distribution each of the principal Clerks is expected to be ready to undertake any business that the Lords or either of their Secretaries shall require.
As the writing all Letters of Issue and most other Letters hath long since been performed by the other Clerks, the Duty of the Chief Clerks in this respect must be supposed to be confined to the examination of such letters previous to their Signature and to the drawing such Letters only as are special.

There can be little doubt that this work demanded discretion and expertise of a superior order, for which years of copying were hardly a good training, and the selection of three outsiders for chief clerkships in 1759 and 1761 is marked by attention to their particular skills. One, Robert Yeates, was a former clerk of the House of Commons and a skilled parliamentary draftsman; his were the duties of the fourth chief clerk defined above. Another was James Postlethwayt, Fellow of the Royal Society, and author of an impressive *History of the Public Revenue* (1759). He was the third of those listed above, but upon his sudden death he was replaced in 1761 by Thomas Bradshaw, an ebullient, pushful War Office clerk, whose abilities were to take him much further. Those rare cases where Treasury clerks rose, not simply to chief clerkships but even to the Secretaryships of the Treasury, must be regarded as remarkable triumphs over circumstance. The great William Lowndes had achieved this in the formative years of the department. So did John Taylor, very briefly, for the years 1714–15. Thomas Bradshaw, who, after becoming Secretary to the Treasury (1767–70), was a Lord of the Admiralty from 1772 until his death in 1774, is another example, although hardly a fair one. This leaves Charles Lowndes – (third son of the great William) who survived over thirty years as an under-clerk and seven as a chief clerk to become Secretary to the Treasury (1765–7) – and Edward Chamberlain. Chamberlain, a cultivated man, Fellow of the Society of Antiquaries and a tutor in the families of Walpole and the Duke of Newcastle, had been on the Establishment as an under-clerk for twenty years when, in 1782, he surprised himself and his colleagues by accepting appointment as a Secretary to the Treasury in the Marquis of Rockingham's administration.* He confided in his fellow-clerk, William Beldam, that he trembled at what he had undertaken, and a few days later, in a paroxysm of anxiety, flung himself from a window.

THE SECRETARIES OF THE TREASURY

This was a rather melodramatic tribute to the comprehensive responsibilities which the Secretaries now bore. Yet, if financial acumen, political sagacity and general administrative ability were to be found anywhere, it had to be with the Secretaries. Experts in a world of amateurs, they were unique among Treasury men in having to bridge the half-perceived but widening divide between permanent 'civil servants' and politicians. The convention was only gradually forming that their political character was paramount, but most of the eighteenth-century Secretaries to the Treasury were Members of Parliament either on appointment or soon after and virtually all were the close political allies of the government of the day. Some began to carry their allegiance to the point of resigning with their colleagues, but their position remained ambiguous throughout this period and was further confused by the intermittent signs of a division of labour between one Joint Secretary and the other – the one, apparently permanent, concentrating on administrative responsibilities, the other, less secure, devoting himself to parliamentary politics. The pattern seemed set during Lowndes's long service as Secretary, since while he survived a series of political upheavals he was yoked to Thomas Harley, Charles Stanhope, Horace Walpole – the cousins and brothers of successive First Lords – who, if they did anything, were likely to do it in the political sphere. The pattern was sustained by Lowndes's successor, John Scrope, in some ways a more remarkable if less celebrated Secretary. Already sixty-two years old on his appointment in 1724, he died in harness at the age of ninety, having been a pillar of strength to Walpole and a rock upon which his enemies were broken. William Pulteney, foremost of his opponents, was prepared to declare 'Mr Scrope is the only man I know that thoroughly understands the business of the Treasury, and is versed in drawing money bills. On

*The selection of Chamberlain for what was described as an 'assistant or Under Secretary'-ship foreshadows the recommendation by a Parliamentary Commission in 1786 for the creation of a non-political, *permanent* Secretaryship. This was not implemented until 1805 (see Chapter 6). The omission of Chamberlain's case is one of the deficiencies of D. M. Clark's study of the Secretaryship: *American Historical Review*, 1936–7.

this foundation he stands secure, and is as immovable as a rock'. While lesser men came and went as Joint Secretary, Scrope remained, serving Walpole's successors equally well. But in the second half of the century the pattern becomes confused, and it is not until 1782, when both Lord North's Secretaries resigned with the government, that their character as wholly political appointments was confirmed. Perhaps that is why Chamberlain had his fit of vertigo: he was stepping across the gulf that was beginning to yawn between the world of officials and the world of politicians. Beldam, cosy in what he liked to call 'my Treasury Den', shuddered at his temerity.*

But in the process of becoming politicians the Secretaries lost little as administrators. None was a sinecurist, few were mediocrities, and several, such as James West, Samuel Martin and Charles Jenkinson, were first-rate men of business who combined a deep knowledge of the political labyrinth with real administrative gifts. Jenkinson (Joint Secretary 1763–5), a Chancellor of the Exchequer *manqué*, reached the second rank of politicians as Secretary at War, was created first Earl of Liverpool and had great influence behind the scenes, but remained essentially 'a born bureaucrat' with a consuming love of administrative detail. Samuel Martin (Joint Secretary 1756–7, 1758–63) gave himself wholly to the minutiae of Treasury business. A bachelor, he told his father of 'my time being wholly engrossed by the functions of my employment . . . from the moment I have breakfasted to my time of dining, and from my return home from dining to the instant of my walk upstairs to bed'.[12]

The functions of the two Secretaries were rather baldly described in the account of 'The Business done in the Treasury by the Officers' already quoted:

> The elder Secretary receives all Papers that are to be brought before the Board – When the Board sits he presents them for consideration, stating the purpose of them – Signs all Letters for the issuing of Money – peruses Warrants prepared for the King's Signature, and superintends all Parliamentary Business.
>
> The other Secretary takes the Minutes of the Board – Signs all Letters written in consequence of the Orders given by the Minutes or otherwise and in general superintends all Official business.

But those vague phrases – 'all Parliamentary Business', 'all Official Business' – have a wealth of meaning. They embraced not only the humdrum routines of the clerical establishment but all the creative, confidential work entailed by the Treasury's responsibilities for the management of finance and the management of Parliament. The

*'It's possible like him I might have been some time or other for the temporary gratification of that Vanity . . . induced to have quitted my Treasury Den and embarked in the open Sea of Politics' – Beldam to Lord Hardwicke, British Museum, Add. MSS. 35, 619, f. 132.

Secretaries of the Treasury were the principal middlemen of eighteenth-century government, the 'fixers' and contact men, operating in the hinterland of politics and finance, where the vanity and vested interests, the idealism and ambitions of peers and M.P.s, merchants and bankers, soldiers, contractors, revenue collectors and plain country gentlemen converged upon the machinery of government. If one wishes to judge the competence of any eighteenth-century administration it is to the Secretaries of the Treasury that one should look first.

Horace Walpole once called them 'the Treasury Jesuits' – 'the Cabinet that governed the Cabinet', but this is not to say that they were all Grey Eminences, hovering behind *fainéant* First Lords. Although they ranked in importance (and in emoluments) above the junior lords of the Treasury Board, they were not only subordinate to the First Lord but in some real sense his servants, often bound to him in a relationship of clientage and dependence with which the eighteenth century was perfectly familiar. As protégés, their opportunities had been created for them, and their merits enhanced rather than diminished the lustre of their patron. Nevertheless, the reciprocal dependence of First Lords and Chancellors of the Exchequer upon the expertise of the Secretaries, with their contacts in the City, their skill as parliamentary draftsmen, their detailed, technical knowledge of the fiscal system, was equally real. After all, even eighteenth-century Chancellors were not really expected to know much about the technicalities of government finance. Henry Bilson Legge, who did, was sneered at by the *Gentleman's Magazine* for his 'clerk-like knowledge of finances'.[13] He had been a Secretary to the Treasury himself, and, as Chancellor of the Exchequer (1754–5, 1756–7 and 1757–61), he had had the sense to learn what the omniscient James West had to teach him.

THE RESPONSIBILITIES OF FINANCE

But in general, the limitations of the senior Lords of the Treasury were less likely to be a reflection of ignorance or of snobbery than of the growing complexity of the financial system. With layer upon layer of tariffs, the Customs laws had acquired an intricacy which defied even the Customs Board, and the system as a whole was no subject for amateurs. Infinitely more important, however, was the degree to which the management of public finance now entailed responsibility for the economy at large. It was not simply that the public revenue tended to absorb an increasing share of the national income. As Sir John Sinclair boasted in his *History of the Public Revenue* (1790), the country was better able to bear a tax burden of £15 million now that the national income was some £120 million than the £2 million it had groaned under in 1688, when he estimated the income to be £43 million. The revenue seemed to have an elasticity which justified Burke in saying, in 1780, 'Taxing is an easy business. Any projector can contrive new impositions, any bungler can add to the old.' It was more significant that government borrowing and the National Debt played such a dominant role in influencing monetary conditions. In the wars between 1688 and 1783 over one-third of government expenditure had been met by loans, and even before 1688 the intermittent demands of Crown borrowing had been seen by men like Locke, Davenant and William Coventry to determine interest rates in the City and provinces alike. After the Revolution, with the creation of the permanent debt and a regular cycle of borrowing and redemption, this relationship had become institutionalized. A stock-market had emerged which, by the accession of George II, revolved confidently around a carefully priced, dextrously manipulated array of government funds. The 'South Sea Bubble' of 1720 was only an incident, although an immensely significant incident, in the gradual process by which the London money market absorbed the long-term liabilities created by the wars of William and Anne. Of course, it is well-known that the South Sea Company's efforts to take over the management of a large portion of the National Debt ended in scandal and disaster. Apart from the ruin of thousands of feverish speculators – some 30,000 individual and corporate interests were affected[14] – it cut a swathe through the government. One Secretary of State died of a seizure, the other of smallpox; the Postmaster General cut his throat, the Chancellor of the Exchequer was sent to the Tower and only Walpole's advocacy saved the First Lord of the Treasury, Lord Sunderland, from a similar fate. Walpole's own reputation for prescience and skill has been stripped bare by his biographer: he was as inept and as unscrupulous as any, and lost heavily on his personal investment.[15] But several good things did emerge from the debris. Firstly, the South Sea Company's legal transactions, authorized by Acts of Parliament, had successfully tidied a large and complex portion of the National Debt into a manageable, redeemable stock. Secondly, the trauma of the 'Bubble' ensured that henceforth the prudent management of the Debt would be a cardinal object of politics as well as of finance. No future government could afford to fail the test of financial competence.

Consequently, the years after 1720 witnessed a succession of Treasury transactions designed to reduce the capital and interest burdens of the Debt. The process had begun in 1714 with the reduction of the maximum legal rate of interest under the usury law from 6 to 5 per cent. A 'conversion' operation in 1717, by which the interest on the medley of national debts was brought into line, created a saving which was the basis of Walpole's famous 'Sinking Fund'. The principle of the Fund was quite simple – perhaps too simple. An Act of Parliament, introduced by the skilful Lowndes, provided that any surpluses arising from the revenues allotted to service these debts were to be reserved 'for discharging the Principal and Interest of such National Debts and Incumbrances as were incurred before the five and twentieth day of December 1716'. But with the same complaisance with which it yielded Votes of Credit, the House of Commons permitted Walpole to divert the growing produce of the Sinking Fund to the relief of ordinary expenditure, rather than raise new taxes. He was bitterly attacked by some critics but the policy was a defensible one. His operations had greatly reduced the capital and interest charges of the Debt, government 5 per cent stock rose above par, and further conversions, to 4 per cent, were possible after 1727. In 1749, Walpole's able successor, Henry Pelham, carried through a major conversion of some £58 millions' worth of 4 per cent stock. They were to yield 3½ per cent until December 1757, thereafter 3 per cent. Meanwhile, the consolidation into a tidy stock of a group of annuities created that historic 3-per-cent stock known as 'consols'. They rose above par almost immediately, reaching a peak not exceeded until the late nineteenth century. These were buoyant years and they reflect much credit on Walpole, Pelham and Treasury administration as a whole.

But underlying this success were indispensable Treasury ties with the City in general and the Bank of England in particular. An arrangement in 1715, by which the Bank took over from the Exchequer the subscription, transfer and general management of nearly all the government's borrowing transactions, marked the beginning of a new era. With its Charter successively renewed in 1713, 1742 and 1764, the Bank's security and efficiency guaranteed the relative cheapness of the 1740s war loans. By the 1750s and 60s its relations with the Treasury had attained a harmony so complete as to seem humdrum. In contrast, there was nothing very tranquil about the City at large. London had been the focal point of the opposition to Walpole's Excise scheme and, although his relations with the moneyed community were good, his successor, Pelham, did well to cultivate even more cordial relations. Within the City, however, rival groups bitterly competed for government favour, for the flotation of public loans – like other forms of government contracting – offered opportunities for patronage which no administration could overlook. It was the established practice for the Treasury to negotiate loans by tender, rather than by inviting open subscription, and the contracts usually went to some favoured consortium of big jobbers, businessmen and their political allies. The City contacts of the Secretaries to the Treasury were particularly important here – Lowndes, Scrope, West were particularly well-equipped with these – and reliance was regularly placed upon well-known City figures such as Samson Gideon, the Jewish stockjobber, or his Quaker-born rival, Sir John Barnard. Charles Jenkinson was carefully coached by Joseph Salvador, another City expert.

Thus, few big loan operations were free of political considerations. No subscription was complete without what was known as 'the Treasury list', some £50–100,000-worth of stock reserved for distribution by the Treasury among dependents, who sometimes included the Treasury staff, and the real or alleged supporters of the administration. Their importunities were incessant. 'I beg the favour you will set me down £5000 in the Treasury List be the terms what they will,' wrote Ralph Morrison to Charles Jenkinson in 1764, 'for I have been in every subscription since the year 1720 . . .'! 'I'd wish to have pretty large sums for 60,000£ or 100,000£ if it could be had', requested John Robinson on behalf of his patron in 1768. The profits they could hope for were juicy. Entering the market as 'stags', having paid up the minimum 15-per-cent deposit necessary to establish their title to the stock, they could sell at the substantial premium which new government stocks generally commanded in the open market. There was clamour, of course, against such privileged profiteering, but in 1757 an idealistic attempt at allowing open subscription by the public failed miserably.[16] In the end it was the enormous premiums yielded by closed-tender loans during the American War of Independence which discredited the system. Lord North's loans, raised at a time when the price of consols had fallen below 60, were extremely costly. The loan of 1781 raised £12 million at a cost to the National Debt of £21 million and a profit to subscribers of 7–11 per cent. Not surprisingly, Coutts the banker could write in 1782 that 'the rage for subscribing continues meanwhile to pervade all ranks of men, and, I believe, they begin to be almost frightened at the Treasury at the amount of the sums offered'.[17] In fact, 2,469 persons were found to have offered over £73 million towards the £13·5 million loan.

In this respect, as in others, the War of American Independence wrought up to a high pitch problems which had been endemic throughout the century. Each eighteenth-century war had occasioned the borrowing of between thirty and forty per cent of its expenditure, with marked effects upon the money market. The improving landlord in search of a loan, the spendthrift in need of a mortgage, the merchant anxious to discount his bills of exchange, were the first to feel the diversion of funds into government loans. The City and West End banks upon which many relied could not afford to miss the profitable opportunities held out by Navy bills, Ordnance debentures and government short-term stock. They drew in their loans, raised their interest rates and moved into the scramble for new subscriptions. Conversely, of course, the drying-up of government issues, the dispersal of the floating debt, liberated funds which flowed back into commercial and agricultural investment – and the general trend in the eighteenth century was for the interest rate to move downwards in sympathy with the yield on 'consols'.[18]

Thus, in both good times and bad, the Treasury's management of government finance had a real significance for the economy at large, and to an attentive moneyed community the Budget began to assume something of its modern significance. The term itself dates from the 1730s, humorously applied to the wallet or 'budget' (*bougette*) from which Walpole, as Chancellor, drew his proposals for the year's finance. And the Chancellor himself, standing, as he now did, at the centre of attention, was more than ever before a man to be reckoned with. Not that his colleagues were prepared to recognize that. He was not regarded as of Cabinet rank, and some third-rate men were appointed with deliberation. Henry Bilson Legge, for example, finding himself ground between a dictatorial Secretary of State (the elder Pitt) and a querulous First Lord (the Duke of Newcastle) wrote peevish letters about the 'latitude' to which a Chancellor of the Exchequer was entitled. Men like William Dowdeswell (Chancellor of the Exchequer, July 1765–August 1766) were used as cat's-paws by their political chiefs, and Sir Francis Dashwood (May 1762–April 1763) has only recently been rescued from the reputation of being the most incompetent politician ever to fill that office.[19] Discussing the claims of the thirty-four-year-old Charles Townshend in 1759, the Duke of Newcastle and Lord Hardwicke agreed that 'that office should be filled by somebody who may in a particular manner be depended upon, of some gravity, known veracity, whose word may be taken and relied upon'. That ruled out Townshend – but in 1766, of course, he did become Chancellor, gambled successfully in East India Company stock and introduced the irresponsible proposals which helped to inflame America.[20]

The turbulent politics and unsettled conventions of mid-eighteenth-century government left the Chancellor vulnerable to less consideration than his responsibilities deserved. But the same is true of the First Lord of the Treasury. As we have already seen, the premiership was not yet rooted in the Treasury. The premiership itself was suspect. The consensus which, in his own day, recognized Walpole as a 'prime minister', saw him not as the first – far from it – but earnestly hoped he might be the last. 'Prime Minister was an odious title', said George Grenville in 1761. This rather disingenuous reluctance to assume a dominant position among the King's ministers after Walpole's fall was sometimes given practical force by the conflict of powerful personalities. Who was to decide the location of the premiership between Pitt and Newcastle in the late 1750s, or between Pitt and Grafton, Grafton and North in the 60s? In these cases a First Lord of the Treasury was being matched by a singularly influential Secretary of State or, in Grafton's case, by an exceptionally trusted Chancellor of the Exchequer. Later, in 1783, the two heavyweights, Fox and North, were to choose the two Secretaryships of State under the nominal leadership of a figurehead First Lord. Most of these permutations were determined, not by personality alone, but by the First Lord's status in the Houses of Parliament. If he was a peer, and therefore detached from the leadership of the House of Commons, then he was at a disadvantage with a commoner Secretary of State. But a commoner First Lord, free to combine that post with the Chancellorship of the Exchequer was almost irresistible. Nothing did more to confirm the political ascendancy of the Treasury in the eighteenth century than the long periods during which the two posts were combined. Walpole (1715–17, 1721–42), Pelham (1743–54), Grenville (1763–5) and Lord North (1770–82), were First Lord and Chancellor of the Exchequer, controlling financial and political policy from their bench in the Commons and their chair at the Treasury Board. Given the King's confidence – and Grenville was never sure that he had it – then they might plausibly be 'premiers' as well.

It is important to retain this sense of uncertainty about eighteenth-century political conventions. They were less rigid, and less formidable, than it is convenient to believe. A particularly notable achievement of modern scholarship has been to modify traditional ideas about the scale and character of the Treasury's 'influence' in managing the parliamentary world. However deft and unscrupulous the means by which Walpole kept his majority together, we should not generalize too freely from the picture of the Secretary to the Treasury handing out guineas to docile Members of Parliament, ticking off their names as they filed past him.[21] The 'secret service' expenditure of the Civil List, so deeply suspected in the reign of George III, appears, on closer inspection, to have been less like a baleful engine of constitutional subversion than a charity for distressed gentlefolk – a kindly resource for peers and M.P.s down on their luck. 'Treasury boroughs' have likewise dwindled – returning barely a dozen Members in 1754 and only five in 1790 – and 'Treasury influence' has shrunk to a routine of calculation and persuasion falling rather short of party organization.[22]

This makes it easier to understand why the activities of the Treasury as a political clearing house did not pervade the permanent staff to any great depth. This work of manipulating the government's electoral interests and marshalling its parliamentary following, though intricate, was manageable by one of the Joint Secretaries to the Treasury, particularly if he was as competent as John Robinson (1770–82). It was the Secretary to the Treasury who issued the circulars which brought government supporters hurrying up to Town for a new session, who summoned them to 'pep-talks' from their leaders at the Cockpit, and while it was likely to be the First Lord who was bombarded with the pretensions and petitions of aspirants seeking, demanding or offering favour, it would be the Secretary to the Treasury who converted all this into the higher arithmetic of politics, who worked out moderately accurate estimates of general election returns, or of votes on some crucial division in the Commons. Aided by the junior Lords of the Treasury and the sinecure Solicitor of the Treasury, he performed all the essential functions of a government chief 'whip'. He drew, no doubt, on the clerical assistance of the permanent Establishment. Not until 1902 did the 'Patronage' Secretary cease to draw one of his private secretaries from the permanent clerks. And no doubt some Treasury clerks engaged themselves very willingly in this confidential political work. But there is little sign that this jeopardized their impartiality in the service of succeeding administrations. There was an ugly phase in the winter of 1762–3 when some of the innumerable office-holding protégés of the fallen Duke of Newcastle carried their loyalty to the lengths of disobeying his successor, the unpopular Lord Bute – but they were taught a sharp lesson. Numerous dismissals in the revenue boards left the Treasury unscathed – but not unwarned. Professionalism had become prudent.

However, professionalism was not the most striking characteristic of the Treasury as British government drifted into ever deeper discredit during the American War of Independence. Of course, there may well be no substance in the contemporary allegations that the Treasury's corrupt use of 'the influence of the Crown' was the only thing that kept Lord North's government in power until 1782. The accusation may be quite false that government war contracts, such as that which made 'Rum Atkinson' a by-word for profiteering, were 'collusively managed by the clerks of the Treasury'.[23] In a recent study of the American war the Treasury's management of strategic army supplies has been praised, and even Lord North's very costly budgeting has found its admirers. But the failure of these incidental charges should not obscure more fundamental faults. Enough has been said to indicate what they were. 'A vicious circle of waste begetting corruption begetting waste', was Burke's way of describing a profound dilemma, rooted in the constitution. By 1780 its solution was long overdue.

SOURCE NOTES

1. Sir R. Clarke, 'The Management of the Public Sector of the National Economy', Stamp Memorial Lecture (1964), p. 7.
2. John Douglas, *Seasonable Hints from an Honest Man* (1761), p. 38.
3. British Museum, Add. MSS., 32, 852, f. 64v.
4. W. R. Ward, *The English Land Tax in the Eighteenth Century* (1953), p. 64.
5. W. Blackstone, *Commentaries on the Laws of England* (1775), vol. I, p. 154.
6. P. Mackesy, *The War in America, 1775–1783* (1964), pp. 65–9.
7. Ward, *op. cit.*, pp. 64, 86, 110, 114; and, by the same author, 'The Office for Taxes, 1665–1798', in *The Bulletin of the Institute of Historical Research,* 1952, p. 206.
8. E. E. Hoon, *The Organization of the English Customs System, 1696–1786* (1938), pp. 198–9.
9. D. M. Clark, *The Rise of the British Treasury: Colonial Administration in the Eighteenth Century* (1960), p. 1.
10. *ibid.,* p. 15.
11. For a concise account of the causes of the American revolution see I. R. Christie, *Crisis of Empire: Great Britain and the American Colonies, 1754–1783* (1966).
12. Cited in Sir L. B. Namier and J. Brooke, *The History of Parliament: The Commons, 1754–90* (1964), vol. III, p. 115.
13. Quoted by J. E. D. Binney, *British Public Finance and Administration, 1774–92* (1958), p. 252.
14. P. G. M. Dickson, *The Financial Revolution in England, 1688–1756* (1967), p. 161. This is the most accurate, analytical study of the crisis. For a vivid account of the background and the personalities involved, see J. P. Carswell, *The South Sea Bubble* (1960).
15. J. H. Plumb, *Sir Robert Walpole. The Making of a Statesman* (1956), pp. 301–28.
16. L. Sutherland, 'The City of London and the Devonshire–Pitt Administration, 1756–7', Raleigh Lecture, *Proceedings of the British Academy,* 1960.
17. Quoted by A. H. John, 'Insurance Investment and the London Money Market of the 18th Century', in *Economica,* 1953.
18. L. S. Pressnell, 'The Rate of Interest in the Eighteenth Century', in *Studies in the Industrial Revolution presented to T. S. Ashton* (1960), ed. L. S. Pressnell.
19. B. Kemp, *Sir Francis Dashwood: An Eighteenth-Century Independent* (1967).
20. Sir L. B. Namier and J. Brooke, *Charles Townshend* (1964).
21. *The Historical and Posthumous Memoirs of Sir Nathaniel William Wraxall, 1772–1784* (1884), ed. H. B. Wheatley, vol, 3, p. 238.
22. Sir L. B. Namier, *The Structure of Politics at the Accession of George III* (1957); Namier and Brooke, *The History of Parliament: The Commons, 1754–90,* vol. I.
23. W. Cobbett, *Parliamentary History of England,* vol. XX, 12 February 1779.

CHAPTER 5

Economical and Administrative Reform: 1780-1866

Economy requires neither superior courage nor eminent virtue; it is satisfied with ordinary energy and the capacitv of average minds.
SAMUEL SMILES, Self Help

'Administrative revolutions' are much in vogue among English historians, and they are quite indispensable to the history of the Treasury. That of the 1530s has been cogently propounded by Professor Elton, and there is a strong case to be made for the rapid developments of the late seventeenth century. But the winter of 1779–80 saw the beginning of a movement which was to produce much more than an administrative revolution. It was to introduce into public life a new morality into finance a new probity and into government as a whole new standards of efficiency and economy. Indeed, it is known as the movement for 'Economical Reform', a rather dreary phrase which scarcely does justice to its full implications. But in 1780 the word 'economy' had a resonance which was almost seismic. 'Oeconomy was the word,' wrote one country gentleman to another in 1781, 'which, like the Sun, diffused its glorious spirit almost instantly over the whole kingdom.' 'The word *economy*,' noted Horace Walpole in 1780, 'has now captivated almost the whole nation'; and in the Upper House Lord Hillsborough lamented a people suddenly 'run mad with virtue'.

An ethic transmuted into a cult, this ideal of economical and therefore virtuous government passed from the hands of prigs like Pitt into those of high priests like Gladstone. It became a religion of financial orthodoxy whose Trinity was Free Trade, Balanced Budgets and the Gold Standard, whose Original Sin was the National Debt. It seems no accident that 'Conversion' and 'Redemption' should be the operations most closely associated with the Debt's reduction. The cult, which obsessed successive generations in the nineteenth century, died some time between the two World Wars. Of course, the Chancellor of the Exchequer still receives his votive offerings, those curious, anonymous bequests to help pay off the Debt,* but one feels that Baldwin's action in 1919, in anonymously donating one-fifth of his substantial fortune for this purpose, was the last grand gesture of the old faith.

This is to look far ahead. In 1780 the motives of 'Economical Reform' were confused, and operated at several levels of sincerity. Probably the strongest common instinct behind them was conservative, for there was no question just yet of a radical reform of the Executive. Those who agitated for the reduction of sinecures, for the expulsion of government contractors from the House, for the disfranchisement of revenue collectors and for the general reform of government finance, lined up behind the classical ideal of the 'balance of the constitution' when they registered their intentions with Dunning's famous motion of 6 April 1780, 'That the influence of the Crown has increased, is increasing, and ought to be diminished'. *Diminished*, not abolished. To have done more would have been to destroy the delicate balance which these constitutionalists were trying to preserve. It was not questioned that the King had a right to the disposal of honours, and there was a strong utilitarian case, which reformers like Edmund Burke were the first to recognize, that the Crown must have pensions and places at its command for the reward of service.

As it is, modern research has shown that the reformers' case was weaker in 1780 than it would have been in the 1760s. The influence of the Crown among Members of Parliament had actually declined since George III's accession, and the Treasury's grip upon its boroughs was manifestly slipping.[1] This does not take into account the vast and mounting scale of monetary influence by way of government expenditure, contracts and loans, but it does indicate how far the reformers were using a vocabulary that belonged to the past.

They were easily outmanoeuvred. By the end of February 1780, supported by a bombardment of petitions from reform associations in the electorate at large, they had given the government advance notice of their proposals. A detailed purge of sinecures on the Civil List, and a Parliamentary Committee of Accounts were moved for, respectively, by the Duke of Richmond and the Earl of Shelburne in the Lords, and Edmund Burke and Colonel Barré in the Commons.

*Officially termed 'conscience money', the rate of anonymous contribution today varies between £500 and £5,000 per annum. The devaluation of November 1967 was followed by a small surge of gifts 'to help with the balance o fpayments' and to reduce the National Debt. Gifts of £500,000 were made in 1927 (the National Fund) and 1929 (the Elsie Mackay Fund). For Baldwin's gift see *The Baldwin Age* (1960), ed. J. Raymond, p. 34.

But on 2 March the premier, Lord North, took the wind out of their sails by outlining his own proposal for a commission of inquiry into public accounts which, unlike that proposed by Shelburne or Barré, was to consist of expert laymen, not M.P.s, reporting independently to Parliament. Given the technical and political advantages of a team of independent experts, free from party rancour, then Lord North's was an infinitely superior conception which in due course was to justify itself magnificently. Spread over seven years, the Commission's fourteen Reports laid down principles which, in their outrageous simplicity – 'every office should have a useful duty annexed to it' – revolutionized British government.

But the Opposition's programme was not wholly sterile. In 1782 Lord North's government fell and the reformers took power under the Marquis of Rockingham. Revenue collectors were duly deprived of the vote, government contractors disqualified from the Commons, and Burke was now able to carry through two important measures. His Act 'Regulating the Office of Paymaster General' endorsed the recommendations of the Public Accounts Commission and established some vitally important principles for the handling of public money. Indeed, its first purpose was to establish that money issued to the Paymaster of the Forces *was* public money and not personal capital to be speculated with at will. His 'Civil Establishments Act' firmly took the King's Civil List in hand, enforcing the novel principle which George III had now conceded – that Parliament was competent to inquire into and regulate abuses in civil expenditure. The Civil List was therefore purged of certain sinecures and redundant posts, among them the Third Secretaryship of State and the whole Board of Trade (among whose salaried but idle commissioners the historian Edward Gibbon was to be found). The remaining annual charges on the Civil List were classified in eight groups, to be paid in strict sequence. As a guarantee that no future deficits would be allowed to accumulate, it was shrewd as well as witty to place the salaries of the Treasury Lords in the eighth and last group.

Unfortunately, Burke's legislation was curiously short-lived. The Board of Trade was resurrected in 1786, and the Third Secretaryship of State in 1794. The Act regulating the office of Paymaster General had to be revised (not for the last time) in 1783, and the Civil List was soon in arrears. Burke is wide open to the criticism that he was an impractical doctrinaire seeking temporary party advantage at the expense of the Crown. But in several vital respects Burke was far-sighted. We have already seen how far eighteenth-century English government was undermined by Parliament's diffidence about its right to amend the Executive. Burke swept those scruples aside and unequivocally asserted that right. It was probably more important for him that the Executive should be reformed by Parliament than that it should be reformed well. And this was not the only profound principle which Burke had grasped. He was the first statesman to envisage a partnership in government between a sovereign legislature and an omnipotent Treasury. He wanted effective Treasury control as a condition of effective parliamentary control. On 20 March 1780 he had asked –

> How could it be expected that the first lord of the Treasury should be responsible, if a variety of lesser treasuries were to exist, each of which would govern the branch of the public expenditure under its direction, just as it thought proper? It would be unfair, it would be unjust, to expect a first lord of the Treasury to be responsible, unless the Treasury was the sole place for issuing public money, and governed the whole expenditure, as well in detail, as in gross amount.

Clearly Burke had penetrated the two fundamental anomalies which had debilitated eighteenth-century government – the doctrinaire divorce between the legislature and the civil executive, and the lack of any responsible, centralized administrative control. The remedies he offered – piecemeal economies in the Civil List, the Exchequer and the great spending departments – do not quite seem to match up to the profundity of his diagnosis, and Burke's actual achievement fell far short of his vision, but he has the considerable merit of having pointed in the right direction and of having broken the spell which had so far paralysed the constitution.

Burke's position gains in clarity when it is compared with that of Shelburne, under whom he refused to serve when Rockingham died suddenly on 1 July 1782. Shelburne was that distrusted animal, an intellectual patrician who had devoted himself to the academic study of politics. Like the seventeenth-century Earl of Shaftesbury, another brilliant outsider and patron of Locke, Shelburne had sought out the most enlightened political philosophers of his age – radical utilitarians like Jeremy Bentham, Joseph Priestley, Richard Price and James Burgh. Thoroughly cosmopolitan, he was equally familiar with European *philosophes*, and, like Burke, he was acutely aware that a resurgent France, under the enlightened financial administration of Turgot and Necker, posed a serious threat to a backward, debt-laden Britain. Shelburne differed from Burke less about ends – if anything he was more radical – than about means, for he was inclined to see administrative reform as a matter for the experts, for civil servants and ministers in a more powerful executive. Setting aside an unpleasant political reputation for deviousness – he was nicknamed 'the Jesuit of Berkeley Square' – it is not difficult to understand why Shelburne was distrusted by parliamentarians like Burke.

THE TREASURY REFORM OF 1782

However, Shelburne had the inestimable advantage, as First Lord of the Treasury between July 1782 and April 1783, of being able to put his ideas into effect, and, despite preoccupation with the peace treaties closing the war of American Independence, administrative reform made swift advances under his direction.[2] In this respect the fact that William Pitt was his Chancellor of the Exchequer is less significant than it may seem. Now only twenty-three years old, the younger Pitt had made his maiden speech on the Civil List and had ardent views on parliamentary reform, but as a financial administrator he was still an unknown quantity. Although the clerks of the Treasury were deeply impressed by Pitt's assiduity – one described him as 'indefatigable in acquiring the Rudiments of Financeering' – he had little opportunity to show his paces before the administration collapsed. It was his successor who presented the Budget of 1783. Shelburne, on the other hand, having bought and studied the archives of James West (Newcastle's veteran Secretary to the Treasury) knew exactly what he was doing. In November 1782, with the assistance of George Rose, one of the ablest Secretaries to the Treasury, he was responsible for what can be regarded as the most important reorganization of the Treasury in that century.

The Minute of 30 November 1782 actually leant heavily on Lord North's Minute of 1776. It endorsed the all-important principle that promotions among the under-clerks should go to those 'who have distinguished themselves most by their Diligence, Attention and Acquirement of the Knowledge of Business without regard to Seniority'. Dismissing a clerk who had not been seen in the department for two years, it reiterated the demand for punctual and personal attendance. But it made two constructive innovations. Firstly, it rearranged business among six 'Divisions', allotting a senior and a junior under-clerk to each. Secondly, it substituted fixed salaries for the variable remuneration from fees. Fees were not abolished; far from it. They were carefully re-assessed. But instead of being collected and pocketed by the individual clerks they were pooled to create a Fee Fund, administered by one of the chief clerks, from which fixed stipends would be paid. It was later provided that any deficiency in the fund would be made good from the Civil List. The joint parliamentary Secretaries, whose incomes had been found to range between a minimum average of £3,414 per annum during the peaceful years 1769–71 to a maximum average of £5,114 during the war years 1779–81, were now given a fixed salary of £3,000 per annum. The four chief clerks, for whom the comparable figures were £853 per annum and £1,278 per annum, were to have £800 per annum. There was no progressive scale among these men, but among the twelve under-clerks a clear hierarchy of seniority was acknowledged. In addition to the basic £100 from the Civil List each clerk received a seniority allowance ranging from £50 to £500 per annum.

The commendable aspects of this reform are fairly clear. The yoking together of senior and junior clerks in a Division enhanced the educational possibilities of specialization, and improved the chances of administrative continuity. The range of Treasury business was not wide enough to permit a functional distribution of business without depriving the Divisions of a balanced diet. Thus, most of them superintended a branch of revenue, all dealt with expenditure and all controlled establishments on the Civil List. But each Division – the Third with Army and Navy business, the Fifth with Customs and Excise – had some solid core of responsibility round which it revolved.

Unhappily, anomalies survived. The clerks still received the traditional New Year gifts from their principal clients in varying amounts which were sometimes large enough to upset the seniority scale. Pluralism among Treasury clerks was to survive for another fifty years. Recruitment was not improved and few promotions flouted the claims of seniority. In other words, the Treasury remained a pleasant haven for gentlemen of good connections and modest abilities, jogging along in the comparative comfort of an assured income and regular hours. Absenteeism was not cured. Hypochondriacs like William Beldam, who had his remunerative by-employment in the Exchequer, pottered on, looking in at the office occasionally for scraps of gossip. The senile were indulged. Thomas Pratt, approaching his nineties, was thought too venerable to sack, although there is little evidence that he had done a stroke of work since the 1760s.

It would be rash to assume that this was an intolerable state of affairs. To believe that the Treasury lords wanted to be served by a troop of nimble-witted young clerks, with thrusting personalities and first-class minds, underrates their ministerial sense of self-importance. Even in Pitt's Treasury, half a dozen first-class minds would have been an embarrassment, over-conspicuous and under-employed. Ability, wherever it could be found in the Treasury, was, of course, noted and rewarded. In the 1780s, at least three very able Treasury clerks were sent out to colonize subordinate departments: Edward Bishop to the Salt Tax Commissioners, G. T. Goodenough as Secretary to the Board of Taxes, and, most significantly, J. Martin-Leake as a member of the new Audit Office Board created in 1785. And, if outstanding ability was usually lacking, the Treasury was at least doing the tasks for which it was intended, drafting warrants, orders, patents, contracts and all the other documentary instruments of routine finance. Nothing more was expected. Indeed, looking at the Treasury in 1784, a Parliamentary Commission of Inquiry into Fees found little to criticize. The reforms of 1782, they remarked in 1786, 'appear to have been wise, judicious and effectual, and at the same time that they have diminished the abuses, have very much added to the accuracy and dispatch in conducting the business of this important public office'. They concluded with the reflection 'how little is wanted for its completion and perfection'! In fact, the Commissioners made a few recommendations which will be considered in due course, but in general their Report faithfully reflects the complacent tranquillity within the department. That is why the forces which were to transform the Treasury's position in government *had* to come from outside.

ADMINISTRATIVE REFORM

By December 1783, when the younger Pitt took office as First Lord of the Treasury (the last hope of a desperate King), Economical Reform was nearly four years old, Lord North's Commissioners were preparing their last reports and the main principles of administrative change were fully defined. At the risk of over-simplification, the purposes of these reforms can be grouped under three heads.

Firstly, *Sincecures*. The abolition of these represented, at worst, the short-term objective of party rancour, anxious to destroy the basis from which a powerful Executive had always domineered. At best – and the implications were gradually realized – it held out the promise of government more cheaply administered. As for efficiency – that was hypothetical, but it was clear that the priorities of eighteenth-century office-holding had to be reversed. The Fourteenth Report of the Commissioners of Public Accounts summed up –

First, No Office should be holden by Legal Tenure;
Secondly, Every Office should have a useful Duty annexed to it;
Thirdly, Every Officer should execute himself the Duty of his Office;
Fourthly, Offices where the Duty is of the same Kind should be consolidated.

This lucid programme speaks for itself. It is of revolutionary significance. In calling for an end to proprietary rights in offices with the declaration that 'the Public have their Rights also, Rights equally sacred and as freely to be exercised', the Commissioners foretold the doom of economic individualism in British administration. Collectivism had been born.

The second area of reform was the question of *Fees*. With the abolition of sinecures most of the dangers implicit in extracting payments from the public for often nominal services would disappear. But it was recognized to be highly undesirable that even those officials who earned their fees should have direct financial relations with the public; the temptations were too great. Carried further, there would have to be a gradation of income calculated in relation to responsibility, and – when the full implications of the abolition of sinecures were worked out – it was conceded that some system of superannuation would have to be supplied. Whatever happened, officials could no longer be allowed to reward themselves by the misappropriation of public money.

The best guarantee against this last abuse fell under the third and most important head of reform – the reform of *Audit*. Ever since the restoration of its control in the mid sixteenth century, the mills of the Exchequer had ground fine but exceeding slow. And they were also invariably grinding the wrong things. Accounts were fed into it, as if into some intricate *oubliette*; twenty or more years later they might re-emerge, their authenticity approved. But it was a spurious authenticity, a mere arithmetical, formalistic check of expenditure against authorization which in no way questioned its wisdom or economy. Even by its own obsolete standards Exchequer audit was a failure, too late to catch up with sub-accountants dead, bankrupt or disappeared.

What was needed was something more fundamental than Exchequer reform; nothing less than a complete re-planning of national accounting, bringing together within one coherent system the whole ebb and flow of expenditure and receipt, subject to independent audit. Without this there could be no real supervision of the validity of departmental needs, and no real calculation of resources. As Burke pointed out on 11 February 1780:

> This much is certain; that neither the present, nor any other first Lord of the Treasury, has been ever able to take a survey, or to make even a tolerable guess, of the expenses of government for any one year. . . . As things are circumstanced, the first Lord of the Treasury cannot make an estimate.

It was desirable, furthermore, that public money should run in fewer and better regulated channels – preferably in Bank of England accounts. There must be fewer and smaller balances lying idle in official hands. The use of these funds for private speculation in land or the stock-market was notorious. Something could be done to curb this if accounting periods were made to conform to a consistent, annual cycle of issue and audit, instead of dragging on from year to year.

This is to put things at their simplest. Some objectives of the reformers were too trivial to note here; some more important objectives had not yet been conceived. The most conspicuous absentee is the idea of a unified, professional public service recruited independently upon ascertainable proofs of merit. As it is, the proposed reforms ran up against quite enough deeply entrenched prejudices. Some challenged that most sacred principle of English law, the inviolability of private property. Sinecures, granted by royal patent and held on 'life' or 'good behaviour' tenure unquestionably fell within that category, however gross their profits at public expense. Pitt himself, not withstanding the recommendations of the Public Accounts Commission, justified the slow pace of reform in 1797 by reminding the House of Commons 'that sinecure offices are given in the nature of a freehold tenure. Parliament has expressly said, they will respect them as freehold property. . . .' In practical terms this meant waiting for patentees to die off before reforming or abolishing their offices, or buying them out at great expense. Both devices were tried but the quick economies envisaged by the reformers were illusory. In 1797, for example, a Select Committee found that while 412 Excise offices had been reduced at a saving to the government of £2,478, 253 new ones had been created at a cost of £40,617 per annum. The unpleasant truth was that in breaking down the old closed shops of sinecures and customary fees the government had exposed itself to the merciless operations of Parkinson's law, at enormous cost to itself.

FINANCIAL REFORM

This serves to emphasize the point that the most urgent problems facing Pitt were, fundamentally, financial and not wholly administrative. The fiscal system and the National Debt were under great strain and both called for radical and imaginative reform. In 1782, for example, a Select Committee of the House of Commons, reporting on loans raised by annuities during the American war, found that the special taxes levied since 1776 had accumulated a deficit of £2¼ million against the interest they were supposed to service. The floating debt was £23 million and the Funded Debt itself had risen £53 million to £177 million. By the time the full cost of the war was absorbed the National Debt exceeded £240 million and half the public revenue was going in debt charges.

Another alarming symptom of exhaustion was the inelasticity of the fiscal system. It reflected weak administration, an enormous rate of evasion and a lack of budgetary ingenuity. In twenty years, half of them at war, Pitt put most of this right. He revitalized the administration of the Tax Office under G. T. Goodenough (late of the Treasury).

He outmanoeuvred the smugglers by reducing customs duties and shifting the burden to assessed taxes on houses, windows, etc., which trebled in 1797–8. Lord North had taxed servants and carriages; he had justified a tax on soap on the grounds that the poor didn't use it: Pitt simply carried this policy to its fullest limits. But it still required an imaginative leap of great political daring to pass from the Treble Assessment of 1797–8 to the Income Tax of 1798–9, the most momentous fiscal innovation since the Excise of 1643.

An undifferentiated 10-per-cent tax on income regardless of source and liabilities, Pitt's Income Tax left much to be desired and it has been plausibly argued that it was Addington, with his Income Tax Act of 1803, who was the real father of the modern system.[3] Equally important in principle, although defective in application, was Pitt's Sinking Fund of 1786. The scheme differed significantly from Walpole's (see p. 112) in that the fund was to be administered independently, under statutory limitations, by National Debt Commissioners with their own account at the Bank of England. The Chancellor of the Exchequer was an *ex officio* member and, it proved, a most attentive one, but the basic principle was to provide an inviolable system by which the dividends accruing on each year's purchase of £1 million-worth of stock should be placed towards the following year's purchases until, by the automatic accumulation of compound interest, the dividends alone were worth £4 million per annum. After that the capital value of the stock would be cancelled. By 1823, when a major reorganization of the Sinking Fund took place, £453 million had been redeemed by this device.[4] But the idea, it is usually pointed out, was not Pitt's own. Few of his innovations were. Shelburne had toyed with several of them. The consolidation of the Customs duties in 1787 was the dusty fruit of an idea produced for the Treasury in 1777, and the Commutation Act, which shifted ineffective duties from tea, was born in the Excise Office. The Sinking Fund likewise owed something to Dr Richard Price, a celebrated dissenting clergyman, as well as to the Public Accounts Commissioners. Indeed, Pitt – like all Chancellors of the Exchequer – was incessantly bombarded with fiscal suggestions, a suspiciously large number coming from half-pay naval officers and curates with huge families. Necessity, in several of its forms, seems to have been the mother of fiscal invention, and it is immensely to Pitt's credit that he was able to sift the rubbish and seize upon the soundest.

Pitt is also incautiously mocked for having maladministered the Sinking Fund, creating an artificial surplus during the war by borrowing large sums at high interest to purchase stock carrying low interest. As a result the Sinking Fund cost more than it redeemed.[5] But this misses the point. Even in peace-time the Sinking Fund was an absurd and masochistic ritual; it was simply a little more absurd in war. But, as a proof of public virtue, the Sinking Fund was of incalculable psychological value. For a government to tie its own hands and yield up, unresisting, any surplus for the redemption of old debt was a gesture of self-sacrifice quite novel in eighteenth-century finance. In this it was characteristic of Pitt. Public virtue was his strong suit. In 1784, for example, he brushed aside the attractive sinecure Clerkship of the Pells to which he was entitled, worth £3,000 per annum. The gesture may not have been wholly artless. Like Pope's nymph, the sprightly Sylvia, who

trips along the Green,
She runs, but hopes she does not run unseen,

Pitt did not expect to go unnoticed. And he was right. He was warmly applauded, and a grateful nation eventually paid his substantial debts.

A little humbug notwithstanding, competence and probity were Pitt's greatest contributions to English public finance. No one sneered at him, or any subsequent Chancellor, for his 'clerk-like' knowledge of finances. He made expertise at the Treasury a political, almost a constitutional, necessity. He cemented the union with the City. To a business world now strongly permeated by evangelical morality, the austere figure of Pitt, his nose sharp with rectitude, was immensely attractive – and with good reason. Among his first measures was the decision to submit public loans and Treasury contracts to truly competitive tenders. William Beldam, prowling round the Treasury for advance news of the next Budget, found himself sharply rebuffed; budget security had arrived.

Unfortunately, Pitt's record as an administrative reformer was not so impressive. Shelburne, the mentor whom Pitt was too proud to have in his Cabinet, was profoundly dissatisfied with the young man, and in 1796 he launched a second Economical Reform campaign. How many of the reform resolutions of the 1780s had been acted upon? How many of the reports of the Public Accounts Commissioners had been implemented? What had been done about the findings of the Commission of Inquiry into Fees in Public Offices? It was difficult for Pitt to give a satisfactory answer. To point out that exports had risen from £14·7 million in 1783 to £27·2 million in 1795 was impressive but irrelevant. Most of the administrative anomalies of the eighteenth century still survived, now greatly aggravated by war. Parliamentary control of military estimates was no more effective in the 1790s than in the 1740s, and the Army's 'Extraordinaries' – that fathomless gulf of unappropriated expenditure – were again enormous. Shelburne (now Lord Lansdowne) called for more exacting Treasury control. Echoing Sir Edward Coke he suggested 'instead of giving the first lord a staff . . . I would give him a knife to cut off every man's fingers that dared thrust his fingers into the public purse'.

Every office [he later said, in a passage which was to be recalled by nineteenth-century reformers], seemed to be the lord of its own will, and every office seemed to have unlimited power over the purse of the nation, instead of their being, as the spirit of the constitution directed, under the constant check of the Treasury. It used to be the distinguishing feature of the British administration that the Treasury was its heart. . . .

Pitt was not disposed to concede much to this view. He was not really 'Treasury-minded'. At least, he rarely entered the office, saw little of the staff and did most of his work at home or through his bosom friends, the Treasury Secretaries George Rose and Charles Long.[6] The novel concept of Treasury imperialism, as propounded by Burke and Shelburne, seems to have left him unmoved. It had already excited resentment. In July 1782, Lord Loughborough criticized the extensive powers of inquisition given to the Treasury under Burke's Civil List Bill, and on 30 June 1783 Lord Stormont attacked the Public Offices Regulation Bill: 'It gave most extraordinary powers to the Treasury, and diminished the necessary power and the dignity of the other offices . . . several of the great offices of the state had ever been distinct and independent; but this Bill gave the Treasury a painful pre-eminence over all of them, and made every one of the rest subject to its control.'

Such a spirit of independent departmentalism was probably not unrepresentative, and helps to explain why the construction of a coherent system of civil service and financial administration under Treasury control was to take so very long. For Treasury control had to wait upon parliamentary control, and it took Parliament more than eighty years to work out its technical basis. The rest of this chapter is devoted to its evolution.

THE EVOLUTION OF PARLIAMENTARY CONTROL

The process was usefully forwarded by Shelburne's revival of Economical Reform in the middle of the Revolutionary war with France. Pitt's answer, the Select Committee on Finance set up early in 1797, produced, in its thirty-six reports, a more detailed analysis of late-eighteenth-century administration than any inquiry to date. Inevitably, its reports lacked the originality of the 1780 Public Accounts Commission, but in reviewing the action taken, or not taken, on earlier recommendations, it gave reform a substantial push forward.

Departmental reorganization, the abolition of sinecures, the introduction of superannuation, the diminution of balances, the speeding of audit – these were the main heads of its proposals. As far as the Treasury Establishment was concerned, dealt with in its Fifteenth Report, it found little to complain about. It remarked on the addition of some fifteen clerks since 1784 – a response to the pressures of war – but found the additional cost to have been absorbed by savings elsewhere. As for old Pratt, 'having been so long a Chief Clerk it was not thought right to superannuate him against his inclination'. However, they successfully condemned the practice of taking New Year's gifts, and for the rest found the 1782 reforms to have been efficacious.[7]

Where the Treasury was thought to be lacking was in the promotion of reforms among subordinate departments, and as proof of its competence it was found desirable to print the Treasury's correspondence on the subject as an appendix to the Report. It is none too impressive. It conveys a formal obedience to the principles of reform but no purposeful or imaginative intentions of its own. As a reforming agency the Treasury still remained passive.

Thus a pattern was set. As long as fundamental anomalies of employment and audit remained unresolved, the government of the day remained vulnerable to the case for administrative reform, and – if the conditions were right, as they were in 1806, 1810 and 1822 – the back-bench pressure for parliamentary inquiry could be made irresistible. It was upon such recurring opportunities that the fragmentary Whig party helped to keep itself alive during the long years of opposition before 1830. Select Committees or Royal Commissions would ensue, breeding reports and, perhaps, some piecemeal legislation. Then the cycle would begin again, with the Treasury often left in possession of some new and unsolicited area of responsibility.

In such circumstances, where developments were the grudging by-product of political opportunism, it is not surprising that of all the objects of reform the abolition of sinecures made the most rapid progress and administrative centralization the least. Thus, the Third Report of the 1807 Committee on Public Expenditure dealt thoroughly with sinecures and led to a Select Committee in 1810 devoted solely to this subject. It uncovered and listed some 242 sinecures worth nearly £300,000 per annum to their owners. But by Queen Victoria's accession, with a few harmless exceptions, they were a thing of the past.

That other bogy of the Economical Reformers, the Civil List, was similarly eliminated as a source of political danger. An important Act of 1816 freed it from many public charges and made them liabilities on the Consolidated Fund, subject to the annual vote and appropriation of the House of Commons. It also authorized the Treasury to appoint an Auditor of the Civil List – a permanent, non-political officer – with responsibility for checking household expenditure, under Treasury control. On the accession of William IV, Wellington's government was unexpectedly defeated trying to resist, but by the time Queen Victoria's Civil List was settled, victory lay with the reformers. The Civil List of £385,900 per annum provided solely for the Privy Purse, the royal household and a very small pension list. Under the head of Miscellaneous Expenditure the costs of civil departments were now all subject to annual parliamentary estimate and appropriation, just as military expenditure had been since the Revolution. At last a comprehensive, unitary system of parliamentary supply was possible – and the ghost of 'the influence of the Crown' seemed finally laid.

It would be rash to take this last point for granted. Queen Victoria was to demonstrate very fully the personal influence of the sovereign in politics, and the consolatory system of honours and awards had a new, rich and apparently still inexhaustible life ahead of it. But in 1822 Charles Arbuthnot, Joint Parliamentary Secretary to the Treasury (1809–23), complained that 'if the just and necessary influence of the Crown' were further reduced 'it will be quite impossible for any set of men to conduct the government of this country'. In this interesting transitional phase, when neither Cabinet nor party solidarity was sufficiently developed to ensure political cohesion, that was fair comment.[8] Clearly, if the Treasury wished to exert the fullest possible influence through the channels still remaining open to it, then it had a vested interest in the kind of co-ordination and centralization of administration which successive Parliamentary Commissions were pressing upon it. It was well advised to collaborate.

The development of superannuation is an important example of the way this was made possible. Pension arrangements had existed for some time in a few of the more professional revenue departments, particularly the Customs. The parliamentary reports of the 1780s and 1790s urged their extension, and in 1803 the Treasury, which had made a few awards to its own personnel in the past, authorized the Customs Board to make pension recommendations in any cases it thought suitable. The awards would be of two-thirds of the retiring salary after twenty years' service, or after fifteen, provided the employee was over sixty. Under sixty, and with ten to twenty years' service, he would get half his salary. The 1808 Committee on Public Expenditure praised these arrangements and in 1810 an Act established this formula as a general principle in the public service, subject to the discretion of the Treasury and annual report to Parliament. It established them too well. In the aftermath of the Napoleonic war, amid vociferous demands for economy, it was alleged that these generous pensions, lavishly distributed, had become regarded as a matter of right, not of grace. The whole system of salary increments established in recent years under Treasury supervision was called in question and suspended. Instead, in 1822, pensions were linked to a compulsory contributory system, which proved vastly unpopular. For the next decade therefore, pay and pensions were at the centre of an interesting three-cornered conflict between Parliament, the Treasury and public servants. Under this parliamentary pressure for strict economy, the embattled government clerks discovered a new sense of identity and the novel concept of a unitary 'civil service' gradually took shape. An Act of 1834 finally settled a revised contributory system, with provision for medical certification. Together with the Act of 1859, which linked qualification (for what should, strictly speaking, be called a Treasury 'allowance', not a pension) with the 1855 Civil Service Commission's certificates, it remains the oldest part of the present superannuation system.

This process had activated and reinforced the Treasury's traditional responsibility for any enlargement of establishments or increases in expenditure. It had obliged the Treasury to enter far more deeply than ever before into the internal staffing arrangements of traditionally independent departments. But the source of this initiative should not be mistaken. It was parliamentary, and *back-bench* parliamentary, pressure that lay behind the stringent economies and reorganizations of the 1820s. In the depressed and anxious circumstances of 1817 a Select Committee on Finance had taken up Shelburne's campaign. In its Sixth Report it 'earnestly recommended . . . that the Lords of the Treasury should call for a return of the present establishments of all the civil offices in the State, the salaries of which have been increased in the last fifteen years; and . . . that they should make a revision of the same, or direct such prospective reductions therein, as may appear to them reasonable'. In response to this, Lord Liverpool's government concerted measures to bring down the inflated salaries and increments of the war years upon lines laid down in Treasury circulars. There was no question of the Treasury imposing absolute uniformity; indeed, there was no question of the Treasury *imposing* anything, except on the subordinate departments of the revenue. Its role was to recommend and to lead, and it did this to some effect in 1821 by making severe cuts in the Treasury Establishment. Here again, the response was to parliamentary pressure. On 28 June and 2 July 1821, respectively, the House of Commons and House of Lords had addressed the Crown to order a minute inquiry into civil departments with a view to reducing expenditure to the level of 1797. To this the government had bowed and the Treasury Minute of 10 August 1821 was the result. It announced cuts which brought the maximnm cost of the revised Treasury Establishment down from

£64,000 to £48,000 per annum. It then addressed itself to all the other departments of state, large and small, and suggested the guiding principles which they should follow in making their cuts. Unfortunately, these economies were linked to a most unpopular (and abortive) scheme for compulsory superannuation deductions, which would have amounted to 7½ per cent, or at least 5 per cent, of existing salaries. Powerful, self-sufficient departments like the Foreign Office and Colonial Office were able to hide their general reluctance to follow the Treasury's sacrificial lead behind the uproar against superannuation. Where cuts were conceded they paid little tribute to the Treasury's moral authority.

Nevertheless, Parliament had successfully nudged the Treasury into taking up a rather more assertive posture towards its responsibilities, and this procedure is paralleled by the third, last and most important line of reform – the reform of Estimates, Accounts and Audit. It was a more hesitant development, painfully slow at times, marked out by a succession of Parliamentary Committees and Royal Commissions – 1810, 1817, 1822, 1828, 1829, 1831, 1847, 1856 – culminating, after much havering and delay in the Exchequer and Audit Departments Act of 1866. Since this is still the cornerstone of modern financial control its origins are of more than academic interest. Unfortunately, they are also confusingly intricate and what follows is a compressed account, which, if tedious, does better justice to the subject than I intended.

COMPLETING THE CIRCLE OF CONTROL

Pitt's contribution to speedier auditing had been an Act of 1785, abolishing the two Auditors of the Imprests (those innovations of 1560) and replacing them with a professional Board of Audit with semi-judicial status. Unfortunately, the departure of the two Auditors – an interesting instance of 'last in, first out' – left in being the far more decrepit structure of the ancient Exchequer to which the Audit Office was now uncomfortably shackled. Side by side with the brisk, direct methods of the Auditors the 'ancient course' rambled on. The Great Roll of the Pipe uncoiled into its eighth century, while the wooden tally system, condemned to extinction by an Act of 1783, only disappeared with the death of the last chamberlain in 1826. Elsewhere, in defiance of the spirit, if not the letter, of the Act, Exchequer officials continued to use the Roman numerals, Exchequer Latin, and unintelligible hieroglyphics that were traditional.

All this *and* the Napoleonic wars proved too much for the Audit Office. By 1806 the Chancellor of the Exchequer, Lord Henry Petty

Fitzmaurice,* could startle the House of Commons with the announcement that some £455 million of expenditure remained officially unaccounted for. A succession of Acts strengthened the Audit Office, simplified its procedures and those of the major spending departments, Army, Navy and Ordnance. Acts of 1806 and 1813 made special arrangements for Army accounting, particularly in Spain, and an Act of 1814 created a Colonial Audit Office. But not until 1817 was the Treasury given full powers to reorganize Exchequer posts as the existing life interests expired. Not until 1821 were some of the ancient audit procedures abolished and the use of English and Arabic numerals enforced. Ten years later the Commissioners of Inquiry into Public Accounts still found the spurious rituals going on, while Bank of England clerks stood by, providing the effectual service of receipt, issue and record. Eventually, in 1833, the structure of the Upper Exchequer was abolished, leaving only the offices of the Chancellor of the Exchequer, the King's Remembrancer and the judicial court of Exchequer pleas, all of which are still incorporated in our administrative and judicial system. And in 1834, the death of the Auditor of the Receipt, Lord Grenville, at long, long last left the way clear for the demolition of the Lower Exchequer. The Act – 4 and 5 William IV c. 15 – brought the seven-hundred-years-old institution to an end.

Yet, like some ancient, legendary tree, crushing those who had dared to fell it, the Exchequer took its appropriate revenge. Board of Works employees, clearing up the mess of old tally sticks in the Exchequer rooms in Palace Yard, overheated the flues of the House of Lords on the afternoon of 16 October 1834, and the ensuing conflagration destroyed the Houses of Parliament, with consequences that are still with us. Pugin's new Palace of Westminster would have been a reasonable price to pay if the Exchequer had been wholly abolished, but it was not. The same Act that killed the ancient Exchequer raised its ghost in the new office of Comptroller-General of the Receipt and Issue of His Majesty's Exchequer. With permanent, semi-judicial status, independent of the Treasury but responsible to Parliament, the Comptroller-General took over the task of being the channel through which the issues and receipts of the government's Bank of England accounts had to pass. It was his particular duty to check the validity of Treasury orders to issue money against the parliamentary authorizations of Supply and appropriation.

This meant that there were still rather too many agencies involved

*Lord Henry, later third Marquis of Lansdowne, closely rivalling Pitt was a precocious twenty-five-year-old Chancellor but, Wilberforce thought, 'not quite first rate'.

in supervising the flow of expenditure. The chain of command ran roughly like this. Firstly, of course, the House of Commons studied the Estimates, voted the Supply, and tied it to the specified purposes with Acts of appropriation. Then the Treasury, responsible for administering these resources, authorized their issue at its own discretion, although in amounts and at times usually agreed with the spending departments. The Comptroller-General of the Exchequer, receiving this authorization, scrutinized it, checking its validity against the parliamentary grants, and when satisfied gave appropriate instructions to the Bank of England. The Bank then transferred the required credits from the Consolidated Fund account – i.e. the great pool of all the revenues which Pitt had created in 1787 from the many distinct streams of taxation hitherto kept in separate Bank accounts – to the accounts of the Paymasters of the spending departments, which drew upon them as instructed by the Treasury. It had been a particular object of the Economical Reformers to keep those Bank account balances as small and as short-lived as possible, so the Treasury's responsibility for careful calculation and timing of expenditure was heavy at this point. However, beyond this, the departments – particularly the Army and Navy – had their own machinery for authorizing and checking the course of spending by a multitude of sub-accountants within their jurisdiction. Ultimately, it was the Audit Office that they had to satisfy with the legitimacy of their transactions, proffering the vouchers and receipts of internal expenditure for their expert scrutiny. But it was well-known, as a Select Committee on Finance had pointed out in 1810, that the Audit Office was usually looking at the carefully doctored end-products of the department's own accounting machinery – 'the officers themselves will be found to be the Auditors of their own Expenditure . . .'!

> The Board of Treasury, to whom this duty might be conceived more immediately to belong, has at no time exercised a systematic control over the Public Accounts; neither would such an employment be compatible with the regular functions and ordinary occupations of that Board, nor consistent with those urgent executive duties in which it is constantly engaged.[9]

Thus, in practice, the chain of responsibility was less effective than it seems; in theory too, there were two conspicuously weak links.

The first of these was the Exchequer, for the formality of its preliminary check upon the validity of orders to issue money was quite spurious as long as it remained unrelated to the retrospective check of the Audit Office. Likewise, the Audit Office check was valueless unless it was submitted to an authority which had a really independent, judicial relation to government expenditure, as well as the power to censure misappropriation. It was no use submitting its reports to the Treasury, as it did, for the Treasury – if it acted upon them at all – was judging in its own cause. The answer clearly lay with Parliament. What was the point of the House of Commons enacting its portentous clauses, appropriating the nation's tax revenue to specific expenditure, if it didn't bother to check that its orders were ultimately carried out? But such was the case. There was no parliamentary follow-up; there was a whole link missing in the chain of responsibility.

This state of affairs has always puzzled posterity. Lord Welby, the great Permanent Secretary of the late-nineteenth-century Treasury, remarked to the 1902 Select Committee on National Expenditure how struck he had been that for 160 years 'the House of Commons, always anxious to establish its control, should have remained all that time under the illusion that it could control expenditure by putting checks on the issue of money from the Exchequer instead of ascertaining how the money had been spent'. It was singular, he said, 'that two of our greatest Chancellors of the Exchequer, Mr Pitt and Sir Robert Peel, did not seize the point'. Actually, this is not quite correct; Pitt did see, if not seize, the point. In May 1796 he told the Commons –

> That it was the duty of the House to superintend the expenditure of the public money, he did not deny; but that it was the duty of parliament to enforce the application of it to the letter of the act, required the command of a retrospective authority which the House had not the means of enforcing.

This threw the responsibility back at the Commons, which in the next seventy years gradually inched its way towards a solution. In the process the concept of Treasury control slowly matured.

The Fifth Report, in 1810, of the Select Committee already cited, pointed the way: 'if Accounts were all under one authority immediately responsible to Parliament, none of these defects would have arisen'. In 1819 another Fifth Report of yet another Select Committee picked up the same thread, deplored the failure of the government to do anything about it and, interviewing the permanent head of the Treasury staff, asked if he thought it advisable to create 'one office upon a great and efficient scale, with a high officer of state, having a seat in Parliament at the head, for the purpose of examining and auditing the accounts of the kingdom?' Unfortunately he did not, and in general took an extremely complacent view of the existing medley of accounting systems. Reform was checked. In 1822 it was only in a footnote to Appendix 54 of the Select Committee on Public Accounts' report that Sir Henry Parnell made another clear statement of the same point. However, in the Second Report of the 1828 Select Committee on Income and Expenditure, under Parnell's chairmanship, the argument came out strongly. It called for the restoration of that 'ancient and wise control vested by our Financial Policy in the hands of the Treasury over all the departments connected with the Public Expenditure'. This could only be effected 'by the House of Commons constantly enforcing its application, by holding the Treasury responsible for every act of Expenditure in each Department'.[10]

Apart from the visionary appeals of individual reformers like Burke and Shelburne, these are the first authoritative parliamentary demands for joint financial control by a responsible Treasury and a watchful House of Commons. They are landmarks of the first importance. At the same time, the Committee nominated several practical objects of reform, all of which were to make great progress in the years before and after the Great Reform Bill of 1832. They included (1) clear, uniform accounting systems in all public departments; (2) the simplification and consolidation of public business; and (3) 'an effectual control in the Treasury over all departments'.

In fact, since 1802 the Treasury had been obliged to present annual Finance Accounts to the House of Commons showing the balance of public income and expenditure, but they left much to be desired. There was no uniformity in the 'financial year' adopted by different departments – some ending in January, some in March, some on 24 December, some on the 31st, and the accounts of income did not properly balance the accounts of expenditure. While the former represented receipts at the Exchequer – i.e. a *net* account, excluding the large sums withheld for expenditure by the revenue departments on salaries, tax rebates, etc. – the latter was not even an account of Exchequer issues but of the sums issued by the spending departments to their agents, and not necessarily spent.[11] From the point of view of both exact parliamentary estimates and coherent accounting this was absurd, yet it was not until 1822 that radical, back-bench M.P.s fomented a first-class row. Cried Joseph Hume, 'There were scarcely two Treasury accounts laid on that table that agreed with each other!' The outcome was the 1822 Select Committee on Public Accounts and the presentation henceforth of properly balanced finance accounts. An Act of 1829 redefined the Treasury's responsibility to submit quarterly accounts of 'actual' receipts and issues. In 1832 the Whig Chancellor of the Exchequer, Lord Althorp, brought the financial year one quarter forward to end on 5 April, but it was not until 1854, with Gladstone's Public Revenue and Consolidated Fund Charges Act that the revenue and parliamentary financial years were at last made to coincide, ending together on 31 March. And it was only by this same Act that *gross* revenue and expenditure figures were presented to the House, making possible a truly comprehensive picture of the financial situation.

A process of administrative consolidation had accompanied these developments. In 1816, as a logical consequence of the 1800 Act of Union, the revenues of Great Britain and Ireland were united in one Consolidated Fund, under the direction of a United Kingdom Treasury (which meant little except the addition of two Irish Treasury Lords to the English Board – and they were soon abolished). Scottish revenue administration was brought under the United Kingdom Treasury's control in 1833. In the same year, the Boards of Stamps and Taxes were amalgamated and in 1849 joined with the Excise Commissioners to form the Board of Inland Revenue. On the expenditure side a single Paymaster of Civil Services emerged in 1834, and in 1835 a single Paymaster General of the Army, Navy and Ordnance. In 1848 the two were combined under the Paymaster General Act, by the terms of which the Paymastership remained a political appointment, tenable by a Member of Parliament. But his assistant was a permanent civil servant and, very often, a Treasury man, so by this means the Treasury secured a useful extension of its command over expenditure.

Elsewhere the Treasury could still only influence by its example. Departmental book-keeping, for example, proved intractable. In 1828 the Treasury commissioned three experts, one of them a senior Treasury clerk, to investigate departmental procedures and make reports, and although they were divided in their recommendations enough were put into effect to give a greater degree of uniformity. Even so, it was not until after 1857 that scientific, double-entry book-keeping was universal in government departments.

THE EXCHEQUER AND AUDIT DEPARTMENTS ACT OF 1866

In most of these developments, back-bench parliamentary pressure was the source of the initiative. It is important to record, therefore, that the decisive breakthrough in the development of parliamentary control was initiated by the Executive, in 1832, in the first fine enthusiasms of reforming Whig government. The First Lord of the Admiralty, Sir James Graham, had ordered his sprawling and unco-ordinated department to submit to him exact accounts of its recent expenditure, and he was startled to find quite flagrant departures from the letter and spirit of parliamentary appropriation. Money voted for victualling, for example, had been diverted to build warehouses at Plymouth. His reaction was to set about sweeping reforms and its first fruit was the Act of 1832 'to amend the laws relating to the Business of the Civil Departments of the Navy'. By clause thirty it required the presentation to Parliament of fully audited accounts showing in detail the correspondence between annual expenditure and the letter of parliamentary appropriation. Thus, the House of Commons had been given, voluntarily, the means of confirming the Admiralty's obedience to its instructions. Yet, it was not until 1846, after prolonged investigation by a Treasury committee, that the same obligation was extended to the War Office and the Ordnance Office, and not until 1861 that it embraced the revenue departments! Once again a clearly marked, logical path of reform proved surprisingly long.

Fortunately, it was during Gladstone's seven great constructive years as Chancellor of the Exchequer (1859–66) that all these separate paths began to converge. In addition, the reforming initiative of a regenerate and purposeful Treasury was beginning to make itself felt. In 1856 an extremely able Select Committee on Public Monies listened to a strongly argued Treasury case for the abolition of the Comptroller-General's redundant functions and their replacement by a more powerful Audit Board reporting regularly to a parliamentary finance committee. In its details the Treasury's case was unacceptable, and it was strongly contested, needless to say, by the Comptroller-General, Lord Monteagle. He professed to see dire constitutional consequences in a measure which 'proposes for the first time in our history to place the powers of issuing public money at the absolute command of the Treasury'. Parliamentary control, he suggested, should be based on mistrust of, not confidence in, the Treasury. In the event, the report of the Committee made recommendations over a wide range of financial procedures, all tending towards greater clarity, uniformity and control. It wished particularly to see the extension of the appropriation audit started by Graham to all the other expenditure of public money, transmitted by a more powerful Audit Office direct to Parliament. The redoubtable Monteagle (who, as Thomas Spring-Rice had been a Whig Chancellor of the Exchequer, 1835–9) stood in the way of more sweeping changes.

But in 1861 Gladstone at last set up a House of Commons Select Committee on Public Accounts and the following year proposed resolutions which made such a committee a permanent part of the machinery of the House. Standing Order No. 90 still provides that 'There shall be a select committee, to be designated the Committee of Public Accounts, for the examination of the accounts showing the appropriation of the sums granted by Parliament to meet the public expenditure'. A few years later the death of Lord Monteagle cleared the last remaining obstacle. The Exchequer and Audit Departments Act of 1866 brought the process to its logical conclusion, tying together the procedures of Estimate, Appropriation, Expenditure and Audit in one coherent system. The Exchequer was now swallowed up by a greatly strengthened Audit Office, their functions united in the new office of 'Comptroller and Auditor-General'. With a salary drawn direct from the Consolidated Fund – that is, free of the annual procedure of a parliamentary vote – holding office during 'good behaviour', the Comptroller's tenure was (and is) as secure and independent as that of the judges. Although appointed by the Treasury, his sole responsibility lay to the House of Commons. As before, it was his particular duty to confirm the propriety of the Treasury's instructions to issue money, and only his signature could make them effectual at the Bank of England. Only with his sanction could the Bank make loans in advance of incoming revenue to bridge any short-term deficiency arising on the quarterly balance of receipts and issues. As heir of the Exchequer he was to receive daily accounts of the gross receipts of revenue and of the issues therefrom. As Auditor the essence of his work lay in investigating the annual appropriation accounts submitted by the departments via the Treasury. Checking the detailed record of issues against the estimates and appropriations voted by Parliament he submitted his findings to the Public Accounts Committee. His own powers of inquisition were considerable: he and his large staff could pursue the processes of expenditure into the departments themselves. Those of the Public Accounts Committee were even greater: 'to send for persons, papers and records' – traditional words to describe a complete inquisitorial authority to which the Treasury and all other government departments have to submit.

In its essentials, the machinery of modern financial control by the House of Commons was now nearly complete. Some of its basic ingredients had been constructed in the seventeenth century – particularly, of course, the fundamental principle that taxation was illegal without parliamentary consent. The reign of Charles II had seen the Commons establish their sole right to initiate financial proposals and thwart any alterations by the House of Lords. Further conflicts, culminating in the Budget struggle of 1909–11, were to deprive the Lords of any effective veto. Meanwhile, the rejection by the Lords of a Paper Duties Bill in 1860 simply stimulated Gladstone to bring budgetary procedures a big step nearer their modern form. Henceforth the annual tax proposals of the Chancellor were embodied in a single 'Finance Bill', and although the timetable of budgetary debates required a good deal of replanning in the late nineteenth and early twentieth centuries, the main forms of procedure had been perfected by the 1860s. The principle had been established in 1667 that Supply proposals – i.e. that such-and-such a sum be voted for such-and-such a purpose – and decisions about

'Ways and Means' of raising that sum, had to be discussed fully and freely after good notice in a Committee of the Whole House. This was balanced by the resolutions of 1706 and 1713 which had conceded the financial initiative within the Commons to the representatives of the Crown – in effect, the ministers of the Treasury. This was decisive in the long process by which the government of the day has gained the dominance of the business of the House, and equally decisive in giving the Secretaries to the Treasury, and the Junior Lords, a major role in controlling the manoeuvres of the ruling party. It is significant that both these principles, of procedure in Committee and Treasury initiative, were restated and amplified in 1866.[12]

However, the Exchequer and Audit Departments Act also had profound significance for the Executive. By creating the first effective machinery for a retrospective, annual audit of government expenditure it put a willing Treasury on its mettle to enforce the strictest standards of financial propriety among the departments. The Estimates and Accounts upon which such an inquiry would be based would have to attain new levels of accuracy, and the Treasury's responsibility for a careful scrutiny of these estimates was now much heavier. But this was all gain to the Treasury. In principle, the relationship of the Treasury to the House of Commons or its watchdog, the Public Accounts Committee, was that of servant to master. It was strictly accountable now for its stewardship of the public purse, and there might well be storms. But the Treasury had also gained a powerful ally. No sanction that the Treasury might bring against the spending propensities of other departments, jealously guarding their autonomy, was more compelling than the ultimate threat of exposure before this parliamentary tribunal. The Treasury's role in the proceedings of the Public Accounts Committee was (and is) often that of prosecuting counsel as well as witness. It was therefore in respect of its new colleague, the Comptroller and Auditor-General, that the Victorian Treasury framed an important statement of the principle of Treasury control. In a Treasury Minute of April 1868, 'my Lords' acknowledged 'that it would be beyond the function of this Board to control the ordinary expenditure placed under the charge of the several departments, within the limits of the sums set forth under the subheads of the several grants of Parliament, and that it is only in exceptional cases that the special sanction of the Treasury should be held to be necessary'. But, 'My Lords consider that such sanction should be required for any increase of establishment, of salary, or of cost of a service, or for any additional works or new services which have not been specially provided for in the grants of Parliament'.

> My Lords therefore desire that, in conducting the Appropriation Audit of the several Votes, the Comptroller and Auditor General will bring to their notice any excess of charge beyond the amount assigned to each subhead of such Votes, or any expenditure which, upon examination, may, in any of the several cases referred to above, appear to have been incurred without Treasury authority, in order that my Lords may determine whether they will sanction the admission of such unauthorized expenditure as a charge against the parliamentary grant.[13]

This Minute is one of the fundamental statements of Treasury control, appearing, appropriately enough, just two hundred years after the first effective affirmation of Treasury authority by Charles II's Privy Council. It is still appealed to today.[14] It was by no means definitive or exclusive of broader interpretations of Treasury control, but as a portent of the fruitful relationship which was soon to develop between the Treasury and the Comptroller and Auditor-General the Minute of 1868 was auspicious. For the Treasury, as for Parliament, the Exchequer and Audit Departments Act was the beginning of a process.

It also marked an end. The circle of control, Gladstone observed, was now complete, and – one is tempted to add – not before time. The fact that the modern foundations of financial control were completed in 1866 ought to be little more interesting than the fact that it took so long. Certain contingencies such as the Crimean War and the life of Lord Monteagle had hindered its completion, and the responsibilities entailed by parliamentary audit seemed to attract the back-bench M.P. far less than the enforcement of a narrow-minded, cheeseparing policy of Supply. The arid technicalities of financial control, then as now, were either boring or confusing. They generated no enthusiasm. No mobs howled outside the Treasury; no pikes were sharpened to enforce an appropriation audit. Unlike Manchester's Anti-Corn Law League, Liverpool's Financial Reform Association appears to have had no direct influence on parliamentary opinion.[15] Yet the creation of a comprehensive system of financial control was an integral part of the movements shaping the reform of the Poor Law, the penal system, local government, banking and the tariff. It was the product of the same principles and the same men – of the 'Classical Economists', Ricardo, Malthus and Wilson; of the radical utilitarians, Bowring, Parnell and Hume; and, above all, of the politicians, Baring, Peel, Graham, Cobden and Gladstone. Nothing could be more expressive than the fact that Cobden, in whom so many of these influences come together, should have been asked by Gladstone to become the first Comptroller and Auditor General.

POLITICAL ECONOMY AND *LAISSEZ-FAIRE*

The association of these men reflects the way in which the nature of 'Economical Reform' had matured since the 1780s. Then it had been an essentially parliamentary philosophy, linked to the static political concept of 'the balance of the constitution'. This element never wholly disappeared: the curbing of an aristocratic executive was more vital to the reforming radicals of the 1830s than it had been to the Rockingham Whigs fifty years before. But the Napoleonic wars had given a new vitality to the cause. For men bearing a tax burden of some £80 million per annum, cowering under a National Debt which had risen from £240 million to £840 million in twenty-five years, economy again excited a sense of urgency close to panic. It is reflected in the level-headed Ricardo's suggestion for a capital levy to clear the Debt in one gigantic act of redemption. It is heard in Joseph Hume's incessant demands for a return to the expenditure levels of 1792. In 1816 an hysterically jubilant House of Commons abolished the Income Tax and ordered its records to be burnt. But the war had stimulated rather more constructive thinking than this behaviour suggests. The Bank of England's suspension of cash payments, authorized in 1797, and the debate over their resumption after 1810, carried British monetary theory to new levels of sophistication. The formal establishment of the gold standard in 1816 and the restoration of normal currency dealings in 1821 mark the beginning of a century of monetary orthodoxy to which the Treasury gave unflinching support. At the same time the commercial blockade of Napoleon's Europe, followed by acute post-war distress, had compelled the entry of 'the manufacturing interest' into nineteenth-century politics. With the principles of Adam Smith's *Wealth of Nations* (1776) now thoroughly absorbed and coursing in their veins they were formidably equipped to contest the case for free trade against an antiquated tariff and the novel degree of agricultural protection provided by the Corn Law of 1815. They were equally disposed to condemn the public expenditure which made these tariffs necessary. Another, more elusive, influence was that of Jeremy Bentham and the radical utilitarians. No generalization can hope to do justice to all their highly idiosyncratic ideas, but their challenge to the pernicious lumber of an archaic social and political system was strong and unequivocal. They could be counted upon to produce the clearest prescription for cheap, minimal yet efficient government.

In such an ideal, *laissez-faire* in government, society and the economy, these lines of thought found a rather precarious agreement. It was by no means unanimous or consistently sustained.

Laissez-faire was never a monolithic creed. Even the classical economists, who tended to forget that Adam Smith had commended state intervention in health and education, public works and the subordination of commerce to the emergencies of defence, were divided over the positive role a government might play in the economy. T. R. Malthus, who looked blandly on famine and plague as the automatic and unavoidable regulators of over-population, seems to have believed that prudent government expenditure might stimulate production and consumption in circumstances of recession. Even *The Economist* (founded in 1843) which condemned the protection of child labour in factories and mines as an intolerable interference in a free economy, found a soft spot for a government-monopoly postal system.[16] But all were agreed – free traders, economists, utilitarians – that the character of existing government administration was inimical to the natural, or even artificial, harmony of human interests. Wasteful and corrupt, government expenditure was fed by a mischievous and irrational fiscal system which hampered trade and diverted investment. This pessimism, unalleviated by any hopes of continuous technological progress, rooted in expectations of diminishing returns from a primarily agricultural economy, was fundamental. No government could hope to do more than tinker in the margins of the social system. Far better that it should leave the economy alone.

Thus the triumph of Ricardian economics over the official mind of nineteenth-century governments is marked – at its narrowest – by what economists have called 'the Treasury view', i.e. 'that government spending, whether financed by deficit or taxation, could do little to lessen widespread unemployment and depression',[17] and – at its broadest – by the belief that the positive role of government lay only in the marginal areas of defence, public order and the administration of a minimal revenue. The triumph was never absolute. As we shall see, nineteenth-century governments intervened in society and the economy to a greater extent than is often believed. But, unquestionably, the body of ideas associated with financial orthodoxy and 'the Treasury view' dominated and circumscribed the range of the Treasury's activities for more than a century. Incapacity and indifference had acquired a rationale.

JOSEPH HUME, SIR HENRY PARNELL AND THE BENTHAMITES

Meanwhile, for a more positive contribution to the evolution of Treasury control one must look to the Benthamite utilitarians – to men like John Bowring, Poulett Thomson and Joseph Hume – and to free-trade reformers like Sir Henry Parnell, Sir James Graham and James Wilson. The fact that most of these men were at the time highly independent Members of Parliament is symptomatic of a distinctive phenomenon in early-nineteenth-century politics. In a period when they were unable to control the House with the discipline of well organized parties, the governments of Lord Liverpool, Wellington and Melbourne were extremely vulnerable to reformers' demands for Select Committees and Royal Commissions, and this type of procedure became the characteristic prelude to all the major and minor achievements of reform. There were over sixty Royal Commissions and 540 Select Committees between 1800 and 1832.

No man exploited these techniques better than Joseph Hume – and it is a minor scandal of historical scholarship that he lacks a biography. He may well be one of the biggest bores who ever left Aberdeen, but in a political career that spanned thirty years he had a remarkable record. Hume was an early and pertinacious spokesman for every worthwhile cause. He fought for the abolition of slavery in the colonies and of flogging in the forces; he spoke consistently for the relief of Ireland and he carried the campaign for parliamentary reform far beyond the Great Reform Bill of 1832. In 1824, Hume and Francis Place (the radical tailor) pulled off the repeal of the 'Combination Laws' inhibiting trade-union organization. Working with Ricardo in 1819 he moved for the elimination of the Corn Laws, and between 1821 and 1823 they mounted a successful attack on the absurdities of the Sinking Fund. Contrary to general belief, Hume's was not a narrow, parsimonious kind of radicalism. He wanted a National Gallery in 1824 and he pressed for the opening of the British Museum to the general public. He deplored the inadequacy of the first government grant for education of 1833. But most typical was his promotion of Savings Banks, for thrift – public and private – was his favourite theme, the only one which he seriously damaged by repetition. Year in, year out, sparing neither Whig nor Tory governments, Hume challenged the Estimates in minute detail. Served by a small group of expert clerks, Hume was a one-man Select Committee on Estimates, capable of producing extremely detailed, carefully worked-out schemes for financial reform. In 1821 his was the pressure which forced on the Treasury the severe salary cuts of August, and in 1822 he helped expose the absurdities of official accountancy. He and Ricardo were members of the 1822 Select Committee on Public Accounts.

Hume's influence on the Treasury is incalculable – regrettably so, because, faced by his nagging pedantry, official opinion hardened against him. It could not ignore him; the whole standard of public finance procedures was perceptibly raised in defence against his probing Argus-eyes; but the response was never cooperative. Even the Political Economy Club, the meeting ground of classical economists and parliamentary utilitarians founded in 1821, blackballed him, and the official Whig verdict on their potential ally was that he 'has many valuable qualities mixed up with some eccentricities which bordered upon moral perversity. As a political associate he was unsafe.'[18]

In this Hume's influence compares unfavourably with Sir Henry Parnell's. Parnell was never quite an outsider, although he was sacked by his Whig Cabinet colleagues after rows over his intrigues with Hume. An Irish Baronet who made his name, as did so many of his contemporaries, on corn and currency questions, Parnell was an ardent economical reformer in office as well as out. He was an excellent choice for the reformed Paymastership of the Forces in 1836. But his greatest influence on nineteenth-century government was probably through his pamphlet, *On Financial Reform,* published in 1830. It contained a clear, cogent prescription for what was to be the fiscal and financial policy of the next twenty years, i.e. a programme of tariff reduction on essential commodities, paid for by the inevitable increase in consumption and supported, when necessary, by the discreet employment of the Income Tax. The simplification and consolidation of the revenue administration would be an incidental part of this programme but he also saw it as serving a major purpose of his plan – the restoration of Treasury control.

Parnell's views on this subject are extremely interesting, not least for their rarity. As a prophet he is in direct line of descent from Burke and Shelburne (whom he quoted). The fact that he was anticipated by the Report of the 1828 Finance Committee is only a tribute to his chairmanship of that body, for in the pamphlet, as in the Report, he deplored the supercession of detailed Treasury control by 'a spirit of profusion' for which Pitt and the war were responsible. He went on to expound the rather touching idea that the eighteenth century had been a golden age of Treasury rigour. This puzzling view is only explained by a footnote in which he cites his authority – 'a MS Treasury Document on the Ordnance Department . . . referring to precedents from 1755'. As we have seen,* it was *only* over the Ordnance Department, of all the great spending departments, that the eighteenth-century Treasury had been able to exercise any effective scrutiny of estimates, although it would be hazardous to deduce that it always did so. Had Parnell looked back to the Treasury of Lowndes, or of Guy, or of Downing, he would have been on

*Above, p. 91. Parnell probably had in mind a memorandum prepared in 1818 by the Assistant Secretary of the Treasury, George Harrison.

better ground. As it is, Parnell's vision of a reinvigorated Treasury authority was based on a rather naïve view of recent Treasury history.

It was none the less effective for that. The years after 1830 saw an active pursuit of financial reforms which all tended to enhance the Treasury's authority. The first appropriation audits after 1832, the abolition of the ancient Exchequer, the consolidation of the revenue departments, the systematization of accounts and the regulation of superannuation all bear the essential characteristics of utilitarian reform – rationalization, centralization, economy. How far they were intrinsically Benthamite is arguable. Bentham's influence always is. It was certainly not as direct as it has been shown to be in the Board of Trade, the Poor Law Board and the Board of Health. But through men like John Bowring, Bentham's literary executor and biographer, and through Charles Poulett Thomson, a close political ally, his contribution was real enough. Bowring was employed by Parnell for the 1828 Select Committee on Finance and later to examine the French and Dutch financial accounting systems. His reports on the much more scientific and coherent systems practised there were a powerful influence in English reforms. In 1848 Bowring was one of the few members of the Select Committee on Miscellaneous Expenditure to make a really probing examination of Treasury control. Thomson, similarly, as Vice-President of the Board of Trade, was able to bring a systematic, Benthamite approach to the problem of departmental accounting. He too served on Parnell's 1831 Commission of Inquiry into Public Accounts and influenced the adoption of scientific book-keeping in the public service.

In the case of the Treasury, as for other departments, to claim too much for Benthamism is to concede too little to common sense, but there are two more good reasons why a case could be made for doctrinaire utilitarian influence upon the course of financial reform. One, which is well understood by historians, is the marked receptivity of the Whig governments of the 1830s to such influences in all spheres of social reform. The other, less often appreciated, is the peculiar susceptibility of Treasury control to utilitarian regulation.

As far as finance is concerned, the eagerness of some of the younger and more conscientious Whigs to equip themselves with the best principles of modern political economy is well conveyed by the holiday reading which Sir Francis Baring, Secretary to the Treasury and shortly to be Chancellor, prescribed for himself in 1835 –

> My general reading must be finance and political economy. Adam Smith I have begun several times and read parts but never finished. Hamilton on National debt, Huskisson on currency . . . Parnell I should like to read, noting what has been already done; Parliamentary Reports such as education, public works and the different subjects relating to commerce . . .[19]

One's heart warms to someone unable to read Adam Smith from cover to cover, but – to take a sterner view – there is more than a hint here of the well-meaning amateurism which was such a disastrous feature of Whig finance. It was, perhaps unfairly, represented by their first Budget, that of 1831. Lord Althorp's appointment as Chancellor of the Exchequer had been approved by his mother – 'Jack was always skilful at figures' – but became an embarrassment to his party, for his Budget – ambitious and ill-considered – was badly mauled and had to be reconstructed. Yet he had been at pains to take the best advice. He had dined and wined all the experts, including Hume, Poulett Thomson, Parnell and other members of the Political Economy Club, and the result was a poor advertisement for political economy. Indeed, the Whigs were never able to extract the full political advantage from their contacts with advanced opinion. While they achieved much that was of permanent value to English society, it was left to the far more expert Peel to snatch the initiative of financial reform for the Conservatives in 1841.

On the second point, it is necessary to recall the way in which increasing statutory responsibilities were defining more exactly the Treasury's immemorial customary control. Most of these were of very recent origin and were plastic enough to take the stamp which the age cared to give them. But, in the event, the age proved deliberately unambitious and, less deliberately, unimaginative. Traditionally, the nature of Treasury control was really negative – the power to give or withhold assent 'to any measure increasing or tending to increase the public expenditure' – and the enormous significance which this power came to have in the nineteenth century is less a reflection of Treasury imperialism than of the organic growth of government fostered by reforming Parliaments. New departments, or expanding departments such as the Board of Trade and Colonial Office, were inevitably forced to cross the Treasury's path in search of larger staffs, larger salaries. Again, thanks to Parliament, the transition from customary fees from the public to regular salaries from the state, the establishment of pensions and the novel submission of civil estimates to the House of Commons had forced the traditionally independent departments more and more within the Treasury's orbit.

The process, as I have emphasized, was one in which the Treasury was passive and unambitious. The major departments lost none of their independence, for the Treasury gained no power to intervene, uninvited, in their internal arrangements – even though the efficiency of those arrangements had a considerable bearing on costs. Sir Charles Trevelyan, permanent head of the Treasury staff between 1840 and 1859, had occasion to lament this to the 1848 Select Committee on Miscellaneous Expenditure. On the seemingly trivial question of stationery expenditure Trevelyan admitted that, while the War Office and Admiralty had condescended to use cheaper paper, the Foreign Office and Home Office continued to use a very expensive quality and there was nothing the Treasury could do about it:

> ... the Secretaries of State have been held in a degree of respect by the Treasury, and we have not felt that we had precisely the same control over them in matters of this sort as over the other offices.[20]

Indeed, departmental autonomy remained so considerable an obstacle that, for the first half of the nineteenth century, it is probably unrealistic to think of 'Treasury control' as distinct from the varying degrees of pressure the Treasury could bring against one department or another.

The principles and prejudices of the age came together to confirm this imperfect state of affairs. Hostility to centralization, a fear of administrative despotism, was common to all parties – Whig, Tory and radical. Even the Benthamite desire for areas of centralized regulation stopped short of a belief in centralized absolutism, and it sometimes seems as if 'the withering away of the State' was a more lively prospect in mid-nineteenth-century England than it has ever been to the most thoroughgoing Marxist.

As a result the new forms of Treasury control were deliberately cast in a narrow mould – essentially negative, harnessed to a defective concept of economy and a static concept of government. They meant adjudication, not inspiration; parsimony not efficiency; conservation, not growth. Where the exercise of control was called for in a new sphere, Parliament was careful to prescribe its limits. This is not yet the age of 'delegated legislation'; the detailed, statutory definition of departmental powers is a characteristic of early-nineteenth-century legislation. A typical example, affecting the Treasury, is the great Municipal Corporations Act of 1835, a landmark in our social history. In this, the power of a reformed corporation to lease, sell or mortgage its property was strictly circumscribed, but where it saw good reason to transgress those limits it was entitled to appeal to the Treasury. By clause 94 the Treasury was empowered to authorize sales or leases on such terms as it approved. But its authority stopped short there. It was not until after 1860 that it was able to regulate the terms of mortgage loans, nor was it able to supervise the appropriation of the money raised with its approval. For much of the century it was obliged to be an impotent spectator of a good deal of municipal mismanagement.

Instances of the debilitating effect of the back-benchers' concept of parsimony and devolution in government could be multiplied, but the most relevant one can be found within the Treasury itself. For of all the departments under attack by the radical utilitarians, the Treasury was the most obvious of targets. Not that its expenditure was large, but, as Hume was quick to notice, it was large in proportion to its numbers and, where better could one begin to set an example? Thus it was the Treasury which bore the brunt of Hume's campaign for economies in 1821 and it was the Treasury Establishment which endured the severest cuts. The result, as we shall see shortly, was to complete the demoralization of the Treasury staff.

So far, I have traced the transformation of the Treasury's position in government almost entirely in terms of the external influences bearing upon it. Since the pre-requisite of effective Treasury control was the creation of statutory control, Parliament and parliamentarians have necessarily dominated the narrative. Less inevitable, but equally significant, has been the incapacity of the Treasury to transform itself. It was a rather passive Treasury which was heaped with new responsibilities and an extremely dispirited Treasury which was made to exercise them. Towards the end of this development signs of a purposeful, imaginative element emerge in the recommendations of permanent Treasury officials to the 1856–7 Select Committee on Public Monies. But the fact that most of those officials were men imported into the Treasury in mid-career serves to underline the nature of the Treasury's demoralization in the preceding decades. As Edward Romilly of the Audit Office pointed out in 1848, 'the truth is we are beginning at the wrong end. Our establishments should first be made efficient, and then they may be reduced.' It is now time to take Romilly's hint. To find the forces which were to create an efficient as well as a parsimonious department it is necessary to leave the history of parliamentary reforms and begin at the other end – inside the Treasury.

SOURCE NOTES

1. I. R. Christie, 'Economical Reform and "The Influence of the Crown", 1780', in *Cambridge Historical Journal,* vol. XII, 1956; Sir L. B. Namier and J. Brooke, *The History of Parliament: The Commons, 1754–90* (1964), vol. I, pp. 124–6.
2. J. Norris, *Shelburne and Reform* (1964).
3. A. Farnsworth, *Addington, Author of the Modern Income Tax* (1951); also A. Hope-Jones, *Income Tax in the Napoleonic Wars* (1939).
4. E. L. Hargreaves, *The National Debt* (1930), p. 149.
5. *ibid.*, p. 136. At the end of the period 1793–1817 the National Debt was £16 million larger than it might have been without the Sinking Fund.
6. D. Gray, *Spencer Perceval: The Evangelical Prime Minister, 1767–1812* (1963), pp. 308, 313.

7. *P.P. 1797–1803*, vol. XII, *Select Committee on Finance, Fifteenth Report*.
8. A. S. Foord, 'The Waning of the Influence of the Crown', *English Historical Review*, vol. 62, 1947.
9. *P.P. 1807–12*, vol. II, *Select Committee on Finance, Fifth Report*, p. 382.
10. *P.P. 1828*, vol. V, *Select Committee on Income and Expenditure*, pp. 7, 8.
11. *P.P. 1822*, vol. IV, *Select Committee on Public Accounts annually laid before Parliament*.
12. Gordon Reid, *The Politics of Financial Control* (1966), pp. 41, 49.
13. The Minute of 1868 is re-printed in the *Epitome of the Reports from the Committees of Public Accounts, 1857 to 1937*, H.C. 154 of 1938, pp. 20–21.
14. See 'Memorandum submitted by the Treasury: Treasury Control of Expenditure', in *Sixth Report from the Select Committee on Estimates, 1957–58*, p. 3.
15. W. N. Calkins, 'A Victorian Free Trade Lobby', *Economic History Review*, 1960, p. 90.
16. S. Gordon, 'The London *Economist* and the High Tide of Laissez-Faire', *Journal of Political Economy*, December 1955.
17. B. A. Corry, *Money, Saving and Investment in English Economics, 1800–1850* (1962), p. 155.
18. *Journals and Correspondence of Sir Francis Baring* (privately printed, 1905), p. 116, n. 1, citing the memoirs of Lord Broughton.
19. *ibid.*, p. 120, cf. p. 114.
20. *P.P. 1847–8*, vol. XVIII, *Select Committee on Miscellaneous Expenditure*, Evidence, Q. 1190.

CHAPTER 6

The Evolution of an Élite: 1805-1914

It was a case of Eton v. *Education, and Eton always won.*
ROBERT LOWE

In an anonymous memorandum, undated but evidently drawn up in April 1821, a discontented Treasury clerk analysed the promotion prospects within the establishment and reviewed, illustratively, the expectations of two of his junior colleagues. Augustus Frederick Pococke (third son of Sir George Pococke, M.P. for Bridgwater), and the Hon. William Rodney (eighth son of the second Baron Rodney) were aged twenty-three and twenty-seven respectively and had served two years in the department already. In current conditions he calculated that they could expect to wait twenty years for their first promotion, earning a basic £120 per annum, and then, after ten to fifteen years more, approaching their sixties, they might hope to succeed to senior clerkships and the giddy heights of more than £600 per annum.

> Such would be the probable official career of two very meritorious young men of high Family connexions. For their mere pecuniary advancement in life their Parents or Friends had better have placed them behind a Counter.

It is not altogether surprising that Pococke resigned in 1824 and Rodney in 1827, escaping from an existence that was as stultifying as it was poorly paid. As late as 1844, the Prime Minister, Sir Robert Peel, casting round for a post suitable for the son of Lord Francis Egerton, decided that only the Foreign Office would do. 'The Treasury offers nothing but the dullest routine – it would give a nausea for public life.'

Of course, things were soon to improve quite rapidly. The reforms following the Northcote–Trevelyan Report of 1854 transformed the Treasury as they transformed other departments, and by 1888 a member of the Royal Commission on Civil Establishments could remark to a witness –

> As you are aware, the Treasury are not satisfied with an ordinary first-class man, but they want a double-first-class man of Baliol [*sic*].

The Treasury establishment had become an exclusive *élite*.

But it would be unwise to take this achievement for granted and most unjust to explain it with vague gestures towards the Northcote-Trevelyan Report. The Report is certainly a great landmark in Civil Service history, but like many historical landmarks it casts a shadow over much that has gone before and gives little guidance to what comes after. It obscures, in particular, the fact that spasmodic and sometimes intensive reforms had been going on in the Treasury since the late eighteenth century. Indeed, that was the whole trouble. The Treasury was demoralized by 'reform' and those associated with Sir Charles Trevelyan were by no means the most beneficial. The regeneration of the Treasury was a long and complex process, but it holds lessons which are of general relevance for administrative history and it deserves to be described.

THE GROWTH OF THE ESTABLISHMENT

Shelburne's Treasury Minute of November 1782 had put the Treasury Establishment one step ahead of the administrative reformers. In terms of staffing, salaries and organization its internal structure seemed sound, and the 1784 Parliamentary Commission of Enquiry into Fees and the 1797 Select Committee on Finance found nothing much to criticize. However, in their report of 20 June 1786 the Commissioners had ventured to make two constructive suggestions. One was that Treasury clerks, like their counterparts in the Exchequer, should be put under oath and made to deposit bonds as pledges of their probity. The other was that one of the Parliamentary Secretaryships to the Treasury should become permanent and incompatible with a seat in Parliament. In a report to the Privy Council, 18 June 1792, both proposals were rejected by the Treasury, and the 1797 Select Committee thought it 'proper to express their concurrence in these objections and in the reasons upon which they are grounded'.

There were indeed sound objections to the form in which the 1786 proposals had been made. No conceivable bond could be large enough to compensate for dishonesty in administering the quite substantial sums which passed through the hands of some Treasury clerks. The embezzlement by a chief clerk of £70,000, discovered in 1812, unpleasantly proved the Treasury's point. Equally, the neutralization of one of the Parliamentary Secretaries was no answer to the increasing burdens which fell on permanent and parliamentary staff alike. It is significant that recent events had sharpened parliamentary distaste for the political activities of the Secretaries to the Treasury.

Although the General Election of 1784 was, to an unusual extent, a triumph for public opinion, it was also quite transparently another triumph for Treasury management. The unique collaboration of John Robinson, the veteran election manager of Lord North's Treasury, and George Rose, his successor, had re-emphasized the potentiality of the Treasury Secretaries as political middlemen. This role, destined to mature into respectability during the next fifty years as Cabinet solidarity and party organization filled the vacuum left by the declining powers of the Crown's 'influence', was still a resented phenomenon in the 1780s.

Meanwhile, the growth of Treasury business, immediately stimulated by the outbreak of war in 1793, was a problem unsolved. The 906 registered papers dealt with in 1767 had grown to 2,892 in 1783, 4,830 in 1796 and 6,180 in 1804. Some enlargement of the Establishment was not only excusable but essential. In 1784 its core still consisted of only four chief clerks, six senior clerks and six junior clerks, plus a minute clerk, two copying clerks, a keeper of papers and the seven clerks of the distinct revenue branch. A small group of five 'extra clerks', a class first created in 1777 as a temporary expedient, helped with copying and registering papers, and two of them dealt with the Treasury's Bills of Exchange. By 1797 these, now indispensable, extra clerks had joined the two copying clerks as full members of the Establishment, the minute clerk and keeper of papers had acquired deputies, and two or three new men filled in as extra clerks.

A general salary increase followed in July 1798, and in May 1801 the chief clerks alone successfully petitioned for a further increase which gave them from £1,200 to £1,400 per annum. The Minute granting it lauded them for the exemplary manner in which they had coped with the vastly increased labour of their offices. But salary increases alone were no answer to the stress of growth; a major reorganization was overdue.

This is what the Minute of 19 August 1805 was intended to provide. Following with significant promptness on the death of old Pratt, survivor of a leisured past, it completely rearranged the distribution of business and radically altered its supervision by making each of the chief clerks individually responsible for one or more of the six Divisions handling it. The enlarged staff, fixed at four chief clerks, six senior clerks, one minute clerk, nine 'assistant clerks' – a new grade – and nine junior clerks (plus the seven Revenue Room clerks), was elevated to a higher salary scale with gradations more closely related to length of service. But the vital innovation which distinguishes this Minute and upon which all else depended, was the creation of a permanent, non-political secretaryship under the title of 'Assistant Secretary and Law Clerk'. As Law Clerk his duties were to assist in drafting financial legislation and to deal with all legal matters which were not worth referring formally to the Treasury Solicitor. As Assistant Secretary his responsibilities were more comprehensive: to attend all meetings of the Treasury Board, take the Minutes, see that they were implemented by the chief clerks, to review all out-going letters and warrants, accept Bills of Exchange, render accounts of special service expenditure, report on any problems referred to him by the Board and 'generally to take care that all Regulations for the conduct of Business are punctually attended to . . .'. In other words, the Assistant Secretary took over effective responsibility for the clerical Establishment, leaving the Joint Parliamentary Secretaries quite free for the political and financial tasks in which they specialized. This latter aspect therefore marks the completion of the process by which the eighteenth-century Secretaries to the Treasury became wholly absorbed by the parliamentary world. Their mobility was not absolutely curtailed; the first Permanent Secretary to the Treasury, George Hamilton (1867–70), had once been a Parliamentary (Financial) Secretary, and it was not impossible to appoint a 'Parliamentary' Secretary who actually had no seat in Parliament. But for all practical purposes the Minute of 1805 served to define a real, functional distinction between the management of a permanent community of bureaucrats on the one hand, and the parliamentary conduct of party government on the other.

Yet for all the detail of definition, the status of the Assistant Secretary remained, initially, rather ambiguous. Was he to be esteemed a 'Third Secretary', as Treasury Minutes sometimes called him, or was he only a glorified chief clerk? His initial salary of £2,000 per annum put him well below the Parliamentary Secretaries at £4,000. And the first incumbent, George Harrison, whose work on the Land Tax and as Counsel to the War Office had attracted Pitt's attention, was a relatively obscure official. But he was an ambitious one who made himself very useful to the Prince Regent, and the upward movement of his salary, to £3,000 in 1809 and £3,500 in 1815 (with a £5,000 bonus thrown in), is some measure of his value.[1] Successive Assistant Secretaries found their own level, usually as highly competent, confidential advisers to the First Lord, and long before the post was given a more substantive character as 'Permanent Secretary' in 1867, its occupants had established it as the repository of the Treasury's professional expertise.

Indeed, it has been suggested that 'the 1805 reform professionalised the treasury',[2] but I think this does an injustice to the pre-1805 Establishment and overlooks the serious demoralization which followed. Aggravated by a sequence of further changes, it took nearly twenty years for the position to become grave, but between 1820 and the 1830s disgruntled chief clerks were almost unanimous in regarding the innovation of 1805 as the root of their ills. Their complaints can be grouped under three heads, none of them very original and none of them wholly attributable to the Minute of 1805. They were: a promotion blockage, an imperfect distribution of responsibility and an inadequate level of remuneration.

On one of these counts it is clear that the 1805 Minute was at fault. In throwing such an enormous burden on the Assistant Secretary it had instantly devalued the four chief clerks. Formerly they had enjoyed a general responsibility for the clerical establishment. Although they had specialized – one in parliamentary business, another in government contracts, a third in departmental accounts and a fourth in Treasury correspondence, they had been equally involved in all aspects of the Treasury's work, drafting Treasury Minutes and, most important of all, having direct and regular access to the Treasury Board. This responsible and stimulating relationship was now severed. They were thrown back on divisional work, forced into a narrow and redundant specialization as overseers of the six senior clerks. This bored the chief clerks and upset the senior clerks. Responsibility for accurate, intelligent work withered somewhere between them.

To understand this and subsequent problems it is desirable to trace some of the routine patterns of Treasury business in its passage through the department. All incoming Treasury papers – petitions, letters, formal applications from other departments – passed first into the Registry room, staffed by two or three clerks who read everything, doketed each item with a précis of its contents, gave it a registration number and indexed it – firstly, numerically, and secondly, alphabetically according to its source. The alphabetical index entries were later endorsed with brief notes of the decision taken and the date of its dispatch. Meanwhile the papers moved on. Before 1805 they would have passed to the chief clerks who, using their discretion and drawing upon their considerable fund of experience, would prepare draft decisions in such cases as they thought fitting. They would present these and all the more difficult business at the next meeting of the Treasury Board, reading the original papers and their draft decisions, and engaging fully in the final resolution. With these noted they would pass the papers to the appropriate Division, placing upon the senior clerk the responsibility for drawing up accurately, according to set forms, the letters, warrants or orders authorized by the Board. Written out fair by the junior clerks, checked by the senior clerk, these would then go back for signature by one or other of the Secretaries in the case of less formal letters, by a quorum (three) of the Treasury lords in the case of all formal instructions to issue money or make appointments, etc. The original minutes would be recorded fully in the Minute Books and copies of the resulting letters, warrants and orders transcribed by junior or extra clerks into the appropriate Letter, Warrant or Order Books.

For the chief clerks, the intrusion of the Assistant Secretary into this pattern, dislodging them from attendance at the Treasury Board and depriving them of their initiative, was quite cataclysmic, but it was part of a more gradual and insidious change. Perhaps before, and certainly after, Pitt's appointment as First Lord, Treasury Board meetings had become more and more of a fiction.[3] Pitt's absenteeism communicated itself to the junior lords and the twice weekly meetings were merely a convenience for obtaining signatures. The real decisions had been reached elsewhere, either by Pitt as First Lord and Chancellor of the Exchequer, or by the Joint Secretaries, and in such a fluid, informal system there was not much point in having four chief clerks bustling about. A single, competent, trusted Assistant Secretary clearly fitted in far better.

This may have made decision-making easier but it certainly multiplied paper work. Much that had been settled before orally now required laborious, hand-written duplication for transmission to the individual members of the Board. The enlargement of the Minute department in 1808 only created a Parkinsonian situation in which, to make themselves useful, the clerks transcribed in detail, not only the Minutes but all the accompanying papers on which they were founded. Whereas one Minute Book had served for four or five years of Treasury business in the 1720s and 30s, and for up to a year in the 1780s and 90s, after 1817 the enormous volumes were filling at the rate of one a month. Much of this additional copying work fell upon the junior clerks of the Establishment. Indeed, it was thought to be wholly good for them that they should learn, by tedious repetition, the exact technical forms of Treasury correspondence, and although some care was still taken to see that they were moved frequently from one Division to another, the monotony and strain must have been considerable.

This was not relieved by the growth of the Establishment. Two new junior clerkships (and two assistant clerkships) were created in 1808, one more in 1811 and four more in 1813. But, as the foot of the promotion ladder grew more thronged, so its higher reaches grew narrow and less attractive. The chief clerks, denied their old initiatives, were now idle, ageing men with little to do but play with their paper-knives, and by 1834, when a clean sweep was made their average age on appointment had risen from about forty to over fifty years. The creation of some new senior posts offered less consolation than provocation. The Assistant Secretary had come, in the first instance, from outside the department, and with two apparent, but not real, exceptions,* this remained the rule until Reginald Welby's appointment as Permanent Secretary in 1885. Meanwhile, in 1815, the great strain falling on the Assistant Secretary was relieved by the appointment of a 'Principal Clerk Assistant to the Secretaries', a title self-explanatory of duties which, with a basic salary of £1,400 per annum ranked in importance above those of the chief clerks. Something more than a private secretary to the Assistant and Parliamentary Secretaries, he was given deliberately vague, general responsibility for Treasury business, and, with full authority to draft minutes, he had the all-important right of access to the members of the Board.

In all but the first instance the post was filled by men wholly trained in the Treasury, but it was recognized to be 'a post of special selection, not of succession', and therefore stood apart from the ordinary ladder of promotion, an object of some resentment. A year later, in August 1816, two more senior positions were created, superior to, and distinct from, the hierarchy that culminated in the chief clerks. The 'Principal Clerkship of the Commissariat' arose from the post-war consolidation of the military commissariat into a department like the Revenue branch, subordinate but closely linked to the Treasury. Unlike the Revenue branch it was never to be integrated with the main Establishment and during the Crimean war its responsibility for financing the clothing and feeding of the Army passed back to the War Office and Paymaster General, but in the meantime there was some small interchange of personnel. The other post was to play a much fuller role in Treasury administration. The Auditor of the Civil List's post had been created by the statute of 1816 with clearly defined responsibility for controlling royal expenditure. But in filling it with a Treasury man, the Treasury Board was careful to extend his responsibility to the general financial work of the department. In 1831 it was officially integrated in the Establishment and by 1834 was held to rank second to the Assistant Secretary. Long after its responsibility for the Civil List had become almost nominal, it was regarded as 'the blue ribbon' of the Treasury.

These developments mark only the beginning of the process which was to supersede the chief clerkships. In 1832 the product of several parliamentary reports and many years of bickering between the Treasury and the Colonial Office was the creation of the 'Princi-

*William Hill (1826–8) and A. Y. Spearman (1836–40) were members of the Treasury Establishment at the time of their promotion to the Assistant Secretaryship but they had begun their official careers elsewhere and could therefore be regarded as intruders.

pal Clerk for Colonial Accounts'. Inevitably, he was an outsider, G. W. Brande, Secretary of the Colonial Audit Office, but he too was rapidly integrated in the department and by 1834 ranked third with the other Principal Clerks. The last step in this process had to wait until 1854 when the Treasury began to absorb the full weight of the administrative burdens being placed upon it by Parliament. The Principal Clerk for Financial Business embodied the Treasury's new responsibility to Parliament for a detailed, comprehensive system of financial control. Once again, it was an outsider, W. G. Anderson, the Assistant Paymaster General, who was appointed. The quartet of Principal Clerks – i.e. Auditor of the Civil List, Principal Clerk Assistant to the Secretaries, Principal Clerk for Colonial Business and Principal Clerk for Financial Business – was now complete and, soon after, the chief clerks had faded away, removed by death or retirement from posts which were never refilled. By this time the regeneration of the department was well in hand, thanks to Trevelyan, Gladstone and other reforming influences, but, while it had lasted, the process of intruding senior appointments into the Establishment, initiated in 1805, had cost the Treasury dear in frustration and resentment.

Reading between the lines of Treasury memoranda, it seems likely that the two careers which occasioned most feeling were those of William Hill and J. C. Herries. Both were quite remarkable. William Hill was brought into the department in 1807 by the Assistant Secretary, George Harrison, to help him with a re-classification of Treasury papers. Already an experienced man of affairs, Hill's first appointment was as a junior clerk, but within a few years he was at the top of the tree. Superintendent of Parliamentary Returns in 1812, it was Hill who was appointed as the first Principal Clerk Assistant to the Secretaries in 1815. In 1816 he moved on to become Principal Clerk of the Commissariat, and in 1826, at a time when his contemporary junior clerks were still either junior, or at best, assistant clerks, he succeeded Harrison as Assistant Secretary. The patronage of Harrison, who brought members of his family into the Establishment, was probably very helpful to Hill's career, but there can be little doubt of his genuine worth, which impressed even Joseph Hume and other hard-bitten 'economist' M.P.s. Unfortunately this meteoric career ended far too aptly in Hill's sudden death, burnt out, in 1828, aged fifty.

The career of Herries, on the other hand, was marked by its longevity. Entering the Treasury in 1798 as a copying clerk, he volunteered for more onerous duties in the Revenue Room in 1799 and soon made himself extremely useful to Pitt. He was private secretary to one of the Parliamentary Secretaries in 1801, and in 1807 to the Chancellor of the Exchequer, Spencer Perceval, who in 1809 became Prime Minister. In 1811 Herries was appointed Commissary-in-Chief and for the next five years handled the extremely complex finance and supply problems of Wellington's Peninsular Army.[4] Some £42 million passed through his competent and unusually thrifty hands. In 1816 it was Herries who became the first Auditor of the Civil List. But in 1823 he crossed the divide between permanent and political appointments and became Financial Secretary to the Treasury with a seat in the Commons. Four years later he was Chancellor of the Exchequer.

It was a remarkable, but precarious, achievement. For all his competence, 'grey-haired, financial Herries' was distrusted, not only by his Whig opponents but by liberal Tory associates like Huskisson, who refused to serve with him. He was believed to be far too compliant to George IV's financial needs, far too intimate with Nathan Rothschild, and far too prosperous, to be wholly reliable. Within five months Herries was edged out of office, and although in the next twenty-five years he held posts at the Board of Trade, the War Office and the Board of Control, he was never again at the Treasury.

With modern examples before us, such as Philip Snowden, John Anderson or James Callaghan, the ascent from clerical posts to the Chancellorship is no longer unique. Nor was it, even in the early nineteenth century, quite outrageous, although it led to gibes about the 'tory clerk' – but for an otherwise stagnant Treasury Establishment these brilliant careers, however well merited, induced a mood of gloomy fatalism and resentment. Sharp salary cuts played their part. The post-war Tory administration made voluntary gestures of economy, and in 1817 tried to suspend the rather generous salary increments of the war years. In 1821, as we have seen, it ran into the powerful economy campaign mounted by Joseph Hume which culminated in the House of Commons Address of 28 June calling for an inquiry into all staffing and salary increases in civil departments since 1797.

The Treasury's answer was to issue on 10 August 1821 a Minute requiring salary cuts in all departments and the establishment of new and considerably shallower salary scales. In the Treasury this hit the junior men most severely. A chief clerk dropped from a generous £1,700 per annum to a comfortable £1,450, and the youngest of the senior clerks fell back from £1,000 per annum to £620, but the foremost of the junior clerks lost forty-six per cent of his salary and a dullard like William Brummell, curtailed of his increments, lost sixty per cent. The prospects for a young man entering the department were now less cheerful – a basic £100 per annum (£90 during probation), and no increments for three years, then a slow climb by

£10 per annum to a ceiling of £200, £320 less than he could have expected before. The effect, in the words of an extremely able assistant clerk, Stephen Ralph Martin Leake, 'tended permanently to paralyse the little zeal still remaining in the department'.

DEMORALIZATION AND REFORM

In this way, two of the distinctive currents in early-nineteenth-century government – radical utilitarianism and incipient Treasury control – came together to stimulate a third, concern for Civil Service recruitment. For the general public, this was an interest slow to evolve as long as the assumption remained plausible that most government clerks were there simply to get some fingers in the till, but for the Treasury it became a matter of urgency when demoralization made itself felt in resignations, absenteeism and flagrant acts of indiscipline.

Indeed, the years between 1821 and the major shake-up of 1834 were rather turbulent ones for the Establishment. A Treasury Minute of 19 March 1822 reduced the junior clerks from sixteen to eleven and no new appointments were made until April 1824. The effects of thirteen resignations, four deaths and two dismissals were therefore all the more marked in an Establishment of thirty-six. Five of the resignations were, in terms of morale, quite healthy since they followed promotion to positions of responsibility outside the Treasury, but seven others (like three of the deaths) can be reasonably described as premature, and only three were plausibly connected with ill-health. It is worth noting here that, on a tentative analysis of the clerks appointed between 1800 and 1850, it seems that, while one quarter left the Treasury for one reason or another within ten years, a third remained there for more than thirty years. More (about seventeen per cent) died in office, than were promoted to posts outside (fifteen per cent) – a sharp contrast, as we shall see, with the generation of 1850–1900. In other words, given good health in the early nineteenth century, the expectations of a long, safe and very dull official life were good.

There were less abrupt ways of expressing dissatisfaction with this state of affairs than resignation. The level of absenteeism was high, it seems, and would have been adequate justification for the Attendance Books ordained in 1830 and 1831 even if they had not been required under the superannuation acts. The traditional formula for Treasury attendance was restated – 'from half past 10 or *11 o'clock at the latest* in the morning until the whole of the necessary Business of the day shall have been executed' – and a severely worded Minute of 12 April 1831 ordered the restriction of holidays to a mere eight weeks! These were the earliest measures of the new Whig brooms and they were properly resented by a department which owed its appointments to years of Tory patronage. The assistant clerks petitioned bitterly against measures which were 'painful and mortifying to their feelings'. Nevertheless, the Whig Treasury Lords did not hesitate to implement their threats. After repeated warnings for absenteeism, William Duke, an assistant clerk with seventeen years' service, was dismissed in 1832 and Charles St John, junior clerk, in 1833. Another delinquent junior clerk, Thomas Bulteel, was pushed into resignation in 1834, while in 1833 Eric Baker, son of an Admiral, retired with what were discreetly described as 'pecuniary difficulties'.

A bundle of documents relating to these cases is, not inappropriately, endorsed 'these naughty boys'! Young they certainly were. The thirty-six members of the main Establishment of 1821 had entered the Treasury at ages ranging between fifteen and twenty-seven, so it is not altogether surprising that the chief clerks were faced with the disciplinary problems that arise in any body of bored, high-spirited young men. Indeed, the atmosphere in any early-nineteenth-century government department was not infrequently reminiscent of the schoolroom and has been immortalized in this mood by Trollope in *The Three Clerks*, by Edmund Yates and by Hertslet.[5] It seems that the young gentlemen of the Foreign Office, like those of the General Post Office, were not above playing with pea-shooters, and there is some hint of ink-pellets. At the Treasury, in more manly fashion, they favoured cricket with young guards officers, played – it is hard to believe – in the attics of the old Treasury building. What turns this horseplay took one can only imagine, but one day in the early 1850s a policeman patrolling Downing Street was rather startled to see a barrel of beer being hauled up to the junior clerks' attic.[6]

These juvenile escapades were not in themselves enough to raise the question of recruitment. Coming from young men of 'high Family connexions' – St John was a nephew of the 3rd Viscount Bolingbroke and Bulteel (Eton and Oxford) came of sound Devonshire gentry – a good deal of nonsense was indulged by the Lords of the Treasury. These youths belonged, after all, to the same social strata from which their political chiefs were drawn.

Nevertheless, the Whig Treasury Lords were determined to press the question of fitness, and in asking the chief clerks in 1831 to explain to them exactly what they did in their Divisions, asked them also what sort of qualities they looked for in Treasury recruits. The replies were remarkably unhelpful. The head of the First Division rambled on about the education belonging to 'a certain station' and 'the habits and associations belonging to that station'; 'that right tone of feeling together with those just and honourable principles ... indispensable for employment'! Only T. C. Brooksbank, the very capable head of the Revenue Branch, offered a precise formulation.

I at once unhesitatingly give my opinion that the general Education of a Gentleman is the best suited for all the purposes of the Treasury.

To be exact, Brooksbank prescribed that an eighteen-year-old candidate should possess –

1. A sufficient knowledge of Classical Literature to pass an Examination for matriculation at Oxford – or for Entrance at the Inner Temple.
2. Arithmetic – including Vulgar and Decimal Fractions.
3. The 5 or 6 first Books of Euclid.
4. Algebra – inclusive of Quadratic Equations.

– a recipe which includes what will seem a healthy standard of numeracy as well as literacy. But, advancing boldly upon what is clearly not an exclusively modern dilemma, he affirmed –

It is easier for a mind of general information to acquire a branch of knowledge which is technical than for a mind which has been confined to one branch to extend itself to a multiplicity of objects.

This was written in February 1831.

Armed with this and much other material, the Whig Treasury Lords prepared for another major reorganization. Its completion was delayed until their legislative programme was enacted, but with the passage of the 1834 Exchequer Regulation Act the time was ripe. The reform was promulgated by the Treasury Minute of 17 October 1834. Laboured on for some months by Sir Francis Baring (Parliamentary Secretary to the Treasury and shortly to be Chancellor of the Exchequer) and the Assistant Secretary, Colonel James Stewart, it is a long and, indeed, long-winded document, designed more to impress Joseph Hume, one suspects, than to revitalize the Treasury. But its objects were simple enough: to rearrange and consolidate the distribution of business, to achieve some immediate economies in manpower and to confirm the place of the new Principal Clerks in the official hierarchy. Thus, the Revenue branch was at last fully incorporated into the salary and promotion structure of the Establishment, and the six existing Divisions reduced to four. Briefly, the *First Division* dealt with business concerning the Army, Navy, Ordnance, Foreign Office and Colonial Office, etc.; the *Second Division* with the Customs, Excise, Post Office, Tax Office and Board of Trade; the *Third Division* with the Bank of England, the Exchequer, the National Debt, Audit Office and Law Courts; the *Fourth Division* with Ireland, the Home Office, the Civil List, Crown lands, Woods and Works; and the *Fifth Division* or Revenue Department with Revenue and Expenditure Accounts, and the formal issue of letters and warrants to the Comptroller-General of the Exchequer or the Paymaster of Civil Services. The Assistant Secretary handled the affairs of the Commissariat, and a Parliamentary Clerk was responsible for all official Accounts and Returns submitted to Parliament. The Registry was given new instructions for the circulation of papers.

Among the chief clerks a death, a retirement and two 'retirements' (a nice distinction) cleared the ground for several promotions, and although there were to be three fewer senior clerks and three fewer assistant clerks, the retirement of a total of seven clerks allowed a general upward movement as well as a saving of nearly twenty per cent in the salary bill. But in confirming the privileged status of the Principal Clerks the Minute slipped in one rather menacing restatement of the principle that senior vacancies would be filled by the persons considered most fit 'whether previously belonging to the Treasury or not'. This, in itself, was a wholesome provision, but the general effect of the Minute was to leave untouched the problems which had damaged the department since 1805. The chief clerks were in no way restored to real responsibilities. Already in their fifties the new men could look forward to nothing but the intrusions of favoured outsiders to the really desirable posts. As for the rest of the Establishment, once the initial changes had been absorbed the promotion rate slowed appreciably and decades of dreary routine remained their prospect. The salary scale offered little comfort.

In such a context of confirmed frustration, the solicitude of Peel for the happiness of young Egerton is easier to understand. What is surprising is the evidence that, during his premiership (1841–6) Peel filled all the seven vacancies that came into his hands with relatives of his own or of his friends. Having found room for a young man to whom he had made some prior commitment, he offered the first unpledged vacancy for a junior clerkship to his sister, Mary Dawson, for one or other of her sons. Another went to the child of his stepmother's nephew, W. H. Clerke. Yet another settled a debt of honour which arose in rather melodramatic circumstances. In January 1843, Peel's private secretary Edward Drummond, a precocious chief clerk at forty-eight, was assassinated, apparently in error for Peel. (The killer, McNaughton, was acquitted with the judgment embodying the celebrated 'McNaughton rule' on diminished responsibility in cases of insanity.*) The vacancy was duly filled with another member of the large Drummond banking clan.

*The name has been variously spelt M'Naughten, M'Naghten and MacNaghten, but for an authoritative verdict in favour of 'McNaughton' see *The Times*, 26 August 1966, 'As it Happens', and 30 August, for correspondence.

Others went to the sons of his old friend Dean (later Bishop) Buckland and his colleague, the Secretary to the Treasury, Sir George Clerk.

These appointments by a man who professed such intense scruples about 'jobbery' may seem to savour of hypocrisy, although no doubt a distinction might be drawn between what were, obviously, personal appointments, and the sort of calculated political patronage which Peel so often deplored. Yet to have garrisoned the permanent Treasury with this little band of Peelites was of no slight political significance. It is not as if the appointments were particularly good ones. W. H. Clerke (later tenth Baronet) and J. H. Cole (grandson of the Earl of Enniskillen) were to have long and distinguished careers in the Treasury – but most of the others were duds, and Alexander Clerk was to be a positive nuisance.

Yet, Peel's record in this respect was no better, and certainly no worse, than that of the Whigs who succeeded him. In the remaining years of personal patronage the Treasury clerkships filled with cadets of the great political houses – a couple of Ponsonbys (one, a son of the 4th Earl of Bessborough, the other, nephew of Viscount Ponsonby and the 2nd Earl Grey), a Plunkett (son of the 4th Earl of Fingall), a Primrose (grandson of the 4th Earl of Rosebery) and a Somerset (son of Lord Granville Somerset). 'Lord John Russell . . . has selected Mr George Russell', reads an unashamed Minute of 1851. It was with material such as this that Sir Charles Trevelyan struggled to reform the Treasury.

SIR CHARLES TREVELYAN, 1840–59

Much has been written about Sir Charles Trevelyan – perhaps too much for a man with such highly developed gifts of self-advertisement.[7] In his innumerable letters, minutes and indiscretions, Trevelyan is still well able to speak for himself. Briefly, his career as an Indian civil servant had been impressive enough to bring him to the Assistant Secretaryship of the Treasury in 1840 at the incredibly early age of thirty-two. His secret – implacable industry, a vigorous intelligence and an ardent faith in what we might prefer to distinguish as Christianity and the *laissez-faire* principles of Political Economy but which for Trevelyan, as for so many others, was one coherent, evangelical creed. Already in India he had made himself notable by the inflexibility of his conscience and the ferocity of his pig-sticking. Bounding through thickets of departmental incompetence like some bureaucratic hound of the Baskervilles, he belongs to that distinctive strain in mid-Victorian England – by Charles Kingsley out of Samuel Smiles – born to do violence to all that was idle, wasteful and ungodly.

There was much in the Treasury to incite him, but it was not until 1848 that Trevelyan could show his hand. The opportunity came with the Select Committee on Miscellaneous Expenditure. Giving evidence on the Treasury's incapacity to exercise real control over a growing array of civil expenditure, Trevelyan readily moved on to a general critique of his own department. The picture is a recognizable one – of redundant chief clerks, dispirited junior clerks and grossly overworked Principal officers. Part of Trevelyan's diagnosis of the Treasury's malaise touched on the question of training:

> the training which the young men on the superior establishment get is not at all such as to fit them for those higher duties. A young man comes from a public school full of energy, intelligence and excited hopes, but after two or three years incessant copying he becomes disappointed and disgusted.[8]

But the heart of his case lay in a simple analysis of the division of labour. All the really important work of the Treasury, he argued, the higher duties of decision-making, administration and control, was done by the handful of men under the Chancellor, by the Principal Clerks, the Law Clerk, the Clerk for Parliamentary Accounts, the head of the Revenue Division, and – he left no doubt – by Trevelyan himself. The rest of the business, handled with varying degrees of competence by junior, senior and chief clerks 'is principally of a mechanical kind, such as copying the minutes, letters and warrants, which would more properly be done by the class of extra clerks'. As a result there was a serious imbalance between the tiny group of hard-pressed administrators and the larger community of under-employed copying clerks; and the effect of this, beyond the demoralization of the department, was to undermine the Treasury's capacity to exercise its proper role in government:

> we have only got strength enough to get through the ordinary current business. If we had more strength in that department of the Treasury, a great deal of business, for which Royal Commissions and Parliamentary Select Committees are now appointed, would be done in the ordinary course of business at the Treasury.[9]

Trevelyan's recommendations were relatively simple. The Principal Clerks should be reinforced by a few of the ablest members of the existing Establishment, and the rest of the clerical hierarchy should be gradually supplanted by men whose lowly vocation was to be copyists and nothing more. Future vacancies in the superior Establishment should be filled by men, not necessarily young but with university education and, perhaps, 'with some experience and success in life'. A select, efficient, economical department would then emerge.

The Select Committee was not disposed to accept Trevelyan's admirably stated case. They had heard a stout defence of the existing organization by past and present Treasury men – all strangely loyal to the merits of a thirty-year apprenticeship in copying work. But what principally inhibited them was the realization that Trevelyan's reforms had implications for the Civil Service as a whole. They were not prepared to face these – yet.[10]

Nor was Trevelyan. Subsequent events have linked his name with the concept of 'open competition' as the basis of a general civil service reform, but this obscures his original position. Competitive entry and the educational philosophy that accompanied it were later accretions which owed less to Trevelyan than to Benjamin Jowett and Macaulay, and the manner in which they captured the movement for Indian and British Civil Service reform offers an interesting case study in political lobbying.[11] But as far as Trevelyan and the Treasury were concerned they were subordinate, if not irrelevant, to the idea of a proper division of labour. In any case, Trevelyan saw the Treasury as a department standing well above the common run of government offices. Its functions of superintendence were to be administered by an *élite* recruited not among the immature, however intelligent and well-examined, but among the ablest, experienced products of the public service. Nor was the Treasury to be a dead-end. He saw it as a finishing school through which first-class men might pass to distinguished political careers beyond. 'The want of a preliminary training of this sort is at present very perceptible in our political official men,' he declared. 'The virtue of the new régime would, therefore, come back through Parliament to our administrative system. . . .'

Thus for the next few years Trevelyan worked with limited objectives, on the regeneration of the Treasury from within. He was a member of a small internal committee, set up on 3 November 1848, which investigated the Establishment and reported on 2 March 1849. Their recommendations led to the consolidation of the four Divisions into two, leaving the Revenue branch intact, but they had no change to propose in the existing system of recruitment. Far more effective were the retirements and promotions made in the following years. Their extent may be gauged if the 1846 Establishment is numbered in order of seniority, from No. 1 (Trevelyan), down to the newest junior clerk, No. 41. By 1856 the highest places under Trevelyan, the Principal Clerkships, were held by the 18th, 11th, 22nd and the 29th members of the 1846 list. A certain amount of leap-frogging, a real application of the principle of promotion by merit, had achieved this result, although not without stress. Its reassuring feature is that, with the exception of the new Principal

Clerkship for Finance, filled by Anderson of the Pay Office, the new senior men all came from within the department. George Arbuthnot, a competent if conservative currency and banking expert, was now Auditor of the Civil List; Charles Crafer, member of a large Treasury clan, became Principal Clerk for Colonial Business after nearly forty years in the department; and W. H. Stephenson, in his path to a knighthood as Chairman of the Board of Inland Revenue, became Principal Clerk Assistant to the Secretaries. These were heartening appointments for the department and, taking a long view of the Treasury's development, seem to mark the beginning of the Treasury's confidence in its ability to fill the highest posts from within.

Trevelyan was still inclined to challenge that confidence. He would have liked to see much more vigorous upheavals, but he was not in a position to secure them. Defending himself from a curiously well-informed attack in *The Times* of 18 June 1855, which put its finger on his poor judgement in selecting outsiders for the Treasury, he protested to Gladstone 'it is unfair to hold me responsible for arrangements relating to the Treasury Establishment, for as you well know, I have no control. If I had, many things would be very different.' He deplored the resentment which Anderson's appointment had caused, but *The Times* letter is only one of the clear signs that Trevelyan was being effectively opposed, both by his permanent colleagues and by his political chiefs.

THE NORTHCOTE–TREVELYAN REPORT

Meanwhile, the broader question of Civil Service reform had really caught fire. It was fed from two sources – the traditional, radical case against aristocratic patronage and privilege, and the more novel educational arguments for social progress linked to a competitive Civil Service entry. Through Macaulay, Jowett and Gladstone, fresh from university reform, the latter had powerful advocates and it was natural that Trevelyan should join them. He was Macaulay's brother-in-law, Gladstone's colleague, and had been profoundly impressed by Jowett's views on Indian Civil Service reform.

Trevelyan announced his conversion with the celebrated *Report on the Organization of the Permanent Civil Service* presented to Parliament in February 1854. Prepared in collaboration with his fellow West-countryman Sir Stafford Northcote, it was ostensibly based on months of detailed inquiry into government departments, but it remains transparently a remarkable piece of propaganda, a brilliant manifesto for views by no means wholly based on an objective appraisal of facts. It began by depicting a profession attractive only to 'the unambitious, and the indolent or incapable', recruited by the importunities of the parents and friends of 'sickly youths' of whom very few chose the profession as an avenue to public eminence. The youth, once appointed, 'the public have him for life'. He could not fail. His wits dulled by years of mechanical labour, he floated gently up a scale of promotion, totally unrelated to merit, into the ultimate haven of a public pension.

From this polemic, mitigated only by the admission that existing civil servants were 'much better than we have any right to expect from the system under which they are appointed or promoted', the Report passed on to detailed recommendations. These amounted to three:

1. The recruitment of a 'thoroughly efficient class of men' by a proper system of open competition.
2. The universal application of the principal of promotion on merit.
3. The introduction of uniform standards of civil service appointment and a proper division of labour between 'intellectual and mechanical work'.[12]

Inevitably, the first part of the Report was sharply resented by civil servants at large and Treasury men in particular. And the second part immediately became the centre of intense public controversy, which cannot be explored here although it brought to the surface some of the profoundest aspirations of mid-Victorian society. Its implications for the Treasury seem largely negative in the first instance. Recent experience, freely adduced, had taught that the Treasury's influence on the Civil Service as the main channel for political patronage, had been often injurious. Edwin Chadwick, the formidable moving spirit of the Board of Health, indignantly cited the case where 'out of 80 clerks supplied by the patronage secretary [of the Treasury] there were not more than 12 who were worth their salt for the performance of service requiring only a sound common education'. With the exception of Edward Romilly, Chairman of the Board of Audit, no one pressed the idea of making a senior, permanent Treasury official responsible for the recruitment, promotion and organization of the Civil Service as a whole. Far from it.

Treasury men, for their part, confined themselves to rebutting the libellous imputations of their colleague. George Arbuthnot, who, as Auditor of the Civil List, felt he had some claim to be the senior civil servant, was particularly vigorous in countering the Report and Trevelyan's accompanying press-leaks. He remonstrated with the Chancellor of the Exchequer, Gladstone, and in an open letter to the Treasury Lords he appealed 'from this Report to Sir Charles Trevelyan himself, if he still recollects the time when he first came to the Treasury, an entire stranger to the Service. . . . He once owned that at that period he found among the gentlemen of this office, intelligence, activity, and that willing aid and co-operation without which he could not have mastered the ordinary details of his duty.' But Arbuthnot's case was largely special pleading and Trevelyan had no difficulty in showing that senior Treasury men were very well aware of grave staffing deficiencies in the higher branches of the department.

Meanwhile, the really effective resistance to the Report's implementation came from the political world. Hard-headed men of affairs threw scorn on Jowett's dream of an educational revolution inspired by the fruits of open competition: it was 'a schoolmaster's scheme'. Party chiefs could not contemplate the abrupt loss of political patronage, and even sensitive liberals shrank from the social implications of a new meritocracy of 'clever scamps'. Gladstone may have shared this fear but he did not share its pessimism. He told Lord John Russell in January 1854 –

> that one of the great recommendations of the change in my eyes would be its tendency to strengthen and multiply the ties between the higher classes and the possession of administrative power. I have a strong impression that the aristocracy of this country are even superior in natural gifts, on the average, to the mass: but it is plain that with their acquired advantages . . . they have an immense superiority. This applies in its degree to all those who may be called gentlemen by birth and training; and it must be remembered that an essential part of any such plan as is now under discussion is the separation of work, wherever it can be made, into mechanical and intellectual, a separation which will open to the highly educated class a career and give them a command over all the higher parts of the civil service, which up to this time they have never enjoyed.[13]

This view was to have interesting implications for Treasury history.

In the event, the Report was not immediately implemented, but in May 1855 an Order in Council set up a Civil Service Commission of three who were empowered to submit all candidates to such tests of moral, physical and intellectual fitness as the departments might choose to prescribe. Indeed, the departments not only set the standard, they supplied the candidates, three of whom would normally be nominated for each vacancy. Patronage was therefore not at an end, there was no question of 'open' competition, and nothing was said about the classification of intellectual and mechanical labour. For Trevelyan it was a bitter disappointment.

RECRUITMENT AFTER 1855

What did it mean for the Treasury? So far in the century the Treasury's recruiting practices had varied between Whig and Tory administrations. As early as 1808 a formal probation period of three months had been instituted to precede the confirmation of junior appointments. The Whig government of 1831 extended this to one year or two, at discretion, and called for a certificate of fitness from the chief clerks. That was the extent of their response to Brooksbank's cogent memorandum. But in September 1834 Lord Melbourne decided to hold examinations. For each vacancy he, as First Lord, would nominate three candidates, and, upon a simple test in précis-writing and arithmetic the Board would select the fittest. For the notoriously lazy Melbourne the scheme had the elegantly simple advantage of killing three importunate birds with each stone, but the Tory governments recognized the test as worthless and reverted to straightforward nominations on probation. Trevelyan occasionally applied tests in spelling, French and arithmetic,* but no more exacting examination was ever considered before 1855. Thus, when in June the Civil Service Commissioners earnestly approached the Treasury to know their entrance requirements, they received a very off-hand reply. The age of candidates should be between eighteen and twenty-five years, with the standards of health and character required in other departments. As for knowledge, the examination should simply ascertain 'whether the Candidate has received a good education and profited by it – the higher duties of the Treasury being of a nature to call for superior cultivation and intelligence'. Only after protest at this absurdly inadequate answer did the Treasury specify its scheme of examination, viz.

1. Exercises to test handwriting and orthography;
2. Arithmetic, including vulgar and decimal fractions;
3. The first three books of Euclid;
4. The History of England;
5. Geography;
6. Translation from either French, Latin, German or Italian;
7. Précis or abstract of official papers.

*The perfunctory departmental examinations were satirized by Trollope in *The Three Clerks* (1858), and even in the Treasury they appear to have resembled that administered by 'Mr Oldeschole' rather than the formidable tests imposed by 'Sir Gregory Hardlines' (a thinly disguised caricature of Trevelyan). See pp. 13–14, 128–31 (World's Classics edn of *The Three Clerks*).

Entire inability in any one of these subjects would disqualify the candidate – but one should have no illusions about the effectiveness of the tests as a bar to favouritism. The candidates, of course, were all carefully selected nominees, and if a favoured protégé failed in competition there was nothing to stop him trying again, perhaps against weaker candidates. Indeed, the Treasury's willingness to manipulate the new requirements barely stopped short of interference with the Civil Service Commissioners, and in 1857, when Palmerston demanded to see the papers of an unsuccessful protégé, he was only momentarily rebuffed, for 'as head of the Government Lord Palmerstone deems it his duty to inform himself of any matters connected with the Administration of the affairs of the Country'.

The Treasury's privileged freedom to manoeuvre against the Commissioners gave rise to one of the more amusing legends of the nineteenth-century Civil Service, the story of 'the Treasury Idiots'. It was alleged that William Hayter, the Patronage Secretary to the Treasury (1852–8), kept two hopelessly stupid young men handy to compete against any favoured nominee. They could be counted on to permit his success. But eventually, the story goes, one of the 'idiots' triumphed and duly received his Civil Service Commission certificate! If the story is true (and it is too good to discard) and if the 'idiot' actually entered the Treasury (which is implausible) then I am tempted to believe it must have been Quentin William Francis Twiss. Twiss entered the Treasury in 1856 and set up some sort of record by remaining there for thirty-five years without promotion. However, on close inspection, Twiss was clearly less an idiot than a kind of clown. Descended from Fannie Kemble and Mrs Siddons, he was a quite celebrated comic actor, whose 'duties as a Treasury clerk', recorded his *Times* obituary, 'fortunately left him a good deal of time to devote to his favourite occupation'. Indeed, Twiss was no fool. A Queen's Scholar and Captain of School at Westminster, a graduate of Christ Church, Oxford, and son of the Vice-Chancellor of the Duchy of Lancaster, his background and attainments were in no way inferior to those of his generation.

Twenty-two men entered the Treasury between 1856 and 1870 under this system of limited competition, and their educational equipment gives some guarantee of an improvement in quality. Nine had been to Oxford, six to Cambridge, compared with only six university men among the generation of 1834–56. Not too much should be read into this. Remarkably few of them bothered to acquire university honours and they were not, in the conventional sense, academically distinguished. Edward Hamilton, a future Joint Permanent Secretary, managed a 'third' in Classical Moderations at Oxford, and even Reginald Welby, a far more distinguished

Permanent Secretary and reputed 'a fairly good classical scholar', seems to have taken a pass degree at Cambridge. Nevertheless, the presumption must be that the majority had been given the opportunity of a first-class education. Nearly all were products of the major public schools – Westminster, St Paul's, Rugby, Marlborough, Charterhouse. No less than eight were old Etonians.

FLOREAT ETONA

The Etonian connection is one of the distinctive features of the mid-nineteenth-century Treasury, and, perhaps, of the higher Civil Service as a whole. In his *Recollections*, written in the 1890s, Sir Algernon West, Chairman of the Inland Revenue and sometime private secretary to Gladstone, contemplated the way in which his generation of Etonians had 'captured the Civil Service by storm' –

> Sir R. Welby was Secretary to the Treasury; Robert Herbert, Under-Secretary for the Colonies; Rivers Wilson, Comptroller of the National Debt; Charles Fremantle, Deputy Master of the Mint; Arthur Blackwood, Secretary to the Post Office; Charles Ryan, Auditor-General of the Exchequer; Whymper was Head Inspector of Factories; Bertie Mitford, Secretary to the Board of Works; and Philip Currie, Under Secretary for Foreign Affairs. As Lowe said, it was a case of Eton *v.* Education, and Eton always won.[14]

Here, ready made, is a splendid conspiracy theory of nineteenth-century government! Need it be taken seriously? Stevenson Arthur Blackwood, who entered the Treasury in 1852, was not the first, and certainly not the last, to find that being at Eton had been 'a great help in rubbing through life'. (A pain in the neck to Trevelyan, who sent him out to the Crimea in the Commissariat, Blackwood was reputed the handsomest man of his day, married the dowager Duchess of Manchester, and became Secretary to the Post Office, a K.C.B. and an embarrassingly ardent evangelical.) In the relatively compact world of high Victorian politics, this legacy of boyhood associations no doubt had the value generally ascribed to it, both to the individuals concerned and, less assuredly, to the smooth running of British government. There seem to be few objective tests of such a possibility. When George Arbuthnot was asked in 1860 if he saw any improvement in Treasury recruits since the introduction of limited competition, he replied – 'I think not a very marked improvement; we generally had a very good selection before. I think perhaps there is rather an improvement; we have had no dunces amongst them.' This, apparently grudging, verdict is borne out by one who was of the new generation himself. Charles Rivers Wilson, of Eton and Balliol, entered the Treasury in 1856 and recorded that 'in making a comparison as to the two systems, nomination or competition, my experience is, that while undoubtedly the new system has raised the average intelligence and ability of the members of the public service, I cannot say that it has supplied better men than some of the best under the old one'.[15]

Yet, in terms of worldly success, the 1856–70 generation was quite impressive. Three of its members, Welby in 1885, Mowatt in 1894 and Hamilton in 1902, became Permanent Secretary to the Treasury, thus confirming the capacity of the Treasury to produce its own masters. It also produced Sir George Lisle Ryder, Chairman of the Board of Customs, 1899–1905; Sir Henry Primrose, Chairman of the Board of Customs, 1895–9, and of the Inland Revenue, 1899–1907; Sir John Arrow Kempe, Comptroller and Auditor-General, 1904–11; and Sir Charles Rivers Wilson, Finance Minister to the Egyptian government and Commissioner of the National Debt Office.

But, to qualify this appearance of success, it is important to note that they were the beneficiaries of something more than education and opportunity. In 1856 and in 1870 the Treasury underwent two further internal reorganizations which at last pulled it clear of the old, built-in frustrations and set it on a self-renewing cycle of efficiency.

The Minute of 4 July 1856 was refreshingly concise. Its objects were:

To secure, by a proper training in suitable duties, a succession of able officers for the highest posts on the permanent establishment;
To secure the prompt and exact execution of the decisions of the Treasury; and
To prevent the waste of intellectual power and money at present caused by an imperfect division of labour.

To achieve this it redistributed business among six Divisions, placed one directly under the supervision of the Assistant Secretary, one under the Auditor of the Civil List, and the remainder under four Principal Clerks. These Divisions, made up of a Principal Clerk, some 'first-class', 'second-class' and 'third-class' clerks, were together responsible for the preparation of minutes 'in immediate personal communication with each other', while most of the routine copying work was now relegated to an enlarged Registry branch of lower-grade clerks. The main Establishment settled down as – one Assistant Secretary, one Auditor of the Civil List, four Principal Clerks at £1,000 per annum × £50 to £1,200; ten first-class clerks at £700 per annum × £25 to £900; sixteen second-class clerks at £350 per annum × £20 to £600; and seven third-class clerks at £100 per annum × £15 to £250.

This Minute, which owed more to the Parliamentary Secretary to the Treasury, James Wilson, than to Sir Charles Trevelyan, is a final comment on the mischief wrought by the 1805 'reform' and its aftermath. For, to restore conditions for the regeneration of the harmony and efficiency of the department, it had reverted to a structure closely resembling that of the eighteenth-century Treasury in which the integration of the clerical hierarchy with the decision-making activities of the Board had been assured. The Principal Clerks of 1856, recruited from, and now working closely with, the main body of the Establishment, were but the old chief clerks writ large.

For the junior men, the situation still left something to be desired. Entering the Treasury in 1867, John Arrow Kempe (of St Paul's and Trinity College, Cambridge) found himself

> one of a body of about forty men, higher division, supplementary clerks and copyists, whose work did not then seem to me of a very attractive or important nature. There was too much useless duplication in the shape of copying out, and making précis in books of decisions and matters which were merely formal.[16]

Yet within a few years all this had changed for the better. The reorganization of 25 May 1870 was made in the light of the government's declared intention (i) to make large cuts in the numbers of pensionable civil service posts, and (ii) to recruit for all permanent posts on the results of an *open* competitive examination.

For a moment, the first requirement was more important because it enforced a much more stringent application of the division of labour. The Minute of 25 May therefore explored the routines of Treasury business which resulted, it will be recalled, in a three-fold record of Treasury papers. The original paper (letter, petition, etc.), with the original Minute made upon it, wound up in the Registry records. The resulting letters or warrants executing the Minute were copied verbatim into the Divisional ledgers, and the Minute itself, copied verbatim, with a précis of any accompanying papers, into the 'Fair Minute' Book (if it was of more than routine significance). Much of this duplication was done by the second- and third-class clerks, as Kempe complained. In addition, they wrote up letters according to the intimations of the 'rough Minutes', and prepared précis and papers for the Principal Clerks – work which required some intelligence and a good deal of practice. But it was decided that a re-routing of decisions could transform this situation. Incoming letters were now to come straight to the first- and second-class clerks in the Divisions for immediate decisions in all routine cases. They would draft replies or other necessary instructions, leaving only the more difficult decisions for the Principal Clerks. The drafts would then pass on to the Secretaries for approval and be left to the lower grade of 'Writers' to copy for signature and dispatch. Only the more novel decisions would be printed and preserved as 'Fair Minutes'.

The saving arising from this ultimate achievement of the division of labour recommended by Trevelyan made possible the abolition of the third-class clerks and a reduction of the 'superior' Establishment from thirty-three to a skeleton of twenty-five: viz., one Permanent Secretary (so called since the Minute of 10 May 1867), one Auditor of the Civil List and Assistant to the Secretaries, four Principal Clerks (at £1,000 per annum × £50 to £1,200), seven first-class clerks (at £700 per annum × £25 to £900) and twelve second-class clerks (at £250 per annum × £20 to £600). The remarkably modest size of this body is a factor of considerable importance, which must be borne in mind in appraising the Treasury's role in late-nineteenth-century government. With up to seven of its younger and ablest men engaged as private secretaries to the Treasury's chiefs, the strength of the department for routine administrative work in the Divisions was extremely vulnerable to stress – with consequences which will be examined later. For the moment it is enough to notice that the reorganization of 1870 placed a high premium on the skill, energy and intelligence of recruits. The Minute appreciated that.

> Looking to the nature of the duties which are imposed upon the Principal Clerks, and to the importance of securing for the discharge of them a succession of properly qualified officers, as well as to the fact that, under the altered organization of the Department, the Clerk, on first appointment, will at once be put to more responsible work, and will receive a higher salary than heretofore, my Lords are of opinion that a high order of examination, which shall test at once the general intelligence and the educational acquirements of the candidates is necessary for admission to the superior establishment of the Treasury.

The minimum age of entry was therefore raised to twenty, the maximum twenty-five, and the scheme of examination given over to the rigours of the Civil Service Commission's open competition.

John Arrow Kempe acknowledged the great improvement resulting from the change, and Laurence Guillemard, coming to the Treasury in 1888 from a rather somnolent Home Office (where he had been advised not to get into late habits: 'I would like you to aim at eleven o'clock') was immediately impressed by the difference in atmosphere and opportunity. 'One felt like coming out of a mausoleum into a busy workshop.' The work, he found, 'was large in volume for our small company . . . and we were all kept pretty busy'. But the distribution of that work gave immediate opportunities for youthful initiative:

The juniors got first bite at the papers: they could put minutes or drafts on them before passing them up to their superiors, thus getting a chance of showing their quality and possibly getting selected for one of the coveted private secretaryships in the office or in Downing Street.[17]

Indeed, the responsibilities and opportunities open to junior Treasury men is another of the distinctive features of the Treasury before the First World War which had equally significant consequences. Entering the Treasury in 1913, Percy Grigg found himself being sent on missions to other departments, 'invariably to see officials very much senior to myself and to lay down the law to them. No wonder the Treasury was disliked in those days!'[18]

More will be said of this in the following chapter, but the point that the late-nineteenth-century Treasury was transformed by *structural* reorganization is worth making now lest it be obscured by the more obviously dramatic consequences of 'open competition'.

OPEN COMPETITION AND THE TREASURY

The Order in Council instituting open competition as the avenue for entry into all departments, save the Foreign Office and a few other specialist posts, was issued on 4 June 1870, and in October 1871 Gladstone could tell his constituents at Blackheath that 'as to the clerkships in my office – the office of the Treasury, and in nearly every other – every one of you has just as much power over their disposal as I have'. This was humbug, of course. It was still open to the Prime Minister to recruit Treasury men, without competition, by the transfer of ex-nominees from other departments, and it proves that the only Treasury appointment made by Gladstone in this period was by the transfer of a young Etonian aristocrat from the Admiralty. Disraeli did exactly the same. Indeed, it was not until 1878 that, after prolonged Cabinet discussions, the Treasury risked recruiting directly upon the result of an open competitive examination – and even then the result looks contrived.

The successful candidate was Stephen Spring-Rice. He was the grandson of the Whig Chancellor of the Exchequer and Comptroller-General, Lord Monteagle. Educated at Eton, he had been President of 'Pop' and the apple of Oscar Browning's eye. He was a Scholar and Fellow of Trinity College, Cambridge, and a member of the 'Apostles'. In every way, Spring-Rice was the fine flower of an aristocratic Victorian education, and, predictably, this paragon – examined for the Civil Service Commission by such giants as Matthew Arnold, Mandell Creighton, Arthur Headlam and Sir Henry Maine – came top in the competition of 1878. Here was a splendid vindication for Gladstone's confidence in the intellectual superiority of the English upper classes! More specifically, Spring-Rice fulfilled the requirements which Robert Lowe, Gladstone's Chancellor of the Exchequer, had unashamedly held out to the 1873 Select Committee on Civil Expenditure. Treasury men, he said, should have 'the best education that England affords; the education of public schools and colleges and such things, which gives a sort of freemasonry among men which is not easy to describe, but which everybody feels'. Because they were daily brought in contact with the upper classes, 'gentlemen and noblemen from all parts of the country and Members of Parliament', 'they should be of that class, in order that they may hold their own on behalf of the Government, and not be overcrowded by other people'. He added, 'It is wonderful how soon a junior clerk in the Treasury, if he is a man of any ability, is brought into contact with the people of whom I speak'.[19]

For how long this philosophy continued to govern the selections of the Treasury is difficult to say. In evidence before the Royal Commission on the Civil Service in 1912 past and present members of the Treasury denied that social influence had played any part in their careers. Asked 'how far would it be fair to say that the Class I examination is devised primarily generally for the sake of drawing men from a certain social and intellectual class?' Sir Robert Chalmers (Permanent Secretary, 1911–13, and 1916–19) answered – 'Intellectual class, certainly; social class, no'. Later in the hearing, Sir George Murray (Permanent Secretary, 1903–11), indicated one good reason for preferring a system of selection to one of pure academic competition by admitting that 'the results of the Class I examination have been rather disappointing as regards the ultimate development of the men', but he was careful to insist that no great weight should be attached to this. Competition, 'tempered' with selection, was not, he admitted, a practical proposition.[20]

Yet, in fact, competition tempered with selection was very much the Treasury's style of recruitment. Of the sixty-one men who entered the department as junior clerks between 1870 and the First World War, thirty-three did so only after service in some other department. Murray himself, equipped with powerful connections and a double third-class degree, was transferred from the Foreign Office at the age of thirty, and there were to be many others who, after passing quite low in the Civil Service examinations, were to be brought into the Treasury upon alleged proof of practical ability. In the 1880s and 90s particularly, direct entry was rare, and as a consequence the average age of first appointment rose to 25·8 years. In the absence of any reliable tests of administrative capability, the Treasury's practice was defensible. It is, to an even greater extent, its practice today, and in the late nineteenth century, with its capacities heavily strained, the Treasury had good grounds to justify its selection of experienced men who could be swiftly absorbed by their duties. Thus, men entered from a wide range of government departments, Admiralty, War Office, Colonial Office, the Board of Trade, Local Government Board and Education Office. Inevitably, this practice gave rise to murmurs, even among those departments from which they came, that patronage was not dead at the Treasury and, taking into account the marked political character of the Treasury (in the 1880s at least), this was not implausible. Yet, a closer look at the Treasury's recruits seems to make the charge irrelevant.

Excluding the first three men appointed in the period 1870–1913 (who were simply redundant products of the nominated competition system transferred, in each case, from a streamlined Admiralty), fifty-seven of the remaining fifty-eight were university graduates – thirty-five from Oxford, nineteen from Cambridge, two from Trinity College, Dublin, and one from London University. Forty of them had received first-class honours at some stage in their degree course, twenty-three of them double-firsts. Sixteen had come top in the higher Civil Service examination. Proof of their intellectual distinction need not stop there. Several, such as the brilliant Llewellyn Davies brothers, were Fellows of their College, with sheaves of university prizes. Others, such as Chalmers with his Sanskrit studies, Heath with his editions of the Greek mathematicians, were to become eminent scholars as well as eminent Permanent Secretaries. The whole generation seems to carry the conventional, worldly emblems of an intellectual *élite*. Through men like Sir Henry Babington Smith (Eton, Trinity College, Cambridge, double-first, Browne Medal, Chancellor's Medal, Winchester Prize, Fellow of Trinity, member of the Apostles) the links go out to that extraordinary, interlaced aristocracy of intellect which has been charted by Lord Annan.[21] At the same time the link with the Bloomsbury of the Stephens and the Woolfs, generally associated with Keynes's entry into the Treasury in 1915, goes back to the arrival of Theodore Llewellyn Davies in 1894 or, at latest, Saxon Sydney-Turner in 1912.

And, with Grigg, the son of a carpenter, and Murray, the heir to a dukedom, the post-1870 generation seems drawn from the broad spectrum of English society – far more varied in background than the generation of 1856–70. With the sons of five M.P.s and five clergymen among the latter, the aristocracy of the 1840s and 50s had clearly given way to politics and piety in equal measure. After 1870 piety won hands down. Apart from ten ministers of the Church of England, dons, civil servants, doctors and commissioned officers are more in evidence than peers in the parentage of the 'competition wallahs'. Evidently, penetrated through the arduous but relatively unsophisticated sieving of the Class I Civil Service competition – with its built-in bias towards the public school Oxonian who had taken 'Greats' – the Treasury had at last become the perquisite of the professional middle class.

In the process, the 'unambitious, the indolent and incapable' had given way to the double-first from Balliol.* Old Etonians were by no means extinct. The products of this large, and no doubt excellent, school were still much in evidence after 1870 and they were not seriously challenged by the handful of men from Manchester – or any other – Grammar School. But enough has been said to indicate that neither 'corruption' nor competition, Eton nor Education, were ever the chief determinants of the Treasury's character. What mattered at all times, in the eighteenth and nineteenth century, as in the twentieth, was the degree to which departmental work provided a healthy correspondence between ability and opportunity. Unquestionably, that relationship had improved vastly in the course of the century. Initiative was now fostered at the earliest stages and Treasury men could look forward to early promotion within or outside the department. The morale, the institutional self-confidence of the Treasury had never been higher.†

It is an elusive phenomenon, this purposeful sense of community among a small body of men, and it would be pretentious to strain after its expression. But, as the early-nineteenth-century history of the Treasury has shown, it cannot be taken for granted. Some of its features were, certainly, well rooted in developments which were common to the Civil Service as a whole. The competitive recruitment of men from the reformed educational disciplines of the universities ensured a new degree of homogeneity in the higher Civil Service. There was indeed, as Robert Lowe had appreciated, a certain freemasonry of education which transcended the widening differences in social background. Equally, the future, in a properly regulated career, offered prospects as bright for the meritorious as they had once been for the favoured. But, beyond this, the peculiarities of individual departments took over. Despite the recommendations for a greater degree of salaried, and organizational, uniformity within the clearly segregated Civil Service grades, put forward by the

*To be precise, Trinity College, Cambridge men (ten) and New College, Oxford men (eight) were more numerous between 1870 and 1914 than the products of Balliol (six). In 1903 'double-firsts' from Corpus Christi College, Oxford, took all three vacancies in the Treasury.

†Of men appointed to the Treasury between 1850 and 1900, over forty-eight per cent were eventually promoted to posts outside. In contrast to the first half of the century (see above, p. 161) eighteen per cent remained for over thirty years in the department and only nine per cent died while in office.

Playfair Commission of 1874 and the Ridley Commission of 1887–8, the Treasury had permitted discrepancies between departments which served to emphasize a distinct hierarchy of esteem. The Treasury was one of the principal beneficiaries of that hierarchy, just as it was the sole beneficiary of its special relationship with the premiership, and with the purse.

Thus, some of the more comfortable aspects of the Treasury's self-confidence were more vulnerable to attack than they had been in the unreformed past. Its select size, its distinctive privileges, the marked ease with which it gained access to the highest fruits of public life, and – above all – its claim to unique powers in relation to its peers among government departments, all these were at the source of an articulate hostility which flows through the late nineteenth century. This criticism has other aspects too, related to much more than the internal characteristics of the department. Thus, in tracing the evolution of the Treasury Establishment, I am aware that I have left unanswered some of the most interesting and important questions which affect it as an institution. For example, if there was at last a correspondence between ability and opportunity within the Treasury, how effective were those abilities and how important were those opportunities? What influence, if any, did Treasury men exert upon politicians, and upon policy? Indeed, what was the Treasury's role in late-nineteenth-century government – and why was it so resented?

SOURCE NOTES

1. Since this was written J. R. Torrance has published a study of 'Sir George Harrison and the growth of bureaucracy in the early nineteenth century' in the *English Historical Review*, vol. 83, 1968.
2. D. Gray, *Spencer Perceval: The Evangelical Prime Minister, 1767–1812* (1963), p. 313.
3. *ibid.*, p. 313. They recovered something of their significance in the early nineteenth century (*Journals and Correspondence of Sir Francis Baring*, p. 105), but were in abeyance by the 1860s.
4. For the Commissariat's duties see R. Glover, *Peninsular Preparation: the Reform of the British Army, 1795–1809* (1963), Appendix A; and for an unfavourable view of its competence, *Autobiographical Recollections of Sir John Bowring* (1877), p.56.
5. For Yates, the theatrical Post Office clerk, see *Edmund Yates: His Recollections and Experiences* (1884), 2 vols. Sir Edward Hertslet, the distinguished Foreign Office librarian, published *Recollections of the Old Foreign Office* (1901).
6. *Some Records of the Life of Stevenson Arthur Blackwood, K.C.B.* (1896), pp. 31–2.
7. On the other hand, there is no modern biography of Trevelyan; but see J. Hart, 'Sir Charles Trevelyan at the Treasury', *English Historical Review*, vol. 75, 1960, pp. 92–110, for a short account of his papers.
8. *P.P. 1847–8*, vol. XVIII, Evidence, Q. 1670.
9. *ibid.*, Q. 1646.

10. *ibid.*, Report, p. xv.
11. R. J. Moore, 'The Abolition of Patronage in the Indian Civil Service', *Historical Journal*, vol. 7, 1964.
12. *P.P. 1854*, vol. XXVII, *Report on the Organization of the Permanent Civil Service*, pp. 3–31.
13. John Morley, *The Life of William Ewart Gladstone* (1903), vol. I, p. 649.
14. Sir Algernon West, *Recollections, 1832 to 1886* (1899), vol. I, pp. 52–3.
15. Charles Rivers Wilson, *Chapters from my Official Life* (1916), ed. Everilda MacAlister, pp. 27–8.
16. Sir John Arrow Kempe, *Reminiscences of an Old Civil Servant, 1846–1927* (1928), p. 34.
17. Sir Laurence Guillemard, *Trivial Fond Records* (1937), pp. 15, 18, 19–20.
18. P. J. Grigg, *Prejudice and Judgment* (1948), p. 36.
19. *P.P. 1873*, vol. VII, *Select Committee on Civil Service Expenditure*, Evidence, QQ. 4543–4452.
20. *P.P. 1912–13*, vol. XV, *Royal Commission on the Civil Service, First Report*, Evidence, Q. 2003.
21. N. G. Annan, 'The Intellectual Aristocracy', in *Studies in Social History* (1955), ed. J. H. Plumb.

CHAPTER 7

The Victorian Treasury and its Masters

Tom drew a line in the dust with his big toe, and said:
'I dare you to step over that. . . .'
MARK TWAIN, The Adventures of Tom Sawyer

On 30 January 1900, the Prime Minister, Lord Salisbury, made an unprecedented attack on the Treasury. The occasion was an important one – the debate on the Address on the Queen's Speech opening the new session – and his words must have been carefully weighed. Enlarging on the changed character of England's 'splendid isolation', now the isolation of inferiority, he had commented bitterly on the areas in which the nation fell short of the other great military powers, lacking as she did a system of conscription, a recognized caste of military experts, an open ladder of promotion and an effective secret service:

> and last of all I feel I am laying my hand on the sacred feature of the Constitution when I say there is the Treasury. At the present time I feel assured that the powers of the Treasury have been administered with the greatest judgment, and the greatest consideration, and do not imagine for a moment that I support the idiotic attacks which have been made on the present Chancellor of the Exchequer. He is a Minister who has filled the office with the greatest consideration to the powers of the Treasury; but I say that the exercise of its powers in governing every department of the Government is not for the public benefit. The Treasury has obtained a position in regard to the rest of the departments of the Government that the House of Commons obtained in the time of the Stuart dynasty. It has the power of the purse, and by exercising the power of the purse it claims a voice in all decisions of administrative authority and policy. I think that much delay and many doubtful resolutions have been the result of the peculiar position which, through many generations, the Treasury has occupied.

Of course, the political world was thrown into an uproar in which outrage and glee were rather unequally mixed. The Chancellor of the Exchequer remonstrated, the Permanent Secretary offered his resignation, and Lord Salisbury took the first opportunity to qualify his remarks. But although he disavowed any reflection on individual officials he reaffirmed his belief that the Treasury had 'gradually acquired a position in regard to the defensive Departments very different from that which the Finance Department occupies abroad, and on the whole I think that, for the purpose of national defence, that is not a satisfactory condition'; adding, 'I think the exaggerated control of the Treasury has done harm'.

This is not the moment to examine the merits of what senior Treasury men thought an absurd and puerile speech. Its immediate interest lies in the circumstances in which it was made and the effects it produced. It was actually not Salisbury's first criticism of the Treasury. In 1895, for example, he had remarked in the House of Lords that 'when the Treasury lays its hand on any matter connected with the future development of the British Empire, the chances of our Imperial policy are small'. Indeed, throughout his public career, Salisbury had a distaste for the Treasury reflected most effectively in his tenure of the premiership as Foreign Secretary rather than First Lord. The long-term constitutional significance of this departure was slight, but the fact that the Treasury was less powerfully represented in the Cabinet during these years is of considerable political and administrative importance. A. J. Balfour was not a combative First Lord; his sympathies lay openly with the military departments, and, as Chancellor of the Exchequer (1895–1902), Hicks-Beach had to fight his battles alone. There were many in this high-noon of imperial aspiration. As recently as October 1899 his relations with Salisbury had reached breaking-point over Colonial Office expenditure, and since the Prime Minister so clearly favoured Chamberlain's pretensions, Hicks-Beach offered to resign. Salisbury replied soothingly enough, but in terms which foreshadow his outburst ten weeks later added –

> I think you do not sufficiently allow for the very peculiar position given by our system to the Treasury, and which is very galling to other departments. That the Treasury should say that any expenditure is excessive or thriftless in regard to the aspects for which it is intended is obviously within its functions. But in practice the Treasury goes much further. It acts as a sort of court of appeal on other departments. Because every policy at every step requires money the Treasury can veto everything: and can do so on proposals which have nothing financial in their nature: and for judgment upon which it has no special qualification. . . . I am bound to say that as a result of my experience during some fifteen years of cabinet office that I think in small matters the Treasury interferes too much. In large questions its resisting power is frequently inadequate.

Since then, of course, some of the worst reverses of the Boer War had taken place and on 30 January the Prime Minister was speaking in the immediate shadow of Spion Kop. Insufficient men, insufficient equipment and insufficient military intelligence were blamed for these defeats, and on all three deficiencies the War Office and Colonial Office could claim they had fought the Treasury to a standstill. Its culpability seemed clear.

The public appeared to think so. Salisbury's speech unleashed a peculiarly bitter onslaught in the correspondence columns of *The Times*. 'Scrutator' drew upon fifty years' experience to denounce an obsolete institution 'which has cramped the exercise and narrowed the scope of British intelligence for generations'. 'A rotten system has been allowed to become part of the national life. No wonder that appalling disasters have overtaken us. The Treasury has no collective discussion, it has not a single expert on its staff. . . . The tradition of the Treasury is to say "No" to all comers . . .', and the vehicle of that tradition was an influence 'as potent and mischievous as any – i.e. the Treasury Clerk. . . . My belief is that he and the Permanent Secretary are more than a match for any Chancellor or Financial Secretary that ever sat in Whitehall.'

Subsequent attacks, and they included a leading article, were depressingly consistent in echoing this theme, that Treasury control was not only an anomaly and a usurpation, but was administered by inexperienced young pedants, remote from the realities of national needs. This insistence on the immaturity of Treasury officials is quite marked and an interesting commentary on the developments analysed in the last chapter. Another is the allegation that many public departments – the Post Office, the Customs, the Inland Revenue, the Mint, the National Debt Office and others – were now quite impotent in the grip of the 'Treasury Ring', controlled as they were by former Treasury clerks and the pampered protégés of successive First Lords.

In making this point, 'Verax' harked back to a similar controversy which had raged through the columns of *The Times* ten years before. The issue then had been the Treasury's control of Civil Establishments and its infuriating refusal to implement fully the recommendations of a recent Royal Commission by levelling up the salaries of the Higher Division Civil Service. 'It is no ordinary storm which has burst upon the Treasury', observed a leading article of 30 January 1890. 'Sluices of bitterness long dammed up' had now poured out, and the ensuing correspondence was marked by considerable venom. Personalities were not spared. A dozen or more Treasury men were cited by name as the privileged beneficiaries of departmental patronage, and it was freely suggested that the 'Treasury Ring' did itself very well, not only from a salary scale pitched higher than that of most other departments, but from pluralism and perquisites denied to the rest of the service. Inexperience, combined with an affectation of omniscience, completed the offensive attributes of the Treasury image.

It was an isolated correspondent who suggested that this uproar was a healthy sign that the Treasury was doing its job. But it was quite clear, and implicitly conceded, that these controversies simply focused the resentments normally generated in the course of financial control. The belief that matters had reached a point of crisis calling for a show-down proved an illusion in each case. For all the resolute posturing of the Treasury's critics, nothing came of these indignant spasms. A question in the House, an abortive motion – and the fuss died down.

Nevertheless, it was (and still is) open to every generation to reconsider the assumptions and techniques of Treasury control. In the late nineteenth century those techniques were still immature and the assumptions were under stress. They were confronted with a rapidly changing situation in government and society, and it was probably inevitable that their application should foster an accumulating legacy of unrest. Wrote 'C' in 1900, 'If the inner history of Treasury tyranny during the last half-century could be told with absolute candour, the British public would be fairly dumbfoundered' [*sic*]. This I cannot guarantee; the history of the Treasury in the second half of the nineteenth century is less outrageous than intriguing. But there can be no better way of understanding its character than to re-assemble the unwieldy context of these fifty years of conflict.

For Salisbury's outburst in January 1900 was the remarkable climax to at least half a century of tension between the Treasury and the great spending departments. It marked also the collision of rival social, political and foreign policies. The issue at stake was essentially the survival of the Gladstonian tradition of rigid economy against the mounting demands of a nearly democratic state. It was an issue of minimal, balanced Budgets against large, continuous programmes of social and military expenditure. It was therefore, an issue of free trade against preferential tariffs, of 'Little England-ism' against expansionist Imperialism. These conflicts cut across party lines. The tariff question divided the Conservative and Unionist party, and it was the Liberal Chancellors, Asquith and Lloyd George, who ushered in the full tide of social welfare expenditure. Thus the fact that the Treasury was so thoroughly permeated by the old Gladstonian tradition increased rather than diminished its isolation. By the end of the century the evolution of English politics had made it, very nearly, an issue of the Treasury *versus* The Rest.

THE VICTORIAN BUDGETARY TRADITION

In order to see how this had come about one must recover the theme which was dropped at the end of Chapter 5 – the evolution of watertight national accounting under comprehensive parliamentary and Treasury control – and add to it another, the Victorian budgetary tradition. Hindsight makes this appear to be wholly Gladstonian, but of course it was not. The tradition was shaped by at least two fundamental obsessions of early-nineteenth-century England – the elimination or reduction of the National Debt, and the attainment and preservation of free trade. The latter objective required, at its simplest, that public income and expenditure should balance at the lowest possible figure; the former, that there should be, if possible, some balance of income over expenditure. Taken together, these requirements hedged budgetary policy into the narrow path of strict public parsimony. Of course, other factors played their part. The resolute application to public finance of private moral virtues such as thrift and probity; the classical doctrines, that money was best left 'to fructify in the pockets of the people', and that public expenditure was but a demoralizing substitute for private initiative, are among the more characteristic. But the Debt and free trade were the major formative influences.

Indeed, the management of the Debt is one of the most readily forgotten feats of nineteenth-century government, monstrously dull in its details no doubt, but expressive of a consistent aspiration. It is not difficult to see why. By 1819, when the full costs of the Napoleonic wars had been absorbed, the gross National Debt exceeded £840 million. In 1914 the comparable figure was £620 million. This unexciting statement is better appreciated in contrast with the sharp upward bounds of the eighteenth-century and twentieth-century Debt: from about £14 million in 1702 to £54 million in 1720, from £132 million in 1762 to £232 million in 1783, and – on a quite different scale – from gross liabilities of £700 million on the eve of the First World War to £7,800 million at its close. The picture of the Victorian National Debt then becomes symbolic of the tranquillity, prosperity and obsessive financial rectitude of the age. It is an inadequate picture, none the less. It is more illuminating, perhaps, to know that charges on the funded debt absorbed a third of gross public expenditure in 1816 and about half in the years before the Crimean War, but by 1880 accounted for only one quarter, and by 1890 only one fifth. This reflects, in part, the successive Treasury operations on the stock of the Funded Debt – Goulburn's 1844 conversion of £250 million of 3½-per cent stock to 3 per cent by 1854, and Goschen's 1888 conversion of £500 million to 2½ per cent by 1903. It also reflects the rise in gross public expenditure.

Between 1792 and 1816 central and local government expenditure rose from nearly £22 million to over £122 million, an increase from eleven to twenty-nine per cent of the Gross National Product (G.N.P.).[1] Between the 1820s and 1850s expenditure remained pretty steady, below £70 million, and accounted for a diminishing percentage of G.N.P. But the advance, from £93 million in 1870 to £130 million in 1890 meant also an increase from nine to fifteen per cent of G.N.P. Defence and social expenditure absorbed a growing share of this total, although for most of this period the impression is one of remarkably controlled stability. After the Crimean War, Gladstone was faced with a legacy of armaments and war scares that kept defence expenditure at nearly forty per cent of the central government budget, but during his first premiership, 1868–74, this had been laboriously dragged down to thirty-three per cent, and thereafter, for twenty-five years, it remained with difficulty at about one third of central government expenditure. But by the 1890s it had begun a climb which not only outstripped Debt charges but was made at their expense. The Sinking Funds – the 'Old' of 1829, the 'New' of 1875 – were progressively curbed and even diverted for the sake of rearmament programmes. It was some justification that, with consols at, or above, par, the process of mechanical Debt reduction had become an increasingly costly and inconvenient gesture. The obsession with Debt reduction as a budgetary and political policy therefore fell into abeyance until the end of the First World War.

This cannot be said of the free trade issue. The passions born in the struggle to reform the tariff in the 1830s and 40s still counted for something in the General Election of 1923. And because the maintenance of what the politicians called 'the free Breakfast Table' necessarily meant the maintenance of a minimal indirect tax revenue, free trade was a consistent budgetary theme for nearly a hundred years, intimately bound up with the history of the income tax, and with the development of the two great parties.

Between 1815 and 1841 some £45 million of duties were remitted and only £8 million imposed, but unfortunately for their reputations, the Whig Chancellors responsible quite failed to combine tariff reform with properly balanced budgets. Deficits piled up year after year, and it was left to Sir Robert Peel and the new Conservative party to recapture the fiscal initiative. Peel's first budget, of 1842, was one of the most important of the century – an act of great daring, greater even than Peel realized, but one amply justified by the results. It revived the buried, dishonoured income tax of 1803–16 for a temporary, three-year period, and we have been nourishing it ever since. Meanwhile, it did its work. The £5 million per annum yield of the tax soon cleared the budget deficit and permitted tariff reforms to which trade generously responded. By the end of Peel's administration he had removed 605 articles from the Customs tariff and had made over a thousand reductions. His tax remissions were worth £2½ million per annum, to which revenue had replied with an increase of £4½ million per annum. The achievement was crowned, by a measure politically more significant than all the rest put together, the repeal of the hated Corn Laws in 1846. Taking full effect in 1849 it left behind only a nominal 1*s*. per quarter registration duty on corn which Robert Lowe cleared away in 1869. It was a harmless item, of no protective significance, but the crisis which accompanied its revival and abandonment in 1902–3 is indicative of the high passions which could still be roused by a tax on bread.

However, by 1852, the evangelical phase of free trade had reached its zenith. All political groups were now regenerate and protection, in Disraeli's robust phrase, was 'dead and damned'. 'It is a pity,' was the Queen's tart comment, 'they [the Tories] did not find this out a little sooner; it would have saved so much annoyance, so much difficulty.' Yet much remained to be done and in his first, great budget of 1853 Gladstone seemed to attempt it all. With the abolition of 123 duties and reduction of 133 he carried tariff reform a substantial step further. And with the elimination of protection on foods, raw materials and partly manufactured goods now virtually complete it was time to turn to the great fiscal engine which had made this possible. Gladstone outlined a programme which would eliminate income tax in seven years; in the meantime he extended its incidence from incomes over £150 per annum to those over £100 (although at a lower rate). In justifying this refusal to concede much to the popular case for some differentiation in assessments according to source, Gladstone stated something of his fiscal philosophy. The income tax, he told the House of Commons,

> has been the instrument by which you have introduced, and by which I hope ere long you may perfect, the reform – the effective reform of your commercial and fiscal system; and I, for one, am bold enough to hope and to expect, that in reforming your own fiscal and commercial system, you have laid the foundations of similar reforms – slow perhaps, but certain in their progress – through every country in the civilized world. I say, therefore, Sir, that if we rightly use the Income tax, when we part with it we may look back upon it with some satisfaction, and may console ourselves for the annoyance it may have entailed, by the recollection that it has been the means of achieving a great good, immediately to England, and ultimately to mankind. [Cheers.]

He admitted to the House of Commons, and indeed regarded as intrinsic, the imperfections of a system of assessment (bearing particularly hard on low professional incomes) which made the tax quite unsuitable as a permanent part of the ordinary revenue. He saw it essentially as a tool of emergency, a weapon of war, a giant called from repose by Peel, which,

> judiciously employed, if unhappy necessity arise – which may God in his mercy avert! – with it judiciously employed you may again, if need be, defy the world! [Loud cries of 'Hear, hear!']

Unhappily that necessity was near. The Crimean War (1854–6) cost nearly £70 million – less than half of which was met by borrowing – brought the income tax from 7*d.* to the maximum war rate of 1*s.* 4*d.* in the £, and 1860, the year in which he had hoped to abolish it, actually found Gladstone raising it to 10*d.* to meet an estimated deficit of £9·4 million. The bitter disappointment was poorly offset by Cobden's free trade treaty with France. But in the great run of budgets which followed (he was Chancellor of the Exchequer, 1859–67), Gladstone exerted his cheeseparing powers to the full. This, after all, was the essence of his fiscal philosophy. 'Economy,' he wrote on one occasion, 'is the first and great article in my financial creed.' On another, he told a Midlothian audience:

> The Chancellor of the Exchequer should boldly uphold economy in detail; and it is the mark of a chicken-hearted Chancellor when he shrinks from upholding economy in detail, when because it is a question of only two or three thousand pounds, he says that is no matter. He is ridiculed, no doubt, for what is called candle-ends and cheese-parings, but he is not worth his salt if he is not ready to save what are meant by candle-ends and cheese-parings in the cause of the country.[2]

This was in 1879, and he was on the defensive. A few years of Conservative government had dissipated his legacy of careful economies with an alarmingly popular policy of imperial expansion and social expenditure. While 1872–3 had given Gladstone's government a realized surplus of nearly £6 million over an expenditure of £70·7 million, 1879, with colonial conflicts going on in several different parts of the African continent, threatened unsecured liabilities of £10 million upon a revenue of £81 million. This put an end to any real hopes of remitting the income tax. Gladstone had come within striking distance of it by 1874 and he tried to fight the General Election on that prospect. But although Disraeli's Chancellor briefly brought the tax down to 2*d.* in the £, the social and military policy of this administration justified all Gladstone's fears that the mere existence of this highly elastic tax was a standing invitation to expenditure.

So far it had achieved much. It had permitted the completion of the free-trade programme. Indirect taxes now fell upon a remarkably narrow range of commodities – coffee, tea, tobacco, wines, spirits, and a few licence duties – and trade had responded in an extraordinary way. The total value of imports rose 143 per cent between 1854 and 1874,[3] and the average rate of growth in the volume of the United Kingdom's international trade was 4·6 per cent per annum between 1841 and 1871.[4] Gladstone's government of 1868–74 had enjoyed the peak of this boom. This was the age of 'leaps and bounds' and, as Robert Lowe observed, it was a problem to know what to do with the budget surpluses that persisted in pouring in upon the Chancellor.

But Disraeli's government was not so lucky. The boom suddenly capsized into slump, and the 1877 budget, when there was no increase or decrease in taxation, was a turning point in revenue history. Thereafter, social and military expenditure advanced and free trade was placed on the defensive. The exploitation of the income tax now became a permanent resource to stave off harmful levies on commerce. Gladstone himself, presenting his thirteenth and last budget in 1882, had to raise income tax from 5*d.* to 6½*d.* in the £.

But the course of the trade and agricultural depression which began in the 1870s made it clear that, even with the permanent support of the income tax, revenue was now drawn from a dangerously narrow range of resources. Some trade recovery spared G. J. Goschen during his six budgets (1887–92), and with reviving prosperity some of the old elasticity returned to the revenue. There was a marked 'run' on drink in 1890 and throughout these decades the costly naval programmes seemed to float upon mounting liquor consumption. But even Goschen had to cut corners by reducing the Debt charges from £28 million to £25 million per annum and his successor, Sir William Harcourt, was inevitably forced upon a major tax change.

Coming within seven weeks of Gladstone's final retirement, Harcourt's Death Duties budget of 1894 was an extraordinary departure from the fiscal principles which he represented. Gladstone had passionately opposed the notion of taxation graduated according to ability to pay. That was 'confiscation'; it opened the path to socialism, to communism. . . . The whole character of mid-Victorian taxation had been coloured by the principle that rich and poor should stand on the same 'manly' footing, paying the same rates of indirect taxation, according to their consumption, and direct taxation regardless of their inequality of means. This led to the effect which the economist W. S. Jevons analysed for the Treasury in 1869. His tentative table of the incidence of tax burdens was as follows:

	FAMILY EXPENDITURE			
	£40	£85	£500	£10,000
TAXES	(per cent per annum)			
On necessaries	2·1	1·7	0·8	0·1
Rates and tolls	2·5	2·4	1·9	1·6
Direct taxes	–	–	2·7	3·7
Legacy, probate duty	–	–	0·8	2·7
Stimulants	5·5	4·1	1·8	0·5
	10·1	8·2	8·0	8·6
Other taxes, say	–	–	1·0	1·0
	10·1	8·2	9·0	9·6

In other words, if the average man (for it was estimated in 1867 that the average income of income-earners in England and Wales was £68 per annum or £32 per head) chose to give up his wilful indulgence in the sort of things that made life worth living then he could bite his nails in the comforting knowledge that he was the most lightly taxed man in the country.

In its application to the income tax, this principle was very slowly giving way, to the extent that the level of total exemption was raised to income of £160 per annum, and abatements of £160 and £100 allowed to those earning under £400 and £500 respectively. But Harcourt's reorganization of the death, probate, succession and legacy duties into a unitary tax which ranged from 1 per cent on estates between £100 and £500, to 8 per cent on estates exceeding £1,000,000, made the decisive breakthrough to graduated taxation. Falling more heavily upon the rich, it opened the way for the contentious budget of 1909, and for the whole future of redistributive taxation. As Harcourt was the first to say – 'We are all Socialists now . . .'.

VICTORIAN CHANCELLORS OF THE EXCHEQUER

The point of this digression has not been to describe revenue history for its own sake, but to convey some idea of the powerful pressures which enforced a policy of the strictest public economy. The Treasury operated within extremely narrow fiscal bounds, and Chancellors could not violate those bounds without shattering the laboriously built, religiously maintained edifice of free trade. It is these inhibitions which gave Chancellors of the second half of the nineteenth century their remarkable consistency, regardless of party, regardless almost of circumstance. And it is this consistency which seems to convey an illusion of Gladstone's vast influence.

It was not quite so. Gladstone himself was the first to praise the reforming governments of Lord Liverpool and Wellington, and it was to Peel, the free-trade convert, that he looked for inspiration. 'He was a rigid economist,' he would recall with relish; 'Oh, he was a most rigid economist!' It was Peel too who had first made the budget a vehicle of long-term public policy, and the fact that he, the First Lord, and not his Chancellor, Goulburn, presented the budget statements of 1842, 1845 and 1846 was expressive of their unusual importance.* On the other hand, it was certainly Gladstone who

*This procedure, although followed by Lord John Russell on behalf of his Chancellor of the Exchequer, Sir Charles Wood, in 1848, was not lasting. Asquith presented the budget of 1908 as Prime Minister because it was essentially *his* budget; he had been succeeded by Lloyd George barely a month before.

dramatized the annual statement in his five-hour meditations upon the nation's economy, conveying in them an extraordinary intensity of moral and intellectual deliberation. In fact, fiscal details fascinated him.

'He had a real intellectual pleasure in inventing and explaining that intricate operation B in the Terminable Annuities Bill . . .', noted Sir Robert Giffen, and Gladstone himself confessed that, however tired he might be, his spirits always rose at the approach of a budget. No doubt he over-dramatized the whole business: sober statisticians like Giffen thought so. But much of the drama was intrinsic to the occasion. The Gladstonian budget was the rehearsal of that great and most popular Victorian morality play, with Thrift vanquishing Extravagance, Industry putting Need to flight, and the customary, concluding apotheosis of British commercial acumen. As Bagehot said of Cobden in 1865, 'There has never, perhaps, been another time in the history of the world when excited masses of men and women hung on the words of one talking political economy'. Gladstone knew he had an enormous audience and he played to it shamelessly.

It was difficult to elude such a spell-binder, and succeeding Chancellors were unquestionably under his influence. In the case of Sir Stafford Northcote, Disraeli's Chancellor of the Exchequer (1874–80), the bond was very strong. Northcote could never quite shake off the deference he felt for the man whom he had once served as a private secretary, and that inclination became more pronounced and more of an embarrassment when he was official leader of the Conservative party. Yet Northcote had some independence of mind: in his *Twenty Years of Financial Policy* (1862) he presented a critically objective account of recent finance, including Gladstone's, and in his own budgets he clashed robustly with Gladstone – who did not fail to let him know that he had seen through the superficiality of his pupil's devices. On balance, Northcote was less unskilful than unlucky to be faced with declining production, wavering consumption and extremely heavy expenditure demands – such as the £4 million Suez Canal shares purchase in 1875, followed by small wars in South Africa and a costly confrontation with Russia in Afghanistan. Taken in conjunction with his avowed reluctance to meddle with the tax structure, they ruined a moderately unimpressive record.

Yet Chancellors more directly under Gladstone's tutelary eye did little better. Robert Lowe (later Viscount Sherbrooke), scholar, wit and Australian politician, who only two years before had led a revolt again his own party's Reform Bill, was a surprising choice for the Exchequer in 1868. He was an albino, and thus a victim of poor sight, brickbats and misunderstandings.* More deadly, he was too clever by half, with a remarkable gift for provoking antagonisms. The fiasco of his 1871 budget, when his proposals – in particular his notorious Match Tax – were contemptuously rejected, was in some degree a popular parliamentary 'come-uppance'. Two years later there was a scandal at the Post Office and Gladstone had to move him to the Home Office, taking the Exchequer upon himself. Yet Lowe was a first-rate departmental chief, greatly admired by his civil servants at the Board of Trade, the Education Office and the Treasury. He was 'very shrewd' said one, 'sees the real point at once, and decides on principle, not on details'. Orthodox in his financial principles, severe in his parsimony, one might best describe him as a Chancellor's Chancellor; at least, Sir George Cornwall Lewis (Chancellor of the Exchequer, 1855–8) said that if he had to be cast away on a desert island he would choose Lowe to go with him.

Although he too admired Lowe's scholarly wit, Gladstone would not have found this idea attractive. Lowe had failed him, and he was no happier with H. C. E. Childers to whom he handed over the Treasury in December 1882. In his inability to defy the defence departments, Childers not only disappointed Gladstone – he disappointed the Treasury. Lingen, the Permanent Secretary, let it be known in 1884 that he had a poor opinion of the Chancellor, and Welby, shortly to succeed Lingen, lamented – 'The Chancellor is not strong backed. His tendency when a difficult case comes up is to find a way of yielding.' This was quite true; Childers's correspondence proves it. Yet there were aspects of his plight which deserve sympathy and which Gladstone should have been the first to recognize. Had not Palmerston's Cabinet forced *him* into vastly increased defence expenditure in 1860? Had not the Services estimates risen under him by nearly £8 million in two years? It was rather tactless of Childers to remind his Prime Minister of this in 1884. The bitter Cabinet conflicts with Palmerston had left wounds over which Gladstone continued to repine until his death. Yet, more recently, in 1874 after he took over from Lowe, Gladstone had been reminded how intractable the military departments could be. His ministers, Goschen at the Admiralty and Edward Cardwell at the War Office, were adamant under his pressure to reduce their estimates and it was their refusal which, as much as anything else, prompted him to the dissolution of Parliament in 1874.

*'Bless his dear old white head' cried a woman to the thirty-seven-year-old orator in Sydney. In England, the peltings he had to endure at the hustings permanently soured his sympathies for democracy.

Had Gladstone been as sensitive to the changing conditions of warfare as to the changing conditions of politics he might have proved more sympathetic to the service departments. It is debatable: morality rather than ignorance determined his attitude to the wasteful blasphemy of war. Yet, by the 1870s, the pressures of technological changes and novel strategic responsibilities were impossible to evade. They bore particularly heavily upon naval policy, for England could not rest indefinitely on the laurels of the Napoleonic wars. The lesson which the nineteenth-century British Navy had to bear in mind was not that of 1805, but of 1781, when the intervention of the combined French and Spanish fleets had ensured the independence of the American colonies. The Royal Navy's numerical strength was not quite enough now that technological change could render a whole fleet obsolete in a year. The French converted the first ironclad warships in 1858–9, and continued to set the pace with heavy guns, torpedoes and submarines. The Royal Navy was never in the technical lead until the launching of the *Dreadnought* in 1906.[5]

It was a defensible policy. It did not pay to render one's own warships obsolete. Let the other chap make the experiments, and, almost certainly, make the mistakes. But this economical policy of shadowing the advances of other navies called for stronger nerves than the country possessed, and from 1860 onwards England was a prey to successive 'scares'. Inspired by French army truculence and the large naval programme of 1859, it was just such a scare which had knocked Gladstone off his feet in 1860. An £11-million fortification programme was the result. The next followed in 1871, fostered by the Franco-Prussian war and an imaginative attempt to apply its tactical lessons to England. In *The Battle of Dorking*, Colonel Sir George Chesney, R.E., depicted a successful German invasion of England, traced with great realism to its humiliating conclusion. Its impact was enormous, and it set an international vogue for fictitious, self-incurred, military Doomsdays. Henceforth, at the level of press sensationalism, military and naval defence fed upon the fears and illusions of a new mass reading public.[6] At a higher level, the academic study of naval strategy moved forward upon the work of men like Sir John Colomb, J. K. Laughton, Julian Corbett . . . reaching its zenith with A. T. Mahan's *Influence of Sea Power upon History* in 1890. Within government, opinion was well-informed. A Royal Commission on Defence, the Carnarvon Commission, had been set up in 1879 on the recommendation of the Colonial Defence Committee. Its findings were so alarming they could not be fully published, but it required little imagination to guess what they were. An over-extended and growing Empire, for all its new telegraph system and coaling stations, lay exposed to surprise by a hostile fleet, tempting and vulnerable. Before the plausible combination of French and Russian (or even French and German) fleets, the Royal Navy was simply not strong enough. A 'two-Navy' standard must be set. In September 1884, in a series of articles in *The Pall Mall Gazette*, W. T. Stead mounted a brilliantly successful press campaign which obtained immediate fruit in increased Naval estimates. In the long term it marked the beginning of organized navalist lobbying and of a succession of further 'scares' – 1888, 1893, 1896 ... 1908.

Thus Childers, and all subsequent Chancellors of the Exchequer, were caught up in a powerful countervailing force, making for expenditure. However, it received an unexpected check in 1886. To the alarm of his colleagues and the dawning delight of the Treasury, Lord Randolph Churchill proved a passionately economical Chancellor. He was no more an 'orthodox' financier than an orthodox politician; his stillborn budget for 1887 would have been a brilliantly radical one. But in his determination to minimize expenditure he yielded nothing to the Gladstonians, and fought the military estimates with all his customary ferocity. Unfortunately, in carrying the fight to the point of resignation, he miscalculated. Lord Salisbury accepted the resignation, and his place was unexpectedly filled by G. J. Goschen.

A Liberal, alienated by the Irish Home Rule question, Goschen's accession to the Conservative ministry in some degree repaid the debt incurred when Gladstone took his Peelite expertise to the Whigs. Of course, Gladstone disowned his former colleague, as financier as well as politician. 'Goschen,' he told a Treasury official, 'was never an Economist. I know that by his Admiralty administration – that is why I never would offer him the Exchequer.' In fact, Goschen was an extremely able Chancellor who did much to adapt government finance to the novel demands of local government and education. An ex-director of the Bank of England, from a banking family, few Chancellors possessed the confidence of the City to such a degree, and few did more to deserve it. But, unquestionably, Goschen's sympathies lay with the great spending departments. He had been a popular First Lord of the Admiralty (1871–4), and it was to the Admiralty that he chose to return in 1895–1900. Not surprisingly therefore, his tenure at the Treasury was marked by a sensational concession to the Navy's demands. The Naval Defence Act of 1889 provided for a five-year programme to build some seventy ships at a cost of £21·5 million. It was the point of 'take-off' from which the defence estimates never recovered. Gladstone's last ministry could do little to stem the tide. The ebullient Sir William Harcourt had bounded into the Treasury in February 1886, swearing he would leave behind 'the reputation of being the greatest skinflint ever known', but in 1892 he knew he could do nothing. His budget of 24 April 1893 was described as 'a sort of swan song on the tradition of economy'.

> I believe the Prime Minister and myself are the last representatives of the vanished creed. . . . Financial economy has gone the way of political economy, and a Chancellor of the Exchequer preaching against extravagance is 'the voice of one crying in the wilderness'. We hear a great deal about the stinginess of the Treasury. I wish the Treasury had a little more power, as it has the will to be more stingy . . .[7]

Only Gladstone refused to submit to the vast new naval programme proposed for 1894. Hunched in his hotel at Biarritz, fierce and excitable, he defied the press, his party and the whole of his Cabinet throughout January and February, returning only to resign his leadership of these clamorous spendthrifts on 1 March. The frivolity of saying '*Après moi le déluge*' would not have occurred to him; he was far too angry. But it was the end of an era.

This, then, was Hicks-Beach's legacy when he entered the Treasury as Chancellor of the Exchequer in Lord Salisbury's administration of July 1895. In certain respects he was well-equipped to cope with it. Dour and tough-minded, 'Black Michael' was a formidable opponent who did not fear unpopularity among his colleagues. He gave short shrift to extravagance wherever it might be found, and he soon secured profound respect from Treasury men. But his difficulties were considerable – and rather peculiar. Like Lowe and Goschen, he was embarrassed by prosperity. An unexpectedly elastic revenue poured in surpluses from several of its sources and the Savings Bank Funds continued to pile up. The National Debt Commissioners paid a peak average of £112 6*s.* 10*d.* for consols in 1898. So there existed the means and even the desirability of some increased public expenditure. There was also the opportunity. At a time when Britain was increasingly embroiled overseas – in South Africa, Egypt, Uganda, China, Turkey, Afghanistan and even South America, the demands of imperial expenditure were pressing. By 1898, the year which saw the battle of Omdurman and the 'incident' at Fashoda, Hicks-Beach seemed to let himself be carried away. 'I do not mean to preach economy,' he said in his budget of 21 April, 'I tried a little sermon on economy two years ago . . . but it had no more effect on the rest of the House, and especially on my own colleagues, than if it had been delivered in church.' Instead he went on to justify defence expenditure with some rather specious figures which showed that although the British Empire spent some £63·5 million on its Army and Navy, compared with £38·5 by Russia, £35·2 million by Germany and £36·3 million by France, this amounted to much less per thousand square miles, or per thousand inhabitants, than for the others.* But 1899 found him tougher. Feeling himself 'milked' by the spending departments and finding the prospects for the year 'very black', he dug in his heels on a number of projects. He had given way on the Prime Minister's Uganda railway project in 1895, but he rebuffed Cecil Rhodes's scheme for underwriting the Bechuanaland railway in 1899. He had recently advanced loans for development in Cyprus and the West Indies but he was extremely difficult about the Colonial Loans Act of 1899. A sequence of obstruction, much of it at Chamberlain's expense, is the immediate background to his resignation threat of October and the proximate cause of Lord Salisbury's attack in January 1900. It restored his reputation at the Treasury and carried the legacy of Gladstonian orthodoxy into the twentieth century.

This short sketch of budgetary policy is vital to an understanding of the late-nineteenth-century Treasury, but it begs the more difficult question of the permanent Treasury's influence upon its masters. It is natural to wonder how far the professional Treasury was really responsible for the strikingly consistent orthodoxy of successive Chancellors, regardless of party. What was it that made Harcourt, so vexing a spendthrift when he was at the Home Office, a 'Cerberus' when he entered the Treasury? What possessed Churchill in 1886? And what kept Hicks-Beach steady through the painful, lonely conflicts with Chamberlain? There is something intrinsically absurd in the idea of men so robust, so inner-directed as these, being mesmerized by the so-called 'mandarins' of the Treasury. The history of the Debt and of free trade already provides one good answer and the question is only worth asking because the Treasury clearly did *something* to its political chiefs. It was not necessarily good. Edward Cardwell, as a Parliamentary Secretary to the Treasury in 1845, was found by his friends to have become suddenly rather 'cocky', and inclined to talk grandly of 'We of the Treasury . . .'![8] But upon a number of others tenure at the Treasury seemed to induce a wholesome maturity. W. H. Smith, appointed Parliamentary Financial Secretary in 1874, told his sister that he found the work rather hard at first, but within a few months a Treasury clerk was reporting confidentially to Gladstone that 'economy in small things reigns in the Treasury; W. H. Smith being a real cheeseparer'. Leonard Courtney likewise developed into an embarrassingly severe Financial Secretary (1882–5) to the dismay of his colleagues and the delight of his officials.[9]

Conversely, Childers, who had been an extremely fertile Secretary

*Viz. per thousand inhabitants the British Empire spent £174, the Russians £298, the French £399 and the Germans £560.

to the Treasury between 1865–6 (he helped the passage of the Exchequer and Audit Departments Act and influenced the creation of the Permanent Secretaryship) clearly did not survive his tenure at the Admiralty (1868–71) and the War Office (1880–82). Goschen likewise was permanently marked by his work at the Admiralty. Yet these were among the exceptions which proved the rule. Treasury officials wrote them off as they wrote off incompetent Chancellors like Disraeli or Sir Charles Wood. They did not lose confidence in their ability to shape a promising newcomer. Reviewing the talent available in 1885 after Courtney's lamented departure from the Financial Secretaryship, Welby weighed up John Hibbert and found him wanting, looked at Wodehouse – 'a good younger man to educate' – and sighed for John Morley, 'He has got go in him'. Unfortunately for Welby he got Hibbert, in both 1885 and 1892. Yet they persevered and rewarded their political champions with unstinted loyalty. Churchill in particular, so surprising, so ardent a convert to parsimony, earned a real devotion in his tragically brief tenure. Reginald McKenna likewise (to take a later example), drew quite gushing valedictions when he left the Financial Secretaryship in 1907, and received a delighted welcome when he returned as Chancellor in 1915.[10] Encomiums of some sort were conventional on such occasions, but in certain cases they clearly transcend the required limits of politeness and reflect a real *rapport*.

Yet, these successful personal relationships do not in themselves demonstrate the nature of professional Treasury influence. If that elusive phenomenon is to be detected at all it must be approached at two levels. Upon the first the permanent officials of the Treasury could commit their chiefs to a policy of routine control, the pettiness and narrowness of which Lord Salisbury was so frequently to condemn. Upon the second one may find, in the higher level of budgetary decision-making, channels by which Treasury men sometimes could shape the policies and even the politics of their masters.

THE PROBLEMS OF TREASURY CONTROL

In 1902 Lord Welby, in evidence given before the Select Committee on National Expenditure, traced the rise and decline of that tradition of parliamentary control which had reached its zenith in the 1866 Exchequer and Audit Departments Act. The turning point had come in the 1880s; since then 'the wind was in the sails of the spending Departments', and 'throughout all parties in the House of Commons I should say the old spirit of economy was very much weakened, with the result that you have a House of Commons I should say very indifferent to economy'. Said Sir George Murray, 'I think the whole attitude of the House itself towards the public service and towards the expenditure generally, has undergone a very material change in the present generation'. 'I think the House of Commons favours expenditure much more', added Sir Edward Hamilton. The implications were clear, although not fully stated. The Exchequer and Audit Departments Act had virtually written economy into the constitution, but although the parliamentary Public Accounts Committee played an indispensable role in maintaining that principle, it really seemed as if only the Treasury and its ally, the Comptroller and Auditor-General (C. & A.-G.) took their responsibility seriously. An orthodox priesthood thus stood at bay, confronting an apostate public and its elected representatives in mute reproach.

Exaggerated or not, such a view helps to illuminate the posture of the Treasury towards all politicians, and in particular serves to explain the very important relationship which had grown up between the Treasury and the Comptroller and Auditor-General's office. Initially, it had been a combative one (see p. 141), but before long the Treasury and the C. & A.-G. had recognized each other as allies: 'We are branches of the same police force', as Sir Francis Mowatt put it. The fact that the C. & A.-G. was (and still is) very often a former Treasury official had strengthened that bond. Statutorily, the C. & A.-G. was judicially independent. Although appointed by the Treasury his responsibility lay to Parliament and it was his duty to report impartially upon the transgressions of the Treasury and other departments alike. More specifically, it was his role to check all expenditure voted and appropriated by Parliament. But in addition the Treasury could direct him to audit such other accounts 'not relating to the receipt or expenditure of imperial funds' as they might specify. Thirdly, and most important, the C. & A.-G. exercised his discretion in reporting on any matter of public expenditure which might tend to economy. Thus, far from being merely a technical check of expenditure vouchers the C. & A.-G. was well equipped to play an invaluable supporting role in general Treasury control. His reports, submitted to the Public Accounts Committee and thrust by them at the Treasury for its comment, apology or action, were an extremely effective device for marshalling the departments into the narrow paths of financial rectitude. He had an initiative to recommend reforms which a preoccupied Treasury could only welcome. Thus the years after 1868, when the relationship was clearly defined by a Treasury Minute,* saw a steady evolution in the techniques and scope of audit and control, curbing the

*Cited above, pp. 141–2.

opportunities for extravagance that were offered by 'Anticipated Savings', 'Appropriations-in-Aid', 'Excess Votes', 'Grants-in-Aid', 'Manufacturing Accounts', 'Virement', 'Votes of Credit', and the rest of the vocabulary of audit.

Some of these deserve elucidation. 'Votes of Credit', for example, were the most remote from the ordinary course of estimate and control. Large, loosely calculated sums – £2 million in 1870, £6 million in 1878, £11 million in 1885 – voted in war-crises, raised by borrowing and spent with alarming freedom by the military departments, they were an irregular outrage to the Treasury's thrifty soul. 'A Vote of Credit,' Welby reminded Gladstone in 1885, 'has the same effect on spending officers as throwing halfpence to a crowd of small boys.' In 1878, £3·5 million had been spent in nine weeks. It had therefore been a great gain to the Treasury that the Public Accounts Committee had repeatedly criticized the latitude of such votes, and in 1879 and 1887 had recommended limitations on their disposition which brought them more fully under Treasury control. In future they would be handled according to a precise, Treasury-framed schedule, or obviated, whenever possible, by Supplementary Estimates.

'Excess Votes' likewise arose in exceptional circumstances, severely condemned, where a department had committed the ultimate offence of exceeding its authorized expenditure and now sought retrospective parliamentary sanction. It required great temerity and some extremely convincing excuse to persuade the Treasury to authorize such a belated application to the House of Commons. Foreseen in good time, the circumstances leading to the excess might have been reasonably covered by a Supplementary Estimate taken in the course of the session before the end of the financial year, but since these Supplementary Estimates might also cover sloppy estimating or careless expenditure they were discouraged no less firmly. Here again, the critical comments of the C. & A.-G. were a useful auxiliary to the Treasury's irritated examination of such applications, and the decline of Supplementary Estimates from sixty-five in 1882–3 to seventeen in 1901–2 is some measure of their success in disciplining the departments.

However, the system of estimate and appropriation could never be impeccable. By 1885, for example, the Civil Estimates were grouped in seven classes, which in turn contained a total of 135 separate votes. The Navy Estimates were covered by seventeen votes and the Army's by twenty-five. Each vote was broken up into a number of sub-heads for the purpose of information, comparison and Treasury (but not parliamentary) control. But some services might prove cheaper than anticipated, leaving a surplus which would have to be surrendered to the Exchequer. At the same time, other services might show signs of moving towards a deficit. Where this happened within a single civil vote the Treasury was empowered to transfer the surplus from one sub-head to meet the deficit on another. This was known as 'virement', and in the case of the Army or the Navy that power permitted transfers from one vote to another – an alteration of parliamentary appropriation which required retrospective parliamentary sanction. Although the ultimate sanction lay with the House of Commons the Treasury's responsibility did not stop short at saying 'Yes' or 'No' to such requests. It called for searching, critical investigation. The Treasury and the C. & A.-G. were on their mettle to detect attempts to bend the rules. At the same time the Treasury had to resist the temptation to regard an accidental saving – where, for example, a strike or a contractor's failure had prevented early expenditure – for a real one. On such a point the department concerned would be quick to enlighten them. Altogether, the question of surpluses, their surrender or retention, was a consistently difficult one, particularly with the military departments, and it grew more acute with the pressure of re-armament. The quickening pace of obsolescence and technical innovation in the Navy greatly strengthened the Admiralty's case for incurring excesses and for setting surpluses aside against depreciation, but the Treasury was very reluctant to countenance such a practice. In 1889 the Admiralty's success in obtaining such transfers received a setback from an unprecedented Treasury refusal. This was upheld by the C. & A.-G., and approved by the Public Accounts Committee. Their Third Report of 1889 noted –

> The Treasury has certainly not, in your Committee's opinion, hitherto been too rigid in the requirements it has exacted from the Departments before consenting to exercise its discretion. Indeed, as Mr Ryder, of the Treasury, stated in his evidence, it is under the influence of criticism from the Audit Office and the Reports of the Public Accounts Committee that the Treasury has of late years 'drawn rather a tighter rein'.[11]

This is sufficient testimony to the nature of Treasury and Public Accounts Committee collaboration. In addition, the C. & A.-G., with a staff of more than two hundred, was equipped to make sorties of his own. Confronted with the vast range of technical expenditure in the military departments, it was extremely difficult to make judgements on cost-effectiveness. In 1902 the C. & A.-G. admitted that he had 'no technical knowledge'. But, by taking an area of expenditure, say naval stores, and making a thorough, concentrated analysis of its conduct, it was possible to establish some piecemeal economies. 'Test audits' such as these made rapid progress after the 1880s and were of immense help in disciplining armaments contracts, stores-purchase, government manufacturing and other elusive processes.

This was work for which the Treasury alone was simply not strong enough.

Unfortunately, the counterpart of this constructive relationship between the Treasury and the C. & A.-G. was a condition of contest between the Treasury and the departments. At best it was a kind of indoor sport with recognized rules and minimal stress. At worst it was a rather bitter conflict with political repercussions, and the severest friction tended to arise in areas where the Treasury was unsupported. The C. & A.-G. had nothing to do with the formulation of financial policy and nothing to do with the framing of Estimates. The staffing and organization of departments was only indirectly his concern. In these large areas of government the Treasury was expected to stand on its own feet.

The surprising thing about the late-nineteenth-century Treasury is that it found this difficult. In the early years of Civil Service reorganization, after 1855, the Treasury and the Departments had been carried along by the reforming current, collaborating harmoniously in a series of Committees of Inquiry which had reviewed the establishments of nearly all the Whitehall empires, great or small. But the impetus slackened after 1865 and the Treasury's relatively weak powers of initiative, let alone compulsion, were exposed. It was prepared to admit this freely, and it did so, for example, before the 1873 Select Committee on Civil Service Expenditure. Speaking as Chancellor of the Exchequer, Robert Lowe depicted an extremely pessimistic view of Treasury control over departmental organization and expenditure:

> [Q.4520.] I do not apprehend that we have at any time any power to re-organize a department without the consent of the head of that department. We have no power *in invitum* over a department at all, except that if the head of a department asks for a fresh expenditure we can either give it or refuse it.

Earlier, commenting on the inability of the Treasury to dislodge an established but redundant item from the Estimates, he had been asked:

> [Q.4494.] Is not that a serious defect in the governing or regulating power of the Treasury? – That is the mistake, we are not to govern; we are only one department, side by side with others, with very limited powers; it is more, after all, by moral suasion and pointing out things that our influence is exercised, than by any large powers that we have.

Lowe was supported by his Permanent Secretary, Lingen, but W. E. Baxter, the Parliamentary Financial Secretary, and Welby, then Principal Clerk of the Finance Division, took a more cheerful view, creating a divergence of opinion on which the Committee was forced to comment. Baxter believed that the Treasury could 'come down upon any department at any time with a proposal for a reduction, if they think it necessary to do so' (Q.4681), and Welby had agreed that 'the Treasury can, if it chooses, at any time review the whole of the expense of every department of the Civil Service' (Q.487). It is not difficult to see that Lowe–Lingen and Baxter–Welby were talking about rather different things – the power to impose, and the power to recommend, an economical re-organization. The confusion in the Committee's mind was probably heightened, unwittingly, by Welby's evidence. Bearing the brunt of the questions, he had shown the Committee that, with the exception of the Judiciary, the Education vote and aspects of the Local Government Board, Treasury control over all classes of Civil Estimates was quite effectual. He could recall that since 1865 the Treasury had reviewed the establishments of the Colonial Office, the Board of Trade, the Poor Law Board, the Mint, the Customs and sections of the Inland Revenue and Post Office. But when confronted with the larger question of the Treasury's power to secure general uniformity by a comprehensive review of all civil establishments he had to admit, 'The Treasury has not the strength . . .'.

Ultimately, this was the calculated import of the Treasury's evidence, summed up in Lowe's complaint that 'the Treasury are accused of many things which really proceed rather from their weakness than from their will'. Consequently, the impression they gave was depressing enough for the Committee's draft report to recommend that –

This impotency or lack of administrative power in the Treasury deserves, in the opinion of your Committee, the serious attention of the legislature.

Had this been implemented then the changes stemming from the Haldane Committee's report in 1919 might have been anticipated. In the event, however, this passage was dropped in favour of a much vaguer expression of confidence in the ability of the Treasury's political chiefs to reconcile 'controversies between the heads of Civil Departments and the permanent officers of the Treasury'.

Their optimism was confounded by events. Out of the next great review of Treasury administration, the 1887 Royal Commission on Civil Establishments, a much more vivid picture of weakness and conflict was to emerge. Opening the batting for the Treasury yet again, Welby, now Permanent Secretary, was asked by Lord Rothschild:

[Q. 8] I suppose we may take it for granted then, that unless there is a demand for increased expenditure, there is virtually no Treasury control? – No; in the main I think that is so. The effective control is applied when an increase is asked for. [Q. 9] And there never is an inquiry as to efficiency in any office . . .? – The

Treasury is of course responsible mainly for economy, and the head of the department is responsible for efficiency; but the Treasury would not, I think, start an inquiry on the subject of efficiency.

Welby's position was less inconsistent than it may seem. What he inferred in 1873 he stated in 1887: that in theory the control of the Treasury was perfect, and that it could not be improved by any formal document or ordinance (QQ.13 and 10,621). But what he was at pains to stress in 1887 was the essentially modest, not to say negative, principle of that control.

[Q. 10,623] My view of the control or check entrusted to the Treasury is that it is purely a financial check, instituted for purely financial purposes, and that from the moment it interferes in any shape or kind with policy it is departing from its proper sphere. [Q. 10,624] . . . I do not think it is the part of the Treasury to say whether the policy which leads to certain expenditure is right or not.

Although hard pressed to admit Treasury intervention in the wider aspects of policy formation, Welby stuck to his guns: Treasury control was solely applied from the financial side.

Thus, in brief, Treasury control was still understood to revolve around that traditional and negative power to give or withhold assent to any *increase* in expenditure. Agreed Welby (Q. 10,648), 'A change of policy that involved a reduction of expenditure, I presume, would not require the assent of the Treasury', and it was almost impossible for the Treasury to insist upon such a reduction. As Sir Algernon West, Chairman of Inland Revenue, said (Q.17,228), 'it is quite impossible that the Treasury can initiate reforms of organization'. It had no ordinary capacity to enforce a review of organization and expenditure, and if it tried to press one, said Welby, it would get snubbed.

This state of affairs undermined the chances of a cooperative relationship between the Treasury and the departments. Unless a department volunteered an invitation to discuss economies (and that was unthinkable), the only opportunity the Treasury had for securing such economies was in quite contrary circumstances – when the department was pressing for an increase! The Treasury was therefore doomed to head-on collisions. This was the central dilemma of the nineteenth-century Treasury, the major cause from which most of its conflicts grew. It deserves to be emphasized. It goes some way towards acquitting the Treasury of the glib and commonplace charges of pettifogging obstruction, particularly when taken in conjunction with two other points which can be stated here only as generalizations. Firstly, that although the Treasury was reluctantly conditioned to the fact that certain areas of government expenditure, such as education, would continue to grow, there was little reason, before the impact of social welfare legislation in the early twentieth century, why the Treasury should have meekly accepted the axiom that departmental establishments were destined to expand at a steady, predictable rate of growth. Gladstone's budgetary achievement had done its best to give the lie to such a prediction, and had made it seem less unreasonable that Estimates could yet be hauled down to levels acceptable some twenty years before. Just as Joseph Hume, in the 1830s, looked back to 1792 for his norm, so, in the 1880s a Gladstonian Treasury looked back to the rigorous years of the 1860s. And this confident nostalgia was linked to a second belief which retained its plausibility rather longer: the belief that the administrative reforms of mid-century were incomplete and that several departments were either fundamentally unsound (e.g. the War Office), or over-ambitious (the Local Government Board). Upon these assumptions the Treasury based its resolute insistence on securing balancing economies somewhere before it conceded any increase in departmental estimates. It was a rule of thumb, firmly applied, and its characteristic effect was to produce a curious departmental shuffle, two steps forward, one back. . . . Its more dangerous effect was to produce extreme irritation.

When pressed, in December 1887, Welby was prepared to say that the Treasury should be invested with statutory power for enforcing economy and governing the Civil Service. And yet he could also say that the theory of Treasury control was perfect . . .? What he meant by this indicates the more positive aspect of his thinking, the belief that financial control was, practically speaking, the self-control of the departments. Already in 1873 he had said:

> The only person who can effectually promote economy, that is to say, that economy which arises from a perfect knowledge of the subject, must be, I think, the permanent chief.

And in 1887 Welby agreed, that

> however good the financial criticism of the Treasury may be, it ought never to supersede an effective financial criticism within the department itself, especially in the case of the great spending departments.

Such a view foreshadows the essentially collaborative theory of modern Treasury control, and it is worth noting that one of the fundamental agencies of that collaboration had been in being since 1872. In a Minute of 14 August it had been laid down as a rule that the permanent chiefs of departments should be nominated as 'Accounting Officers' – i.e. as the officer responsible for the Appropriation Accounts presented to the C. & A.-G. Since that responsibility extended beyond mere technical accountancy to the economy and efficiency of departmental business it was clear that it must be inseparable from the duties of the permanent chief. Today, this responsibility is regarded as one of the best guarantees that the interests of Treasury control will be best served by the departments themselves.

CONFLICT

Unfortunately, late-nineteenth-century practice did not quite attain that ideal. The irritant factors already noted proved too powerful, and the evidence to the Royal Commission of 1887–8 was full of the reality of conflict. 'As a matter of fact we know there have been constant conflicts of view between the Treasury and the departments?' – 'Yes,' answered Welby. From Board of Trade representatives came a pungent whiff of battle-smoke. Treasury control was a sham, insisted the Assistant Secretary Robert Giffen: 'You do not get any criticism at the Treasury – none whatever. You get refusals, but you do not get any discussion, and they are not in a position to discuss.... Treasury "reasons" are not worth considering at all. . . . Reasons founded on entire ignorance . . . nothing can be more useless and absurd even, because the Treasury, as a department, are absolutely without information on the subject . . .'!* Sir Thomas Farrer, former Permanent Secretary of the Board, made a point which has general relevance when he said, 'We can cheat them in big things; they may bully us in little things'.

Other departments were less pugnacious. 'We have no complaints to make at present', conceded the Colonial Office witness. But the War Office spoke acidly of petty controls and the First Lord of the Admiralty expressed the ever-popular opinion 'that if you take the best managed private yard in the world and put it under Treasury control you would make it bankrupt'.

As proof of the reality of conflict, such evidence is not unique. 'Atrocity stories' of oppressive, or at best unimaginative, Treasury control are easily found in the annals of nineteenth-century government. They are, one comes to feel, an intrinsic feature of all departmental evolution, and indeed, the ingenious and entirely plausible theory has been advanced that Treasury obstruction was a positive stimulus to departmental creativity. At least, it seems that by forcing the Board of Health upon novel organizational shifts it saved it from a rigid and perhaps stunted centralized structure.[12] Such experiences were probably common to all the infant agencies of

*It ought to be mentioned that Giffen had some purely personal grudges against the Treasury, arising from quarrels over the distribution of honours and Giffen's close ties with the financial press.

social welfare, for whom Treasury control added specific content to what are aptly called 'growing pains'.

But the severest friction was invariably generated between the Treasury and the defence departments. There were special reasons why this should have been so. The War Office and Admiralty still preserved a larger degree of financial autonomy than civil departments. Although scrutinized by the Treasury in detail their aggregate Estimates were settled at Cabinet level and presented to the House of Commons by their ministers, independently of the Treasury. As already noted, they had a greater latitude to depart from the letter of parliamentary appropriation between one vote and another, and they had larger discretionary powers to incur expenditure on works, etc., without prior Treasury consent. In addition, the sheer size and unco-ordinated character of these departments rendered them suspect, and although each had its own machinery of financial control – actually much larger than the whole Treasury establishment – the Treasury was not satisfied with the economy of their administration. Lastly perhaps, although not least, their very being was distasteful to the pacific, civilian soul of the Victorian Treasury.

Thus when Goschen came to the Treasury in 1887 he put on record, 'while my impressions are still fresh, . . . that I have been rather struck by the uniform and almost constant attitude of positive hostility in language taken up by various officers of the Treasury towards Naval and Military Officers generally'. He was not alone in commenting upon this; it was a consistent theme of all the Treasury's critics and deserves illustration. In 1891, for example, Goschen himself had occasion to correct a particularly stiff draft Treasury letter to the Admiralty. 'The draft is too strong,' he wrote, 'not for what the Admiralty deserve, but for what is prudent. The receipt of such a letter produces anger, not penitence or shame. . . . A quieter draft (not without ironical innuendo) would in my judgment be more effective.' It was good advice, but a year later the same senior Treasury official, G. L. (later Sir George) Ryder, Principal Clerk of the Second Division, again let himself go against the Admiralty. This time Welby thought the letter 'well deserved – though perhaps it may be softened in one or two places'. In both cases the Admiralty had retreated from an agreement on pay and establishments, making economies, upon which a balancing increase had already been granted. Ryder was furious at what was bound to seem a calculated deception, and Welby was sympathetic: 'our friends over the way think they have a large stock of credulity here to draw on'. Thus, although the letter was altered by Sir John Gorst, the Parliamentary Financial Secretary, it remained cutting enough to draw a strong protest from the Admiralty on 'the tone which it has been thought fitting by one great Department of State to assume, in dealing with a question put before it by another great Department'.

A similar conflict arose in 1903 when the Secretary of State for War vainly demanded the withdrawal of an expression 'which he can only regard as offensive'. In this case the War Office had distributed to Yeomanry Regiments a number of surplus horses raised for the Boer War – not in itself an act of extravagance since the mounts were in lieu of hiring charges, but a transfer of charges which required prior Treasury consent.

> Mr Brodrick [Secretary of State for War] regrets that through inadvertence the matter was not referred for their Lordships' approval before steps were taken to distribute the animals, and fears that it is now practically impossible to call upon individuals to whose care they have been entrusted to return them.

The Treasury pencil's angry underlining of the words 'inadvertence' and 'before', the bitter tick beside 'impossible' were preludes to a letter which observed that 'My Lords'

> have no option but to acquiesce in the accomplished fact, on the definite condition that no further alienation of public property will be made on this basis.

From this expression they refused to retreat.

Were these just storms in a Treasury teacup? They are bound to appear so, but, even in the curious budgetary conditions of the 1890s, disputes over £2,000 or £3,000 – all that was involved in these cases – were by no means petty, and the examples were not chosen for their triviality. They are representative of a consistently sour relationship, and are expressive of the difficulties which political chiefs, such as Goschen and Gorst, faced in mitigating the rigours of Treasury control. They reflect the singularly unfortunate disposition of the permanent Treasury to prefer long-range verbal bombardments to the kind of personal inter-departmental relations which would have eliminated this bickering at an earlier stage.* Associated with that disposition was an affectation of 'tone' which so vexed its victims. Its origins cannot be precisely located; the Treasury has always adopted a certain bluntness of manner in defending the public purse. But there are clear signs that it sharpened in the course of the nineteenth century, taking its passion from Gladstone, its acerbity from Lowe. The Permanent Secretaries, Lingen and Welby, made their distinctive contributions, which in Lingen's case proved a positive embarrassment to his political chiefs. By 1883 the Chancellor of the Exchequer was complaining that Lingen – whom even Gladstone described as 'a ferocious economist' – had made himself so unpopular with departmental heads that it was extremely difficult to

*By the 1890s, inter-departmental conferences with the War Office are alleged to have alleviated this situation: Sir Thomas L. Heath, *The Treasury* (1927).

work through him.* That was never said of Welby; his were usually sins of omission. But when Lord Salisbury was privately reproached for his outburst in 1900 he said it was Welby he was getting at, and, reminded that Welby had retired six years before, he refused to be shaken; the wounds still ached.

THE LATE-VICTORIAN ESTABLISHMENT

This lamentably sterile aspect of the Treasury's role is related to something more important than the vigorous temper or barbed wit of its personnel. It is rooted in the impotence to which Trevelyan and later Welby had so freely testified in 1848, 1873 and 1887 – 'The Treasury has not the strength . . .'.

This was true, not only because the Treasury was harnessed to a negative concept of control, but in the simpler sense that the department was undermanned. This was a deficiency far more absurd, far more culpable than any lack of powers – derived as it was from a wilful, and even conceited, addiction to false economies. Asked in 1873 if the Treasury was not a 'model Department', Welby coyly declined to answer, but the fact that the Treasury Establishment Vote had fallen from £49,000 in 1853 to £48,000 in 1873 was thought sufficient proof that this was so. Figures for the rest of the century were compiled by the Treasury in 1904 and were as follows:

YEAR	TREASURY VOTE Upper Establishment	Total	TOTAL CIVIL SERVICE ESTABLISHMENTS
1862	£21,835	£52,683	£7,665,377
1872	18,671	45,218	10,645,544
1882	19,142	48,219	16,087,104
1892	18,933	51,174	16,516,029
1902	18,018	51,860	23,630,120

This is a striking and yet ignoble record. It is important to see what it meant.

For the Upper Establishment it meant an administrative staff fixed by the re-organization Minute of May 1870 at one Permanent Secretary, one Assistant Secretary, four Principal Clerks, seven first-class clerks and twelve second-class clerks. Under them worked the 'Supplementary Department', consisting of the Accounts Branch (seven clerks), and the Registry Branch (seven or eight clerks), and with them were associated the staff of the Treasury

*While they were together at the Education Office it was already discerned that the more biting snubs emanated from Lingen rather than Lowe.

Solicitor (about a dozen) and the County Court Department (another dozen, among whom Q. W. F. Twiss was quietly parked). However, this analysis is primarily concerned with the Upper Establishment of twenty-five upon whom fell the brunt of the administrative work of the Treasury.

By the terms of the 1870 arrangements they were distributed in five Divisions:

First (or Finance) Division	= '1D'
Finance generally, Banking and Currency; the Mint, Exchequer and Audit Department, Bank of England, National Debt Office, Public Works Loan Commissioners, Estimates, etc.	1 Principal Clerk 2 first-class clerks 2 second-class clerks
Second Division	= '2D'
Foreign Office, Colonial Office, War Office, Admiralty, Woods, Municipal Corporation, etc.	1 Principal Clerk 1 first-class clerk 1 second-class clerk
Third Division	= '3D'
Home Secretary, India Office, Privy Council Office, Works, Channel Islands, Education, Science and Art Department, Poor Law, etc.	1 Principal Clerk 1 first-class clerk 1 second-class clerk
Fourth Division	= '4D'
Revenue Departments, Post Office, Board of Trade, Superannuation, Telegraphs, Civil List Pensions, etc.	1 Principal Clerk 1 first-class clerk 2 second-class clerks
Fifth Division	= '5D'
(known as the Department of the Auditor of the Civil List and Assistant to the Secretaries until 1881)	
The Royal Household, Legal Establishments and Courts of Law, Criminal Prosecutions, Sheriffs' Accounts, etc.	1 Auditor of Civil List or Principal Clerk 1 first-class clerk 1 second-class clerk

This left one first-class clerk free to serve as 'Parliamentary Clerk', working closely with the Parliamentary Financial Secretary in superintending the passage of Treasury business through the legislature, scrutinizing any Public or Private Bills that might entail a charge on the public purse, and keeping the Principal Clerks informed of legislation that might affect their areas of responsibility.

(Some indication of his responsibilities is suggested by a lapse in 1893 when a Bill for the Education of Blind and Deaf Children, entailing expenditure of £16–20,000 per annum, was allowed to pass all its stages without the attention of the Chancellor of the Exchequer or the Financial Secretary being drawn to it.)

This distribution also left some five second-class clerks free to supplement the Divisions or to serve as private secretaries.

Contemplating this skeletal organization it is a little difficult to appreciate why 'those among us who know', like Sir Algernon West, could regard its chief, Welby, as 'easily the most powerful man in the British Empire'. True, here was a man of formidable intellect and great personal influence, and even if the Permanent Secretaryship of the Treasury did not yet carry the amplitude of authority that came after 1918 (together with the controversial title of 'Head of the Civil Service'), there can be no doubt that his position was enormously strong. But the fact that Welby seemed to insist on seeing every file that passed through the Treasury was a loss, not a gain, in omnicompetence, for he was also a dilatory man, expansive, ruminative, easily side-tracked. His room became a kind of gigantic 'In-tray', and it was a Treasury joke, upon the occasion of a celebrated murder, that if the criminal had had the sense to conceal the body on Welby's desk he would have certainly escaped detection. Not surprisingly, urgent business tended to by-pass Welby in a way which drew down occasional, protesting Minutes. But even if business had been expeditiously handled in the Treasury it is difficult to believe that it could have been handled well. Its complexity and volume were always mounting, while the Treasury's strength remained much the same. Divisional work was not the sole charge upon the department's resources. Imperial commitments, international and domestic committees, conferences and commissions of inquiry tended to draw ever more heavily upon the Treasury's time. In 1867, for example, the International Monetary Conference in Paris was attended by Rivers-Wilson. W. B. Gurdon was the Treasury's representative in Paris in 1878. A year later Gurdon was posted to the Transvaal to investigate the accounts of recent war expenditure, and, being a man whose passion for economy was described as 'almost Quixotic', he did work there which pleased Welby enormously. Returning via India in 1881 he was able to see his colleague Henry Primrose who had been seconded as private secretary to the Viceroy after accompanying Rivers-Wilson to Egypt in 1878. Twenty years later, a Treasury official (E. G. Harman) was in the Sudan, keeping an eye on Kitchener's administration, while in the years after the Boer War two more (Henry Higgs and J. S. Bradbury) spent long spells in Natal. But the strain on the Treasury's manpower was considerable. It was possible to spare someone for the Seal Fisheries dispute in Canada in 1892; ten years later they could not send a man to Australia. It was not until 1904 that the undermanning of the Upper Establishment was attended to and then only to the extent of creating an extra first-class clerk. It took the novel demands of Liberal welfare legislation, the Old Age Pension and National Insurance administration in particular, to force the Treasury upon appreciable increases.

Seen in this context the five or more private secretaryships appear to have made a disproportionate demand upon the Treasury's strength. They were highly prized, of course, and keenly sought after. Personal service to the head of government and his colleagues was a reasonable summit to any young man's ambition; and no one could tell what might lie beyond. Past experience left it in some doubt whether unique abilities or unique opportunities had carried former private secretaries like Disraeli's protégé, Montagu Corry, or Gladstone's, Algernon West, to honours and high places in public service. But it is far less clear that they were of equal administrative value to the Treasury. Work in the private office of the Chancellor, of the Financial Secretary and the Permanent Secretary was certainly of real importance to both servant and served. Although they might share their privilege with the sons, nephews and remoter relatives of their political chiefs, private secretaries drawn from the Treasury were generally relied upon to provide the expertise which the amateurs lacked. It was rare to get personal private secretaries of the calibre of Arthur Godley (later Lord Kilbracken) or Alfred Milner (later Lord Milner). But the secretaries to the First Lord and the Patronage Secretary appear, in certain cases, to have been little more than high-class clerical valets, whose duties tended to render them unfit for return to the humdrum work of the divisions. Edward Hamilton, for example, after five happy years as one of Gladstone's four private secretaries (1880–85), in which time he docketed and answered his letters, chose his wine, found his spectacles, bought his railway tickets, felt he could no longer face the ordinary duties of the Treasury and contemplated resignation. Happily he had found great favour. A C.B., promotion to first-class clerk, and appointment as Principal Clerk of the Finance Division all followed within less than six months. Sir Edward Hamilton was later to prove a conscientious Permanent Financial Secretary, but at this stage in his career one must doubt whether he knew one end of a terminable annuity from another. 'I foresee that I have much to learn . . .', he wrote on his promotion.

Private secretaryships were furthermore related to a slightly sinister phase in Treasury history, for in the twenty years after the

Civil Service was thrown open to competition they tended to reflect the political complexion of successive administrations. This is an interesting development, in odd contrast to the mid-nineteenth century when Treasury clerks with marked political backgrounds like George Arbuthnot appear to have served Whig and Tory governments with consistency and impartiality to the satisfaction of both parties. Disraeli must bear some of the responsibility for the change, although he had some excuse in seeking to counter the predominantly Gladstonian character of the department. Between 1874 and 1880 he made strenuous efforts to recover for the First Lord such Treasury patronage as he could legitimately claim, and his choice of private secretaries reflected the same frank partisanship. Not all the Treasury clerks were the 'damned Gladstonians' which Randolph Churchill amiably dubbed them, and it was possible for Conservative governments to choose men like Algernon Turnor, Frederick Clay or John Arrow Kempe, with sound Tory backgrounds. Indeed, in 1888, when Welby wished to promote, prematurely, the thirty-two-year-old Spring-Rice to the Principal Clerkship of the Fourth Division, the Conservative leader W. H. Smith intervened in Kempe's favour and Welby was eventually over-ruled at Cabinet level. Likewise V. D. Broughton's promotion to the Deputy Mastership of the Melbourne Mint (where he went mad) was condemned as 'one of Lord Beaconsfield's most scandalous appointments'; 'he was an electioneering Treasury clerk' complained Childers in 1884. Soon after the Liberal chiefs were harshly prompt in demanding Gurdon's resignation when he announced his candidature (as a Liberal) for the next General Election.*

These seem to have been isolated incidents; they belong to a limited phase of political history, and party differences in no way soured internal Treasury relations. But it would be unwise to suppose that the introduction of open competition immediately dispelled the legacy of patronage. Products of the nomination system, in the persons of Sir Edward Hamilton and Sir George Murray, continued to govern the Treasury until 1911. And appointments of Treasury men to posts outside still carried the distinctive brand of patronage. They were to be found planted out in the Customs, Inland Revenue, National Debt Office, Post Office, Paymaster's Office and the Office of the Comptroller and Auditor-General, usually in the

*The Treasury Minute arising from this appears to have established the general rule for the Civil Service that resignation should precede the acceptance of a parliamentary candidature. Gurdon eventually became a Member for North Norfolk. A. G. V. Peel, in 1895, and Henry Higgs, in 1921, resigned to contest elections. They were unsuccessful. So much for Trevelyan's ideal that Treasury men should fertilize parliamentary politics.

highest positions. This was (and is) not simply a legitimate but a necessary distribution of Treasury-groomed talent. However, some appointments were ambiguous. Not all were promotions, and it was no secret that places on certain boards marked the dignified disposal of someone with no future in the Treasury. Maurice Headlam, despairing of advancement, cheerfully went off to be 'Treasury Remembrancer' in Ireland; at least he could fish . . .*

Indeed, at this point it is fair to recall the accusations against the Treasury and acknowledge that there was a case to answer, even though it need not be framed in quite the same terms as the letters to *The Times*. Treasury control *was* imperfect, both in theory and in practice. The department itself was prepared to admit that. An undermanned establishment, strenuously administering a negative principle, seemed well designed to impede, with the maximum of friction, and poorly equipped to collaborate in purposeful government. It was at the same time an over-privileged and over-paid *élite*, thoroughly permeated by the prejudices of one political party.

But there are some more positive aspects of the late-nineteenth-century Treasury, and the phenomenon of Treasury patronage among the revenue departments is a timely reminder that the Treasury's resources were never wholly confined to its own divisional strength. The Inland Revenue Board was unquestionably the Treasury's most important auxiliary. Gladstone never confessed for the Treasury the 'idolatrous adoration' he declared for the Inland Revenue! The Customs, presiding over a vestigial tariff, was for obvious reasons less warmly favoured. Gladstone claimed 'he had never had any help from the Customs' and he would have liked to see it swallowed up by the Inland Revenue. Nevertheless, it was expert and indispensable, managed by former Treasury clerks. Thus, Sir Edward Hamilton, preparing budget proposals for Hicks-Beach in 1900, could turn with ease and familiarity to old colleagues like Sir Henry Primrose and Bernard Mallet at the Inland Revenue, Sir George Ryder and John Arrow Kempe at the Customs and G. W. Hervey at the National Debt Office. In the City, A. S. Harvey, Secretary of Glyn, Mills & Company, but a former Assistant Accountant in the Treasury's Supplementary Branch, gave invaluable assistance on monetary questions.

And beyond this innocuous Treasury ring lay other allies and advisers. The expertise of the Parliamentary Counsel's Office was

*Maurice Headlam, *Irish Reminiscences* (1947), p. 88. It is a significant comment on the preceding paragraph that Headlam observes, of the manner in which he was passed over for promotion in 1912, that if this had been done to him by a Conservative instead of a Liberal administration there would have been accusations of political jobbery: *op. cit.*, p. 24.

of enormous importance. Founded by Treasury Minute on 8 February 1869 it was Robert Lowe's greatest contribution to the Treasury, while the first Parliamentary Counsel, Henry Thring, was one of the ablest draftsmen of the age, concise, lucid, vigorous. In 1886 he found worthy successors in Sir Henry Jenkyns and, later, Sir Courtenay Ilbert. Then there was Arthur Godley, Lord Kilbracken, whose association with the Treasury dated from his private secretaryship to Gladstone in 1872 and 1880. One of Gladstone's best 'finds' – his first appointment was pure patronage – he passed through the Inland Revenue to be Permanent Under-Secretary at the India Office, to which his great abilities were by no means confined. At the War Office, Sir Ralph Henry Knox, the Permanent Under-Secretary, was a useful ally, and, on a quite different footing of self-interest and social intimacy, there were the Treasury's City friends.

There had always been wider contacts than the official ones with the Bank of England, and they were reinforced by certain personal ties. These belong to a tradition which runs back through Peel and Pitt to the less impeccable associations of Walpole and Stanhope. It suffered a slight setback from Gladstone who distrusted the City despite his friendship with Lord Overstone and Lord Wolverton (George Grenfell Glyn, of Glyn, Mills, Secretary to the Treasury, 1868–74). But Goschen, like J. C. Herries, was born into the banking world, and unlike Herries this was not held against him. The City helped him with his 1888 conversion and he did something to repay the debt with passive government support during the Baring Crisis of 1890. Other personal ties passed through Edward Hamilton, that assiduous socialite who seemed to know everyone. The Rothschilds, whose record of personal intimacy with successive Treasury administrations was consistently good, were among his closest friends, although in his official capacity he was not above playing them off against Lord Revelstoke of Barings', or J. S. Morgan.

SIR EDWARD HAMILTON AND BUDGETARY POLICY

Significantly, most of these relationships belong to the sphere in which the Treasury's authority was not seriously challenged – the control of public finance. Its competence here was founded not only upon customary and statutory sanctions far more positive in content than those which regulated its control of government establishments, but also upon a formidable tradition of expertise going back to those little-known chiefs of the eighteenth-century Revenue Room and, ultimately, to Lowndes and Downing. In the critical years of the early nineteenth century that tradition had been reinforced by the currency expert, James Pennington (1777–1862), who gave advice to Huskisson and Goulburn on a footing which rather resembles that of the modern Economic Adviser to the Treasury. He was Auditor of the Civil List from 1835 to 1851, and 'was my first tutor in currency matters', wrote George Arbuthnot, who succeeded him and carried the tradition of monetary orthodoxy into the 1860s. Another mentor of the Treasury was Walter Bagehot. Nephew of Vincent Stuckey the banker, who had been Pitt's currency expert, and son-in-law of the particularly able Parliamentary Financial Secretary, James Wilson, Bagehot had natural Treasury ties. His public and confidential advice to Gladstone's Treasury as Editor of *The Economist* ranks him high in the line which links John Locke to Keynes.*

Meanwhile, theoretical sophistication had been balanced by the great organizing capacities of A. Y. Spearman, Assistant Secretary, 1836–40, and William Anderson, who came to the Treasury in 1854 as Principal Clerk, Finance Division, after a career in the Admiralty and as Assistant Paymaster General, 1838–54. It was of such men that Reginald Welby was the heir when he became Principal Clerk of the Finance Division in 1871, at the age of thirty-nine. He was to make his own distinctive contribution, ushering in Walter Bagehot's brain-child, the 'Treasury Bill', in 1877, and confirming, by day-to-day, detailed decisions, the hard outlines of Treasury control. This sort of work does not lend itself to illustration; it was humdrum; but Welby's penetrating, analytical mind was an unfailing resource to governments until his retirement in 1894 and it is fascinating to trace through his correspondence with Gladstone the developing maturity which links some rather amateurish calculations on price fluctuations in the 1860s to the masterful memoranda on the Naval Defence Acts of the 1880s and on the financial implications of Irish Home Rule.

But with Welby's successor, Edward Hamilton, one must hesitate. Like Welby, he was an extremely popular bachelor-dilettante, a devoted Gladstonian, well-connected, moving in the very best social circles. Where Welby was an epicure, keeping a superb table, Hamilton was a virtuoso, belonging to another Treasury tradition which is worth recording in parentheses. It had unfortunate beginnings. Philip Cipriani, chief clerk in the Treasury (which he entered in 1782) 'was a skilful performer on the flute, and his private concerts were admirable treats for his friends', noted his obituary in 1820, but his contemporary, William Chinnery, ruined himself with his elegant Regency music parties, embezzled £70,000 and absconded. However, with Frederick Clay (Treasury, 1857–74), author of

*Contributions from such economists as W. S. Jevons, Alfred Marshall and Leone Levi are also to be found among Treasury files.

several operettas and the immortal melodies of '*I'll sing thee songs of Araby*'; with W. H. D. Boyle (Treasury 1888–97), who compiled the King's College, Cambridge, chant-book; and with Sir Thomas Little Heath (1884–1919), a precocious devotee of Brahms, the tradition recovered its respectability. Hamilton studied with his friend Arthur Sullivan, and it is a pleasing fancy to think of him composing songs like '*By the River Side*' or '*Little Ditties*' during Welby's Old Etonian boating parties at Datchet.

Yet, although gifted, even his friends did not credit Hamilton with more than a decent mediocrity. 'He was not in the first class for intellectual gifts,' wrote Lord Kilbracken, who had served with him as one of Gladstone's private secretaries, 'but he was very industrious, painstaking, accurate and obliging.'[13] However, this is less a reflection on Hamilton than a comment on public finance. By later standards, and even by the standards of the eighteenth century, the management of late Victorian government finance placed modest burdens on the Treasury. Peace, prosperity, the reformed simplicity of the system crowned by the Exchequer and Audit Departments Act had minimized the stress of annual financing. Large areas of responsibility had been tidied up by the Coinage Act of 1816, the Bank Charter Act of 1844, the Local Loans Act of 1887. The Treasury's own demands were few. Between the limited emergencies of the Crimean War and the Boer War it made no large-scale calls upon the money market. The £11 million purchase of the electric telegraph system in 1869, the £4 million purchase of the Suez Canal shares in 1875 created two of its largest needs. Rare budget deficits were occasionally met by the issue of medium-term Exchequer Bonds, but thanks to the predominance of surpluses and to small-scale funding operations the government's floating debt was very modest. The foundation of the Post Office Savings Bank in 1861 brought substantial borrowable funds within the Treasury's reach, and the creation of the Treasury Bill in 1877 gave it easy access to the short money market. Its posture towards the Bank of England was therefore transformed. 'A Chancellor now never had to beg',[14] and Welby followed Gladstone in letting the Bank know its master. The payments made to the Bank for its services were successively reduced in 1861 and 1892. In 1885 there was even talk of raising 'Ways and Means Advances' – i.e. short-term loans in advance of revenue receipts – in the open market.

At the same time the principles of monetary orthodoxy tended to minimize the Treasury's responsibility for public finance. 'The best thing undeniably that a government can do with the Money Market is to let it take care of itself', wrote Bagehot in 1873; and on the whole it did. The mechanics of currency management through adjustments of the Bank rate were a matter for the Bank alone, supplemented only in emergencies such as 1847, 1857 and 1866, by Treasury authority to exceed the fiduciary issue of notes permitted under the Bank Charter Act of 1844. Otherwise, the system was a self-regulating one, revolving under the automatic disciplines of the gold standard. The question of bi-metallism – i.e. the idea of a silver-and-gold standard – was summarily dismissed by the Treasury whenever it arose in the 1880s and 1890s. Even the literature of public finance, as distinct from political economy, was sparse. C. F. Bastable, in 1892, could fairly claim that his study, *Public Finance*, was the first systematic contribution on the subject to appear for fifty years, and it remained unmatched for a decade or more.

Thus Hamilton's abilities were not greatly dwarfed by his responsibilities, and he produced much useful work. He did a good deal to promote Goschen's operations on the National Debt in 1888 and published the best short account of its technicalities – *Conversion and Redemption*. Unlike his colleagues – he was the son of a bishop – he was not greatly amused to learn that this was being sold on stalls of religious tracts. Later in his career he was to produce major reports on the financial implications of Home Rule (with Welby), on Local Taxation, and on Old Age Pensions. For the rest, his work as the Chancellor's principal adviser followed the routine cycle of the financial year: watching the quarterly flows of revenue and expenditure, and the state of Exchequer balances; assessing the need for deficiency loans and arranging the issue of Treasury bills at the Bank. As the financial year moved towards its last quarter these tasks grew more urgent. What were the prospects for the final outturn of the year? Would there be a surplus, and if so, how large? What natural or artificial factors were affecting the flow of revenue returns? These were uneven at the best of times and as a basis for future fiscal decisions it was vital to assess them properly. This was where the Revenue Boards and the Statistical Department of the Board of Trade came in, for the Treasury had long ago declined to set up its own statistical department. Basing himself upon their detailed appraisals of present and future trends, Hamilton would begin to project the outcome of the year ending 31 March and begin deliberating the possible outlines of the next budget.

The degree to which he could influence the shape of the budget necessarily varied with political circumstances and the character of individual Chancellors, but as Hamilton developed his competence there are clear signs that Chancellors were increasingly inclined to accept his guidance. He had found it difficult to keep pace with Goschen's endless prevarications, but Harcourt was more amenable. 'Harcourt is most laborious over his Budgets,' recorded Hamilton in his diary, 'more so than any other Chancellor of the Exchequer with whom I have had to do. He takes my brief – *and that is practically an invention of my own*,* at least in a complete form – and from it he writes out *verbatim* what he intends to say. When he has finished it after a good deal of re-writing and correction, he has it type-written, tables & all. Fancy Pitt or Mr G. composing a Budget like that! They would have scorned almost to have a brief given them.' This was fair comment. Although Welby took an authoritative tone when telling Gladstone what rates he should offer on Treasury bills, even he did not presume to outline his, or his successors' budgets. Nevertheless, Hamilton's briefs continued even with the robust Hicks-Beach, and it is through this channel that one may trace an example of Treasury influence upon the course of policy and politics that is both striking and apt.

It is apt because it marks a climax to the conflicts with which this chapter began, producing a collision between Hicks-Beach and Chamberlain in which the fiscal tradition of the last half-century was put to its severest test. It is striking because the effects of this collision were decisive for both the political parties and for several of their protagonists. I refer to the tariff crisis which arose from the Corn Duty of 1902.

It cannot be argued that Hamilton deliberately sought to embarrass the Conservative party; the episode is better proof of misjudgement and naiveté; but the idea would be easier to dismiss if the political affiliations of leading Treasury officials had been less near the surface. In the 1880–85 administration, for example, Welby had tried hard to make Gladstone seize the political opportunities offered by local government reform. He failed, and it was left to the Conservatives to reap the benefits of the 1888 County Councils Act. Hamilton's own ideas of Civil Service impartiality were curious. He believed in it wholeheartedly and, more than a decade after the Ballot Act of 1870, thought the principle was best served by not voting in elections! Yet, like Welby, who on his retirement immediately entered politics in the House of Lords and the London County Council, Hamilton was deeply committed to the fortunes of the Liberal party. He worked passionately for his school-friend Rosebery's succession to the leadership. Perhaps he did not break any rule of impartiality by his work behind the scenes, but it led him into a curious double-life in which there was some element of self-deception.

His Cabinet memorandum of July 1895 – *Some Remarks on Public Finance* – is a symptom of this. It concluded –

> that these remarks are not made in any pessimistic, much less alarmist, sense; particularly at this moment when the prospects of an improving revenue are

* My italic.

decidedly good. They are intended to be precautionary, and to point out that, unless the brake is applied to the spending propensities of the State, which in the last fifteen years have resulted in a growth of public expenditure amounting to no less than £22,000,000, the Government may ere long find themselves confronted with a choice of evils involving serious changes in our fiscal system, and consequently formidable Parliamentary difficulties.

Ostensibly an objective appraisal, it was significantly timed to serve warning on the new Conservative government of July 1895 and to strengthen the Treasury's free-trade-orthodox position against such dangerous spendthrifts as Goschen and Joseph Chamberlain. In the event, Hamilton's predictions of a fiscal crisis proved right only because of the Boer War. It was not until 1901 that the Chancellor was forced to broaden the basis of taxation, introducing a sugar duty (as Hamilton had recommended) and a highly controversial coal export duty. In 1902, with peace in prospect, it was necessary to go still further, for there was likely to be a £45·5 million deficit. By 5 February 1902 Hamilton had made up his own mind:

I have finished my Mem. on Budget prospects. There must be increased taxation and the conclusions which I lead up to are (1) that if the Chanc. of the Exchequer wishes to be heroic, he should increase the income tax by a penny, remodel or graduate the House Duty and impose 2/– a quarter or 6d a cwt on Corn; and (2) that if he does not wish to be heroic he should content himself with remodelling & graduating the Income tax and with imposing 1/– a quarter or 3d a cwt on corn. I am convinced that the re-establishment of an old duty which was allowed to continue during the hey-day of free trade down to 1869 will give rise to much less difficulty than the imposition of some new and more or less fancy tax.

Hamilton stuck to that view; Hicks-Beach was less sure. The prospect of peace made him waver over such radical proposals. He did not like the Corn Duty but the Cabinet accepted the proposal in March and it went forward into his budget of 14 April. The ingredient which provoked most hostility turned out to be Hicks-Beach's own idea of a doubled cheque duty and this had to be dropped.

Blinded by his conviction that what had been good enough for Gladstone between 1846 and 1869 could not do harm in 1902, Hamilton did not appreciate that a major error in fiscal strategy had been committed. But others were quick to see that the Corn Duty had reopened the tariff question, giving a valuable hostage to Chamberlain's campaign for imperial preference. For it was now possible to cement imperial unity with a *differential* Corn Duty, lowered in favour of colonial corn imports. Sir Wilfrid Laurier, the Canadian premier, saw this and Chamberlain quickly seized the opportunity. By the summer of 1902 it was clear even to Hamilton that the movement had derived new strength from the strange apostasy of a free-trade Treasury.

At this point Hicks-Beach decided to get out: he was exhausted and embittered by his lonely Cabinet conflicts. But who could succeed him? Hamilton had firm views on that. The Financial Secretary, Austen Chamberlain, was out of the question, although very able:

I have said I shall resign if Hanbury [Financial Secretary, 1895–1900] is appointed and I have lodged a protest against Ritchie. George Hamilton [Secretary for India] would probably be the least bad appointment or J. W. Lowther whom some people talk of. The first qualification required is to be a gentleman.

C. T. Ritchie, then Home Secretary, had been responsible for the 1888 Local Government (County Councils) Act as President of the Local Government Board. A bluff, heavy man, he had a manufacturing background and in the opinion of Hamilton (whom Beatrice Webb had set down as 'a flashy fast Treasury clerk') was distinctly *not* a gentleman. His appointment was therefore a blow to Hamilton – 'a great come down for any one like oneself' . . .; but he consoled himself that Ritchie, probably 'being somewhat lazily inclined I expect he will be keen to be led & to concur'. Hamilton grossly miscalculated yet again. Ritchie proved 'sound', likeable and completely determined to thwart his colleague, the Colonial Secretary. The Treasury, now thoroughly alive to the preferential danger, agreed with Ritchie that the Corn Duty must be withdrawn, and by 1 November Hamilton had completed a strong brief against preference which Ritchie largely adopted for the memorandum he submitted to the Cabinet. It was rejected and Chamberlain was able to leave for a visit to South Africa in the belief that preference might figure in the 1903 budget.[15]

Throughout the winter of 1902–3 Ritchie and the Treasury worked hard to pull the mat from under Chamberlain's feet. A leading part was played by Hamilton's senior colleague, the Joint Permanent (Administrative) Secretary, Sir Francis Mowatt. Another ardent Gladstonian free-trader, it was Mowatt who coached the rebellious young Winston Churchill in orthodox liberal economics, and it has been generally accepted that in canvassing political support for Ritchie, he transgressed the normal limits of official impartiality. However, those who comment on his retirement in 1903, apparently under a cloud, seem unaware that Mowatt had been due to retire in January 1902, had been asked to stay on, and therefore had nothing much to lose (except, perhaps, a peerage). Hamilton, and the forty-four-year-old Assistant Secretary, Robert Chalmers, were more at risk for their advocacy, for all the 'little conversations' they had with Balfour and other politicians in these vital months.

It was a risk worth taking. By the time Chamberlain returned from South Africa he had lost this crucial round. Ritchie, choosing his time well, made it clear to the Prime Minister that if the Cabinet did not drop preference and accept the repeal of the Corn Duty he would resign. Luckier than Randolph Churchill, his blackmail succeeded. In the budget of 1903, based on another of Hamilton's detailed drafts, the government withdrew the Corn duty, sweetening their retreat with *4d.* off income tax. It seemed a victory for orthodoxy and a victory for the Treasury; and it cost the Conservative and Unionist Party dear.

In the first place, the imposition of the Corn Duty (the very idea of which Hamilton had dismissed in 1895) had proved more unpopular with the electorate than even Balfour's controversial Education Bill, and its repeal (Hamilton had intended it should be permanent) laid the government open to damaging charges of inconsistency. In the interim it had raised fundamental questions of imperial and social policy which deeply divided the party and threatened ruin to its leaders. Balfour's reaction to this débâcle was quietly savage. By the end of 1903 five of his Cabinet had gone, among whom Chamberlain resigned and Ritchie was dismissed. The Liberals, on the other hand, reunited in defence of free trade, had been placed on strategically strong ground, and the electoral landslide of January 1906 had been brought that much nearer.

There are several, rather obvious, comments which could be made on this episode, but one of the more important is that, in defeating Chamberlain's programme for tariff reform, the Treasury could be said to have defeated a programme for social reform. For, intimately bound up with Chamberlain's vision of imperial unity cemented by preferential duties was his hope that the new revenues would serve to meet novel welfare expenditure, particularly on old age pensions. Hamilton was not unaware of this. He feared the development of social welfare expenditure precisely because it would jeopardize the free-trade fiscal system. Commenting on the 1899 Report of the Select Committee on Old Age Pensions, he wrote 'one might almost imagine that what H. C. [Henry Chaplin, chairman of the Committee] has had in his mind is to force up the State's expenditure to such an extent as will necessitate the re-imposition of a tariff, or at any rate a duty on corn'. Ironically, Hamilton was shortly after appointed chairman of an inter-departmental committee instructed to look into the financial feasibility of the Chaplin scheme. It reported in predictably gloomy terms.

THE TREASURY AND LIBERAL REFORMS, 1906–14

On the surface the Treasury's restiveness under the Conservative administration contrasts with its seemingly docile response to the far more radical innovations of the Liberal government which came into power at the end of 1905. Non-contributory Old Age Pensions were introduced in 1908, national insurance for sickness and unemployment in 1911, and – at the heart of this expensive revolution in the state's attitude to social welfare was the sensational 'People's Budget' of 1909 with its equally revolutionary adoption of a discriminatory, re-distributive tax system. A vast new naval re-armament programme, which forced defence estimates up from £59 million in 1906–7 to £68 million in 1910–11, completed a situation which was profoundly uncongenial to the traditions of a Gladstonian Treasury.

However, the contrast is not a fair one. In 1902–3 the Treasury had been given the chance to exploit a divided Cabinet in favour of the orthodox *status quo*. After 1906 it did its duty to a united government with an overwhelming mandate, pursuing policies to which the Treasury, if pessimistic, was by no means a total stranger. Throughout the century the Treasury had been exercising a greater degree of direct and indirect responsibility for financial aspects of economic and social welfare than is often appreciated.

Sometimes it was very indirect – indeed, involuntary. The practice by which the Treasury, through the National Debt Commissioners, used the surplus funds of the Savings Banks to manipulate government stock and Treasury Bills resulted, by 1857, in a deficiency of over £5 million against the liabilities owing to the Savings Banks.[16] To the extent that this was the result of paying a higher rate of interest on Savings Bank deposits than was justified by the yield of government stock it might be said that the Treasury subsidized Victorian thrift. Likewise, the introduction of the penny post in 1840, during Rowland Hill's brief and uncomfortable association with the Treasury, resulted in such a disastrous drop in Post Office revenue that it did not regain the level of 1839 until the mid-1870s. The telegraph system, which the state bought in 1869, also brought losses and scandals in its wake. Not surprisingly, the Treasury approached international cables and telephones with great caution.[17]

Meanwhile, in 1817 – one of the formative years of *laissez-faire* economic philosophy – the Poor Employment Act implicitly recognized the state's responsibility to curb unemployment and systematized the practice, which had been regular since 1793, of making government loans to assist social and commercial investment in canals, roads and public buildings. Treasury loans, raised by the issue of 2½-per-cent Exchequer bills, were to be made available at 5 per cent up to a total of £1¾ million in Great Britain and Ireland. If anything, the Act reduced the Treasury's direct administrative responsibility by placing the loans in the hands of commissioners responsible to Parliament, and this relationship was eventually institutionalized in 1875 with the creation of the Public Works Loan Board. But all the regulations issued by the Board were subject to Treasury approval, and the Treasury had wide powers to regulate the rate of interest. After 1871, though the Local Government Board now sanctioned borrowing by local authorities under the Public Health Acts, the Treasury retained its general responsibilities for municipal borrowing and had a particularly close superintendence of the London County Council after its creation in 1888. 'The glamour of the Imperial Treasury's superintendence,' the Treasury told itself, 'adds a certain weight to their stock in the market and to their dignity among municipal authorities.'

Then there was Ireland. Nineteenth-century Ireland presented peculiar difficulties which could only be faced if it was agreed that the ordinary laws of political economy did not apply. Ricardo himself recognized this with greater willingness than the Treasury which, in the person of Sir Charles Trevelyan, added its own terrors to the great famine of 1845–7. In these years, it is true, Trevelyan worked himself and his subordinates nearly to death dispensing the thin gruel of Treasury aid to a starving population, but he did so with the pessimistic belief that it was an expensive folly to interfere in this way in the 'natural' workings of supply and demand, and he threw all his weight against indiscriminate state charity.[18]

It is greatly to Lord Monteagle's credit that he could write, in 1846 – 'I am both an Economist and a Treasury man, but after what I have seen and know the government must be prepared to face much responsibility if they wish to keep society together.'[19] To some small extent the Treasury did attempt to meet its responsibilities. It directly controlled some six of the twenty-nine Irish government departments, and continued to administer loans and relief funds in aid of drainage, housing, education and railways. Indeed, in 1868 a Treasury-appointed commission reported favourably on the possibility of nationalizing the Irish railways. But its grudging supervision was always marked by an exasperated conviction that Irish administration was feckless, corrupt and utterly demoralizing to the Irish themselves. Hamilton himself wrote once that 'administrative acts in Ireland almost constitute synonyms for blunders', and it was a question of Irish education that gave rise to one of the most flagrant instances of intemperate language by a Treasury official that I have come across. F. A'C. Bergne, a particularly peppery Principal Clerk who cast his blighting influence over all the vulnerable areas dealt with by the Third Division in the 1880s – Local Government Board, the Office of Works, Education, Ireland, the Isle of

Man, etc. – had written of a plea to increase Irish teachers' fees that 'the proposal is bad enough as a sample of the indifference of the Irish offices to public interest when it clashes with the petty perquisites of a class of officials, but it seems to me to be also demoralizing to the teachers themselves. I assume that for the most part they are Romanists. . . .' Welby deplored this innuendo and Bergne promised to tone down the memorandum here and there – and then burst out 'but it is no use shutting our eyes to what is certain to happen if you put it in the power of low-class Irishmen to plunder the public'! For this the incorrigible Bergne was heavily censured by the Chancellor.

But the real significance of the episode is that it was not only Ireland but education which excited the Treasury's passions. The first state grant in aid of elementary education had been made in 1833 – a mere £20,000. In 1839 the administration of the grant was taken over by the Privy Council Committee of Education and by the 1850s the annual parliamentary vote towards education had risen to £700,000. This was a very large sum, vulnerable to proof of incompetent administration. Appropriately, it was the future Treasury team of Robert Lowe and Ralph Lingen, then Vice-President and Secretary of the Education Office respectively, which in 1861 introduced the harsh, economical formula of 'payment by results' as the basis of the education grant – 'results' which by 1864 had justified an immediate drop of one quarter in the parliamentary vote. But, ultimately, growth in the education vote was inevitable and uncontrollable, and its administration scarcely fell within the Treasury's jurisdiction. Welby therefore deeply resented the education vote being included in calculations of the growth of civil expenditure because it was not open to administrative economies. Hamilton also saw it as another of the displeasing growths which menaced the fiscal system and would have liked to see it cut out of the central government budget in much the same way as the ever-growing state grants in aid of local expenditure were cut out by Goschen (with Hamilton's help) in 1888. Finally, it was in a scribbled minute rejecting a salary increase in the Education Office that, in 1871, Robert Lowe succinctly stated what I take to have been the late-nineteenth-century Treasury's general attitude to socially beneficial expenditure – 'It is not our business to make things pleasant all round'!

The Liberal government of December 1905 did something to change that. The upheaval was rendered slightly less painful by Asquith's tenure as Chancellor of the Exchequer. His first budget of 30 April 1906 was a heartening Gladstonian performance which declared a return to a 'more thrifty and economical administration the first and paramount duty of the Government', and his second firmly guaranteed the compatibility of social reform with the maintenance of free trade. But social reform there must be and Asquith was soon in disagreement with his Treasury chiefs over the price that had to be paid. Against his proposal to introduce the principle of graduation, as well as a differentiation between earned and unearned income, into the income tax, he met with orthodox Gladstonian objections. However, these were outmanoeuvred with the aid of a Select Committee, and the budget of 1907 duly embodied relief for earned incomes below £2,000 per annum and a much steeper, graduated estate duty. Less dramatic than Lloyd George's budget of 1909, that of 1907 is a landmark for having made it clear that 'ability to pay' would be the measure by which the nation henceforth contributed to the support of its elderly, its sick, and its unemployed. This in itself was a social revolution.

The 1908 Old Age Pensions Act made a modest start. Its 5*s*. a week (8*s*. 9*d*. for a married couple) was intended for 'the aged deserving poor' – a limiting concept which restricted the full rate to respectable hard-working seventy-year-olds with incomes well below a ceiling of £31 10*s*. per annum. Its execution at local level was to be by 'pension officers' and pension committees under the central direction of the Local Government Board. But it was the Treasury which appointed the pension officers, determined the conditions of payment and, in conjunction with the L.G.B., made the regulations necessary for its detailed enforcement. There was therefore an immediate impact on the internal organization of the Treasury.

On 26 October 1908, the Permanent Secretary submitted to the Board that 'the additional work imposed on the Department by the Old Age Pensions Act, together with the close attention which is now being paid to Naval and Military expenditure, make it advisable to strengthen the establishment of the Treasury by the constitution of a new (or Sixth) Division'. Characteristically, however, there was to be no overall increase in numbers. With that special parsimony it reserved for its own numbers – if not for its salaries – the Treasury carved the new Division out of the existing personnel.

But recent years had seen some increase in the elasticity of the department. In January 1902 the 'Patronage' Secretary to the Treasury had relinquished his claim to a private secretary drawn from the Establishment – a significant gesture, finally severing the ancient links between the political and administrative dimensions of the Treasury staff. For some decades now, the development of professional party organizations among the electorate had helped to insulate the departmental Treasury from the conduct of national politics. Meanwhile, the humbug of pretending that the junior Treasury lords were of the slightest administrative significance had been exposed by Trevelyan in evidence to the 1847–8 Select Committee on Miscellaneous Expenditure. True, they might attend occasional board meetings, make comments, sign things, but the 1849 Treasury Instruments (Signatures) Act reduced the legal quorum necessary to authenticate formal documents from three Commissioners to two, and the number of junior Treasury lords was cut from four to three. Later, Gladstone was to make junior lords useful as financial assistants to the Parliamentary Financial Secretary, but for the most part they were worthy Phineas Finns, loyal, obscure, aspiring to make their way as parliamentary Whips whose sole *raison d'être* was 'to make a House, to keep a House, and to cheer the Ministers'.

Other ambiguities were slowly disappearing. The vestigial 'secret service' money, once the bane of eighteenth-century politics, had survived until 1886 as a useful perquisite of £10,000 per annum, but after that date the modest expenses of the Patronage Secretary's office had been placed on the Treasury vote. Likewise, the advent of open competition had cut swathes through the resources of an office-holding party. What was left was remarkably large. In 1885 the Patronage Secretary still had 20,000 places in his gift – the majority of them in the Post Office.[20] But these nominations were gradually given up and on 15 August 1912 the Patronage Secretary formally relinquished his remaining rights over an infinite number of porters, typists, messengers and functionaries in government departments. It was the end of an era, although one would be naïve to suppose it was the end of official patronage.

Meanwhile, the Treasury had recovered the services of one of its junior officials, and in September 1903 an additional second-class clerkship was created (making eleven in all). In October 1904 a carefully considered reorganization added another first-class clerkship (making eight). This, in some measure, reflected the declining powers of Sir Edward Hamilton, who had been a sick man for some time, but in allotting the new post to the Finance Division it fairly recognized the mounting pressure on that side of the Treasury's work. Likewise the division of senior command in 1902 between Joint Permanent Secretaries had been a disguised concession to Hamilton's incapacitation, and on his retirement in October 1907 the sole Permanent Secretaryship had reverted to Sir George Murray. But subsequent permutations in the senior posts show that deliberate efforts were being made to spread the load of ultimate responsibility. For example, while Murray retained a particular supervision of the work of '2D', on Army and Navy affairs,* two new Assistant Secretaryships divided between them the financial and ordinary administrative sides of the Treasury's business. Immediate responsibility remained, as before, with the Principal Clerks at the head of the Divisions, but the trend towards a functional distribution of ultimate responsibility was beginning to emerge, as may be seen from the position at the end of 1908 (see Table on p. 230):

*It was presumably in this period that Murray dealt with a request from the Army Council to spend £6–700 on a subway under Whitehall for the secret disposal of War Office archives in the event of an invasion. 'This application must be refused', wrote Murray: 'The last objective of any intelligent invader of this country would be the War Office.' The story is told in H. H. Asquith's *Memories and Reflections* (1928), vol. I, p. 256.

THE UPPER ESTABLISHMENT OF THE TREASURY

AUTUMN 1908

Consisted of: 1 Permanent Secretary, 2 Assistant Secretaries, 4 Principal Clerks, 8 first-class clerks, 1 acting first-class clerk, and 10 second-class clerks – a total of 26 distributed as below. (*Note.* The Assistant Secretaries were directly responsible for 1D and 3D respectively, but superintended 4D and 5D. The Permanent Secretary superintended 2D and 6D.)

	Division	*Staff*
Assistant Secretary (1D + 4D)	*First (or Finance) Division* Finance generally; Banking and Currency; Mint; Exchequer and Audit; Paymaster General; Bank of England; National Debt Commissioners; Public Works Loans Commissioners; L.C.C.; Estimates; etc.	(1 Assistant Secretary) 2 first-class clerks (1 acted as *Estimate Clerk*) 3 second-class clerks
	Second Division India Office; War Office and Admiralty; Chelsea Hospital	1 Principal Clerk 1 first-class clerk 1 second-class clerk
	Third Division Board of Trade; Civil Service Commission; Privy Council Office; Board of Agriculture and Fisheries; Education, etc.; and Scottish and Irish departments	(1 Assistant Secretary) 2 first-class clerks (1 acted as *Parliamentary Clerk*) 1 second-class clerk
Permanent Secretary (2D + 6D)	*Fourth Division* Post Office; Local Government Board, England; Office of Works; Registrar-General; Friendly Societies; Isle of Man; Channel Islands; Duchies of Lancaster and Cornwall, etc.	1 Principal Clerk 1 first-class clerk 1 second-class clerk
	Fifth Division Superannuation; Workmen's Compensation; Customs and Inland Revenue; Old Age Pensions	1 Principal Clerk 1 acting first-class clerk 1 second-class clerk
Assistant Secretary (3D + 5D)	*Sixth Division* Foreign Office; Home Office; Colonial Office; Law Courts and Legal Establishments; etc.	1 Principal Clerk 1 first-class clerk 1 second-class clerk
	Private Secretaries	
	To First Lord of the Treasury	1 first-class clerk
	To Chancellor of the Exchequer	*nil*
	To the Financial Secretary	1 second-class clerk
	To the Permanent Secretary	1 second-class clerk

The absence of a private secretary to the Chancellor of the Exchequer between October 1908 and September 1910 is a fleeting symptom of the sort of changes which followed Lloyd George's arrival at the Treasury in May 1908. From what was, essentially, a marked change in personality flowed changes in the manner of conducting business and, to some extent, in the business itself. For a start, it is probably fair to say that Lloyd George was not congenial to the gentlemanly Liberalism of the Treasury. That Liberalism had already received shocks from Asquith, mitigated only by Reginald McKenna's too brief tenure as an ideal Financial Secretary. But it took much more to get used to a Chancellor of the Exchequer who could later confess 'I am the only Chancellor who ever began by saying and meaning to spend money'. Equally disconcerting were Lloyd George's methods of business. It was reasonable, if unusual, that he should prefer to bring to the Treasury his own devoted private secretary, W. H. (later Sir William) Clark of the Board of Trade. Later, under the stress of the war, it was still more reasonable that he should supplement his official advisers with a motley group of personal assistants – even though a confusingly large number were called 'Davies'. However, as a Treasury official later recorded, 'the peculiar mental equipment of Mr Lloyd George . . . had affected the whole system. He disliked, he often would not read, minutes; he insisted on oral advice. . . .'[21]

It is not easy to see what was 'peculiar' about such a preference, but it is easy to imagine how disconcerting it was to a tradition of leisured introversion, confided to paper in only the most faultless of prose. It was particularly upsetting for someone like Sir Thomas Heath, 'always more at ease on paper than in debate'. And Heath, Joint Permanent Secretary, 1913–19, was not the only senior Treasury man to be 'upset' by Lloyd George. The retirement in 1911 of Sir George Murray (1849–1936) was by no means conspicuously premature, but the chequered career of his successor, Sir Robert (later Lord) Chalmers, is rather less ambiguous and a good deal more significant.

In 1910, Chalmers – who entered the Treasury in 1882 – was Chairman of the Board of Inland Revenue. His situation is best described by one who worked very closely with Lloyd George:

> There had been friction between L.G. and Sir George Murray, then head of the Treasury, and Chalmers had gone in for a good deal of short circuiting of Murray. Traditionally the Commissioners of Inland Revenue used to report to the Chancellor of the Exchequer through the Treasury, but Chalmers, having direct access to L.G. dispensed with this formality, and L.G., not getting very much help from Murray, turned to Chalmers on other than Revenue matters, and also used Bradbury in the Treasury rather than Murray. . . . Thus Chalmers was getting a reputation with L.G. for getting things done.[22]

Chalmers was one of those senior Treasury men who, as a passionate Liberal partisan, is said to have been deeply disappointed with the government of 1906. However, as an official his instincts were strongly engaged by the 1909 budget struggle, and when the House of Lords rejected it he was heard to shout 'I should like to festoon this room with their entrails!' He seemed well suited to serve the resolute Lloyd George. Yet, his appointment as Governor of Ceylon in 1913, while maliciously apt for an Oriental scholar like Chalmers, clearly marked a breakdown in his relations with his chief, and it was not until the end of 1915 that McKenna, now Chancellor, was able to arrange his return as Joint Permanent Secretary to the only work with which he was really happy.

This sort of gossip about individuals is rather unsatisfactory as evidence, but even if unfounded – which it is not – it would reflect the significant idea that the certainties and self-sufficiency of the late-Victorian Treasury were breaking up under the pressure of radical policies and uncompromising personalities. Ironically, perhaps fortunately, this was taking place at a time when the quality of the Treasury's personnel had never been higher. The whole of the administrative establishment was now the product of open competition and contained men of exceptional ability. In 1910 the Finance Division alone contained J. S. Bradbury, R. G. Hawtrey, O. E. Niemeyer, J. H. Mc. Craig and F. W. Leith-Ross – men whose names will recur in this narrative as they would in any history of the modern Treasury.

But although the Treasury had creamed off the most brilliant entrants to the Civil Service, taking all those who had passed top in the Civil Service examination between 1906 and 1913, it had no monopoly of ability and, more seriously, it remained under-strength. Added to the well-established practice of referring specialized fiscal problems to the revenue departments, it is this fact which supports the impression that Lloyd George habitually felt obliged to by-pass the Treasury in working out his radical policies. Thus, in one biography, we have the vivid picture of him throwing together his great 1909 budget during a week-end at Brighton, aided only by W. H. Clark and J. S. Bradbury.[23] We have the even more striking picture of him giving birth to the welfare state at Nice, assisted this time only by 'W. J. Braithwaite, a junior clerk in the Treasury'.*

*A. J. P. Taylor, *Lloyd George: Rise and Fall* (Leslie Stephen Lecture) (1961), pp. 7–8. If one accepts Taylor's (or, rather, Braithwaite's) view that 'Braithwaite created the National Health System almost single-handed under Lloyd George's inspiration', then some of the beauty of the situation is lost by calling him 'a junior clerk in the Treasury'. This is verbally correct, but Braithwaite was, in fact, an Inland Revenue clerk, temporarily given a room in the Treasury.

It would be unfortunate if these enjoyable vignettes obscured the protracted and complex drudgery which actually lay behind the achievement, drudgery performed in the Treasury as well as in the revenue departments. But it remains substantially true that in a period of intricate, radical innovations which placed a premium on imagination and initiative the Treasury was momentarily eclipsed. Other departments, other men, were setting the pace. There was Robert Morant, Permanent Secretary of the Board of Education, architect of the great Education Act of 1902 and a bitter opponent of Treasury control. There was William Beveridge, in his twenties, carrying away the Webbs and, ultimately, Churchill with his visionary scheme for labour exchanges. Both these men came into public administration from adventurous careers outside, but within the static, divided ranks of the Civil Service young men of ability were being brought to the fore by the challenge of the new legislation. John Anderson, twiddling his chilblained fingers in the Colonial Office, and Arthur Salter, moored in his Admiralty backwater, began their distinguished ascent to ministerial rank on the fresh tide of National Health administration. Its fiscal counterpart, the novel taxes introduced in 1909 and later, proved the youthful powers of Inland Revenue men like Richard Hopkins, Josiah Stamp and Warren Fisher. All were to rise to the highest places in public life, and their names, particularly Fisher's, are a portent that the Treasury was on the eve of another transformation.

SOURCE NOTES

1. The figures in these paragraphs are based on B. R. Mitchell and P. Deane, *Abstract of Historical Statistics* (1962); A. T. Peacock and Jack Wiseman, *The Growth of Public Expenditure in the United Kingdom* (1961); and J. Veverka, 'The Growth of Government Expenditure in the U.K. since 1790', in *Public Expenditure – Appraisal and Control* (1963), ed. A. T. Peacock and D. J. Robertson.
2. Cited by F. W. Hirst, *Gladstone as Financier and Economist* (1931), p. 243.
3. W. Ashworth, *An Economic History of England, 1870–1939* (1960), p. 13.
4. P. Deane and W. A. Cole, *British Economic Growth, 1688–1959* (2nd edn, 1967), p. 29, Table 8.
5. G. S. Graham, *The Politics of Naval Supremacy. Studies in British Maritime Ascendancy* (Wiles Lectures) (1965).
6. I. F. Clarke, *Voices Prophesying War, 1763–1984* (1966).
7. A. G. Gardiner, *The Life of Sir William Harcourt* (1923), vol. 2, 231.
8. A. B. Erickson, 'Edward T. Cardwell: Peelite', *Transactions of the American Philosophical Society,* New Series, vol. 49, Part 2, 1959, p. 7.
9. G. P. Gooch, *Life of Lord Courtney* (1920), pp. 168–9, 210.
10. S. McKenna, *Reginald McKenna, 1863–1943: A Memoir* (1948), pp. 44, 227.
11. *Epitome of the Reports from the Committees of Public Accounts, 1857 to 1937* (H.C. 154, 1938), p. 225.

12. R. Lambert, *Sir John Simon, 1816–1904, and English Social Administration* (1963), p. 458.
13. *Reminiscences of Lord Kilbracken* (1931), p. 121.
14. Sir J. Clapham, *The Bank of England: a History, 1694–1914* (1944), vol. 2, p. 274.
15. The fullest account of this episode – A. M. Gollin's *Balfour's Burden: Arthur Balfour and Imperial Preference* (1965) – unfortunately makes no use of Hamilton's diary.
16. H. O. Horne, *A History of Savings Banks* (1947), pp. 160–62.
17. H. Robinson, *Britain's Post Office* (1953), p. 194.
18. C. Woodham Smith, *The Great Hunger: Ireland 1845–9* (1962).
19. R. D. Collison Black, *Economic Thought and the Irish Question, 1817–70* (1960), p. 116.
20. H. J. Hanham, 'Political Patronage at the Treasury, 1870–1912', *The Historical Journal,* 1960, p. 80.
21. M. F. Headlam, 'Sir Thomas Little Heath', *Proceedings of the British Academy,* XXVI, 1941.
22. *Lloyd George's Ambulance Waggon; the Memoirs of W. J. Braithwaite, 1911–12* (1957), ed. Sir H. N. Bunbury, p. 68.
23. F. Owen, *Tempestuous Journey: Lloyd George, his Life and Times* (1954), p. 170.

CHAPTER 8

The Treasury in War and Peace: 1914-47

... Some considerable time ago I had been thinking to myself, 'It is a modern world of finance and economics when it is not actual war...'.
SIR WARREN FISHER, in 1936

THE FIRST WORLD WAR AND ITS AFTERMATH

War has always been the principal catalyst in the Treasury's development. The 'rougher hands' of 1667 were called upon to redeem the disasters of the second Anglo-Dutch War, and the Treasury of Lowndes and Godolphin reached maturity in the crises of the War of the Spanish Succession. 'Economical' and administrative reform sprang from the loss of the American colonies, and was pushed to its climax by the disgraceful revelations from the Crimea, while the great war with Revolutionary and Napoleonic France helped to transform the terms of economic debate as well as setting in motion the internal reorganization of the department. In almost every case the stimulus of conflict had presented much more than problems of finance. It had called for administrative flexibility in the institution and creativity of mind in the personnel. It had sometimes meant a fundamental readjustment of the Treasury's place in government.

The First World War fits into this pattern, but in a rather less convincing way than one might expect. As Lord Bridges – who entered the Treasury in December 1917 – has written, 'looking back today it seems that the First World War, as compared with the Second World War, resulted in few far-reaching changes'.[1]

It is the Second World War and its aftermath which made the Treasury the co-ordinating centre of government activities in the economy. However, the conflicts of 1914–18 were accompanied by, and did to some extent stimulate, an important line of development in the Treasury's administrative powers. In addition, the war abruptly pitchforked the department into a responsibility for aspects of the British economy which, although modest, was quite novel and which it has never since relinquished.

'HOW WE SAVED THE CITY'

In August 1914 the Treasury was unprepared for the administration of a great continental war. Recent reforms and reorganization in the War Office and Admiralty meant that in military terms the nation was probably better equipped than it had ever been – which is saying very little – but although a sub-committee of the Committee of Imperial Defence had considered the economic problems of war in 1911–12, the Treasury itself was not equipped with anything like blueprints for emergency action. Likewise the City of London, secure in its prosperity, confident in its leadership of world finance, was relatively oblivious to the dangers which might flow from a major European conflict. But, following the Austrian ultimatum to Serbia on 23 July 1914, the continental bourses began to close and within a few days the London money market was in difficulties. Although Great Britain's position as a creditor nation was very strong, the City's short-term liabilities to other countries, and its inability to meet its obligations in London, meant that on balance London was likely to be left dangerously exposed. The City found itself rapidly embarrassed by a contraction of credit, and on Friday 31 July the Stock Exchange was abruptly closed down for the first time in its history. Banks called in their short-term commercial loans, holding up gold payments to their customers and drawing heavily from the Bank of England. The whole structure of financial credit seemed jeopardized by the imminence of panic.

Fortunately, it was a Bank Holiday week-end which began on 1 August, and in this breathing space – extended by proclamation for an extra three days – the government and the Bank of England organized their emergency measures. Legislation was rushed through announcing a one-month moratorium (later extended) on all contractual payments – except, of course, government debts, wages, salaries, banknotes and debts under £5. Arrangements were simultaneously made at the Treasury to issue a new paper currency of £1 and 10*s.* 'Treasury notes', fully convertible to gold on demand at the Bank of England. The Bank rate was raised, inevitably, and the Bank was authorized to exceed the normal limits of its legal note issue. On 13 August the government published an agreement with the Bank, guaranteeing it against loss if it undertook to purchase any of those bills of exchange for which the City was liable and upon which so much of its international credit depended. Later, in September, the Bank was to extend its support to those City accepting houses hard-hit by the difficulties of their European clientele. But by then the worst of the crisis was over. Credit was maintained, the public appeased, and within the limits set by the extended moratorium and the continued closure of the Stock Exchange, it was very nearly 'business as usual'. Collapse had been averted.

'How we saved the City' is the way Lloyd George entitled this episode in his *War Memoirs*[2] and the exaggeration is pardonable. The Chancellor's actions were extremely vigorous, and he was very strongly supported, not only by the Governor of the Bank of England and other City leaders, but also by two former Chancellors of the Exchequer, Austen Chamberlain and Lord St Aldwyn (formerly Hicks-Beach). Above all, there was the Treasury under Sir John Bradbury, Joint Permanent Secretary at the age of forty-one. His own role in contriving the emergency measures was to be publicized by his signature on the new Treasury notes, £4 million of which were designed and rushed through for issue by 7 August. Inevitably, they were known as 'Bradburys', and had a currency which continued into the 1930s.*

And behind Bradbury there was the tiny '1D', the Finance Division, under Malcolm Ramsay and Basil Blackett. It rose to the occasion superbly. Its lucid formulation of policies which would relieve panic and ensure normal gold and currency dealings had a great influence on Lloyd George, who was soon – noted Blackett – 'in a fair way to becoming quite a currency expert'.[3] And it was at Blackett's invitation that, on Sunday 2 August, J. M. Keynes, then a young Cambridge don, made his first informal appearance in the counsels of the Treasury. With Blackett he helped to draft those papers which began Lloyd George's education in high finance. Later, being quite unattached officially, it was open to Keynes to publish his own account of the crisis, and he did so in the September issue of *The Economic Journal*.[4] His verdict there was scathing on what he thought to be the vacillation, timidity and dishonourable self-seeking of the City institutions. It was, he wrote, 'the staunchness of the Bank of England . . . and the good sense of the Treasury' which had saved the City from counsels of great folly.

This summed up an episode which one must suppose to have had a profound effect on the Treasury mind. Coupled with the evident success of its own improvised measures, the discovery that the City (whose representatives Asquith shortly described as 'the greatest ninnies I ever had to tackle') was morally and intellectually leaderless, gave an inexperienced Treasury a sense of confidence in monetary management which practice soon turned into authority. No wonder that a financial commentator could write in 1916 that the Treasury 'was more apt to exceed its duty than to fall short of it'![5] The characteristic optimism of the modern Treasury in the ability of its

*The issue of Treasury notes continued until 1928. They ceased to be legal tender in 1933.

'intelligent laymen' to master the intricacies of financial administration may have its roots in August 1914.

WAR FINANCE

But, having said this, it is important to stress that there was no immediate question of the government taking large powers to control the war-time economy. Initially, that seemed to offer few difficulties. Britain's creditor position and the scale of her short-term claims on the rest of the world meant that sterling was buoyant in the first phase of the war. The dollar rate for the pound rose from its normal $4.90. But early in 1915 it became clear that Britain's imports from dollar countries were not being balanced by the ordinary course of trade. The exchanges turned against her and it was necessary to organize support for the pound. Gold shipments and the sale of some dollar securities didn't help, but in October 1915 an Anglo-French Commission raised a $500-million loan in New York, and soon after the Treasury began to organize a comprehensive 'Mobilization of Securities Scheme'. Actually there were two schemes: Scheme A of December 1915, inviting the sale or loan to the Treasury of sound dollar securities (barbed by the budget of 1916 with a penal tax on those not forthcoming), and Scheme B, of August 1916, for further loans which, in January 1917, became compulsory. This marked the climax of a rather terrible period in which the British supply of dollars had been very nearly exhausted, but the Treasury had been determined to maintain the position of the pound by orthodox dealings, and it did not reveal the gravity of the situation to its ministers. Keynes described the climax in December 1916:

> 'Well, Chalmers, what is the news?' said the Goat [Lloyd George]. 'Splendid,' Chalmers replied in his high quavering voice; 'two days ago we had to pay out $20,000,000; the next day it was $10,000,000; and yesterday only $5,000,000.' He did not add that a continuance at this rate for a week would clean us out completely, and that we considered that an average of $2,000,000 [was] very heavy. I waited nervously in his room, until the old fox came back triumphant. In fact the drain did dry up almost immediately and we dragged along with a week or two's cash in hand until March 1917 when U.S.A. came in and that problem was over.[6]

At the time this happened Keynes had been in the Treasury for nearly two years, his position regularized by a Treasury Minute of 26 March 1915 which recorded that he had been assisting the Treasury at the Chancellor's request since 18 January. But this was only one of the special measures taken within the department. On 14 September 1914 a Minute observed that the disturbance of the complex machinery of international trade and commerce by a war in which all the principal industrial communities of Europe are engaged has raised difficulties in connection with currency, banking, international exchange and credit generally, which are unlikely, whatever may be the course of the conflict, to exhaust their effects for many years to come. The result has been that the intervention of the Treasury has been invoked in regard to a great variety of matters which have hitherto been regarded as outside the province of the Government, while at the same time the ordinary finance business of the Treasury has increased in importance and responsibility by reason of the necessity for providing money for the expenses of the war and for the relief of distress and for the assistance of our less wealthy allies . . .[7]

Ramsay was promoted to an Assistant Secretary in charge of Finance, but on 24 March 1915 it was decided to go further and set up a special statistical unit under a 'Director of Financial Enquiries' to co-ordinate information on foreign exchanges, currency, banking, international movements of capital and the public expenditure and borrowing of other governments. It was to work in close touch with the Board of Trade, the revenue departments and the Foreign Office. The first appointment as Director went to Hartley Withers, financial editor of *The Morning Post*, and his assistant was Dudley Ward, of St John's College, Cambridge, formerly correspondent of *The Economist* in Berlin. Keynes, after assisting Sir George Paish, the official adviser to the Chancellor, took over as acting first-class clerk in 1D while Blackett was on a mission to the U.S.A. From this temporary vantage point he quickly built up his authority on questions of overseas finance. He organized the system of British loans to allies (which by the end of the war exceeded British borrowing from America, Canada and other neutrals) and was particularly active in the Treasury's foreign exchange operations. Early in 1917 a whole new unit – called 'A' Division – was carved out of 1D to contain Keynes and his growing body of assistants.

However, there is another side to this picture of a dynamic Treasury, pushing its way forward into new realms of expertise. The Bank of England not only retained the initiative in handling the early sterling crisis but jealously preserved its autonomy under its very independent Governor, Lord Cunliffe. While Lloyd George was Chancellor this seems to have worked well, and Cunliffe was in tears at the Chancellor's departure in May 1915, but with his successor, the Treasury favourite, McKenna, a deterioration soon followed and in September 1915 the Bank withdrew its support from the sterling–dollar rate, which fell heavily.[8] Cooperation was eventually restored by the creation of the London Exchange Committee, on which the Bank – but not the Treasury – was heavily represented. Put bluntly by Lord Beaverbrook, this meant that 'power over Government assets passed from the Treasury to a privately operated banking company in the City – the Bank of England',[9] and to some observers, like Montagu Norman, seemed conclusive proof that the Treasury didn't know what it was doing. Unfortunately for the Bank, Cunliffe finally overstepped the mark in July 1917 when, without consulting the Chancellor, he interfered in the gold dealings between the government's American agents and the Treasury representative in the United States. By the time the consequent row had subsided the Chancellor was in possession of the Governor's full submission and the Treasury's command of its overseas financing seemed fully guaranteed. The episode finally broke Cunliffe's authority with his colleagues, although not – as Montagu Norman's career was to demonstrate – the Governor's authority with the Treasury.

This triumph tends to obscure the possibility that the novice Treasury was – for all its self-confidence – rather less successful in its direction of war finance, but the possibility is reinforced by consideration of budgetary policy, where its responsibility was unshared. Its achievement seemed formidable enough – a tax revenue raised from a peace-time £160 million to £1,000 million by 1919–20. But this fell far short of requirements. Lloyd George's two war budgets of November 1914 and May 1915 were peculiarly timid, and even the more vigorous measures of his successors, McKenna and Bonar Law, did not raise the average revenue contribution to war expenditure, 1914–20, above thirty-six per cent. The balance, met by some rather costly war loans, totalled £7,186 million and fell upon posterity – an unprecedented burden accumulated at a rate which compares badly with British war finance before and since.[10]

Direct taxation certainly bore real burdens. Income tax was raised by stages from a basic 1*s.* 2*d.* to 6*s.* in the £, and – with matching increases in super tax – this levy became more markedly redistributive than ever before, ranging from 13 per cent on earned incomes of £500 per annum to nearly 43 per cent on earned incomes of £10,000 per annum. Up to 80 per cent was levied by the Excess Profits Duty and this proved particularly productive. But indirect taxes made little impact and the uproar over the controversial 'McKenna duties' of 1915 – introducing import duties on manufactured luxuries such as watches – was an expression of outraged free-trade principles, not of injured consumption. Inflation therefore remained a serious danger, and this was the phenomenon for which orthodox opinion thought the Treasury most culpable. It seemed directly related, not only to such questionable innovations as the Treasury note-issue, but to serious technical mistakes in the Treasury's financing of short- and long-term deficits which, in general, was thought to be too costly and mistimed. However, although the rise in prices and purchasing power (which doubled) was clearly attributable to a scale of expenditure vastly in excess of anything that could be financed by ordinary savings, monetary factors alone have been discounted as a cause of war-time inflation.[11] And some factors which clearly did make for price rises – panic buying, acute competition for raw materials and manpower, shipping losses and rocketing import costs – were eventually brought under government control, as, from 1916 onwards, a fairly comprehensive system was built up under the Defence of the Realm regulations. The question of manpower was, of course, dependent on recruitment policy, but some months before conscription was introduced in 1916 the problem of moving unskilled and female labour into war-work created a problem with the unions which only the government could solve. Negotiations between Lloyd George and the union leaders culminated in the historic bargain known as 'the Treasury Agreement' of March 1915.

In fact, this was just a convenient label to describe a characteristic Lloyd George *coup* which had little to do with the departmental Treasury. The Treasury was much more intimately involved in other aspects of control. It administered the trading-with-the-enemy regulations and, to protect the exchange rates, supervised the foreign purchases of the new trading departments. Likewise, when the Stock Exchange re-opened in January 1915, it assumed control over all new borrowing for domestic investment. Foreign investment, it announced, 'would not normally be allowed at all'. Furthermore, although the operation of the gold standard was not formally abrogated, the Treasury's restrictions on gold shipments were an effective alternative. Finally, the Treasury collaborated with the Bank of England, in manipulating the domestic money market in favour of the high interest rates to attract and retain foreign funds. Treasury bills, attractive for short-term investment, were permanently 'on tap' after April 1915, and as a result of this huge presence in the money market the Treasury's interest rates effectively supplanted Bank rate as the regulator of demand.[12] Never before had the Treasury exercised such influence in domestic finance.

Some of its measures could be fairly described as deflationary, for by 1917 price controls were working effectively and a larger share of purchasing power was being absorbed by the national savings movement. But the almost unanimous verdict of economic historians is that the Treasury's fiscal policy, particularly under Lloyd George, signally failed to impose a tax burden sufficiently heavy or well-designed to absorb the wealth and excess demand created by war expenditure, and from this failure flowed all the inflationary evils of later years. The Treasury's inability to control that expenditure seems to go without saying.

THE RECONSTRUCTION OF TREASURY CONTROL

Yet, this inability is closely bound up with changing techniques of Treasury control promoted in the light of war experience. The Ridley Commission in 1888, as we have seen, had noted that the Treasury was unable to promote organizational uniformity in government departments without a good deal of friction. It had therefore recommended that Orders in Council should be the vehicle for all general regulations governing the Civil Service, and that the conformity of individual departments should be superintended by a 'Permanent Consultative Committee' on which the Treasury and four other departmental chiefs should be represented.[13]

Treasury disapproval helped to give rise to the storm in *The Times* already described, and was only overborne by an Order in Council of 15 August 1890 which actually set up such a Consultative Committee. But over the next four years the Committee completely failed to settle the problems of departmental organization set before it, and after 1894 it was never again called upon. Instead, on its own initiative, the Treasury made greater use of *ad hoc*, interdepartmental committees to solve problems of supply and organization, and in evidence before the 1902 Select Committee on National Expenditure the Treasury witnesses gave a favourable verdict on their effectiveness as a means of checking even the defence departments. Yet, in its report of 7 July 1903, this Committee – which was more concerned to reinforce the mechanics of parliamentary control – recommended that the Treasury should, at fixed periods (perhaps once in five years), exercise the right to review and revise the staffing of the various departments.[14]

Not until 1910 did an Order in Council declare that '*it shall be competent for the Treasury to direct, should they see cause, that inquiry be made at intervals of not less than five years into the pay and numbers of officers employed by any department of State*'. And in the investigations of the important 'MacDonell' Royal Commission on the Civil Service of 1912–14 it was once again revealed that the Treasury's strength still fell short of real control over an homogeneous Civil Service. The Commission's Fourth Report, in 1914, inferred that 'whatever may be its indirect influence, the Treasury does not, in practice, exercise a sufficiently effective control over the organization of departments unless a question of finance is involved'. 'We therefore recommend the creation within the Treasury, and subject to its administrative orders, of a special section for the general supervision and control of the Civil Service.'[15] Its functions would be to investigate and supervise the conditions and activities of the Civil Service, to make recommendations to heads of departments, foster the reward of merit and promote transfers of personnel between departments and, finally, 'to carry out inquiries and investigations into any matters connected with Departmental administration or methods of working'.[15]

The First World War interrupted consideration of this report but also lent urgency to its implementation. The proliferation of government departments which had begun under the demands of social welfare was now greatly accelerated by war-time controls. Ministries of Munitions, of Labour, of National Service, of Blockade, of Food, of Shipping, and other evanescent departments came into being, and they all raised problems of pay, organization and control which were normally the responsibility of the Treasury.* At the same time, ministers were learning the hard way the importance of co-ordination in the machinery of a government under siege.

Consideration of all these problems began to converge between 1916 and 1919. On the one hand, there was one of the nation's earliest, horrified, investigations into the scale of war-administration by the Select Committee on National Expenditure, set up in July 1917. Examining the War Office and Ministry of Munitions it found that while the Treasury controlled appointments above a certain level and supervised purchases abroad with an eye to foreign exchange, it exercised no powers over contracts or capital expenditure. Although it was represented on interdepartmental committees it seemed quite unable to stop competitive, and therefore inflationary, buying by rival departments. Finally – and it should come as no surprise to the reader – the Committee discovered that the Treasury was absurdly understaffed, with barely thirty-eight members in the administrative hierarchy as compared with thirty-three before the war. Its recommendations therefore called for the recruitment of more experienced men, a more active application of sound financial controls and a regular series of investigations into clerical organization. A reflection on the damaging in-fighting that had been going on between Lloyd George and McKenna was its comment that 'in the exercise of a proper financial control the Chancellor of the Exchequer should be enabled to feel that he has the support of the Cabinet, with whom the ultimate decisions rest'.†

*Under the terms of the statutes setting up the Ministries of Pensions [6 & 7 Geo. V. c. 65] and of Labour, Food, Shipping and the Air Board [6 & 7 Geo. V.c. 68] the Treasury was given the authority to determine the pay-scales of the departments but not their numbers or organization.

†*P.P. 1917–18*, vol. III, *First Report from the Select Committee on National Expenditure*, p. 15. Not until 1924 was the Cabinet rule clearly formulated, that 'no memorandum is to be circulated to the Cabinet or its Committees in which any financial issue is involved, until its contents have been discussed with the Treasury'.

Meanwhile, it is pleasant to record, the Treasury's own initiative had made itself heard in a memorandum presented to the Financial Secretary, Edwin Montagu, shortly before he became Minister of Reconstruction in 1917. Commenting on the wasteful overlapping of functions among the old and new departments it called for a comprehensive review of government organization, and it is this which, it is suggested, led to the appointment of a reconstruction sub-committee on 'The Machinery of Government', the celebrated Haldane Committee which reported on 7 January 1919.

THE HALDANE COMMITTEE

The Committee, whose members included Beatrice Webb, Sir Robert Morant and Sir George Murray, as well as Lord Haldane, is a major landmark in British administrative history and the Report was itself an admirable advertisement for the ideal which it extolled – the recognition of 'investigation and thought as a preliminary to action'. Its significance for the Treasury is that, after laying down in Part I some of the basic principles of sound government – a select, effective Cabinet, equipped with a secretariat and statistical information, formulating and co-ordinating the policies of a rationally integrated departmental system – it moved on in Part II to examine the best way of distributing functions in such a system. As for finance, it conceded 'the Department of Finance must necessarily have an exceptional position among all the State Departments', and that 'on the whole experience seems to show that the interests of the tax-payer cannot be left to the spending Departments'. But, in passages apparently drafted by Sir Robert Morant – who had suffered much from Treasury control – it looked very critically at the manner in which the system was applied. It was all very well for the Treasury to set up rigid financial limits within its own sphere of budgetary control, but it was clearly the duty of the Chancellor of the Exchequer to provide funds necessary for the execution of policies agreed upon by the government, and 'the obligation upon the spending Departments to formulate a full and reasoned statement of their proposals must be recognized as placing upon the Treasury a corresponding obligation not to assume a negative attitude in the first instance towards suggestions for improving the quality of a service or the efficiency of the staff which administers it'. Control must be exercised 'in a sympathetic spirit and with an adequate knowledge of the circumstances and difficulties of the other Departments'.[16]

To deal with the awkward problem of the Treasury's 'manner' it suggested that 'the traditional attitude of antagonism between the Treasury and other Departments which so often manifests itself might be substantially modified if the officers of the Treasury could establish closer personal relations with the several Departments with which they deal, and acquire a fuller knowledge of their work and their difficulties. It is clearly desirable to dissipate the tradition that all Departments have a natural disposition to extravagance and that the Treasury is irreconcilably opposed to all increases of expenditure.' To be more precise, it thought the Treasury's knowledge might benefit from the establishment of an Advisory Committee which it could consult either on general questions affecting the public service or on specific departmental proposals. Financial control could be improved by strengthening the internal finance branches of the departments, and – finally – in a sequence of most important proposals on staffing and organization it suggested that:

> In the Treasury there should be a separate branch specializing in this 'establishment' work, and studying all questions of staff, recruitment, classification, etc., and routine business generally. Such a branch would be in close touch and constant communication with the officers in other Departments charged with the duty of supervising the 'establishment' work. It would also keep itself acquainted with what was being done in business circles outside, and perhaps in foreign countries. Probably special arrangements would be required for recruiting the staff of this branch so as to provide the necessary expert knowledge.

One does not have to be familiar with the modern development of the Treasury and Civil Service to recognize the importance of these ideas. In clarity and cogency they compare well with Burke's programme of administrative reform, and, like that programme, it is taking more than one generation to fulfil their vision.

Meanwhile, the Haldane recommendations coincided with some being evolved almost simultaneously by a departmental Committee of Inquiry into the Organization and Staffing of Government Offices, sitting under Bradbury's chairmanship. It was looking at the results of a war-time situation in which 'the permanent Civil Servants for the first time in their lives could settle their arrangements without reference to the Treasury'. Normal Treasury control over staffing and even pay had been waived in many cases and there had been no central organization at the Treasury or anywhere else to keep trace of staffing statistics. The consequences had been made clear in overstaffing, the overlapping of functions and wide disparities in remuneration. Its recommendations were, therefore, the full restoration of Treasury control but based upon sympathetic collaboration with a reformed system of functionally integrated departments. The Bradbury Committee explicitly aligned itself with the recently published Haldane report and echoed its call for the creation of a special 'Establishments Division' within the Treasury. But it concluded emphatically that the business of superintendence and research into establishments could not be divorced from the Treasury, which had all the necessary powers of review under the Order in Council of 1910.

These reports marked the climax of the protracted and rather repetitious sequence of deliberations which helped to drag the early twentieth-century Treasury clear of its stultifying legacy. Within a year action was taken and the Treasury entered on a new phase in the formation of its present character.

CONTROL OF THE CIVIL SERVICE

First of all, in February 1919, an Establishments Division was quickly set up in the Treasury under Sir Malcolm Ramsay. But this was soon overtaken by a major Treasury reorganization in September 1919 from which emerged, not a Division, but a whole 'Establishments Department' of five Divisions covering the whole range of Civil Service pay and organization. Among the significant functions of one of these Divisions was

> Routine, i.e. questions of office machinery, the keeping of registers, records and statistics, the employment of labour-saving appliances in the Public Service.[17]

This represents the frail beginnings of what is now known as 'O. & M.' – Organization and Methods, or the application to public administration of scientific techniques of management and routine. But the full realization of its potential lay in the future. The half-hearted employment during the inter-war years of an insignificant handful of technicians recalls the furtive way in which, in 1889, two lady typists had been allowed to tip-toe into the Treasury attics, past the dozing satyrs of the five divisions. Of more immediate importance to the Treasury was the appointment in all the major departments of Establishment officers responsible, with the Treasury, for the supervision and organization of personnel. And this was accompanied by a fundamental reclassification of the career structure of the Civil Service. From the old, confused hierarchy of grades – First Division, Second Division, assistant clerks, boy clerks, typists, messengers, etc. – emerged the principal career grades which are familiar today – Administrative, Executive and Clerical. Within these comprehensive categories uniform scales of pay helped to consolidate a new degree of homogeneity, transcending old departmental variations. Unfortunately, the inadequacy of those pay-scales had already done much to unify the service with a profound sense of grievance, but the Treasury was now moving away from its old, stony-faced posture towards clerical associations. Their petitions were no longer filed away, automatically marked 'nil'. The post-war Treasury sought to set the pace with national developments in improved labour relations and set up the complicated but ultimately successful machinery of Whitley Councils for negotiation and arbitration between the 'official side' representing the government as employer, and the 'staff side' representing civil servants as the employed.

All these measures, which transformed the Civil Service, were well designed to supplant the old idea of a despotic and inflexible Treasury with its new image as a creative agency of co-ordination. There was a greater interchange of personnel, and to meet its own expansion – from thirty-three in 1913 to nearly eighty by 1927 – the Treasury recruited widely from experienced members of other departments. It became deliberate policy to make first appointments to the Treasury only from among men who had served a promising apprenticeship in other government departments, and by 1942 twenty-two of the thirty-one most senior Treasury officials were found to have begun their careers elsewhere.

But while the implementation of these long-deliberated measures was leading to a broadening of the basis of civil service control, another line of development was tending to concentrate powers in the Treasury more narrowly than ever before. Its origins also lie in the war-time relaxation of Treasury control which had given departments considerable latitude to dispose their financial resources as they thought best. In place of the exact schedules of Estimates, approved by the Treasury and the House of Commons in detail, war expenditure had been granted by huge Votes of Credit upon which the Treasury had imposed only broad distributive limits. But the Comptroller and Auditor-General and the Public Accounts Committee had not ceased their vigil. Already in 1917 they were calling for a return to stricter control, and in the course of their inquiries they found plentiful evidence that departments had abused their freedom. In several cases, not only had legitimate Treasury control been flouted, but the protests of departmental finance officers had been over-ridden by ministers and senior officials.

This helped to emphasize the sophisticated concept that policy decisions and financial considerations should be inseparable. Already in 1872, as we have seen, the principle had been laid down by Treasury Minute that 'Accounting Officers' – i.e. the official responsible in each department for its efficiency and economy, as well as for the appropriation accounts it submitted to the C. & A.-G. – should be the permanent head of the department.

But this principle had been rather lost sight of by the First World War, and although in six cases out of ten the Accounting Officers were heads of departments, the exceptions included most of the major departments, particularly of defence, where any conflict of interest between economy and policy was likely to be most dangerous. The Treasury therefore firmly restated the principle in 1920, and, although the Public Accounts Committee questioned its wisdom on the grounds that Permanent Secretaries were already overworked, it was eventually conceded as the proper basis for departmental self-control. Henceforth, Permanent Secretaries have borne the full weight of responsibility for their department's economy and financial propriety, and it has ever since been axiomatic that 'finance is something integral with policy and cannot be dissassociated from it'.[18]

Like the creation of Establishment Officers, this reinforcement of the status of Accounting Officers helped to strengthen the collaborative element in Treasury control. But it must be seen in conjunction with the three final measures which were taken in 1919–20, each vitally important to the authority of the modern Treasury.

(1) The Treasury reorganization of 4 September 1919, which had divided the establishment between three functional Departments – Finance, Supply and Establishments – had put at the head of each a 'Controller' who was to rank in status with the Permanent Secretary of any other department of government. By implication, this itself elevated the Permanent Secretary to the Treasury to a new level in the Civil Service hierarchy, and, to spell it out, a Treasury Circular of 15 September informed the departments that he was to 'act as Permanent Head of the Civil Service and advise the First Lord in regard to Civil Service appointments and decorations'.

(2) Furthermore, on 12 March 1920 another Treasury Circular announced that the consent of the Prime Minister was required to the appointment or removal of Permanent Heads of Departments, their Deputies, Principal Finance Officers and Principal Establishment Officers.

(3) Finally, on 22 July 1920 an Order in Council consolidated the Treasury's authority over the Civil Service with the ordinance that '*the Treasury may make regulations for controlling the conduct of His Majesty's Civil Establishments, and providing for the classification, remuneration, and other conditions of service of all persons employed therein, whether permanently or temporarily*'.

Separately promulgated, these measures were well designed to form an interlocking whole, and they achieved for the Treasury, at long last, what the Exchequer and Audit Departments Act had achieved for the House of Commons – a completed circle of control.

The importance of this can hardly be exaggerated. At no time in the past had the relationship of Treasury control with the machinery of government been so logically formulated or so clearly enunciated.

While the customary and statutory authority of the Treasury had not been inflated in any way, its effectiveness had been considerably reinforced. The transformation was comparable in degree with the measures of 1668. Then, however, the Treasury's achievement had been by way of gaining some effective independence from the casual will of the Crown. Now its gain was by way of reintegration with the central will of government, particularly that of the Prime Minister. This relationship had been damaged in the recent past by dissensions between Chancellors of the Exchequer and Prime Ministers, but in 1919 the circular of 15 September was a clear reminder that the Permanent Secretary to the Treasury was also Permanent Secretary to the First Lord, and this was peculiarly timely in a period which had seen the sudden war-time development of a Cabinet secretariat and of the influential body of private advisers round Lloyd George known as 'the Garden Suburb'.

Indeed, taking stock of the changes which had accompanied the First World War, it is this which seems the most decisive development for the Treasury. Certainly, the way in which a section of the Treasury had been obliged to concern itself with problems of foreign exchange, currency, credit and price control, was historic and foreshadowed the developments with which the second half of this chapter will be concerned. But the body of regulations which consolidated the Treasury's position at the head of a reshaped Civil Service marks a point of maturity in the principles governing a major aspect of the Treasury as we know it today.

THE 'HEAD OF THE CIVIL SERVICE' CONTROVERSY

Unfortunately, the novelty of this achievement made it controversial, and criticism soon began to concentrate upon the ambiguities of the title 'Head of the Civil Service'. Its implications are still open to debate today for, as we shall see, there are perfectly reasonable grounds for questioning the present system of disposing senior Civil Service patronage. But it is significant that in the two periods when the Permanent Secretary's 'Headship' has been most stormily discussed – in 1926 and 1942 – the debate has been tainted by considerations which did not fully appear – considerations of politics and considerations of personality. It is not surprising that the author best equipped to discuss the issue, Lord Bridges, has done so with a certain scrupulous detachment. 'So many people have trampled about on the evidence that it is difficult to know what, even now, will be accepted as a fair summary of the position.'[19] That is fair comment. More nonsense has been written on the 'Head of the Civil Service' title than on any other aspect of the Treasury, and it is dangerously easy to add to it. But a few points about the controversy ought to be registered.

For example, the debate in the House of Commons on 14 April 1926 should be recognized as, primarily, an effort to add yet further discredit to the record of the late Lloyd George Coalition government. Based upon Sir Henry Craik's innocuous motion, 'that, in the opinion of this House, the Civil Service has merited the gratitude of the nation, but that its continued efficiency depends upon the control of that Service by His Majesty's Ministers . . . the debate was designed to condemn the administration for a thoroughly unwholesome and unconstitutional innovation in creating a new 'Headship'. How far it was, or was not, unwholesome was not seriously discussed, but its character as an innovation gave rise to some rather curious interpretations of Treasury history. Lloyd George quite correctly testified that it had always been the practice for the Prime Minister to call upon the Permanent Secretary of the Treasury for advice on senior Civil Service appointments. But he was skilfully disingenuous when he said 'I have never heard that there has been any new practice. The right hon. Gentleman referred to something in 1919, when the present Foreign Secretary [Austen Chamberlain] was Chancellor of the Exchequer, but he initiated no new practice – none. I cannot imagine what the right hon. Gentleman has in mind. . . .'[20] This evaded any reference to the novel Treasury Circulars of 15 September 1919 and 12 March 1920 of which the House of Commons seemed totally ignorant. However, the Treasury spokesman, the Financial Secretary, seems genuinely to have believed that the origins of the 'Headship' lay with the creation of the Permanent Secretaryship in 1867. He cited circumstantial evidence from 1872 and 1889 to prove that the title 'Head of the Civil Service' had always been linked to the Permanent Secretaryship, although it was impossible for him to be more exact because the original Treasury Minute creating the post had disappeared!

This seemed ludicrous enough at the time. It seems even more so now when it is known that copies of the original Minute were available elsewhere in Treasury papers. However, if found, the Minute would have caused even greater confusion for it has nothing at all to say about the 'Headship' of the Civil Service. Its nearest approach to the concept is to say that 'he [the Permanent Secretary] will have particular regard to all increases of establishments and salaries in the public service'.[21] It could not be known on the basis of this that the first, rather obscure, incumbent – G. A. Hamilton – did indeed see himself as the potential co-ordinator of a unitary Civil Service, and that his more notable successors, Lingen and Welby, were regularly described as 'Head of the Civil Service' in contemporary, semi-official documents. But this usage, of which the cases cited from 1872 and 1889 were a fair reflection, does not explain what was thought to be the content of the phrase. Was it any more than a reflection of the Treasury's self-esteem, an informal deduction from the Treasury's special status as the department of the premier?

There need be no doubt that, in this role, the late nineteenth-century Permanent Secretary did sometimes perform the sort of functions now associated with the Headship. Welby, 'the most powerful man in the British Empire', was regularly consulted by Gladstone about senior appointments and the distribution of honours, and this relationship was most likely to arise between a First Lord and the head of the Treasury establishment. It was less likely when the premiership was held outside the Treasury, and it was precisely this which clouded the relationship in the last decade of the nineteenth century, and the first of the twentieth. Thanks to Lord Salisbury, not much is to be heard of the 'Head of the Civil Service' in those years.

There is a similar imprecision in the sense in which the title was used to indicate an effective command of the permanent Civil Service. The Permanent Secretary's power (which was essentially the Treasury's traditional power) to adjudicate on 'all increases of establishments and salaries' certainly gave him an unrivalled authority and breadth of concern for the Civil Service which justified a reasonable interpretation of the title, 'Head'. But how limited the authority, and how modest the interpretation the evidence in the last chapter will have indicated. To add to it, here is a gloomy minute which Lingen wrote in his last months as Permanent Secretary, in 1884 (on a file dealing with the terms of service of Metropolitan Police Court messengers):

> The only mode at present by which uniformity can be introduced into any of the details of the Civil Service is by Order in Council, and even after such an Order has been agreed to by the Cabinet (which is necessary if it is to bind Ministers and others at the head of Departments) there is no security for its observance, unless it involves some payment which must be audited by the Comptroller and Auditor General. Probably there are many details connected with the organization of the Civil Service which the Treasury might usefully be empowered to regulate. But at present the Treasury has no such authority and its *advice* has a very limited operation against departmental interest or amour propre.

All this should reinforce the significance of the developments of 1919–20. By underlining the special relationship with the premier and consolidating the Treasury's authority over the Civil Service, they amounted to a substantially novel departure which Lloyd George could have been proud to confess. The post-war Civil Service had acquired a healthy new identity and its 'Headship' a positive new content. What had been, at best, a rather imprecise aspiration had become a serviceable reality – and the first beneficiary was well equipped to make the most of it.

WARREN FISHER, 1919–39

Warren Fisher came to the Treasury as Permanent Secretary on 1 October 1919, after barely sixteen years in the Civil Service. At the age of forty he had already put his mark on the infant National Health Commission and, as Chairman, on the Board of Inland Revenue. His evidence had had a strong influence on the recommendations of the Bradbury Committee (of which he had been a member) and it was his pressure which led the Public Accounts Committee to accept the reinstatement of Accounting Officers at the highest level of authority. But he took no responsibility for the peculiar reconstruction of the Treasury in September 1919. That was how he found it, and he didn't much like the arrangement which, he said, left the Permanent Secretary 'deliciously vague, floating somewhere rather Olympian'. It therefore cannot be assumed that 'he got himself designated Head of the Civil Service'.[22] It was Lord Milner, that formidable graduate of Gladstone's secretariat, who – in the finance committee of the Lloyd George Cabinet – framed the details of the September reorganization.[23]

Nevertheless, Fisher's energy and idealism were perfectly suited to his new status. He had a visionary faith in an integrated Civil Service which would rank in patriotic esteem beside Army, Navy and Air Force as one of the four Crown Services. This meant, for a start, breaking down all relics of complacent departmentalism, creating a new degree of mobility between departments for the Administrative grade and opening up recognized avenues of promotion to the highest positions for all ranks, high and low. Fisher was particularly attentive to the welfare of the lower grades of the Civil Service, which had been neglected for so long. He wanted their welfare and recreations attended to in the same way that the Forces attended to their own, and he pushed his campaign for Civil Service sporting facilities to quite unorthodox lengths. He told the Public Accounts Committee in 1936 – 'I have had myself to go round almost with a barrel organ and a monkey for these poor fellows to get things . . .'.[24]

The breeziness and exaggeration are fairly typical of the vigorous style in which Fisher tackled bigger problems. He was the quintessential new broom, and he sustained this zest for years.

For the Treasury Fisher's views were of particular significance, for he was wholly opposed to much of its nineteenth-century legacy. He utterly condemned the negative conventions of old-style

Treasury control, conveyed from the heights by chilly letters from 'My Lords Commissioners of H.M. Treasury'. He wanted it replaced in the Haldane image, by the friendlier concept of departmental collaboration in financial restraint, and that collaboration was to be worked out, face to face, by 'lively and vigorous discussion with other officers'.

Indeed there could be no more effective way of changing the character of Treasury control than by changing the character of the men who administered it. Fisher clearly detested the in-bred exclusiveness of the old Treasury *élite*. He shared much of that suspicion of Treasury men's narrow immaturity which had emerged so often in the correspondence columns of *The Times*. Instead, he wanted the Treasury recruited from men who had already served seven or eight years in other departments – men who therefore knew and understood their problems. It was no use taking them straight from the Civil Service Commission examination. 'If you do that, they then get to work and take their little pens in their infant hands and they write away little criticisms of every sort and kind, very clever ones no doubt, but there is no training for constructive work, or work that would enable them to get the practical experience that might make Heads of Department. . . .' The Treasury should be instead a clearing house, or – in his favourite metaphor – a General Staff, amicably co-ordinating the departments by constant discussion.

Of course, it could be (and it has been) said that Fisher was working off old scores. Once a clerk in the Inland Revenue he had experienced the rougher side of Treasury manners and, seeing the system from below, had learned to detest it. He was not, he sharply reminded a Royal Commission, a 'Treasury man'. But there was nothing narrow or destructive about his approach to Treasury reform. It fitted naturally into a coherent concept of the public service, and it is this – the breadth and humanity of his vision – which makes his the greatest single contribution to Treasury development at any time.

By 1930, when he was giving evidence to the Tomlin Royal Commission on the Civil Service, some of the fruits were already mature. His fellow-Permanent Secretaries were apparently happy with the new order, liking the new mobility of the administrative grade and the ease of consultation with the Treasury. And by 1936, when he was interviewed by the Public Accounts Committee, he could announce that he had overcome most of the inherent organizational defects of the Treasury as he had found it. The rigid, tripartite division of the Treasury instituted in 1919 had been broken down and instead of three Controllers of Finance, Supply and Establishments ranking as independent Permanent Secretaries, Fisher now had a more flexible, unitary system with a higher degree of interchangeability between the personnel of the Divisions. There had also been recruitment to the highest levels from outside the Treasury. Sir Robert Russell Scott, for example, had come from the Admiralty to be Controller of Establishments in 1920, and R. V. N. (later Sir Richard) Hopkins had followed closely in Fisher's footsteps, coming from the chairmanship of the Inland Revenue to be Controller of Finance and Supply in 1927. By 1931, two of the three Under-Secretaries of the Treasury were post-war additions to the Treasury with wide experience outside.

Perhaps it is significant (particularly for the discussion of the Treasury's economic policies, which follows shortly) that the pre-First World War generation of Treasury men remained most strongly entrenched in the pure finance side of the department. But it is also from this branch of the Treasury that there was a conspicuous flow of traffic going the other way, often to employment outside the Civil Service. In 1919, for example, there was an early symptom when H. A. Siepmann, a relatively junior official, threw up his Treasury post and shortly after joined the Bank of England.[25] This route was to be followed in 1927 by the Controller of Finance himself, Sir Otto Niemeyer, and two years later Sir Basil Blackett was enticed away from his distinguished career in the public service to join the Bank and other City boards. Meanwhile, Lord Bradbury, the youngest of the three Joint Permanent Secretaries displaced in the 1919 reshuffle, had been followed as Official Director of the Anglo-Iranian Oil Company by Sir George Barstow, Controller of Supply Services in the Treasury, 1919–27.

Internal upheavals were not the only price the Treasury had to pay for Fisher's dynamism. Nor was it merely his habit of commenting loudly and unflatteringly upon his contemporaries which made him enemies. Fisher put himself and the Treasury at the centre of controversy by entering forcefully into fields which were traditionally alien – those of defence and foreign affairs. Yet one must credit him with higher motives than self-aggrandizement. As 'Head of the Civil Service' he had set out with a low opinion of the professional leadership of the three armed forces, and, in the context of German rearmament in the early 1930s, this was overtaken by a profound anxiety about British defences, particularly in the air. It is ironic therefore that circumstantial evidence should have linked Fisher with the policy of appeasement after 1937.[26] This has to be squared with his highly constructive labours to equip Britain, not only with more air squadrons, but with the basic administrative machinery of defence. It was at his prompting that in 1933 the Defence Requirements Sub-Committee, with representatives of all four 'Crown

Services' (including Fisher for the Treasury), was set up to examine the whole problem of imperial defence. Linked to a Cabinet committee on defence it was reconstituted in 1935 as part of the urgent new policy of rearmament shortly announced in the Defence White Paper of March 1936. Fisher's own strong convictions of the German danger had some difficulty in making themselves heard in official declarations, but the White Paper presaged his most valuable contribution to defence preparations – the Treasury Inter-Services Committee, set up by Treasury Minute on 4 March 1936. Consisting of representatives of the defence departments under Treasury chairmanship, it was empowered to review defence requirements and sanction contracts and expenditure in advance of formal Treasury approval. This did not mean the abandonment of Treasury control; decisions were not reached by majority verdicts. But it did speed up the route by which the armed services made their needs known to the Treasury and introduced greater flexibility into the techniques of sanction. It was accompanied by a general relaxation in the atmosphere of inter-departmental relations. Negotiations on staffing and pay were, increasingly, carried on in the friendlier medium of semi-official correspondence, and decisions were reached at a lower level in the official Treasury hierarchy. Although defence ministers and service chiefs could still find Treasury control extremely irksome it does appear that it was wisely and deliberately prepared for the much more modest role it would perform in any future war.[27]

FISHER'S SUCCESSORS

None the less, evidence of Fisher's high-handed ways remains irreducible,[28] and it is easy to understand why he was believed to exercise a baleful political influence behind the scenes. Baldwin may never have said to him, as he said to Vansittart, permanent head of the Foreign Office – 'You are the most powerful man in the country . . . and you may boot me out if you like',[29] but Fisher exercised great influence on ministers, particularly on Neville Chamberlain. This adds plausibility to the charges of appeasement, but they appear to be more appropriate to Fisher's friend and successor, Sir Horace Wilson.[30] Wilson, who became Permanent Secretary to the Treasury in February 1939, had been a special adviser to the Prime Minister since 1935. It was in this role, which came to an abrupt end with Churchill's arrival in 1940, that he was actively involved in the diplomacy of Munich. It had nothing necessarily to do with his position at the Treasury as 'Head of the Civil Service'.

Nevertheless, his retirement on 1 June 1942 was the signal for another major onslaught on this title. For six months 'the sluices of bitterness' again flowed through the correspondence columns of *The Times*, and the troubled waters were assiduously fished from both Houses of Parliament. Fresh force was given to the torrent by a report of the Select Committee on National Expenditure which was highly critical of Treasury leadership in the Civil Service. Looking at the progress which had been made since the Haldane and Bradbury Committees, it reported that 'as far as the Treasury was concerned, the period from 1919 to 1939 was marked by an almost complete failure to foster the systematic study of organization as applied to Government Departments'. The handful of 'Treasury Investigating Officers', skilled in the application of labour-saving office machinery, were thought to be a derisory response to the demands for expert analysis of organizational problems. 'As a result of twenty years' neglect, the outbreak of war found the Treasury insufficiently equipped to deal with the problems of administrative organization which were forced upon it.'[31]

The Committee also looked at the crucial issue of the Treasury's supremacy, in the Civil Service as in financial control. Though it realized that 'there have indeed been times when antagonism between the Treasury and other Departments has been both an embarrassment and a hindrance to the work of Government', it felt that the Treasury's central position, its wide view of the whole range of government activities, gave it unique advantages which should not be wasted. Appearing at a time when feelings were running very high against the Treasury, this was a valuably balanced conclusion and probably the most constructive thing to come out of the controversies of 1942. About the newspaper correspondence, a significantly large proportion of which came from the disgruntled partisans of the diplomatic service, the less said the better. Arguments were again rather venomous and there was much inaccuracy of fact and illogicality of thought. But in the course of debate in the House of Lords on 25 and 26 November 1942, there emerged a formidably reasoned defence of the Permanent Secretary to the Treasury as 'Head of the Civil Service'. A few dubious historical arguments were effaced by the practical advantages which were shown to exist in a special, confidential relationship between the Prime Minister as First Lord of the Treasury (statutorily recognized as one and the same by the Ministers of the Crown Act of 1937) and his Permanent Secretary. Reflections on past occupants of that office were avoided and there seemed to be a general confidence in the future of a flexible, responsible advisory system centred on the Treasury.

This was soon justified by events. The uncontroversial tenure of

Sir Richard Hopkins, Permanent Secretary to the Treasury from 1942 until 1945, did much to allay the old resentments. Succeeding him at the end of the war, Sir Edward (later Lord) Bridges was sufficiently sensitive to his embarrassing legacy to make a personal point of not using the title 'Head of the Civil Service', but he found it to be a popular label which could not be easily abandoned.[32] He had only himself to blame. Returning to the Treasury, which he had served for twenty years, from 1919 until 1939, he brought with him the considerable trust and respect which he had earned from senior statesmen as Secretary to the Cabinet, 1939–45. There seemed to be no better justification for associating the leadership of the Civil Service with the head of the Treasury than the character and aptitudes of Lord Bridges.

This foundation was further reinforced by Sir Norman Brook (later Lord Normanbrook) who had also graduated from the confidential role of Secretary to the Cabinet, either as deputy or jointly with Bridges since 1942. But with his appointment to the Treasury in 1956 there was a significant change. His was a joint appointment with Sir Roger Makins, who was to be solely responsible to the Chancellor of the Exchequer for financial and economic affairs. Brook not only remained Secretary to the Cabinet (the post in which he had been specially retained by Churchill in 1951) but was designated Head of the *Home* Civil Service, responsible for the Establishments side of the Treasury's work.

This was a significant compromise with the claims of the Foreign service, and, occurring under Anthony Eden's premiership, was not to be wondered at. Of more lasting significance was the division of senior responsibility between the economic and the Establishments side of the Treasury's work. In 1962, when the next major reorganization took place, the dual arrangement was perpetuated. While Sir William Armstrong was appointed head of the Finance and Economic side of the Treasury, Sir Laurence Helsby became 'Head of the Home Civil Service', directing the Pay and Management Side.

That remained the position until 1968, and it has had its critics. But before reviewing the current organization of the Treasury it is necessary to pick up a cue from the way in which the 1956 appointments recognized the problems of economic and financial administration as a vast and distinct area of responsibility. It is not only the responsibility which bulks largest in the public image of the Treasury today but the one which directly and indirectly governs policy in the Pay and Management Side. The modern Treasury is therefore quite unintelligible without some idea of the scope and history of this task.

THE TREASURY AND THE ECONOMY

Fortunately, there can be no question of fitting a narrative of the last fifty years of British economic history into the scope of this chapter. It would be quite legitimate to begin an explanation of the Treasury's role as a ministry of economic affairs either with the budget of 1941, which was the first to be based upon a concept of national (as opposed to government) expenditure and resources, or in 1944, with the avowal of full employment as the official goal of public policy, or – most plausibly – in 1947, when the Treasury eventually acquired the statistical and administrative apparatus of national economic planning.

But the inter-war years cannot be written off as some meaningless dark age. Their memory continues to exert the influence of revulsion upon modern policies. They saw the painful and laboured reassertion by the Chancellors of both governing parties of the Gladstonian tradition of public finance, and they saw its ultimate eclipse. They also saw the formulation, notably by Keynes, of a radically different philosophy of financial management, and the tentative beginnings of its application. These historic shifts of opinion and policy produced remarkably few changes in the institutional character of the Treasury, but they eventually transformed its role in the 1940s and beyond.

The hollowness of the First World War slogan 'business as usual' did not invalidate the intention to get things back to normal as soon as the conflict was over. The immediate post-war boom shook prices loose of all restraints, the improvised system of state trading was hurriedly dismantled, and the slump of 1920 gave new urgency to the demand for slashing cuts in public expenditure. The authentic note of public opinion, loudly echoed from the press and political platforms, was sounded in 1920 by the Fourth Report of the Public Accounts Committee:

> The imperative necessity for securing economy in every department of public (as, indeed, of private) life, if national bankruptcy is to be avoided, is not yet sufficiently recognized. Nothing will accomplish it but a return to the almost forgotten tradition established by Mr Gladstone, and carried on by Sir Michael Hicks-Beach, under whom the financial policy of the State was 'by saving numerous pence to spend effective pounds'.[33]

Meanwhile, a less representative but just as influential definition of policy had been propounded by the Cunliffe *Committee on Currency and Foreign Exchanges after the War* in its interim report of August 1918. Charged with the same veiled nostalgia as the call for Gladstonian economies, it was a sober rhapsody on the pre-war gold standard system which, it insisted, 'should be restored without delay'. This meant, essentially, a system in which inflationary conditions in the British economy would be curbed by the harsh but almost automatic disciplines of free, international movements in gold. The Committee therefore argued for a restored gold standard with the prospect of a favourable balance of trade stabilized at the price of intermittent slumps, low wages and a flexible margin of unemployment. To the Committee, to the Treasury and to a wide range of opinion in public life there was no doubt that the price seemed worth paying.

However, there could be no easy return to normality. Indeed, in March 1919 the Treasury replaced its informal restraint on the working of the gold standard by a formal prohibition of gold exports, and the issue of Treasury notes had to be continued. But other measures were quickly taken to reduce inflationary pressures. The Bank rate was raised to 7 per cent and the Treasury bill rate became 6½ per cent. Strenuous efforts were made to reduce the gigantic burden of war debts and expenditure, which stood at roughly ten times their pre-war level. Of the £7,830 million National Debt in 1920 only £315 million was properly funded, and of central government expenditure – over £1,600 million in 1920 – about forty per cent was going in debt charges. It was in this situation that Stanley Baldwin made his anonymous gift of £120,000 towards the redemption of the National Debt.[34] Never, since Edward Chamberlain threw himself out of a window, had a Secretary to the Treasury made a more futile gesture. But it expressed the rather desperate sacrificial mood in which responsible men approached the financial situation, a mood in which there was much anguished talk about the *inadequacy* of conventional Treasury control. Thus, in August 1921, the businessman-Chancellor, Sir Robert Horne, set up a businessmen's committee under Sir Eric Geddes (formerly Minister of Transport) to supplement the normal Treasury efforts to pare down Estimates for the coming year. Set a savings target of £100 million they earned their keep by working out cuts of at least £86 million of which a heavy proportion (£18 million) was to be suffered by expenditure on education, compared with £21 million and £20 million from the Army and Navy respectively. In the event the government could only endorse a proportion of these cuts but the £6½ million taken from education undermined it for a decade and is a symptom of the generally regressive attitude to social expenditure in the early 1920s. That expenditure had, of course, grown enormously during the war, from a gross total (central and local) of £63 million in 1910 to nearly £300 million in 1920.[35] This reflected not only war pensions and automatic increases but enlarged commitments such as the emergency housing policy begun in 1919 and the five-fold extension of unemployment insurance in 1920. Its scale was unquestionably novel and frightening, vulnerable to panic economies. At the very least, orthodox monetary thinking and the vociferous public demand for tax alleviation ensured that welfare policy and welfare needs met each other in headlong contradiction.

Budgetary policy in the 1920s was therefore tormented by dilemmas all too familiar since, requiring the reconciliation of desirable levels of domestic expenditure with the maintenance of 'sound' currency policies abroad. Faced with the problem of huge debt repayments to domestic and foreign creditors there could be little hesitation over priorities; the pound's stability could not be jeopardized by inflationary budgets. Yet, even in this restrictive context, the budget of the first Labour government in 1924 strikes a curious note – a piece of deliberate antiquarianism, idiosyncratic of its author, Philip Snowden. With remarkable deftness the former Inland Revenue clerk affirmed the hallowed verities of orthodox nineteenth-century finance – maximized debt redemption, minimized defence expenditure, and, to crown it all, free trade. In abolishing the war-time McKenna duties Snowden severed his party from any remaining hopes of meeting new levels of welfare expenditure with the yields of protective tariffs. The climax soon followed. Presenting the Conservative government's budget on 28 April 1925, Winston Churchill announced the immediate return to a gold-exchange standard with the pound statutorily valued at its old parity of $4.86.

OVERSEAS FINANCE AND THE RETURN TO GOLD

This controversial decision, from which flowed so much distress, immediately opens up the question of Treasury policy, for it has long been part of the legend surrounding the episode that Churchill was 'led astray' by his official advisers. This view, first pronounced by Keynes, was one which Churchill himself came to believe,[36] but it should none the less be treated with caution. Churchill was certainly a novice, surprised by the offer of the Chancellorship (which he had taken to mean the Chancellorship of the Duchy of Lancaster!) and over-anxious to redeem the promise of his father's blighted career. But the notion of an administrative innocent being misled by 'evil counsellors' has been effectively questioned, notably by Professor Sayers.[37] Churchill was advised, of course, but by more than one set of advisers. There was, for example, a notable dinner-table debate between, on the 'old parity' side, Lord Bradbury and Sir Otto Niemeyer, and, on the critical side, McKenna (then Chairman of the Midland Bank) and Keynes. With McKenna's grudging agreement that 'you have to go back; but it will be hell' the 'Ayes' had it.[38] And there was much more to the debate than that. An early return to the old gold standard was not peculiarly a Treasury objective; it was explicit in all public policy since 1918, rendered imminent by the expiration of the Gold and Silver Export Embargo Act, and prefaced by the formal deliberations of yet another Bradbury Committee set up by Snowden in June 1924. This heard evidence from two former Chancellors of the Exchequer (McKenna and Horne), three economists (Professor Cannan, Sir George Paish and Keynes) as well as the Governor of the Bank of England and business representatives. It would seem fair to say that alternative views were not strongly, if at all, represented in the Treasury. The Treasury was indeed very deeply committed to the restoration, and, as Niemeyer admitted to the Macmillan Committee in 1930, he thought it should have been done sooner – in 1921 perhaps. As Controller of Finance, Niemeyer's impressive powers as an advocate almost certainly had a large share in convincing Churchill, permitting him the subsequent luxury of feeling 'misled'. Indeed, evidence now available makes it clearer than ever that Churchill fought with great prescience against the 'orthodox' policy and its consequences. However, the moralists have always been harsh on those who do wrong, even harsher on those who do wrong against their better judgement. The peculiar morality of ministerial responsibility has been no kinder to Churchill.

The aftermath of the return to gold was to reinforce the Chancellor's bitter complaint that the Treasury seemed blind to the domestic implications of its policy. Yet, in this respect, an important point ought to be stressed about the inter-war Treasury. To a degree which was quite novel in its history, and which was scarcely matched by any source of financial influence other than the Governor of the Bank of England (Montagu Norman), the Treasury's Finance department was now thoroughly cosmopolitan in its outlook. The insularity which had been a normal feature of its nineteenth-century forebears had been replaced by an active concern with problems of international monetary stability, and at any one time several of its members might be engaged in financial diplomacy abroad.

The Paris Peace Conference had started the trend by making heavy demands on 'A' Division. Keynes served there in several capacities, and it was Blackett who drafted the compromise reparation proposals on which the Allies eventually managed to agree. Bradbury meanwhile had become the chief British Delegate on the Reparation Committee (1919–25) and Andrew MacFadyean, of the Treasury,[39] initially secretary to the British Delegation, succeeded Arthur (later Lord) Salter of the Admiralty as Secretary General of the Commission in 1922. When MacFadyean became

Commissioner of Controlled Revenues in Germany in 1924 he was succeeded by yet another Treasury official (Armitage-Smith) while F. (later Sir Frank) Nixon followed Salter as Director of the Economic and Financial Section of the League of Nations. But the career which best demonstrates the Treasury's widened horizons is that of F. W. (later Sir Frederick) Leith-Ross, who was Deputy Controller of Finance in the Treasury, 1925–32, and Chief Economic Adviser, 1932–46.[40] He was a Treasury representative on the Finance Board of the Reparation Commission, 1920–25, British Financial expert at The Hague Conference of 1929–30, Chairman of the International Committee on Inter-governmental Debts and a member (and chairman) of the Economic Committee of the League of Nations, 1932–9. Meanwhile he went on the Treasury's War Debts Mission to Washington in 1933, negotiated a Financial Agreement with Germany in 1934, another with Italy in 1935, and, from 1935 to 1936, led a Financial Mission to China. Indeed, throughout the 1930s there were permanent Treasury representatives, at Assistant Secretary level, stationed with British Embassies in Berlin, Paris, Washington and the Far East. They were all part of an important new dimension in the Treasury's character which reflected the breadth and complexity of Britain's monetary problems.

Unfortunately, one of the most significant international ventures of the post-war Treasury was also the least successful – the Genoa Conference of 1922. This was called, at British initiative, to consider the economic reconstruction of Europe, and although America had now withdrawn from these post-war deliberations, the scope of the conference was large enough to consider the possibilities of world-wide financial cooperation. Indeed, on the financial side, the programme it adopted was close to being the international implementation of the Cunliffe Committee's report. The resolutions of the preparatory Finance Commission set out the urgent priorities of currency stabilization, under the direction of politically independent central banks, upon the basis of a restored gold standard. This, it urged, should be made a major objective of government policies. But, inflation – fed by government expenditure – stood in the way. 'The most important reform of all must therefore be the balancing of the annual expenditure of the State.' 'The balancing of the budget will go far to remedy an adverse balance of external payment by reducing internal consumption [Resolution 7].'[41]

As in the Cunliffe report, a restored gold standard and deflation – with its accompaniment of lowered prices, wages and some incalculable degree of under-employment – were implicit in the formulation of 'sound' financial policy. However, the visionary core of the proposals lay in Resolution 9, urging the creation of some international convention by which the world's demand for gold could be co-ordinated in such a way as to avoid violent fluctuations in its purchasing power. If the collaboration of central banks could be matched by deliberate government policies stabilizing national currencies at an agreed parity with gold then there might be some hope of maintaining steady prices and steady production, eliminating thereby the more painful consequences of the dreaded trade-cycle of boom and slump. The technical key to this solution would lie in the novel 'convention', supporting the gold-exchange standard with some system of international credit; but the basis would still rest upon orthodox budgetary restraint. That was indispensable.

The British representative on the Commission of Financial Experts at Genoa was Sir Basil Blackett, but the resolutions owed most to Sir Ralph Hawtrey, Director of Financial Enquiries at the Treasury since 1919. The problems surrounding his scheme are most interestingly set out in his books *Monetary Reconstruction* (1923) and *The Gold Standard in Theory and Practice* (1927). Unfortunately, the Russo-German agreement at Rapallo invalidated the Genoa Conference and subsequent events obstructed the chances of any international convention. As Montagu Norman explained in 1931, he had been unable to comply with the Genoa Conference's request that the Bank of England call a meeting of central bankers 'for the excellent reason that the people would not come'.

In addition, Britain was now forced to abandon her hopes of a comprehensive settlement of inter-allied debts and German reparations. Since her war-borrowing from America had been balanced by her loans to other allies – £1,030 million from the one, £1,740 million to the other – a comparatively simple cancellation on both sides of the account would have made good sense, but the U.S. government found this quite unacceptable. It had a mandate to treat European debts on a strict business footing and it was on this basis that Britain was obliged to negotiate. Inevitably, controversy surrounded the agreement which Baldwin eventually made in Washington in 1923 – even the Prime Minister denounced it. It seemed clear to the British public that, 'hard-faced' or not, the men who had done well out of the war were not on this side of the Atlantic. But the agreement to pay up at a rate rising from 3 to 3½ per cent over sixty years (which was abrogated by Britain in 1932) was another symptom of Britain's anxiety to re-establish the integrity of financial relations between nations, whatever the cost. The return to gold in 1925 was part of the same self-conscious policy – a high-minded gesture in 'setting an example' to the rest of the world.[42]

THE TREASURY AND THE SLUMP

Unfortunately, it was becoming increasingly difficult to reconcile the nebulous international benefits of this policy with the very palpable effects on the domestic economy. By 1921 unemployment had reached the unusual height of twenty-two per cent and thereafter it levelled off at 9–13 per cent (16–17 per cent among the insured), compared with a pre-war average of 4½ per cent. This reflected a seemingly permanent depression in the old staple industries which deepened rapidly after the return to gold. It soon became clear that the pound had been over-valued by some ten per cent, with the result that British exports were seriously handicapped by high prices in their shrinking overseas markets. The coal industry, already tormented by conflict, suffered further decline which, with its consequent wage cuts and lock-outs, was the immediate cause of the General Strike of May 1926. Thereafter, the British economy entered a slough of despond from which it did not emerge until the late 1930s, and although the pattern of causation is complex and controversial the return to gold has a secure place in the chronicles of error.

The ultimate relevance of all this to the Treasury is that it gave fresh vigour and much wider appeal to the dissenting arguments which were being worked out by J. M. Keynes. His dissociation from official policy had begun in 1919 when he resigned from the Treasury and published his *Economic Consequences of the Peace*. This shattering attack upon official Allied policy towards German reparations did not in itself mark a breach with his former Treasury colleagues. They too were committed to a reasonable estimate of Germany's capacity to pay as £2,000 million – the figure Keynes so cogently propounded in his book. Some, like P. J. Grigg, may have deplored the effect of Keynes's sensationalism on American opinion;[43] others, like H. A. Siepmann, may have found him personally insufferable; but the conflict of views on financial policy was slow in forming. Keynes thought highly of Hawtrey and their views had much in common in the early 1920s. Both emphasized the importance and potential of international monetary policy in eliminating the blind fatality of the old trade cycle. Both renounced passivity in the face of mass unemployment. But already in 1923, Keynes's *Tract on Monetary Reform* explored some areas of divergence between his views and Hawtrey's. He questioned the optimism of the Genoa resolutions and suggested that Hawtrey's ideal of a gold standard managed in conjunction with America 'retained too many of the disadvantages of the old system without its advantages'.

He argued instead for the maintenance of *internal* price stability by an enlightened Treasury and an active Bank of England. *Exchange* stability should be the secondary objective, but if compelled to choose between the two, 'the former is generally preferable'. The automatic, autocratic, gold-standard system was a barbarous relic which Keynes wished to see scrapped with all the other shibboleths of *laissez-faire*. This was heresy, of course, from which the high priests of City and Treasury alike were bound to recoil. But it was only the point of departure for his positive proposals. By 1924, his biographer has recorded, 'Keynes had completed the outline of the public policy which has since been specifically associated with his name – credit control to eliminate the credit cycle, State-sponsored capital development and, for a country in Britain's position, some check upon the outward flow of capital'.[44]

Of these, state-sponsored capital development revealed the most striking divergence with official Treasury policy, for, clearly, any extension of the already large scale of government investment in services and welfare would have run counter to the careful, deflationary budgeting which was leading up to the return to gold in 1925. For this decision Keynes therefore reserved his bitterest attack. In *The Economic Consequences of Mr Churchill,* a piece of widely publicized journalism, he made no bones about denouncing official Treasury advisers for having led Churchill astray. They had seriously miscalculated, overlooking the ten per cent disparity between the actual exchange valuation of the pound and the artificial valuation established by the Gold Standard Act of 1925. The consequence had amounted to 'a policy of reducing everyone's wages by 2*s*. in the £ ... for he who wills the end wills the means'. And the means necessarily included the deliberate intensification of unemployment. Keynes therefore measured out in human terms the sacrifice being made to the economic juggernaut of the gold standard. The underpaid miners, he wrote, 'represent in the flesh the "fundamental adjustments" engineered by the Treasury and the Bank of England to satisfy the impatience of the City fathers to bridge the "moderate gap" between $4.40 and $4.86. *They* (and others to follow) are the "moderate sacrifice" still necessary to ensure the stability of the Gold Standard.'

Keynes's proposals necessarily placed their emphasis on the human and social, rather than the purely economic, benefits of a deliberate policy of employment fostered by credit expansion and higher rate of government expenditure. But it would be an unpardonable caricature of the Treasury to suggest that it was blind or hostile to such ends. From the beginning of the severe unemployment of 1920 the extension of unemployment insurance had been accompanied by programmes of public works in addition to large existing schemes of capital investment. An unofficial Cabinet committee on unemployment was set up, together with a Treasury grants committee which distributed funds to local authorities for the employment of labour. It approved schemes totalling £115 million between 1921 and 1929, largely on road construction.

Unfortunately, this was just a drop in the ocean, providing work for a mere four per cent of the unemployed.[45] And even this was undermined by deepening Treasury pessimism about the efficacy of such a highly artificial stimulus to employment. As a short-term palliative, diverting resources from the tax-payer and stealing work from the future, state aid in public works appeared a highly questionable expedient which was paying diminishing returns. Thus, scepticism was the essence of the so-called 'Treasury view', and it was roundly stated by Churchill in April 1929 when he defended 'the orthodox Treasury doctrine which has steadfastly held that, whatever might be the political or social advantages, very little additional employment and no permanent additional employment can, in fact, and as a general rule, be created by State borrowing and State expenditure'. Even Hawtrey, who was one of the few economists to favour liberal monetary policies as the cure for stagnation, described public works as 'merely a piece of ritual convenient to people who want to be able to say that they are doing something, but otherwise irrelevant'.[46]

The Treasury view was directly challenged in 1929 by a Liberal party pamphlet embodying an ambitious Keynesian programme of public works. But a real confrontation between Keynes and the representatives of the Treasury had to wait until the inquiries of the Macmillan Committee on Finance and Industry, set up by Treasury Minute in November 1929. Its deliberations, which lasted until 1931, mark an historic confluence of orthodox and radical ideas on monetary management, and the encounter which is generally held to be the significant high point in its proceedings was that between Keynes (as member of the Committee) and Montagu Norman (as witness). In forcing the Governor to admit, eventually, that unemployment was the deliberately calculated price paid for the Bank of England's operations on the foreign exchanges, Keynes is generally held to have exposed the fundamentally malign nature of 'sound' monetary policy.[47] This may be so, but it oversimplifies the relationship between two modes of experience which had few points of contact. Keynes was expounding an hypothesis of monetary management which was daring and quite unproved. Norman took his stand on the instinctive judgements of a professional banker, and there is little sign that he comprehended the premisses from which Keynes questioned them.

In much the same way, the Treasury's official witness, Sir Richard

Hopkins, retreated as Keynes pressed him for some objective standard by which the value of a public works programme could be measured. Was it one which did most to reduce unemployment? Was it one which yielded a four per cent return rather than three per cent? 'Oh! no,' answered Hopkins, 'I see the logical dilemma into which you are endeavouring to drive me.' Instead, Hopkins claimed to take into account such imponderables as the 'atmosphere' in which schemes were started, their effect on public opinion, as well as practical estimates of their yield, their effect on unemployment and savings in dole. Ideally favoured were schemes which 'are in a natural development of a programme of economic development in the country', but he admitted, 'once you begin to apply a theory like that, personal judgment comes in'. This was the revelation of the Treasury's evidence, the flexible empiricism of the 'Treasury view'. 'It is not a rigid dogma,' said Hopkins, 'it is the result of the views that we take as to the practical reactions of the scheme.' 'It bends so much that I find difficulty in getting hold of it,' answered Keynes.[48]

Some commentators on this episode have accepted the Chairman's verdict that it was 'a drawn battle'. This may be a little generous to Hopkins, who did not choose to meet Keynes on his own ground. And Keynes's concession that 'the Treasury view has been gravely misjudged' may have been less magnanimous than some have supposed. What had emerged, surely, was that in the absence of any 'rigid dogma' there was the absence of anything in the Treasury view which could be given systematic theoretical expression. In thinking that there might be, Keynes had paid the Treasury an undeserved compliment which he withdrew with ambiguous courtesy.

This is not to say that the Treasury view was lacking in wisdom. Practical wisdom was its essence, and there is much of it to be found in the evidence given by Hopkins, Sir Otto Niemeyer and Sir Ralph Hawtrey (the last two speaking as private individuals). What seems lacking, in retrospect, was the degree of optimistic theoretical sophistication shortly to be supplied by the concept of the 'multiplier' – articulated by R. F. (now Lord) Kahn in 1931 and quite vital to the later writings of Keynes. This demonstrated that by setting up a sequence of economic activity, a certain degree of public expenditure in circumstances of stagnation had finite repercussions far in excess of the initial investment. This seemed the complete answer to the Treasury's pessimistic view that it was a lot cheaper and wiser to keep a man on the dole than to finance his artificial employment.

Yet fate was kind to the Treasury view in the 1930s. While the Macmillan Committee was still sitting the world economy tumbled into the 'Great Depression', and in Britain unemployment again rose steeply, placing an intolerable burden on government funds. With an unfavourable balance of trade, a budget deficit and a minority Labour government the country soon faced an international crisis of confidence. There was a heavy drain on gold. Conditions were therefore lamentably suited to the conventional disciplines of Treasury parsimony. Snowden, playing Gladstone to Churchill's Disraeli, advanced grimly on the public purse, bringing with him yet another businessmen's committee. The 'May' Committee, set up in March 1931, produced recommendations more alarmist, more severe, than those of its Geddes predecessor. Feeding the panic it was supposed to allay, it joined all the other pressures which forced Britain off the gold standard on 21 September 1931.

Thereafter, government policies were marked by a paradoxical yet viable adaptation of principles which, while not yet quite Keynesian, were no longer wholly orthodox. On the one hand, the final departure from the gold standard opened the way for a managed currency, by which the domestic economy could be protected from unfavourable fluctuations of the foreign exchanges. In 1932 the machinery of such management was created in the 'Exchange Equalisation Account' – initially £150 million, later £550 million – with which the Treasury could direct the sale or purchase of gold and currency to counteract speculative pressures on the pound. It is a vital part of our monetary defences today. At the same time, the final adoption of 'Imperial preference' and a system of protective tariffs in 1932 severed further mystical links with the orthodox past. Tariffs actually made little contribution to trade recovery but they were a necessary counterpart of other domestic measures of industrial reconstruction. For some years there had been tentative and rather grudging Treasury aid to business. The Trade Facilities Acts of 1921 onwards had provided cheap loans in aid of exports, and the Agricultural Credit Act of 1928 offered similar Treasury support for the farmer. Marketing agencies were set up under government initiative, and new areas of activity such as broadcasting and civil aviation joined old ones, such as shipping and railways, in receiving Treasury subventions. In 1929 a large measure of de-rating relieved agriculture and industry from tax burdens at the Treasury's expense.

The 1931 crisis and the May Committee enforced some cuts in these programmes, but most of them were eventually renewed and extended. Agriculture, housing, specific industries and 'special areas' received support channelled directly or indirectly from the Treasury. Above all, there was 'cheap money'. From 1932 a policy which lasted until 1951 kept interest rates down to 2 per cent. This not only helped investment, it relieved the Treasury. In 1932 a great War Loan Conversion reduced some £2,000 million of the National Debt from 5 to 3½ per cent, and the share of Debt servicing in government expenditure dropped dramatically from nearly 28 per cent in 1928 to 13·4 per cent by 1938.

At this point, the Treasury's economic policies can be seen to have been consistent with some of the old techniques of orthodox finance. Its essence, balanced budgets pruned of all vulnerable excess, was deliberately nourished by Snowden and his successor, Neville Chamberlain. Between 1931 and 1939 there was only one year of budget deficit (1932–3) and although public expenditure rose steadily, from over £800 million in 1931–2 to over £900 million in 1937–8, heavier taxation exerted an effective deflationary influence and there was no slackening of debt redemption. Unemployment benefits were first cut (as were salaries among civil servants, teachers and other public employees) and then restrained, and although the Unemployment Act of 1934 was a healthy measure of consolidation its main objective was economy. Housing experienced a great boom under 'cheap money' and state subsidies, but despite aid to special areas of depression there were no further large-scale programmes of public works. Apart from the effect of the re-armament programmes which began after 1936, government policy has been found to have exercised no positive influence on economic recovery,[49] and Britain entered the Second World War with 1,300,000 unemployed.

The implications of this state of affairs, in human terms of suffering and economic terms of wasted resources, make up the substance of posterity's indictment of official policy. Certainly, with public expenditure accounting for thirty-three per cent of the Gross National Product in 1938, it is impossible to discount the potential influence which government policies might have exerted upon the economy. Indeed, through control of 'cheap money' a new era in the possibilities of monetary policy had begun. Initiative had shifted, insensibly but decisively, from the Bank of England to the Treasury. By 1937 even Montagu Norman was willing to describe himself as 'an instrument of the Treasury'.[50] With the abandonment of the gold standard, he said, 'there took place an immediate redistribution of authority and responsibility, which deprived the Bank of some of its essential functions. Foreign Exchange became a Treasury matter and perhaps it still remains to be seen what other responsibilities pass with it from Threadneedle Street to Whitehall.'

But the ultimate comment upon the Treasury's all-too-modest economic role is provided by the Treasury Establishment itself. In 1936, of its eleven Divisions, only two were involved in pure financial policy, as distinct from the mixed financial and administrative responsibilities of the Social Service and other 'Supply' Divisions, and these two were seriously overworked. Warren Fisher expressed alarm about them to the Public Accounts Committee in that year. '2D', for example, responsible for overseas finance, was physically dispersed around the world, highly expert and irreplaceable. '1D', on the other hand, was bowed under the weight of domestic finance,

ORGANIZATION OF THE TREASURY ESTABLISHMENT IN 1936[51]

			Division		PAS	AS	P	AP/SO
		FINANCE	–1D	Home Finance	1	–	4	4
		–Under Secretary–	–2D	Foreign Finance	1	[4]	2	1
			–FE	Financial Enquiries	–	1	–	1
	–Second Secretary							
		SUPPLY	–3D	Social Services: Health, Labour, Pensions, etc.	1	–	1½	1
		–Under Secretary–	–4D	Education; B. of Trade; Agric. and Fisheries; etc.	–	1	2	1
PERMANENT SECRETARY			–5D	Defence; Dominions; Foreign Services; Colonies; etc.	–	1	4	
		ESTABLISHMENTS	–6D	Superannuation	–	1	2	4
			–7D	Civil Service	1	–	2	2
			–8D	Defence personnel	–	1	2	3
		–Under Secretary–	–9D	Post Office; Works; etc.	–	1	1½	1
			–10D	Other establishments	1	–	2	2
			–11D	Other establishments	–	1	2	2
		PRIVATE SECRETARIES:		Prime Minister: First Lord;		1	1	1
				Chancellor of the Exchequer		1	–	1
				Ld. President of the Council		–	1	–
				Financial Secretary		–	–	1
				Permanent Secretary		–	1	–
				Second Secretary		–	–	1

Key: PAS = Principal Assistant Secretary; AS = Assistant Secretary; P = Principal; AP = Assistant Principal; SO = Staff Officer

Notes: Owing to vacancies and absences the numbers given above do not account for the authorized establishment of the Treasury, which consisted of: 1 Permanent Secretary; 1 Second Secretary; 3 Under Secretaries; 1 Director of Women's establishments; 6 Principal Assistant Secretaries; 15 Assistant Secretaries; 28 Principals and 27 Assistant Principals or Staff Officers (regarded as interchangeable for organization purposes). The Assistant Secretaries [4], in 'Foreign Finance' were serving abroad, and one Principal divided his time between 3D and 9D. The 'Organization and Methods' investigating officers were directed by the Principal Assistant Secretary of 7D.

dealing with parliamentary supply business, public accounting, loans, currency, banking and the work of the Revenue Departments. It was also the watchdog for the financial aspects of the work of the Supply Divisions. Matters affecting the Exchange Equalization Account were dealt with at high level, by the Under-Secretary (Sir Frederick Phillips) or by the Second Secretary (Sir Richard Hopkins). Yet, judging from the evidence Fisher gave to the Public Accounts Committee, there seems to have been little place in this grossly undermanned organization for the broader, deliberative tasks of long-term planning – unless it was in the Financial Enquiries Branch.

But this consisted of little more than a man and a boy, the diminutive empire of R. G. Hawtrey and one assistant. Sir Ralph Hawtrey has been, of course, a remarkably productive financial theoretician. In addition to countless articles and learned papers he produced several of his major works between the wars and built up a substantial academic reputation. Between 1928 and 1929 he was a visiting Professor of Economics at Harvard. But it is not quite clear how seriously he was taken in the Treasury. Grigg has recalled how Churchill would demand, jestingly, that 'the learned man should be released from the dungeon in which we were said to have immured him, have his chains struck off and the straw brushed from his hair and clothes, and be admitted to the light and warmth of an argument in the Treasury Boardroom with the greatest living master of argument'.[52] Fisher, likewise, was a little jocular about Hawtrey, 'who works away on metaphysics and writes learned books and concerns himself primarily with the theory of higher finance. It is very difficult to define his duties, because, as I say, they always strike me as a bit metaphysical. . . . He is not engaged on any actual positive clearly defined practical functions the whole time in the way 1D and 2D are. . . .'[53] So much, it would seem, for 'investigation and thought as a preliminary to action' in the Treasury – although the impression is almost certainly unfair to Hawtrey's real influence on monetary theory.

Nevertheless, the axis round which financial policy formed was an extraordinarily frail one, and it was insecurely geared to the machinery of government. Warren Fisher, preoccupied with administrative and political affairs, cheerfully disavowed any competence to deal with financial technicalities: he left those to Sir Richard Hopkins, as did Sir Horace Wilson.[54] But Hopkins in his turn evidently lacked the confidence of his Under-Secretary for Finance as an arbiter of overseas financial problems. The latter, Sir Frederick Leith-Ross, felt himself frustrated by the narrow chain of command which led through Hopkins and Fisher to the Chancellor, and found relief only by transfer in 1932 to the post of Chief Economic Adviser.

But no hopes should be raised by that portentous title. We have Leith-Ross's word for it that it was a misnomer.[55]

If there is a paradox in the influence which this lightweight, ramshackle structure was able to exert upon ministerial policies then the clue probably lies close to the career of Montagu Norman. Recent studies of Norman have modified the myth of a Svengali, dominating stout-hearted Chancellors by black and irresistible arts. Arts there certainly were, worthy of a *prima donna*, but, in the face of them, Chancellors proved remarkably susceptible.[56] By the same token it was the deference of their masters which did most to guarantee the authority of the Finance Divisions. Nothing in the story of the 1929–31 crisis is more remarkable than the submissiveness with which the Cabinet received the most unpalatable of Treasury memoranda. The posture was broken only by rare and equally discreditable spasms of petulance.[57]

Meanwhile, outside the Treasury, there was a growing demand for a greater degree of co-ordination and planning of the government's role in the economy. Representatives of some parties – Ernest Bevin, Harold Macmillan, Sir Oswald Mosley – and the whole of the Liberal party, made it their major theme, yet remarkably little came of their efforts. In 1925 a Committee of Civil Research was allocated the duty of 'giving connected forethought from a central standpoint to the development of economic, scientific and statistical research in relation to civil policy and administration', but proved a rather frail and ineffectual vehicle for the now frail and ineffectual Lord Balfour. In 1930 it was supplanted by a body rather more impressive in its membership – an Economic Advisory Council. Keynes, G. D. H. Cole, R. H. Tawney, Josiah Stamp, Bevin and Citrine were among its non-ministerial members, and its secretariat included economists of the calibre of Hubert Henderson, Colin Clark and H. V. Hodson. Unfortunately, the kind of dissensions which were aired before the Macmillan Committee proved just as irreconcilable in the Council. And, if there had been a greater degree of unanimity on economic policy it would have found difficulty in communicating itself to ministers. The machinery of government was not yet linked to the power-supply of economic enlightenment – and the Council became a cipher.

THE SECOND WORLD WAR

It was the approach of the Second World War which injected new urgency into the demand for the co-ordination of the economy at the highest level of authority. For some months there was talk of an Economic General Staff, or a Ministry of Economic Affairs. And a significant trend appeared in these recommendations – a trend of hostility to the Treasury which can only be understood in terms of the controversies discussed earlier. From 1939 until 1942 the Treasury was under a political shadow which not only diminished its customary prestige and authority but disqualified it from access to the new centres of deliberation. At the very least, the Treasury was the victim of enduring prejudices against its supposedly old-fashioned, negative role. 'The primary function of the Treasury,' wrote *The Times* on 31 January 1940, 'is to say "No" . . .', and while this was generously conceded to be an admirable function performed by extremely able men, 'the qualities bred by it are hardly those required to transform our peace-time economic system into the kind of organization we need if all our resources are to be used effectively'.

The emphasis on 'resources' was rightly placed. It had long since been foreseen – indeed, the First World War had taught – that the key to any future war-effort would lie in the control of physical resources. The supply of raw materials, the co-ordination of transport, the organization of manpower and the direction of industrial production were likely to prove far more critical tasks than any manipulation of the foreign exchanges. The future clearly lay with such departments as the Board of Trade, the Ministry of Food, the Ministry of Labour, the Ministry of Shipping, the Ministry of Production . . . or, at least, with some novel authority of Cabinet co-ordination.

Thus, once war had broken out, the Treasury retained its central position only until May 1940 and Churchill's arrival at No. 10. Thereafter it was supplanted, at ministerial as well as official level, by other ministers and other departments. The Chancellor of the Exchequer, Sir Kingsley Wood, ceased for a while to be a member of the War Cabinet, and the Permanent Secretary's *entrée* to occasional Cabinet meetings was lost to the Permanent Under-Secretary of the Foreign Office. Minister and civil servant both lost their leading positions on the important inter-departmental committees of economic co-ordination, such as the Economic Policy Committees and the Production Council. Simultaneously, new agencies of economic planning grew up without formal ties to the Treasury. In November 1939 a Central Economic Information Service had been established under Lord Stamp, who was the residuary legatee of the Economic Advisory Council, and from this sprang, in January 1941, the Economic Section of the Cabinet Office and the Central Statistical Office. Churchill meanwhile had gathered round Lord Cherwell a small group of young economists who, in due course, became the Prime Minister's Statistical Section.

The success of these new agencies of professional, academic economists in establishing themselves within the machinery of government justly reflected the urgency of their tasks and the distinction of those who performed them. But in a period which saw the rise and fall of a great many *ad hoc* bodies their survival was very largely helped by force of personality in the minister who co-ordinated their work – Sir John Anderson (later Lord Waverley), Lord President of the Council. A superb administrator who had risen to the top of the Civil Service tree as Chairman of Inland Revenue and Permanent Secretary at the Home Office, Anderson was now at the height of his powers and, in Churchill's phrase, virtual 'Prime Minister of the Home Front'. His exceptional qualities ensured that 'the Lord President's Committee', set up in May 1940, emerged as the effective co-ordinator of economic policy. And this achievement gains in importance in the light of his appointment as Chancellor of the Exchequer in September 1943, for he took some of his responsibilities (e.g. for manpower) and all his influence with him. The 'renaissance' of the war-time Treasury is held to date from his appointment.

The way in which the Treasury (or any other institution) can be transformed or energized by the impact of strong personalities is a point always worth emphasizing, but it has its obvious dangers. In this case it risks obscuring the crucial importance of the work which the Treasury was doing, very successfully, before as well as after Anderson's arrival. However unpopular the Treasury might be in the short term, nothing could deprive finance of its central position in economic relations, and the course of the war very soon established the Treasury's primacy in certain lines of policy. Abroad, there was the vitally important conduct of 'dollar diplomacy' with the United States administration, and the organization of sterling area finance elsewhere. At home, in addition to the fundamental tasks of budgeting for a war, there were the urgent problems of borrowing, price-control and other counter-inflationary policies, and it was from these that one of the most decisive developments in the Treasury's modern role was to emerge when the budget of April 1941 clearly acknowledged the Treasury's concern for the balance of resources and demand in the economy as a whole.

This sounds commonplace enough but it reflected a revolution in the Treasury's budgetary thinking. Hitherto, the orthodox tradition, fundamentally unaltered since the nineteenth century, had based the annual budget statement upon (1) a straightforward assessment of the out-turn of Exchequer income and expenditure in the past financial year, (2) an estimate of the coming year's expenditure requirements, and (3) the proposal of fiscal changes such as were necessary to meet those requirements. This was what the Chancellor of the

Exchequer had described in 1939 as the 'annual problem play' in three acts.[58] It was, of course, part of a much larger drama – standing in relation to the production and consumption of the British economy much as a mere housekeeping account might stand in relation to the total earnings and expenditure of a large family – but the Treasury had nothing to do with that. Set in its nineteenth-century mould the early twentieth-century budget statement was, until 1940, primarily an Exchequer account unrelated to the sophisticated arithmetic of national accounting.

In fact, in 1940 that arithmetic was none too sophisticated, but it was developing swiftly at the hands of just those economists and statisticians who had been recruited to the government service. In addition, Keynes had turned his attention to the problem in the course of three newspaper articles, later reprinted in February 1940 as *How to Pay for the War*. In this, and a privately circulated 'Budget of National Resources', Keynes tried his hand at producing a national balance sheet of resources and the war-demands likely to be made on them. 'The problem,' writes his biographer, 'was how to prevent the total stream of effective demand, viz. that part of private income directed to consumption plus government expenditure, exceeding the resources available to meet it at existing prices.'[59] If they did exceed resources then they would set up that dangerous inflationary spiral of higher prices, higher wages, higher costs . . . with all that that would mean in labour unrest, social distress and a bankrupt war-effort. The first object, therefore, was to establish by this tentative arithmetic the 'inflationary gap' between demand and resources, and then set out to close it by taking the steam out of demand from private income with heavier taxation and voluntary savings. Certain irreducible pressures like scarcity, forcing up the cost-of-living, could be mitigated by subsidies, particularly on food.

These, in their bare essentials, were the administrative implications of the new approach. They required from the Treasury an attentiveness to the economy as a whole, not just to the public sector. They required some degree of responsibility for price levels, savings inducements, capital investment and other key financial factors in a healthily balanced economy. Fiscal policy was therefore completely reorientated, directed away from the stultifying concept of a balanced Exchequer account, to achieving the larger ideal of an overall balance of resources and demand. In inflationary conditions this could mean deliberate budgeting for an Exchequer surplus – extracting excess demand from the public by heavier taxation than expenditure strictly required. In recession it could mean (what had been so unthinkable in the 1930s) a deliberate budget deficit – priming the pump of economic activity with government expenditure markedly in excess of its income. That, of course, was the shocking reversal of the whole Gladstonian budgetary tradition, and, in so far as it was now accepted by the war-time Treasury, marked the long-deferred triumph of the Keynesian philosophy over the nineteenth-century orthodoxies.

To be fair, it marked a collaborative success for both the new vanguard of academic economists working for the government and the veteran representatives of the professional Treasury. Sir Richard Hopkins, shortly to succeed Wilson as Permanent Secretary, had fully grasped the significance of the new approach and he took the lead in pressing it upon the Chancellor.[60] He encouraged Keynes, who had re-entered the Treasury as an unsalaried adviser in the summer of 1940, and the basis of the 1941 budget was worked out in collaboration between Keynes, the Treasury's other economic advisers, and the staff of the Central Statistical Office. It was from the latter that the historic White Paper on National Income and Expenditure, which accompanied the budget, emerged.[61] Few, if any, war-time developments were more significant for the future of the Treasury.

It was complemented, however, by many other changes in fiscal and social policies, all symptoms of the same basic revolution in the priorities of financial administration. Purchase tax and pay-as-you-earn were devices which vastly broadened the base from which the state took; while food subsidies, and the comprehensive ideal of social welfare embodied in the Beveridge Plan of November 1942, similarly broadened the base to which it gave. At the same time, the range of technical financial devices which the Treasury could apply to the supply of credit and liquidity was greatly extended by a versatile National Savings movement, by skilful use of Treasury bills and the novel 'Treasury Deposit Receipts' to mop up any remaining loanable resources. Less important as finance for the Exchequer than as a curb to inflation these measures helped to justify the verdict that 'in the sense that financial obstacles were never allowed to obstruct the war effort, British policy in the Second World War was undoubtedly successful'.[62]

Nevertheless, although domestic policy spared the country the worst effects of inflation, there was high price to pay in terms of overseas trade and finance. Entering the war from a less robust position in the world economy than that of 1914, Britain's deficits were soon graver than any that could be solved by a freebooting, amateur 'A' Division. The creation of the Sterling Area by a series of regulations which culminated in September 1939 provided the basis for one part of the answer. A club of nations, not necessarily confined to or including all the Commonwealth countries, content to waive gold and use the pound sterling as their common trading and reserve currency, the Sterling Area reinforced London's traditional role as an international banker. In this role it had the inestimable trading and investment benefits of the sterling balances deposited with it, and during the war these balances grew huge as areas like India, the Middle East and South America accumulated credits representing British purchases and defence expenditure. By the middle of 1945 Britain's external liabilities totalled £3,355 million, and of the £2,723 million owing to the Sterling Area £1,732 million is estimated to have been incurred by Britain's defence of the countries owning them.[63] They constituted a huge liability on Britain's post-war trading position.

They were dwarfed, of course, by the volume of dollar aid received from the U.S.A., which amounted to some £5,000 million under the terms of Lend-Lease alone. Against this, the United Kingdom had provided £1,200 million in reciprocal aid, but – more important – had entered into agreements with the U.S. government which fundamentally adjusted her post-war trading and monetary policies. In the Atlantic Charter of August 1941 and the controversial Article VII of the Mutual Aid Agreement of February 1942, the United Kingdom pledged herself to reverse the kind of preferential tariff policies she had evolved since 1932. At Bretton Woods, in 1944, the agreement to set up the International Monetary Fund and the Bank for Reconstruction and Development, while designed to increase world monetary stability, also entailed some sacrifice of autonomy in British exchange policy. Enforced by America as a condition of the desperate 1945 Loan Agreement it directed the British government down a hazardous and, as it proved in 1947, a disastrous path. In the longer term, however, when alleviated by the Marshall Plan, the policies embodied in the General Agreement on Tariffs and Trade (GATT) and the International Monetary Fund have proved healthy, although by no means ideal, features of the post-war world.

But for the purposes of this narrative it is worth recording that they involved the Treasury in some peculiarly arduous negotiations. For, in addition to American neutralism and a real hostility towards the policies and being of the British Empire, there was a certain distrust of the British Treasury to be overcome. It is an ironical comment on all those efforts which had sought to produce in 'the Treasury man' the acme of cultivated intelligence that the American negotiators seemed to distrust him as 'too clever by half'. Consequently, behind the technicalities of Anglo-American negotiations there were some unexpected problems in human relations to be solved.[64] That they were overcome, most commentators seem to agree. Treasury officials, like Sir Frederick Phillips, Sir Wilfrid Eady and Sir David Waley, played important and fruitful roles in the course of this 'dollar diplomacy', and they were powerfully assisted and often led by temporary advisers like Keynes, who, if he created some of the peculiar difficulties in human relations, also did more than his fair share in solving them. He was the indispensable architect of the Anglo-American agreements which rescued Britain from her financial Dunkirk, and his sudden death in 1946 was not the least price paid for the Treasury's strenuous war-efforts.

To sum up, the war and its economic consequences – stated in the crude terms of monstrous debt, devastated resources and a shrunken capacity for recovery – absolutely determined the role of government in managing the immediate future of the British economy. There could be no question this time of a quick return to 'business as usual'. Direct controls of imports, consumption and savings were bound to remain in force for some time. But while all this could be foreseen with pessimism, there was a brighter side to the state's new responsibilities. Months before the General Election of 1945 committed the country to socialist policies of welfare planning, the Coalition government had pledged its successors – regardless of party – to the maintenance of a high and stable level of employment after the war. This meant, necessarily, a permanent commitment to government intervention in the peace-time economy, and for that reason the White Paper on Employment Policy of 1944 has been justly described as 'perhaps the most important single landmark on the way to the post-war policy of managing the economy'.[65]

For the moment, it meant no dramatic change in the Treasury's role. As long as economic management entailed a system of physical control on imports, manpower and production, the dominant tasks were those of the appropriate departments such as the Board of Trade and the Ministry of Labour. The Lord President of the Council in the new government, Herbert Morrison, retained the same co-ordinating functions which Attlee had lately performed under the Coalition, and although the Prime Minister's Statistical Section was disbanded the Economic Section and the Central Statistical Office remained distinct agencies attached to the Cabinet office rather than the Treasury. Later, in 1947, with Morrison's illness and amid economic crisis, the machinery of co-ordination was further elaborated without specific reference to the Treasury. An Economic Planning Staff of departmental officials was set up in May under the chairmanship of Sir Edwin Plowden, who had been designated 'Chief Planning Officer'. In June a new Economic Information Unit was created to advise the Lord President, and in July an Economic Planning Board (of employers, trade unionists, Permanent Secretaries and Planning Officers) was named to advise the government on the best use of economic resources for the short-term and long-term planning of the economy. Finally, on 29 September, as the climax to this sequence of improvised measures, Sir Stafford Cripps was appointed to the new post of 'Minister for Economic Affairs', presiding over the Economic Planning Staff, the Economic Information Unit and the Economic Section of the Cabinet office. The ailing Lord President thus lost his co-ordinating role. As for the Treasury, that too was supposed to be a department co-ordinated with the general plan – but that concept, suggests his biographer, 'was clearer to Sir Stafford Cripps than to his colleagues'.[66]

In fact, although King George VI advised Bevin that 'the treasury is only an accountant's job', Dalton, as Chancellor of the Exchequer, had soon acquired all the conventional autonomy of his office and clearly revelled in it. Like Snowden, he appears to have been readily captivated by the Treasury ethos, self-consciously enrolling himself in that great tradition which led back through Gladstone to Pitt. He was the kind of Chancellor who could not resist reflecting, as he revised the lower range of the Estate Duty scale in 1946, that he was treading on ground last visited by Harcourt. In April 1947 he triumphantly unveiled a balanced budget! Unfortunately, his ultimate contribution to the Treasury's development was to be a good deal less deliberate than that of the great Victorians. On 12 November 1947, shortly before delivering his autumn budget, he indiscreetly outlined its contents to a lobby correspondent who published it within the hour. The following day Dalton resigned. He was succeeded by Cripps, who took with him to the Treasury all the authority and apparatus which he had recently acquired as Minister for Economic Affairs. Only in this curious way, quite fortuitously, did the Treasury gain the essential ingredients of its modern character as a department of economic co-ordination.

SOURCE NOTES

1. Sir E. Bridges, *Treasury Control* (Stamp Memorial Lecture) (1950), p. 8.
2. *War Memoirs* (1933), vol. I, p. 61.
3. Sir R. Harrod, *The Life of Keynes* (1951), p. 197.
4. 'War and the Financial System, August 1914', *The Economic Journal,* September 1914, pp. 460–86.
5. W. R. Lawson, *British War Finances, 1914–15* (1916), p. 8.
6. Harrod, *op. cit.,* p. 205.
7. *Treasury Arrangement Book,* vol. VII.
8. Sir H. Clay, *Lord Norman* (1957), pp. 94–5.
9. Lord Beaverbrook, *Men and Power, 1917–1918* (1956), p. 99.
10. W. K. Hancock and M. M. Gowing, *British War Economy* (1949), pp. 3–12.
11. S. Pollard, *The Development of the British Economy, 1914–1950* (1962), p. 69.

12. S. E. Harris, *Monetary Problems of the British Empire* (1931), p. 125; E. V. Morgan, *Studies in British Financial Policy, 1914–25* (1952), p. 143.
13. *P.P. 1888*, vol. XXVII (Cmd 5545), *Second Report of the Royal Commission on Civil Establishments,* p. xii.
14. P.P. *1903*, vol. VII (H.C. 242), *Report from the Select Committee on National Expenditure,* p. iv.
15. *P.P. 1914*, vol. XVI (Cmd 7338), *Fourth Report of the Royal Commission on the Civil Service,* p. 86, paras. 96–9.
16. P.P. *1918*, vol. XII (Cmd 9230), *Ministry of Reconstruction: Report of the Machinery of Government Committee,* Part II, pp. 17–21.
17. Sir Thomas L. Heath, *The Treasury* (1927), p. 122.
18. 'Treasury Control of Expenditure', Memorandum submitted by the Treasury, *Sixth Report from the Select Committee on Estimates* (1957–8), p. 3, para. 20.
19. Lord Bridges, *The Treasury* (2nd edn, 1966), pp. 173–4.
20. *H.C. Debates, 1926* (5th Series, Vol. 194), cols. 331–4.
21. The Minute of 10 May 1867 creating the Permanent Secretaryship to the Treasury is printed in Appendix VII to Bridges, *The Treasury*, p. 233.
22. P. J. Grigg, *Prejudice and Judgment* (1948), p. 51.
23. See Sir H. P. Hamilton, 'Sir Warren Fisher and the Public Service', in *Public Administration,* vol. XXIX, spring 1951, p. 11, quoting evidence given by Lord Geddes in the House of Lords, 26 November 1942.
24. *P.P. 1935–36*, vol. V. *First and Second Reports from the Committee of Public Accounts,* Evidence, Q. 4480.
25. In a curious story, involving Keynes and hot-water bottles, Siepmann's brother has shed some light on this resignation: E. O. Siepmann, *Confessions of a Nihilist* (1955), p. 41.
26. See, for example, Lord Avon, *Facing the Dictators* (1962), p. 447; I. Colvin, *Vansittart in Office* (1965), pp. 147–8; D. C. Watt, 'Sir Warren Fisher and Rearmament', in D. C. Watt, *Personalities and Policies* (1965), p. 115.
27. J. D. Scott and R. Hughes, *The Administration of War Production* (1955), Chapter 15; W. Ashworth, *Contracts and Finance* (1953), Chapter 2. Both these volumes are part of the Official History of the Second World War, U.K. Civil Series. For more critical, private views on Treasury control of defence see R. J. Minney, *The Private Papers of Hore-Belisha* (1960), pp. 170–77.
28. See, for example, *The Memoirs of the Rt. Hon. the Earl of Woolton* (1959), pp. 138–9.
29. Colvin, *op. cit.*, p. 31.
30. M. Gilbert and R. Gott, *The Appeasers* (1962).
31. *P.P. 1941–42*, vol. III (H.C. 120), *Sixteenth Report from the Select Committee on National Expenditure, 1941–42: Organization and Control of the Civil Service.*
32. Bridges, *The Treasury*, p. 176.
33. *Fourth Report of the Public Accounts Committee* (1920), para. 43.
34. See 'Baldwin and the Right' by R. Blake in *The Baldwin Age* (1960), ed. J. Raymond, p. 34.
35. U. K. Hicks, *The Finance of British Government, 1920–36* (1938), Appendix Table 6, p. 383.
36. *Memoirs of the Rt. Hon. the Earl of Woolton* (1959), p. 374; Grigg, *op. cit.,* p. 180.
37. R. S. Sayers, 'The Return to Gold, 1925', in *Studies in the Industrial Revolution* (1960), ed. L. S. Pressnell.
38. Grigg, *op. cit.,* p. 184.
39. Sir A. MacFadyean, *Recollected in Tranquillity* (1964).

40. Since this was written, Sir Frederick Leith-Ross has published his autobiography: *Money Talks* (1968). Some comments drawn from this useful record are inserted, below, pp. 271–2.
41. *P.P. 1922*, vol. XXIII (Cmd 1650), *International Economic Conference, Genoa: Resolutions of the Financial Commission*, p. 3.
42. For the concept of setting an example, see the evidence of Sir Robert Kindersley to the Macmillan Committee (Evidence, Q. 1575 *et seq.*) cited by A. J. Youngson, *The British Economy, 1920–1957* (1960), p. 236.
43. Grigg, *op. cit.*, p. 104.
44. Harrod, *op. cit.*, p. 350.
45. K. J. Hancock, 'The Reduction of Unemployment as a Problem of Public Policy, 1920–29', *The Economic History Review*, 1962, pp. 335.
46. K. J. Hancock, 'Unemployment and the Economists in the 1920s', *Economica*, 1960, p. 311.
47. Harrod, *op. cit.*, p. 418; Youngson, *op. cit.*, p. 252.
48. Committee on Finance and Industry, 1931, Minutes of Evidence for 16 and 22 May 1930 (evidence of Sir Richard Hopkins), QQ. 5625, 5627.
49. H. W. Richardson, *Economic Recovery in Britain, 1932–9* (1967), p. 230.
50. Clay, *op. cit.*, p. 437.
51. *P.P. 1935–36*, vol. V. *First and Second Reports from the Committee of Public Accounts*, Appendix VIII.
52. Grigg, *op. cit.*, p. 82.
53. *P.P. 1935–36*, vol. V. *First and Second Reports from the Committee of Public Accounts*, Evidence, Q. 4529.
54. See *Public Administration*, summer 1956, for an appraisal of Hopkins's career.
55. Leith-Ross, *op. cit.*, pp. 144–6. (For '1938' in the second paragraph on his p. 144 read '1928'.)
56. A. Boyle, *Montagu Norman* (1967), p. 150 ('Sir Robert Horne, a fairly malleable character whose docile reactions to the magnetic charm of the Governor resembled those of a favourite pupil to a benevolent headmaster'); p. 179 ('Now Norman found Churchill in the receptive and responsive mood of a backward pupil who was willing to be taught'); p. 242 ('In 1929, as in 1924, Philip Snowden at once succumbed to the charm as well as to the policy of the Governor').
57. R. Skidelsky, *Politicians and the Slump* (1967). For examples of Cabinet submissiveness, see pp. 101, 217–18, 240, 388, 391; for remarkable instances in which Snowden, as Chancellor, and MacDonald, as Prime Minister, dissociated themselves from official Treasury policies, see footnote 2, p. 288.
58. Quoted by Bridges, *The Treasury*, p. 89.
59. Harrod, *op. cit.*, p. 492.
60. R. Stone, 'The Use and Development of National Income and Expenditure Estimates', in *Lessons of the British War Economy* (1951), ed. D. N. Chester, p. 85.
61. Stone, one of the authors of the survey, describes its creation in the essay cited above.
62. R. S. Sayers, *Financial Policy 1939–45* (1956), p. 21.
63. *ibid.*, p. 439; Hancock and Gowing, *op. cit.*, p. 111.
64. On this interesting and peculiar problem see Sayers, *op. cit.*, p. 380; R. N. Gardner, *Sterling-Dollar Diplomacy* (1956), pp. 111, 201; and Harrod, *op. cit.*, pp. 506–7, 529, 557.
65. Bridges, *The Treasury*, p. 92.
66. C. Cooke, *The Life of Sir Richard Stafford Cripps* (1957), p. 362.

CHAPTER 9

The Treasury and the Post-War Economy: 1947-68

Ignorance is not so damnable as humbug,
but when it prescribes pills it may happen to do more harm.
GEORGE ELIOT, Felix Holt the Radical

THE BEGINNING OF AN ERA

The ministerial arrangements of November 1947 might be argued to mark some sort of climacteric in the Treasury's evolution. Here, one could say, the Treasury attained a zenith of responsibility and power which, in the broad context of several hundred years, resembles a terminus to developments that got under way in the late seventeenth century. Given the economic, social and political compulsions that now required the state to regulate the national economy, then the measures which consolidated this task in the Treasury have a logical finality which subsequent events, such as the creation of the Department of Economic Affairs in 1964, have not undermined. The twenty years since 1947 acquire the characteristics of an epilogue.

But that would be a crassly academic point of view which I do not propose to endorse. The arrangements of 1947 had some logic but no necessary finality, and to think of the years since as an epilogue empties them of their significant content. They have been years which have seen a unique intensity of challenge to the assumptions and conventions which govern the Treasury, and there have been responses, rather less vigorous but no less important, from the Treasury itself. Twice, in 1956 and 1962, the Treasury has experienced noteworthy internal changes. Repeatedly, its relationships within the machinery of government have been adjusted. The concept of Treasury control has been refined and the techniques of economic management progressively developed under stress. 1947 marked a beginning, not an end.

Unfortunately, that makes it difficult to wind up this long narrative of evolution. Nothing could be more convenient at this point than a belief that the British financial system is in a high degree complete, sacrosanct – requiring nothing more from its historian than a reverent valediction. Indeed, a book of this kind should be the last to deny that the system, from the quaintly named 'Chancellor of the Exchequer' downwards, is only intelligible in terms of its centuries of development. A glance at the parliamentary context in which the Treasury exercises its powers will reveal all the traditional features of the system crowned by the Exchequer and Audit Departments Act of 1866. That is still the keystone of the system of estimate, appropriation and audit, and it is flanked by the complementary pillars of Victorian financial propriety, the Comptroller and Auditor-General and the Public Accounts Committee. Even older are the conventions which still govern the supply procedures of the House of Commons. They are basically those of the late seventeenth, and early eighteenth, centuries, manipulated by those residuary legatees of Hanoverian politics 'My Lords Commissioners of Her Majesty's Treasury'. Here and there in its proceedings language floats to the surface which would have sounded sweetly in the ears of Queen Elizabeth I, and one may even catch an occasional glimpse of what seems to be the very ancient prerogative of the Crown in the power of the Treasury to sanction expenditure in advance of parliamentary authorization. It is a power circumscribed by statute; the Civil Contingencies Fund from which the Treasury produces its extra-parliamentary resources is a sum now limited to £75 million and the issue is subject to retrospective parliamentary approval. But some have seen in this the vestigial authority of the Executive to act, in emergency, as it thinks fit,[1] and it is certainly a commonplace that 'Treasury control' has immemorial foundations in the prerogatives of the Crown.

But this sort of antiquarianism is not a particularly helpful approach to the forces which are shaping the late-twentieth-century Treasury. Anachronisms may form part of its fabric, but – though cynics will question this – they scarcely embody the spirit or even the letter of current practices. The Exchequer and Audit Departments Act, for example, was significantly amended in 1921 by an Act of the same title. It liberalized the Comptroller and Auditor-General's duties, giving him greater freedom to pursue a selective audit of a range of departmental activities far wider and more complex than anything which had been dreamed of in the days of Gladstonian 'candle-ends'. The consequence has been less pedantry and more penetration in his inquiries. Meanwhile, his parliamentary counterpart, the Public Accounts Committee, strengthened from an original nine members to fifteen in 1893, has been joined by an Estimates Committee, appointed to 'examine such of the estimates presented to the House as may seem fit to the committee, and report how, if at all, the policy implied in those estimates may be carried out more economically'. First set up in 1912, on lines recommended by the 1902 Select Committee on National Expenditure, it nearly withered under the chill breath of Treasury disapproval, but is now vigorous and mature, deploying some thirty-six M.P.s in specialized committees of inquiry.* There will be more to say about it and the 1956 Select Committee on Nationalized Industries in another part of this chapter, but reference to these institutions indicates that the machinery of nineteenth-century financial control has been overlaid, if not superseded, by change. Subtler changes have also modified the supply procedures of the House of Commons, although for political rather than administrative motives. In the process, the Executive has acquired mastery of the business of the House at the expense of those heroes of nineteenth-century parsimony, the back-benchers, whether on the government or the opposition side. It is now an academic question, in more than one sense, whether parliamentary financial control has any substantial meaning.[2]

But, has there been a similar transmutation of the Treasury? How far removed is the Treasury of the 1960s from – say – the Treasury of the 1930s? What has happened in the last twenty years to modify its institutional character?

An answer could plausibly begin with the matter of scale. A Department now numbering over 1,700 (about 170 of them in the Administrative grade) is virtually unrecognizable to any veteran of the pre-war Treasury, and the physical changes go further than the removal of the establishment from its elegant eighteenth-century home, Kent's Treasury, to the extravagantly gaunt chambers of the New Public Buildings in Great George Street. With five ministers, two of them in the Cabinet, with about thirty-five divisions, and a complex distribution of functions, the structure of the Treasury is more intricate than it has ever been. But it soon becomes obvious that explanation must begin at a different level, with the scale of the state's involvement in the economy at large, now of such an order that it has compelled qualitative changes in the character of Treasury control. This, more than anything else, has modified the Treasury's historic functions and come near to severing it from its past. And another phenomenon, closely related to it, has made an unwelcome contribution to the Treasury's modern image: the recurrence of crisis in the post-war British economy. Much has followed from this. The increased range of government intervention in the economy is

* Between 1960 and 1967 its membership stood at forty-three, but in the Session of 1967–8 the numbers were reduced to thirty-six in anticipation of the appointment of two or three new specialist committees, for Science and Technology, for Agriculture and perhaps for Education. *First Special Report from the Estimates Committee* (1967–8), 29 November 1967.

more obviously an effect than a cause of this state of affairs, and we have not yet seen the end of the development. In addition, it has set up a dialogue of criticism which has subjected the Treasury to an unusually intense scrutiny. So far as it has led to constructive reforms, this urgent debate must be counted as one of the major factors shaping the life of the department.

I propose to deal with these two themes – scale and crisis – in that order. Each relates to the two main dimensions of the Treasury's work: the first, to its control of Supply and Establishments, the second to its management of the public sector of the national economy, and although it is artificial to separate them in this way there may be some consequent gain in clarity.

THE REFORM OF TREASURY CONTROL, 1947–64

THE GROWTH OF PUBLIC EXPENDITURE

The growth of the public sector in relation to Gross National Product is a phenomenon common to all advanced economies in the twentieth century. The increasing wealth of the community, accompanied usually by intensified urbanization, tends to create needs for government services, such as communications, education and welfare services, at a faster rate than it eliminates other needs, such as poor or unemployment relief. Simultaneously, with or without inflation, prosperity draws a steeply rising volume of income within the orbit of a tax system which is significantly slow to adjust itself downwards, and revenue, as Gladstone understood so well, creates its own expenditure.

In the United Kingdom, war, in particular, increased public expenditure – not just by creating defence needs and huge debt problems, but because the social and administrative circumstances of war are favourable to growth, or promises of growth, in social welfare services. Unemployment relief, health and education services have been the principal beneficiaries of both World Wars, raised by political decisions far further than could have been predicted from their pre-war rates of growth. And this has led to a change in the proportion that one form of government expenditure bears to another. Debt repayments, once so large a part of nineteenth-century government expenditure, have fallen from over forty per cent in the 1840s, twenty-five per cent in the 1930s, to less than ten per cent in the 1960s, while social services (thirty-two per cent in 1910, forty-seven per cent in 1961) have long since outstripped defence (twenty-seven per cent in 1910, twenty per cent in 1961). The administrative costs of government, fourteen per cent in 1910, are a relatively tiny item at seven per cent in the 1960s.[3]

Local government expenditure, as a proportion of total government expenditure, has declined from its high point in the late nineteenth and early twentieth centuries, when it was between forty and fifty per cent, to barely twenty-five per cent in the 1960s,[4] implying a greatly increased degree of centralization in the control of the public sector. How far the nationalized industries fit into this picture is arguable. Although publicly owned they are administratively autonomous and their current expenditure (if not their deficits) is their own responsibility. They (and that 300-years-old government monopoly, the Post Office, is joining them) are required to make profits like any other commercial undertaking – profits from which they can help to finance their own capital needs. But those needs do require Treasury loans, and although they do not constitute a tax burden (unlike their deficits), being raised in the ordinary market, the fact that the capital requirements of the nationalized industries accounted by 1955 for forty-four per cent of the public sector's capital formation is a significant point, for the public sector, in its turn, accounted for forty-five per cent of domestic capital formation. Briefly, this is all part of a secular process in which United Kingdom public expenditure has been seen to grow from fourteen per cent of Gross National Product in 1900 to thirty-eight per cent in 1961. The rate of increase, according to the same source,[5] has been 3·7 per cent per annum over the period 1890–1961, compared with the slower cumulative growth rate of 1·5 per cent in G.N.P.

This phenomenon has been the point of departure for successive appraisals of the Treasury's modern role, such as the 1961 Plowden Report on the *Control of Public Expenditure* and the 1964 Stamp Lecture by Sir Richard Clarke. In *The Management of the Public Sector of the National Economy*, Clarke (then a Second Secretary in the Treasury) depicted the novel critical approach which management studies and cost/effectiveness research brought to bear on the large-scale use of national resources. He also noted the continuity of thought between his approach and that of a 1950 Stamp Lecture on *Treasury Control*. In this, Lord Bridges had assessed the implications of the war-time revolution in budgetary concepts which meant that the Treasury's 'prudent housekeeping' was now a 'judicious blend' of departmental self-control and Treasury supervision. On this crucial role Lord Bridges championed the Treasury man as arbiter; a lay-critic dealing with experts, perhaps, but skilled in 'weighing up facts and testing evidence and judging men' against common-sense administrative standards. He concluded on a note of nostalgia for the sturdy traditions of old-style Treasury control. It is reasonable, therefore, to feel some gap, not continuity, between the approaches of 1950 and 1964. Writing on Treasury control in 1954, ex-Treasury official Sir John Woods suggested that the increase in government expenditure had 'not yet been matched by a sufficient adaptation of the rules governing Treasury control', and he was shortly to argue this before a most influential Parliamentary inquiry.

THE ESTIMATES COMMITTEE REVIEW OF TREASURY CONTROL, 1957–8

At the end of 1957 the Select Committee on Estimates deputed a sub-committee to make an inquiry into Treasury control of expenditure. It took evidence between January and May 1958 and reported in late July. From it stemmed the Plowden inquiry into the control of public expenditure, the major Treasury reorganization of 1962 and a whole sequence of change which we are still absorbing.

The report of the Select Committee and the often entertaining, always interesting, evidence given before it is therefore essential reading for anyone concerned with the recent evolution of the Treasury. At least it succeeded in penetrating the character and vocabulary of Treasury control more effectively than any preceding parliamentary inquiry – although that is not saying much. Though it had its own limitations it became the healthiest post-war dialogue between the Treasury and its parliamentary masters. They forced the Treasury to think again. In fact, the Treasury had been thinking quite hard about the special problems of Treasury control in the post-war world, with its vast, complex and often quite unpredictable expenditures on defence and social welfare. As far as administrative reform was concerned, the Treasury could boast that it 'had had a hand in the setting up of Committees of Enquiry into the top structure of almost all the major Departments over the past ten years'.[6] It had even reviewed itself, albeit with 'comforting' results! As for expenditure, it could tell the committee that a technique of 'forward looks' and long-term planning was being evolved, and that the extent of the financial responsibility that could be 'delegated' to the departments was under constant review. Indeed, relations between the Treasury and the departments seemed generally good, as several were to testify. When the Permanent Secretary of the Ministry of Health was offered an idea which thousands must have savoured at some time or other – i.e. suppose the Treasury was blown up overnight, how would you feel? – he replied without irony 'Total regret . . . I should feel a great many helpful friends had been removed from us, whom we would miss in our official life' (Q.1234, 1236; but cf. Q.2417). Other officials were to endorse this sense of collaborative intimacy. 'The Treasury division is so close to us,' said the Permanent Secretary of the Ministry of Agriculture, 'that I do not believe that if the head of the division sat in the office instead of near his superiors, he would know any more or be any more effective' (Q.1174). Cooperation on policy was such that 'it is not always quite easy to determine from where the initiative actually comes' (Q.1101). Even the witness for the Foreign Office warned the committee against regarding the Treasury and the Foreign Office 'as being on opposite sides of the table in day-to-day work. We work very closely with the Treasury' (Q.1452).

It would be too much to suppose that all was harmony between the Treasury and the departments, only six of which gave evidence. 'Differences of view – sharp differences of view – do arise. I do not think we are a gutless Department,' said the principal Treasury witness. But this evidence on Treasury–departmental relations makes pleasanter reading than anything comparable before 1945. It demonstrates the considerable progress which had taken place since the advent of Warren Fisher or, indeed, since the Second World War.

However, the Select Committee deferred the large question of Treasury control of Establishments to a later inquiry. Their immediate object, as it seems to emerge from the questions, was to pin down a suspected inconsistency between the ideal of departmental self-control – long since extolled by the Haldane Committee and by Warren Fisher – and an actual practice of Treasury control which was feared to be 'niggling' and short-sighted.

But, for a proper understanding of their approach, it would be well to adopt the useful analytical framework used in the Report, which wisely began by noting the absence of anything like a coherent *system* of Treasury control. 'What is called "Treasury control" is better described as a complex of administrative practice that has grown up like a tree over the centuries, natural rather than planned, empiric rather than theoretical.'[7] Founded on no single statute, it was only partially defined in such documents as the Exchequer and Audit Departments Act of 1866 or the Treasury Minute of 1868. Its boundaries were blurred and curious anomalies limited its scope. At one extreme there was the Admiralty with large powers to incur refit-expenditure under an authority which dated back to the days of James II. At the other, there was the Ministry of Works with its unchartered freedom to replace electric-light bulbs in government departments without Treasury authority. In between lay vast tracts of expenditure in which the departments might, or might not, move without Treasury sanction. They had to be explored with care.

However, the committee clearly discerned the four levels at which Treasury control had to operate.

First the Treasury must play a part in deciding the total of expenditure on all services. Secondly the Treasury must be concerned that there is a proper balance of expenditure *between* services, so that greater value could not be obtained for the total expenditure by reducing the money spent on one service and increasing expenditure on another. Thirdly they must help to determine the total of expenditure on individual policies and services. Finally, having decided how much should be spent on each service, the Treasury must have a continuing concern in seeing that the money is being spent as wisely as possible by Departments responsible – that there is a proper balance of expenditure *within* services.

And in practical, administrative terms the committee found it convenient to think of four stages, not necessarily consecutive or always distinct, but helpfully defined for analytical purposes by the Treasury's memorandum on 'Methods of Treasury Control'.[8] They were:

(a) Treasury control in relation to policy decisions,
(b) Treasury control over programmes of expenditure and annual Estimates,
(c) Treasury control by prior sanction of new projects, and
(d) Treasury interest in continuing expenditure on services previously authorized, in matters falling within the limits of Departmental authority and in the Departments' own methods of financial control.[9]

The character of Treasury control may have changed appreciably in the years since 1957 but it is still worth following the committee's inquiry through these four stages.

(a) The first belongs to that exalted and opaque sphere where Cabinet discussions emerge as policy decisions. *Treasury control* here ultimately means such influence as the Chancellor of the Exchequer is able to bring upon his colleagues – an influence which is, and always has been, a variable in our constitution. As it happened, January 1958 saw a striking instance of its failure when the resignations of the Chancellor (Peter Thorneycroft) and the two Parliamentary Secretaries to the Treasury (Enoch Powell and Nigel Birch) marked a defeat for their stand against rising public expenditure. It was a rare, and, in its scale, unique instance of the ultimate ministerial sanction being thrown, unsuccessfully, into the balance on the Treasury's behalf. In 1951, on the other hand, Aneurin Bevan and Harold Wilson had resigned from their ministerial posts (the Ministry of Health and the Board of Trade respectively) in protest against Hugh Gaitskell's budgetary policy, which seemed to sacrifice welfare services for a quite unrealistic scale of re-armament expenditure. Normally, however, the 1924 rule that 'no memorandum is to be circulated to the Cabinet or its Committees in which any financial issue is involved, until its contents have been discussed with the

Treasury' provides an effective guarantee that Treasury control can be brought to bear, collaboratively, at the earliest stage – at the point where a proposal has not yet become a policy. It also permits the permanent officials of the Treasury to perform their duties at the first of the levels indicated above – in matching the overall distribution of required expenditure with the fiscal and economic resources available. The decisions, ultimately, are political ones taken by the Chancellor and the Cabinet, but the spadework belongs to the intricate network of official and ministerial committees which binds Whitehall together. The Select Committee was left in no doubt that 'Treasury control is a real factor at this stage'. For example, although defence policy had always had a special status, with its global totals agreed at Cabinet level, they heard a good deal of interesting evidence on the Treasury's involvement in its formulation. Nor was this function performed only within the narrow limits of annual Estimates: it was a matter of long-term planning, framed by continuous review of 'forward looks' three years ahead.

But, as the Treasury pointed out, it ran up against real limits on its freedom to control the quantum of expenditure.[10] The government itself was bound by certain international agreements. And within social expenditure there were huge areas governed by statute, such as pensions, National Assistance and housing subsidies, that were not susceptible to economies. Other national policies – the health service, atomic energy development or weapon research – had such large elements of the incalculable that they seemed to defy planning, let alone control.

(b) Some of these difficulties flowed over into the next stage – *Treasury control over programmes of expenditure and annual Estimates.* But in general the scrutiny of programmes offered the best of all opportunities for pinning down investment plans on such things as roads, schools, hospitals or warships to specific limits of total and annual expenditure. Here again, defence seemed to lead the way with its draft programmes reviewed annually for the three years ahead, with detailed attention to the sums that would be required for the next year's Estimates. But, as the Committee was told (Q.458) and then forgot,[11] civil departments were also in the habit of supplementing their annual estimates with forecasts submitted to the Treasury each January 'of what the Parliamentary Estimates are likely to be for two years ahead'.

The fuller development of techniques of forward planning lay in the future, with the impetus given by the Plowden report. The past, in the traditional form of the annual Estimates-cycle, was still more in evidence. Programmes phased over several years to mounting levels of expenditure still had to be fitted within the annual cash-supply procedures of the House of Commons, and this had some of its old shortcomings as a device for control. The Treasury's scrutiny of Estimates submitted to it in early December had to be hurried through for submission to Parliament by early February. ('I do not know whether you can visualize what the Treasury is like in December and January,' said an old Treasury hand, 'but it is absolutely chaotic' (Q.2420).) But, as another Treasury witness was to say, nearly everything came through the Treasury's hands at Estimates time and this was allegedly the starting point for a thorough, unhurried inquiry into the general standards of economy, good sense and efficiency of a department (Q.209, 212). The process of sieving through the Estimates each year, *in conjunction with other techniques of control*, was an unquestionably fertile phase of the Treasury's procedures.

The italicized proviso is important, for, as we have seen in Chapter 5, it is a fundamental axiom of Treasury control (which the committee seemed to find difficulty in accepting)[12] that the provision of money in a Parliamentary Estimate does not itself convey authority to spend it. The Exchequer and Audit Departments Act of 1921 had spelled out the rule of specific sanction more clearly – viz. that any audited expenditure 'shall, unless sanctioned by the Treasury, be regarded as not being properly chargeable to a Parliamentary grant, and shall be so reported to the House of Commons'. Of course, it might easily happen that items would have to be rushed into the Estimates to which the Treasury had not yet given its *prior* approval, and specific sanction for the expenditure would clearly have to follow, but this was by no means the full limit of the principle. Any item, approved by Parliament, still needed the Treasury's specific 'go-ahead' for expenditure – at least in theory. 'The present day practice,' stated the Treasury's memorandum, 'can probably best be described briefly by saying that Treasury approval is necessary for every new item of expenditure, for any new service, or for any change of policy which involves an increase in expenditure, subject to any delegated authority which may have been given to particular Departments in particular fields of expenditure.'*

(c) This brings us to the third and most controversial stage – *Treasury control by prior sanction of new projects*. In their answers the Treasury witnesses were at pains to stress the tact and prudence with which this large authority was administered. They were acutely aware of its dangers. 'A tendency to ask "niggling" points, to try to impose too detailed a control is a very natural fault for one to fall into, particularly when one's duties are of a critical character.' . . . 'I

*The derivation of this definition from the Treasury Minute of 1868 will be obvious. See above, pp. 141–2.

do not say the Treasury ever has been, or ever will be, wholly free of that fault till it is staffed by archangels, but I will say it is a fault which the Treasury recognizes and devotes a great deal of attention to avoiding' (Q.265).

In fact the Treasury went a good deal further than this disarming piece of self-criticism. To mitigate the dangers and wasted time entailed by its powers of detailed review it had long since developed a system of 'delegation' by which the Treasury conferred on a department the freedom to incur expenditure on specific items or services within a fixed limit. Since 1950, the ceilings on 'delegations' had been progressively adjusted. They could be as high as the £250,000 permitted to the Ministry of Transport for individual road construction projects, or the £60,000 limit on hospital building schemes. The Ministry of Supply possessed several £250,000 delegations, and some of its transactions could be undertaken without limit.[13] At the other extreme, for less demanding departments, delegations might seem absurdly meagre. For some time the committee was to be hilariously misled by the (erroneous) example of the Foreign Office's liberty to provide two, but not more, bicycles for consular staffs without the Treasury's specific approval! (QQ. 293, 313, 377). In general, however, the critical principles governing the scale of delegations were the same for all items, large or small – 'Is a proper balance being struck between (a) the need for the Treasury to maintain a sufficient control in its own hands for the discharge of its proper responsibilities and (b) the need to avoid slowing down the tempo of public business and consuming too much manpower, both in the Treasury and in other Departments, in the submission and scrutiny of cases?'[14]

Other large areas could be dealt with under codes of practice built up by experience – where only the exceptional cases needed the Treasury's detailed attention. The Treasury's particular task was to be wary of the long- as well as the short-term implications of sanction. It was not only a question of the prudence and economy of a particular item of expenditure but – what sort of precedent did it establish? How, as an item of continuing expenditure, would it fit into the future provision of departmental resources?

(d) This leads to the last stage of concern – *Treasury interest in continuing expenditure on services previously authorized*. The committee recognized that 'the total of continuing expenditure for which Departments are primarily responsible is too large to be left, without oversight, in the hands of the spending Departments alone'.[15] It was therefore an essential part of the Treasury's duties to keep the flow of departmental expenditure under constant review – questioning its validity and economy where suspicion seemed justified. Here in particular its advantages as the central department of state equipped it with the kind of critical standards which could enlighten one department with the experience learned from another. Indeed, the committee was anxious to know how the Treasury kept departments and their Accounting Officers (usually the Permanent Secretary) up to scratch – and in answer were given assurances on the frequency and penetration of Treasury inquiries. Mismanagement, falling standards, were said to be quickly spotted, and – as they were darkly told – 'We have our ways of persuading Departments' (Q.105). But, if that conveyed any suggestion of friction between the Treasury and the departments, it was a little off-key. The essence of the evidence given, by the departments as well as the Treasury, was the *collaborative* character of Treasury control.

In working their way through these categories the committee found plenty of room for criticism – although the first stage of Treasury control, which entailed Cabinet and ministerial decisions, presented them with difficulties which could only be overcome by a more detailed, expert and privileged inquiry. Accordingly the ultimate recommendation of the Select Committee's Report was 'that a small independent committee, which should have access to Cabinet papers, be appointed to report upon the theory and practice of Treasury control of expenditure'.[16] From this the Plowden committee was to arise. Otherwise, their major criticism boiled down to the view that 'the old theory of "candle-ends" economy has not wholly been abandoned, and the new theory of Departmental responsibility and partnership may not have been wholeheartedly accepted'.

Coming seventy years after Welby's declaration that 'however good the financial criticism of the Treasury may be, it ought never to supersede an effective financial criticism within the department itself', this seems a rather shocking indictment. Could it really have taken the Treasury so long to comprehend a principle actually laid down in the high-noon of Gladstonian parsimony? Had the Treasury really remained deaf to a warning pronounced by its leaders decades before Warren Fisher's day? Yet, one may reasonably suppose that the Estimates Committee of 1957 was not overburdened by its knowledge of nineteenth-century parliamentary reports and that it saw itself as giving fresh life to an essentially modern concept. The Treasury itself, unduly apologetic about its own past, had done much to promote the misconception that Haldane's Report and Warren Fisher's rule had seen the birth rather than the maturity of the ideal of financial self-control among the departments. As for the *practice* of self-control, which is rather a different thing, the Select Committee's criticism about 'candle-ends' would have been fairer comment if this point had properly emerged from the evidence, but it had not. On a dispassionate reading and re-reading of the 3,000-odd questions and answers one must say that a different impression is given, and that the Treasury's defensive *Observations* on the Select Committee's Report are understandable.

What *had* emerged was that the departments – or at least the six questioned – generally found 'Treasury control' in its various forms to be a helpful and healthy part of normal administration. As the Permanent Secretary to the Ministry of Health put it – 'It is a very desirable discipline ... – a severe financial discipline'. Other witnesses were to take up and expand this ideal of 'useful discipline' – but the committee soon seized on one of its dangers. Was it not possible that the Treasury's presence as a kind of 'long-stop' (the metaphor is theirs, not mine) always there to check the 'byes' of administrative imprudence, undermined the wicket-keeping department's sense of financial responsibility? However, the majority of witnesses had no hesitation in declaring that the obligation to submit proposals to the Treasury's scrutiny was a stimulus they valued. Furthermore, they magnanimously suggested, it *educated* the Treasury in the nature of their problems (QQ. 1252, 1257, 1279, 1526).

But did the Treasury's purview of the whole vast range of public expenditure make it anything more than 'an intelligent lay-critic' when it came to dealing with a specific problem of departmental policy? Was it not likely to be 'blinded by science' when it sought to judge the merits of some technical item of – say – defence expenditure? On this important concept of the Treasury as 'lay-critic', which got a badly-needed airing, the departmental witnesses gave forth an uncertain sound. Indeed, the Foreign Office witnesses had a field-day. 'The cases in which the Treasury suggestions or criticisms really make much difference in the long run to the amount spent are pretty rare,' said one (Q.1525). 'I do not think they would claim to give expert advice,' said another (Q.1576). 'It makes a certain amount of unnecessary work,' they explained; 'a good many things go to the Treasury on which one cannot really expect the Treasury to have a very valuable opinion.' Of course, 'they are very helpful on things like office organization. We might be glad to have their expert advice,' but 'if Treasury control at that stage were removed, if there were no control really between the Estimates stage and the Accounts stage at the end, probably so far as the Foreign Office were concerned you would find that it would not make very much difference to the amount of money that was spent' (QQ. 1596, 1516). Yet, they generously concluded, 'the Treasury control, annoying though it may seem and although it may be a waste of time and rather unproductive, is by and large serving a useful purpose' (Q.1589); 'the value of consulting the Treasury at that stage is, perhaps, from our point of view – one does not want to put it rudely – an educative one; in other words, keeping the Treasury informed of how things are going on and how foreign policy works. . . . That does help the Treasury to exercise their function as lay-critic intelligently' (Q.1526).

It was left to the Treasury's principal spokesman to make the best defence of this vulnerable concept:

> Finally, I ought to say just a word about this phrase 'lay-critic'. It is a phrase we have used, and it perhaps is a little glib. Of course, we in the Treasury, from the Chancellor downwards, are laymen in the sense that we have not got, except incidentally, the qualifications of lawyer, scientist, architect, and so on, but lay criticism does not mean ignorant criticism.... We have a certain expertness of our own, because we have got special advantages in our central position, and in the apparatus of experience and comparative knowledge which we wield. Although we do not know as much about agriculture as the Minister of Agriculture, or as much about works as the Minister of Works, we know more about works than the Minister of Agriculture does. We have got a central position which gives us the comparative faculty and we are, I think, able to guide Departments and make points which they could not make themselves [Q.1050].

In the light of the continued criticism of Treasury 'amateurism' and the frailty of its defence, it is interesting that the Select Committee's Report accepted this doctrine, for 'it would be both impossible and undesirable to staff the Treasury divisions with experts on all the problems that arise'.[17] However, they were alive to the danger that 'laymen may be examining proposals submitted by laymen, while the technical officers who initiated the proposals and who really understand the details, remain behind the scenes'. They urged a much closer relationship between the technical and financial considerations bearing upon a decision.

This is only one instance where a specific recommendation of the Select Committee makes better sense than their ultimate conclusions – which might just as well have been drafted before the inquiry began. Indeed, there were many points on which they clearly scored against the existing practices of Treasury control. At the highest level of policy-making they were not satisfied with the scope or effectiveness of forward planning, particularly on civil expenditure – and subsequent developments show this unease to have been understated. At the second stage, the deficiencies of the annual Estimates procedure came in for some well-deserved criticism. Its haste, its selectiveness, its tendency to concentrate attention on increased rather than static items of expenditure, were points which might well have been made at any time since the mid-nineteenth century but were none the less timely in 1958. Likewise, at the third stage, they seized upon the dangers which had always been implicit in detailed

Treasury control. Its 'educative value' for the Treasury and its 'useful discipline' for the departments they accepted – but as a means to 'specific economies' it was open to question. Of a sample of 213 projects of civil expenditure submitted for Treasury sanction in 1957–8 only one, costing £250,000, had been withdrawn as a result of Treasury probing. In the defence field a secret memorandum showed Treasury control to have achieved substantial economies, but a doubt was bound to remain whether the existing scale of prior sanction requirements was really necessary. Accordingly, the Report recommended 'an increase in the delegated financial authorities of spending departments, particularly in relation to projects specifically forming part of agreed programmes or fully covered by previously determined totals of expenditure'[18] – in other words, a shift in the weight of Treasury control from the third to the second of its stages. That would promote the all-important practice of departmental responsibility without seriously jeopardizing the Treasury's budgetary control over public expenditure. Nor need it be inconsistent with a more scrupulous view of continuing expenditure. The committee rather feared that established policies and programmes were being allowed to go on, unchallenged – 'living on their legends' – without anyone saying – 'Why are we doing this?'. The essential message from this intricate inquiry was, therefore, that efficiency and economy could clearly be served by a tightening as well as a liberalization of Treasury control.

THE PLOWDEN COMMITTEE, 1959–61

The Treasury's *Observations* on the Report, published in June 1959, have naturally been accused of complacency. They were certainly not submissive. They could point to some misunderstandings, to some failures to probe deeply enough. But it was difficult to quarrel with a Report which had found that 'the system appears to work reasonably well', and the general drift of the Treasury's response was towards agreement that 'the operation of Treasury control, both in general and in particular, must constantly be reviewed and brought up to date'.[19] The Treasury consequently took up the proposal for an expert inquiry and made it its own. It envisaged a broad investigation, not simply into Treasury control, but into the 'central processes of Government' – parliamentary as well as ministerial. Nothing less could reveal the multiplicity of pressures which now determined the scope and effectiveness of the government's financial control. However, if the inquiry was to have access to Cabinet papers and the inner councils of government it would have to be a government inquiry, conducted under the authority of the Chancellor of the Exchequer. Its reports would be confidential – although its conclusions could be reported to Parliament 'in due course'.

Under these limitations, Lord Plowden (the Chief Planning Officer of yesteryear but since then Chairman of the Atomic Energy Authority) was brought in to head a small committee of three businessmen – all with some Civil Service experience. Five anonymous senior civil servants also took part in their deliberations and after meeting fortnightly over a period of two years the group produced a series of confidential reports and, in June 1961, the published summary of their conclusions which we know as the Plowden Report.[20]

This was to be greeted by the literary equivalent of a slow handclap. Expecting the red meat of controversy, the cognoscenti of public administration felt themselves fobbed off with a mere vitamin capsule of consensus. Close textual analysis revealed to them that Whitehall re-drafting had emptied the report of all life. 'The sharp edges, the pungent phrases and any handles to outside critics were all removed'; the end-product was 'muffled', 'obscure'. But it was not a bromide. As D. N. Chester, the most penetrating of these critics, has pointed out, the Report was unusual among the products of official committees of inquiry in marking an effective change of heart. Its conclusions had been absorbed, its recommendations were being implemented. 'It was in effect a statement of Government policy.'[21]

In this case an impression of the Report's significance is not conveyed best by a summary of its conclusions. Seen in the sequence of post-Haldane investigations into the machinery of government which includes that by the 1957 Estimates Committee, the Plowden report is really distinctive for being the first to take the Keynesian revolution as its point of departure. As we have already seen, it sets its inquiry in the context of public expenditure which, at forty-two per cent of G.N.P., dominated the whole economy. Traditional assumptions, associated with a minimal, passive role for government finance, were now quite invalid and it was long since time to dismantle the administrative and parliamentary framework in which they had been sustained. From a stand-point as lofty as this, any bickering about the boundaries of Treasury control was likely to seem rather parochial.

Interestingly enough, the Plowden Report echoed the Estimates Committee in its findings on Treasury control: 'the system seemed to us to be working reasonably well'.[22] It agreed in approving the 'educative' value of some degree of Treasury control (para. 39), but seemed to have little time for the 'useful discipline' argument. The Treasury–departmental relationship 'should be one of joint working together in a common enterprise' (para. 34), and as for anything resembling the search for 'specific economies', 'the Treasury should express its views about the administration rather than about the individual submissions themselves' (para. 39). The scope for delegations, they hoped, would gradually widen.

All this followed from the Report's central recommendation – that public expenditure should be considered 'as a whole, over a period of years ahead, and in relation to prospective resources' (para. 12). This required the Treasury to re-direct its energies to the two top levels of control – the 'policy' and the 'programme' stages (paras. 79, 80). The sort of planning and 'forward looks' applied to defence expenditure should be extended to other fields 'into a system of provisional and tentative departmental allocations five years ahead; firm for the first year, firm for the second year subject to major changes in the military and economic situations, provisional for the third year and tentative for the fourth and fifth years' (para. 20). But, of course, it recognized that all this required a technical revolution in the Treasury methods – 'a wider application of mathematical techniques, statistics and accountancy to problems of public expenditure' (para. 30). Quantitative estimates which made sense in terms of economic resources, rather than fiscal policy, would have to become the regular basis of administrative decisions.

And this revolution should be carried over into the parliamentary language of financial control, for despite the reorientation of budgetary thinking which had taken place since 1941 the documentation of government expenditure was still framed after nineteenth-century patterns. The printed Estimates and the consequent Appropriation Accounts were set out under headings quite unrelated to the economic categories used in the National Income and Expenditure Blue Books (paras. 27–9). Furthermore, the adaptation to long-term planning as the basis of administration suggested a similar adaptation of parliamentary procedures. Perhaps the House of Commons should move over to a two-year or eighteen-month cycle of Estimates, Budget and Appropriation (para. 62)? Perhaps they should adopt the American system of programme-appropriation, and tie-up long-term commitments years ahead (para. 72)? The Report examined these ideas, but rejected them. In what amounts to a remarkable testimony to the nineteenth-century patterns of Parliament's financial control they decided, on practical grounds, in favour of the traditional *annual* cycle of cash-Estimates, Appropriations and Audit (para. 75). This need not be inconsistent with the government's long-term planning. The government would have 'to develop means of informing Parliament and enabling it to consider and approve the broad issues of policy involving public expenditure for some years ahead at the time when the effective decisions are taken'. Adaptation could be more effectively undertaken by the parliamentary review committees – the Public Accounts Committee (P.A.C.), the Estimates Committee and the Select Committee on Nationalized Industries – so that their pressure could be exerted at the points where it did most good (para. 78). The Report noted that the P.A.C., for example, originally concerned with fairly narrow questions of propriety and technical accountancy, was already shifting the emphasis of its attention to the efficiency of departmental management.

This was in the right direction, for 'management' was the other key concept of the Plowden Report – and one vital to the Treasury. The Report was most emphatic in upholding the Treasury's central responsibility for the control of pay and conditions of service, and although it discreetly acknowledged evidence of friction arising from the Treasury's supervision of departmental establishments it concluded that 'something very like the present arrangement is inescapable' (para. 40). Management likewise, although the primary responsibility of individual departments, could only be advanced through the centralized promotion of new techniques and services – scientific, statistical, 'O. & M.', etc. On these the Report had a good deal to say, stressing the need for a cross-fertilization of ideas and experience with commerce and industry (para. 58) and applauding the Treasury's pioneer work in the field of automatic data-processing 'which is clearly in the forefront of national progress' (para. 53). It expected, none the less, that further development along the lines envisaged in the Report would impose heavy additional responsibilities on the Treasury, and from this would follow 'considerable changes in the nature and pattern of the Treasury's work'. A review of the Treasury's organization seemed clearly necessary (para. 59).

THE TREASURY REORGANIZATION OF 1962

In fact, a major reorganization of the Treasury was announced within twelve months of the Report's publication – but to assume a narrow sequence of cause and effect has its dangers. On the one hand, the Report's implications belong to a wider context than administrative reform. On the other, the reorganization was more sweeping than any that could have been envisaged on the basis of the Plowden Report alone.

Of course, Treasury men are most anxious to stress that the changes announced on 30 July 1962 went beyond the text handed down on the Plowden tablets. But to the layman the new structure of the Treasury which came into operation on 1 October 1962 seems to mirror very exactly the two main themes of 'Plowden'. It was a kind of diarchy – with the cleavage pushed far deeper than the 1956 division of responsibility between Joint Permanent Secretaries. In 1962 the Treasury was split from top to bottom into two 'sides' – the 'Pay and Management Side' and the 'Finance and Economic Side' – and so complete and logical was the division that the Treasury was immediately on its guard against any assumption that this presaged their ultimate divorce. As it was, the two halves remained closely knit by collaboration, personnel and sentiment. Below the level of 'Sides' the interaction between their subdivisions ensured that this would be so.

There were to be five 'Groups' within the two 'Sides'. The 'Pay' and 'Management' Groups accounted for one; 'Finance', 'Public Sector' and 'National Economy' Groups made up the other. Within these, notwithstanding several 'branches', one 'service' and the Economic 'section', the usual nomenclature was preserved for the basic administrative unit – the division – of which there were now about thirty-five. But 1962 is significant for a transformation in the content of divisional business. The tradition, going back (as we have seen) to their eighteenth-century origins, had been of specialization in terms of other departments – one division, for example, dealing with all the business of the defence departments, another with all the aspects, such as pay, superannuation and expenditure, of some civil departments. Approached from the other direction this had meant that a government department usually had only one Treasury division to deal with. But this distribution, modified before, was now abandoned. Divisional responsibilities were carefully re-allocated in terms of functions – for example, the *expenditure* of defence departments, of social service departments, of nationalized industries, etc., being the concern of several distinct divisions of the Public Sector Group, while the *pay, promotion, organization* and *superannuation* of these departments were to be dealt with separately by divisions on the Pay and Management Side, the overall effect being a considerable multiplication of contacts as the price for some hoped-for gain in Treasury expertise.

That remained to be seen. For the Treasury the immediate implications were unprecedented upheavals – a physical upheaval of thousands of files, and of furnishings and phones – and a conceptual upheaval which shattered the specialisms of once-compact divisions. For example, no less than nine new divisions inherited pieces of the old 'Government and Allied Services Division', while in other cases it took six cannibalized old divisions to provide one new one with its reconstituted diet.[23] But from this chaos of fragments many new concentrations of specialized activity emerged, and among the most significant were those which provided centralized services for the Civil Service as a whole. Five of them were in the Management Group – viz., the Treasury Medical Service concerned with general and particular problems of health among civil servants; the Training and Education Division, responsible for the growing range of formal training courses and further education provided, in particular, for the Administrative grade; the Management Services (General) Division, which was to co-ordinate research and reform in the techniques of public administration; and two Organization and Methods units – the Office Machines Division and the Training and Information Branch – which provided consultancy and supervisory services on the technical aspects of Civil Service administration. It was these – and some of the Public Sector Group divisions – which most clearly reflected the new light of the Plowden gospel, and it was therefore these which post-Plowden apologists like Sir Richard Clarke were particularly anxious to set in the front of the Treasury's reorganized shop-window.

This was legitimate, for the reorganization of 1962 mattered less as an elaborate exercise in the efficient reapportionment of functions than as a visible demonstration of the underlying conceptual revolution which had been taking place since 1958, and which made 'management' the purposeful, creative successor of old-fashioned, negative 'control'. 'This means,' said Clarke, 'that the Treasury's job is not to act as a censor, or as a back-seat driver, for the Departments. It must satisfy itself that every Department's management is as adequate as the resources of the Service permit; and that the techniques of management are being steadily improved and extended. Instead of being a back-seat driver, the Treasury's job is to ensure that every Department has the best possible cars and drivers and is properly equipped with maps.'[24]

But, as he also said, the 'confrontation of prospective public expenditure against the prospective national resources is the heart of the matter',[25] and that is a timely reminder that this theme of administrative reform makes complete sense only in association with the concurrent developments in economic planning which are to be dealt with later. However, within the boundaries set by the economic policies of the early 1960s, one can usefully isolate some of the technical aids which accompanied the new conceptual approach. Indeed, it is arguable that the technical revolution implicit in electronic data-processing was the parent rather than the child of that approach, for the range and sophistication of the technique of 'cost/benefit analysis' are scarcely conceivable apart from the computer, and it is that range and sophistication which have made possible the new breadth and penetration of expenditure control. To quote Clarke yet again –

From time immemorial, the opening move of anyone whose duty is to control expenditure or to allocate resources is to meet any proposal with the question, 'What would happen if you did not get it (or *x* per cent of it)?' Then the question, 'Could you not get the same result by doing *y* or *z*?'[26]

Now, the novelty of cost/benefit, or cost/effectiveness, analysis arises primarily from the precision with which data-processing techniques of statistics, costing and accountancy can predicate the financial implications of *y* or *z* (to say nothing of *x*) and from the flexibility of its provision for the sort of variables which complicate any kind of decision-making process. Translated into defence terms this could mean, for example, a straightforward assessment that policy A would produce 100 units of defence gain for £50 million while policy B would achieve the same at twice the cost. But, suppose B – a hypothetical missile system – has greater reliability, and/or greater versatility, and/or greater immunity across a wider range of circumstances? So far as these variables can be assessed in financial terms, rigorous cost/effectiveness analysis can produce helpful foundations for expenditure decisions. It is no substitute for decisions, or for thought. Part of its value seems to lie precisely in the exacting demands which data-processing makes upon prior logical analysis; the rest upon its success in substituting dubious 'hunches' and sloppy compromises with concrete foundations for choice.

As in America, this technique was to make its first impact on British defence expenditure and by February 1965 a Defence White Paper could announce – not before time – the adoption of functional costing and the decision to create an establishment for defence operational analysis 'which, among other tasks, will participate in cost-effectiveness studies for all three Services'. But clearly the approach was valid for a wider range of government expenditure, notwithstanding the difficulty of producing appropriate financial yardsticks of welfare value.[27] In fact, education, the social services, agriculture and transport are areas which have been, and are being, submitted to this kind of analysis, and although, in the nature of things economic and political, it will take some years for these reviews to work their way through to acceptable formulae, the process itself has had immediate and pervasive effects upon the methods and personnel of the Civil Service.

For example, one may deduce that in any area of government expenditure where cost/effectiveness analysis has been applied the scale of inter-departmental collaboration has been greatly enlarged. There has been much wider consultation with external advisers and experts. The exchange of ideas and research between the Civil

Service and the universities has been increasingly fertile, almost catching up in the social science field with the long-established links between scientific research and defence. But the process tended to expose rather than eliminate the traditional barriers which inhibited flexible interchange between the Civil Service and the outside world. Mounting anxieties about this were not greatly allayed by the announcement in June 1964 that six posts at Principal level and three at Assistant Secretary level would be made available for men or women aged between thirty and thirty-five or forty and forty-five respectively. The rider, that 'a knowledge of economic, industrial, commercial or financial matters would be an advantage', has an inexpressible pathos in face of the need.

Consequently, as the implications of the Plowden Report sank in, there was growing unease about the ability of the Administrative grade to meet its challenge. 'Management', with its profit-motive, commercial connotations seemed thoroughly alien to the alleged mandarin traditions of the higher Civil Service. 'Some fifteen years ago,' wrote an Assistant Secretary in 1964, 'nobody talked about management', and even now he felt it rated low and ambiguously in the attractions offered to the graduate entrant. Response to what was now in essence the task of many government departments – i.e. the running of very big businesses – seemed lacking. Yet, at the same time, no one seemed to doubt that the Executive grade, trained on the job, had acquired high degrees of competence in managerial roles which ranked with anything in private industry.

The creation of the Treasury Centre for Administrative Studies in Regent's Park, announced on 23 May 1963, was an attempt to bridge the gap between the special abilities of young Administrative grade civil servants and the sort of managerial roles they could now expect to perform. The lecture curriculum of the original fourteen-week course included – Public Administration (principles and techniques), Structure of Industry, Operation of Business Enterprise, Science and Technology, the International Scene, Micro-Economics (theory and concepts), Statistics and Macro-Economics (National Income, Finance, International Trade and Economic Policy). By 1965 the basic course had become twenty weeks long, with its emphasis placed heavily on economics and statistical and mathematical aids to administration. Written exercises and practical work on computer-programming and network analysis now formed an important part of a course which was highly responsive to the demands of its own students.[28] Assistant Secretaries and other civil servants in mid-career discovered a strong incentive to join in, if only to acquire the same standard of technical literacy as their juniors.

Meanwhile the Treasury O. & M. divisions recovered an initiative they had seemed in danger of losing twenty years before. In the post-war period most of the larger departments had developed their own O. & M. branches – but the smaller ones continued to rely on the Treasury's advisory services, and with the development of electronic computers the whole Civil Service came to depend on the Treasury's resources of information and expertise. Indeed, the Treasury's inquiries into the sort of data-processing equipment appropriate to departmental tasks were not only a useful exercise in cost/benefit analysis, they were a desirable form of financial control over these extremely costly items of investment.* Hence the Plowden accolade, which clearly encouraged the institutionalization of this advisory service in the Treasury's Management Services (General) Division. Set up in the 1962 reorganization, the infant division established an ascendancy by sheer professionalism – and success. A Treasury manual on Organization and Methods techniques became a Stationery Office best-seller and its *O & M Bulletin*, founded in 1945, passed on from strength to strength. It is from this that one can learn something of the measurable benefits of the Treasury's O. & M. work. For example, a quantitative study by the O. & M. (General) Division faced up to the difficulty of costing gains in efficiency but found that in 1962 and 1964 about half its assignments (taking thirty-five per cent of its time) had yielded identifiable savings of 250 per cent on the cost of the inquiries. The remaining sixty-five per cent of staff effort was not really measurable, but if the value of incomplete assignments and future savings were estimated the total gain seemed impressive. Among those assignments, incidentally, was the modernization of the Chancellor of the Exchequer's office. 'A new filing and indexing system, better copying methods, desk intercommunicating equipment and special furniture all led to speedier business with less effort.'[29]

This may fall short of Keynes's breezy ideal that any Treasury man worth his salt could save £1 million per month, but in an interesting way it demonstrates how the Treasury's new collaborative techniques could achieve the sort of valuable piecemeal savings which were once the painfully-fought objects of 'niggling' Treasury control.

Unfortunately, these responses to the challenge of the times were not enough to disarm an increasingly vocal criticism of the Treasury's Civil Service leadership. To some critics, even Plowden's bright ideas looked a little faded in the light of reforming proposals going back to the 'Assheton' Report on the Training of Civil Servants presented in 1944. Not for the first time, the pressure for radical

*The first computer for office work was introduced into the Civil Service in 1958. By 31 March 1966 the Civil Service had fifty-eight computers for office work, forty-eight for scientific work and twenty-eight on order.

change in the Civil Service outstripped the response by an uncomfortable margin.

A particularly significant symptom of the post-Plowden disillusion is a Fabian Society tract – *The Administrators* – published in 1964. Drafted with the help of career civil servants, it welcomed Plowden's analysis and the subsequent changes, but found them nothing like adequate. It sharply questioned the Treasury's confirmed ascendancy over the management of the Civil Service, and made the transfer of its 'Establishments' work to a reformed Civil Service Commission the first of its specific proposals. Others touched on recruitment, training, grading, specialization and policy-making – a litany of complaints which sprang from the glaring paradox between Civil Service amateurism and Civil Service rigidity.

Rigidity at the highest level seemed to begin with the recruitment by examination of sixty per cent of the Administrative grade, for too high a proportion of that percentage came from the narrow 'Oxbridge' element in the educational spectrum. (The figures for 1957–63 showed that 'Oxbridge' provided 64·3 per cent of candidatures and 85·3 per cent of successes.) Amateurism likewise seemed to originate with the preponderance of 'arts' graduates within that element – 30·6 per cent of the successful having read History at University, 24 per cent of them Classics. And this background was not thought to be amended by the brief courses laid on at the Treasury Centre for Administrative Studies. The few weeks spent there by Assistant Principals of two years' seniority were only part of a series of frequent transfers which kept junior administrators on the move as a deliberate antidote for premature specialization. In the Treasury, with its deliberate policy of indirect recruitment via other departments, the pattern of transfer had seemed specially disturbing to the 1957–8 Estimates Committee, for fifty-five of its seventy-four Principals and twenty-four of its thirty-two Assistant Secretaries had under two years' experience in their present divisions.

Of course, the authors of *The Administrators* were not hostile to flexibility within the career structure of the Civil Service provided it was of the right sort. The recruitment from the Executive grade of the other forty per cent of the Administrative grade's annual intake was a most healthy practice, but they wanted to see a much greater interchange between business, industry or the professions and the Civil Service – with an accent on specialist competence at high levels. In practical terms this would mean, among other things, relaxing the pension rules which inhibited civil servants gaining experience outside in mid-career. As it was, temporary secondments were far too rare. The administrative hierarchy was 'as closed and protected as a monastic order. A young man enters at 21 or so, and is virtually locked in until 60', and there could be no doubt that this stultifying prospect was a real deterrent to broad recruitment. In spring 1965 the inquiries of the Estimates Committee revealed that a hostile caricature of the higher Civil Service was deeply etched on the minds of provincial undergraduates – precisely that quarter where the largest untapped resources of ability were thought to lie. Thus, entering a fiercely competitive market where those graduates not attracted into the academic world were scooped up by the sophisticated recruitment techniques of large-scale industry, the Civil Service Commission was yearly failing to meet the service's manpower requirements by 30–40 per cent. And, since a belief that the higher Civil Service was an 'Oxbridge' preserve was one of the deterrents to recruitment, something like a vicious circle was being set up as the socially and educationally unrepresentative character of the intake grew more and more pronounced.[30]

The immediate responsibility for coping with this state of affairs was, of course, the Civil Service Commission's. Another of our lasting monuments to mid-Victorian ideals of the proper relations between government and society, its duties – though amended as recently as August 1956 – were still essentially those defined under the Order in Council of 4 June 1870. But under the Order in Council of 1956, as under its predecessors, the wider responsibility to regulate the structure and conditions of the Civil Service was unquestionably the Treasury's, so the problem of recruitment inevitably turned back on the whole question of the Treasury's regulative and managerial duties. On these the Fabian authors had no doubts: 'Take personnel management and concern with the structure of the Civil Service out of the Treasury altogether.' It was a view which was to acquire powerful support.

Yet in May 1964, after its long-promised inquiry, the Estimates Committee came out with a striking affirmation of faith in the Treasury's control of Civil Service Establishments. It 'categorically' deplored 'the suggestion implied in the Report of the Committee on Control of Public Expenditure [Plowden] that the Treasury and Departments have equal standing in the control of numbers in the Civil Service'. This 'revealed a complete misconception of the historic role of the Treasury and the Chancellor of the Exchequer . . .'.[31] Instead, far from yielding to any modish tendencies to discard traditional canons of administration, the Committee took its stand on the control procedures last defined by a 1949 Treasury circular. Also, in contrast to its 1957–8 predecessor, it was prepared to take at its face value any evidence on the merits of Treasury control. 'In written evidence submitted to Sub-committee C the majority of Departments welcomed Treasury initiative in the field of management; and in no sense did they regard the Treasury as interfering with or usurping their own responsibilities.'

Now this favourable verdict on Treasury control of Establishments was not necessarily inconsistent with the earlier, critical verdict on Treasury control of expenditure. In 1964 the Estimates Committee could applaud the rapid and successful adaptation of the Treasury to its modern managerial role. But there remains a fundamental shift in critical standpoint between the Estimates Committee of 1957–8 and that of 1963–4, and an explanation will have to go further than the turnover in membership.

However, it may be unnecessary to look further than its senior partner, the Public Accounts Committee. Wedded to the principles and machinery of the Exchequer and Audit Departments Act, the P.A.C. has always been constitutionally pledged to the stricter requirements of Treasury control. Year after year, with a more stable and concentrated membership than the Estimates Committee, the P.A.C. traverses scattered tracts of government expenditure, firing away at the peccant game put up for it by the Comptroller and Auditor-General. The sport is meagre enough at times – obscure technical breaches in the nineteenth-century code of accounting propriety – and on occasions the Committee has revealed a petty spirit of parsimony which would have shocked even Joseph Hume. Might we not, they once asked of that admirable enterprise in collaborative scholarship, the History of Parliament Trust, 'save something like £900,000 or possibly more by stopping the thing now?'[32]

But with increasing frequency since the late 1950s the P.A.C. has been dealing with problems rather than peccadilloes – problems of expenditure which have far-reaching implications for the nature of financial control. This is not purely a question of scale – such as the £20 million profits of the independent television companies, noted in 1958–9, or the 1¼ million surplus army boots of 1957. Even the sensational £5·7 million Ferranti profits on the 'Bloodhound' missile (eighty-two per cent on costs, forty-five per cent on selling price), mattered less for their size than for their demonstration of the peculiar difficulties involved in the contracting for sophisticated items of defence hardware. Already in 1959–60 the P.A.C. drew attention in its Second Report (para. 45) to the obdurate fact that 'development contracts on the present scale are something new in the financial history of this country: open as they inevitably must be to abuse, they call for new methods of supervision and co-ordination at the highest level'.

This was just one straw in a wind which has been blowing through the whole structure of British defence from 1961 to the present day – transforming its policy, its organization and its expenditure levels.

The gale has owed its strength to several pressures, not least to brute economic necessity, but among institutional influences that of the P.A.C. should rank high. And it may also be significant that a vigorous pursuit of these novel expenditure problems coincided with Harold Wilson's tenure as Chairman of the P.A.C. from December 1959 to February 1963. Unquestionably, he brought a new cutting edge to its proceedings. Slicing through verbiage, he was not averse to a little verbal by-play of his own,* and a new menace was added to the traditional terrors of the Committee. But most important was the fact that between 1959 and 1964 the House of Commons was given a series of object lessons in the incapacity of some government departments to keep their financial houses in order. The ideal of departmental self-control in matters of expenditure began to look a little sick and in the nature of things this rebounded on the Treasury. For while it is the Permanent Secretary of the erring department to whom the P.A.C. hands the suave hemlock of its disapproval, it is the Treasury which must answer at the inquest. There was, therefore, in these years an appreciable stiffening in parliamentary attitudes to the principles and practice of Treasury control – and the Estimates Committee was not out of step. Early in 1964 it castigated the Treasury for failing to exercise a proper supervision over the vastly expensive Anglo-French Concorde project. Unconsulted from the outset, the Treasury had been left out of the negotiations which culminated in the agreement of 29 November 1962. Even in 1964 its authorization had not yet been given, although (the Committee reported) 'as Treasury witnesses admitted, the Government is now so fully committed that the authorization of the project "is to some extent a formality"'. It concluded –

> Parliament is entitled to believe that, when decisions of this kind are under consideration by the Government, the Treasury are actively concerned at every stage and insistent on the kind of elementary safeguards to which your Committee have referred . . . the apparent failure of the Treasury to fulfil its obligations to the public revenue requires explanation.[33]

Naturally, the Treasury was badly shaken by this red-hot broadside from an Estimates Committee which had suddenly turned into

*Examples from an interrogation of the Permanent Secretary of the Ministry of Aviation should demonstrate this point adequately.

(a) Q. 2706: 'What I am really getting at is, are you satisfied you are getting adequate competition in the matter of design? – It is an issue we constantly bear in mind.'

Q.2707: 'I want more than "bear in mind". Are you doing it?'

(b) Q.2891: 'You have used this phrase "inertia guidance". Would that be a proper description of the relations between the Ministry and the contractor during the whole of this operation? – That is rather unfair, Sir . . .'

(*Public Accounts Committee* (1961–2), Evidence, 22 March 1962.)

'Gladstonian counter-revolutionaries'. 'In appearing to seek to defend these things I find myself, I assure you, in a most unfamiliar position,' complained the Joint Permanent Secretary to the Treasury. But later, in its rather testy written answer to the Concorde criticisms, the Treasury gestured towards the Plowden Report. Had not the House of Commons endorsed the principle of departmental self-control set out there and in the Chief Secretary to the Treasury's speech of 24 January 1962 where he had emphasized that 'the Treasury cannot both place the chief responsibility for sound and economical administration on each Department – which I am sure is right – and at the same time retain all the strings in its own hand and keep tugging at them'?

No doubt the Treasury felt hard done by, but the severity of its critics should not be misunderstood. These were not irresponsible assaults on the character or being of the Treasury. They conveyed, rather, the earnest desire that the Treasury should perform its tasks as effectively as possible. But which tasks? The belief was now clearly growing that even the reorganized Treasury could not perform *all* the roles with which it was charged. Early in 1964 Mr Harold Wilson expressed the view – 'and as a former Chairman of the Public Accounts Committee I've good reason to say this, that the Treasury in the last few years, because of its widespread responsibilities, has not been doing its traditional job of economizing and cutting out waste'.[34]

This was one part of a broadcast interview in which some of the administrative reforms of the prospective Labour government were given a preliminary airing. For example, Mr Wilson's anxieties about the limited range of economic and scientific expertise in the Civil Service were cautiously expressed – it was really a matter for the Civil Service Commission – but he hoped to see a much greater interchange between civil servants and outside experts (for example, between the Treasury and the Bank of England, or with the nationalized industries) on a temporary basis. He also left little doubt that by strengthening the Prime Minister's secretariat he would make the premiership the effective, informed centre of government, immune to railroading by any department, however powerful. As for the overloaded Treasury, he was quite explicit: 'I would suggest that the Treasury on the one hand does money, that is taxation, control of expenditure, and responsibility for monetary management – the national debt, responsibility for the foreign, the overseas balance of payments. On the other hand your Ministry of Production or Planning, if this is what we finally decide, would be responsible for co-ordinating decisions about expansion in the physical field . . .'

Foreshadowing the creation of the Department of Economic Affairs from a pair of the Treasury's lower ribs – the two National

Economy Divisions set up in 1962 – this passage was interesting and important. With the benefit of hindsight, the whole interview is significant also for what it omitted – any reference to the future of the Treasury's controversial functions as the head of the Civil Service. Towards a subject which was to need very careful review this showed a sensible reticence in the future First Lord of the Treasury.

But, of course, it was open to other politicians to voice their opinions, clearly if not harmoniously. When the Estimates Committee Report on Treasury Control of Establishments was debated in the House of Commons, on 23 February 1965, sharp divergences of attitude were revealed which, in the nature of debates on the Estimates Committee's work, owed nothing to party prejudices. On the one hand there was the same guarded satisfaction with the Treasury's superintendence that had been voiced in the Report. Mr William Hamilton (Labour M.P. for West Fife and the new Chairman of the Estimates Committee) echoed his Conservative predecessor in seeing Treasury control as the indispensable guarantee of responsible administration. 'Each Government Department must clearly understand that the Treasury has the right to inspect regularly and to root out quite ruthlessly any inefficiency which it sees. In this respect, as the Estimates Committee said, the Treasury must be the agent of the House of Commons. This House is not a body which can do that kind of thing, and we have to rely on the Treasury to do it on our behalf. It can be done without hostility.' But a younger generation within his own party was less sanguine about the Treasury's authority and a good deal more assertive of parliamentary competence. Dr Jeremy Bray (Labour M.P. for Middlesbrough West) warned the House, 'It would be a mistake for the House to undermine the principles of the Plowden Report and the divisions of responsibility between the Treasury and the Department [*sic*]. In particular, it would be a pity for the House to build up the Treasury and the responsibility of the Treasury to a level higher than the present one.' As for public expenditure, 'if we need five-year reviews and the authorization of commitments, is it not proper that Parliament should be involved in authorizing those commitments?' Admittedly, Plowden had rejected the possibility, but 'I do not think that the House should accept that position. We should examine whether we can institute some form of review of commitments to spend as distinct from merely a review of the annual estimates.'

Here, in the demand for something resembling the United States Congress's informed control of long-term policy budgets, one can recognize a characteristic aspiration of the House of Commons in the 1960s. It was capable of extreme expression. In the speech preceding Bray's, Mr Ian Lloyd (Conservative M.P. for Portsmouth, Langstone) had cheerfully expounded the prospect of 'a battery of large-scale great power computers throwing up on a screen in this building movements in national income and expenditure not for last week or last month or last year, but for today, during the last hour ... and the sooner that we recognize that this is coming and that it will be possible, the better qualified we in this House will be to conduct the government of the nation'. Dr Bray was not prepared to go along with that Orwellian vision of direct parliamentary government, but pursuing his own idea of a re-shaped machinery of government he asked – 'Is it good to associate the financial and economic influence of the Treasury with the question of administering the personnel policy of the Civil Service?'

This last remark had special importance because Bray was now Chairman of the Estimates sub-committee inquiring into recruitment to the Civil Service. Naturally enough, he took the opportunity to press his view, at the highest level, upon the Head of the Home Civil Service, Sir Laurence Helsby:

Q.36: If one does not have an independent Civil Service Commission and it does concentrate both control of personnel and control of finance in a single department, do you think this makes for health in government? – I think the management of the Service is most effective when it is combined with day-to-day contacts with the sort of work that is being done, so that one is not given a managerial responsibility *in vacuo*, as it were. Indeed, this is surely the experience of all outside organizations. The Treasury as a central Department on financial matters, which after all is the one kind of concern that runs right across the whole pattern of government, is a very convenient centre also for management.

Q.37: Do you think they necessarily have to go together? – Not necessarily, but if management were not to be linked to that, I would want it to be linked to some other function which was equally all-pervasive, if I may put it so.[35]

The Treasury view was, in fact, the traditional one, although it no doubt owed more to Sir Laurence's common sense and experience than to any formal tradition of orthodoxy. Finance and efficient management simply seemed to him, as they have to many others, naturally linked, and despite the functional division of the 1962 reorganization Sir Laurence was not prepared to regard the hiving-off of the Department of Economic Affairs from a small section of the Treasury as a significant precedent for isolating the Pay and Management Side from the rest of the Treasury.

Ultimately, the Committee's Report did not pursue the wider question 'whether the final responsibility for recruiting policy and management should remain with the Treasury, whose primary responsibility is for finance'. Indeed, beyond a few specific, short-term recommendations it could only urge that the whole question of Civil Service structure and management and recruitment be referred to a Plowden-style committee – i.e. an internal government inquiry with the sort of access to information which could not easily be made available even to a Royal Commission.

This proposal was accepted by the government, for there were by now overwhelming pressures inside and outside politics for a thorough overhaul of Britain's administrative machinery. On 8 February 1966 the Prime Minister was able to announce the appointment of a committee under Lord Fulton which, it was hoped, would join the great tradition of historic inquiries such as the Tomlin Commission of 1931 or the Northcote–Trevelyan Report. So, for two years, the question of the Treasury's control of the Civil Service was virtually *sub judice*, and there for the moment I must leave it.

THE MANAGEMENT OF THE ECONOMY, 1947–64

INTRODUCTION

It is now time to break off the pretence that the Treasury's recent evolution has taken place in some kind of vacuum, insulated from the stress of external emergencies. One hardly needs the detachment which only time can give to recognize that the developments of the last twenty years are inseparable from events which have had all the pace, hazard and sickening urgency of a runaway roller-coaster.

But this otherwise sterile progression along the 'Stop-Go' switchback of economic policy has set up a curiously syncopated rhythm of innovation in management, following belatedly and too often feebly in the wake of balance-of-payments crises, which has none the less left its mark on the machinery of government and the character of the Treasury. It is these changes which I now have to describe. As for the detailed chronology and analysis of post-war economic policy, I must refer the reader to other authors. This is not simply an evasion! The large and growing literature of comment performs a dual role, whether it means to or not. Proffering a committed and often passionate diagnosis of the British economic disease it is, at the same time, one of its more hopeful symptoms. On both counts it deserves attention.[36]

However, skeleton calendars of events accompany this brief commentary on the main phases of economic management in the last twenty years. Two of the main divisions correspond, as one might expect, to the abrupt transition between governing parties – Labour to Conservative in 1951, and Conservative to Labour in 1964. But – and cynics will applaud – the importance of this need not be taken for granted. The 'Stop-Go' cycle has sometimes moved in unashamed harmony with the election cycle, but the drearier characteristic of recent economic policy has been the uniformity of style imposed on Chancellors of all kinds by the procrustean bed of the balance-of-payments position. The Gaitskell of 1950–51 therefore merged insensibly into the Butler of 1951–5, and something called 'Butskellism' was born. Similarly, it might be argued that the real differences between Mr Maudling and Mr Callaghan may matter less for the history of institutional change in the Treasury than the transition from Mr Heathcoat Amory to Mr Selwyn Lloyd. Along these lines, Mr Samuel Brittan's perceptive analysis of successive Conservative Chancellorships is a splendid vindication of personality as a significant variable in economic management, and disproves the conventional humbug that the departmental policies of the professional Treasury are inseparable from those of the Chancellor of the Exchequer. The possibilities – and actuality – of dissonance give a more than notional importance to the comings and goings of Chancellors in recent years.

Another kind of landmark also lacks a consistent significance. The 7 per cent Bank rate of September 1957 retains the historic importance it was recognized to have at the time. At its highest level since 1921 it marked the climax to a period in which monetary measures – such as hire-purchase controls, the restraint of bank loans and Bank rate adjustments – had had an unusual significance. But the 7 per cent rates of July 1961, November 1964, July 1966 (to say nothing of the 8 per cent of November 1967 and February 1969 – unequalled since the outbreak of the First World War) are merged with some more meaningful measures. Indeed, one of the most important developments since 1961 has been the attempt by both parties to achieve the kind of economic management which precludes abrupt landmarks of discontinuity. They have failed, of course, but in the process even the April budget had lost some of its traditional magic as the only solstice of the financial year.

Indeed, the boundaries are much less important than the continuity of the experience. Half battlefield, half playground, the chronology of the last twenty years seems bleakly littered with discredited weapons and discarded toys – and the retrospect has considerable poignance. But for the Treasury, as for the government and the nation, the unique experience of post-war economic management has been a continuous education in the urgency of change – and there are still lessons to be learned.

CALENDAR OF EVENTS
THE LABOUR GOVERNMENT 1945–51

Note: The bracketed figures accompanying the budgets indicate the net estimated effect of tax changes in a full year; + = net increase, — = net reduction.

1945	5–26 July	*General Election:* overall majority of 136 for Labour Party. *Dalton* Chancellor of the Exchequer.
	21 August	End of Lend-Lease announced.
	13 October	*Budget:* (—£385m.) surtax raised; income tax, excess profits and purchase taxes reduced.
	6 December	U.S. loan agreement signed.
1946	1 March	Bank of England nationalized. Lord Catto appointed Governor.
	9 April	*Budget:* (—£146m.) purchase tax reductions; income tax allowances increased.
	21 April	Death of Lord Keynes
1947	1 January	Nationalization of coal industry.
	February	Fuel crisis.
	22 February	First *Economic Survey* published.
	21 March	Plowden appointed Chief Planning Officer.
	15 April	*Budget:* (+£54m.) death duties, profits tax, purchase tax, stamp duty and tobacco duties raised.
	7 July	Economic Planning Board announced.
	15 July	Convertibility of sterling inaugurated.
	21 August	Convertibility of sterling withdrawn.
	29 September	Stafford Cripps appointed Minister of State for Economic Affairs.
	12 November	*Budget:* (+£197m.) profits tax, purchase tax, drink duties raised.
	13 November	Dalton resigns. *Cripps* Chancellor of the Exchequer.
	6 December	Douglas Jay appointed to new post of Economic Secretary to the Treasury.
1948	1 January	Railways nationalized.
	February	White Paper on *Personal Incomes, Costs & Prices.*
	March	U.S. loan exhausted.
	6 April	*Budget:* (+£49m.) capital levy; tobacco and drink duties up; Pools betting tax; income tax relief; nationalization of electricity.
	May	Nationalization of transport.
	July	Health Service inaugurated.

	November	Board of Trade controls 'bonfire'.
1949	1 March	Mr Cobbold succeeds Lord Catto as Governor, Bank of England.
	6 April	*Budget:* (−£92m.) income tax relief; beer and wine duties reduced; betting tax and death duties raised; food subsidies cut.
	29 August	Cabinet decision on devaluation.
	18 September	£ devalued from \$4.03 to \$.280.
	24 October	Economy cuts announced. £140m. cuts in capital expenditure, £120m. cuts in current expenditure. Bank loan restrictions. Building controls.
	November	Agreement with trade unions on wages standstill.
1950	23 February	*General Election:* overall majority of 5 for Labour Party.
	1 March	Mr Gaitskell created Minister of State for Economic Affairs; Mr Jay appointed Financial Secretary to the Treasury.
	18 April	*Budget:* (−£1m.) income tax reduced; fuel tax, purchase tax raised.
	June	Korean War begins.
	3 August	Defence estimates trebled.
	19 October	Cripps resigns. *Gaitskell* Chancellor of the Exchequer. (Minister for Economic Affairs abolished.)
	December	Economic Information Unit becomes Treasury Information Division.
1951	February	Steel nationalized.
	10 April	*Budget:* (+£387m.) increased income tax, purchase tax, petrol duties. Health Services charges. Bevan and Wilson resign.
	17 April	Capital issues control.
	26 July	Restrictions on Bank credit, dividends and prices.

PERIOD I: THE LABOUR GOVERNMENT, 1945–51

Some of the worst moments of this period, which saw a remarkably steady recovery of the domestic economy, were provided by unavoidable, if not unforeseeable, external contingencies like the abrupt end of Lend-Lease and the severe terms of the United States Loan Agreement in 1945, or the United States recession of 1949, or the Korean war and the Persian oil dispute. But this does not acquit the Treasury of mismanagement. The most striking thing about the 1947 convertibility crisis is not its inevitability but the foolhardiness with which it was approached. Dalton's 'serious fears' about our obligation to make the pound convertible under the Loan Agreement were offset by official reassurances from the Treasury and the Bank of England which, in retrospect, he was to denounce as 'a profound error of practical judgment'. He rejected, but did not fail to mention in his memoirs, the suspicion among his friends of 'a plot by my advisers to deceive me'.[37] Thus, right at the outset of its post-war economic management, the Treasury was at the centre of another conspiracy theory. Yet another Chancellor of the Exchequer left office weighing the possibility that he might have been 'misled' by his official advisers. It was a bad augury for the new era which opened with the arrival of Cripps.

As we have seen, this meant the incorporation of large new responsibilities in the Treasury's sphere. Cripps brought with him, for example, the responsibility for the Regional Boards for Industry which he had recently acquired from the Board of Trade as Minister for Economic Affairs. He also brought into the Treasury the newly-fledged Central Economic Planning Staff under Sir Edwin Plowden and the Economic Information Unit which, in December 1950, was to grow into the Treasury Information Division. Yet all this involved relatively little structural change in Treasury organization. Certainly there was the creation of an Economic Secretaryship to the Treasury, the first addition to the ministerial command structure of the department in the twentieth century – but not the last. Shortly, in 1950, with Gaitskell's appointment to this responsibility it was up-graded to Minister of State for Economic Affairs, with Cabinet rank (though not actually in the Cabinet). Also, there was the creation of a statistics section in the already large Overseas Finance Division of the Treasury – a confession of, as well as a remedy for, what had gone wrong in August 1947. But otherwise the Central Economic Planning Staff was easily absorbed as another division of the Treasury.[38] Its work of co-ordinating the economic activities – particularly investment – of other departments kept it at the centre of the network of inter-departmental committees, but it would be a mistake to confuse this with a powerful long-term planning role. The C.E.P.S. consisted largely of lay-administrators, rather than economists. The Economic Section of professional economists, serving the whole machinery of government, remained in the Cabinet Office until 1953, and although its relations with the C.E.P.S. grew ever closer it was ironic that Aneurin Bevan should have complained in April 1951, after his resignation, that 'there are too many economists advising the Treasury'.

In fact, as far as planning was concerned, the role of economists at the Treasury was not yet very significant. Planning itself was becoming less and less purposeful.[39] It made some unhappy gestures. The first *Economic Survey* of February 1947, although the beginning of an admirable enterprise, had the ill-luck to coincide with that triumph of non-planning,, the fuel crisis. Indeed, it scarcely sounded a clarion call with its confession that 'the task of directing by democratic methods an economic system as large and complex as our own is far beyond the power of any Governmental machine'. Cripps, it is true, published a 'Long Term Programme' in 1948 to which actual economic performance conformed remarkably well – but this document had been a window-dressing contribution to the Organization for European Economic Co-operation and the achievement of aims has been written off as 'to some extent an accident'.[40] Cripps himself hoped to see planning as 'a simple matter of general indications by the Government in its annual Economic Survey'[41] and his speeches, with their appeal to the nation's moral, ethical and religious ideals, seemed to owe more to Law's *Serious Call* than to Keynes's *General Theory*.

Probably, when the internal history of the post-war Treasury can be written authoritatively, it will be agreed that the centre of gravity, in terms of capacity as well as achievement, now lay in the large Overseas Finance Division of the Treasury. Inheriting the experience and much of the personnel of the war years it was a highly professional unit, specializing either on a territorial basis – the sterling area, dollar countries, etc – or functionally, on the balance of payments, exchange control, import programming. It was this wing of the Treasury which had to face the external crises of 1946–51 and to assist in the international monetary reconstruction which produces the O.E.E.C. and the European Payments Union.

Home Finance, on the other hand, though deeply involved in digesting the large short-term war debt as quickly as possible, displayed no special inventiveness in these years. It was scarcely permitted to. Dalton's adherence to his increasingly unpopular 'cheap money' policy was followed under Cripps by an absence of any monetary policy at all.[42] Bank rate, held at 2 per cent since 1939, played no active part in regulating the economy. A degree of voluntary wage restraint was a valuable feature of these years but it was principally fiscal policy and physical controls which had to hold down the enormous inflationary pressures of post-war demand, and by 1949 these restraints were beginning to slip. The 30 per cent devaluation of the pound to 2·80 dollars, if it did not actually mark the failure of domestic policy, marked the beginning of its decay. 'It was inevitable,' as the Radcliffe Committee Report later put it, 'that sooner or later fresh thought should be given to more serious monetary restraints than the very mild ones that had been employed as auxiliaries in the early post-war years.'

PERIOD II: THE CONSERVATIVE GOVERNMENT, 1951–7

Fresh opportunity, if not fresh thought, was to be the privilege of the Conservative government of 1951. Uncontaminated by the disasters of the late 1940s they were soon free to manoeuvre in a rather kinder international climate, gradually dismantling the second generation of physical controls occasioned by the Korean war. The recession of 1952 was followed by the recovery and expansion of 1953. By 1954 the Chancellor of the Exchequer, Mr Butler, could hold out the prospect of doubled living standards in the next twenty years.

The end of this euphoria came with a series of balance-of-payment jolts, expensively recorded on the Bank rate seismograph, and it is the use of this instrument which holds the clue to the special character of the Conservatives' economic management. The spell-breaking increase in the Bank rate to 2½ per cent in November 1951, and to 4 per cent in March 1952, was, the 1952 *Economic Survey* claimed, 'the most significant change in monetary policy since the beginning of the war', for it ushered in a period of activity in the financial authorities quite unequalled since the 1930s. More important for this narrative, it involved a reapportionment of initiative within the Treasury, and between the Treasury and the Bank of England. It meant a revival of authority in the Home Finance side of the department, and it put the leadership and status of the Bank to their first serious test since the nationalization of 1946.

CALENDAR OF EVENTS: THE CONSERVATIVE GOVERNMENT, 1951–7

1951	25 October	*General Election:* overall majority of 17 for Conservative Party. *Butler* Chancellor of the Exchequer; Salter Minister of State for Economic Affairs.
	7 November	Bank rate raised from 2 per cent to 2½ per cent.
1952	29 January	Credit restrictions on hire purchase; import restrictions.
	February	'Robot' scheme mooted.
	11 March	*Budget:* (–£67m.) Food subsidies cut; income tax relief; Bank rate raised to 4 per cent.
	24 November	Mr Maudling appointed 'Economic Secretary to the Treasury'; Salter Minister of Materials.
1953	14 April	*Budget:* (–£412m.) 6*d.* off income tax; purchase tax reductions; investment allowances.
	May	Transport and steel denationalized.
	September	Plowden retires from Chief Planner's Office. Cabinet's Economic Secretariat moves to Treasury.
	17 September	Bank rate reduced to 3½ per cent.
1954	6 April	*Budget:* (–£10m.) 'No changes' (investment allowances adjusted).
	13 May	Bank rate reduced to 3 per cent.
	June	Chancellor holds out prospect of doubled living standards in twenty years.
	July	Food rationing ends.
	19 August	Hire-purchase restrictions lifted.
1955	27 January	Bank rate raised to 3½ per cent.
	24 February	Bank rate raised to 4½ per cent; hire-purchase restrictions. (STOP.)
	April	Anthony *Eden* Prime Minister; Sir Edward Boyle Economic Secretary to the Treasury.
	19 April	*Budget:* (–£155m.) 6*d.* off income tax. (GO.)
	26 May	*General Election:* Overall majority of 58 for Conservative Party.
	25 July	Credit restrictions on hire purchase, Bank loans; education cuts. (STOP.)
	14 September	I.M.F. conference at Istanbul. Convertibility of £ postponed.
	27 October	*Budget:* (+£113m.) purchase tax, profits tax increased; housing cuts.

	20 December	Butler resigns; *Macmillan* Chancellor of the Exchequer.
1956	16 February	Bank rate raised to $5\frac{1}{2}$ per cent; public investment cuts; hire-purchase restriction.
	March	White Paper on the *Economic Implications of Full Employment*.
	17 April	*Budget:* (−£2m.) income tax reliefs offset by profits tax, tobacco duties; premium bonds scheme.
	26 July	Suez crisis begins.
	1 September	Sir Norman Brook and Sir Roger Makins Joint Permanent Secretaries to the Treasury.
	October November	Suez invasion.
	November December	Petrol rationing. Drawing from I.M.F. to support £.
1957	13 January	Eden resigns; Macmillan Prime Minister; *Thorneycroft* Chancellor of the Exchequer; Powell Financial Secretary; Birch Economic Secretary.
	7 February	Bank rate reduced to 5 per cent. (GO.)
	25 March	Treaty of Rome signed; inauguration of E.E.C.
	5 April	Cuts in defence expenditure.
	9 April	*Budget:* (−£131m.) surtax relief; company tax concessions; purchase tax reductions.
	3 May	Appointment of the Radcliffe Committee on the Monetary System.
	11 August	Devaluation of the franc.
	12 August	Appointment of the Council on Prices, Productivity and Incomes. Rumours of devaluation of the £.
	19 September	Bank rate raised to 7 per cent. Emergency credit controls, cuts in public expenditure. (STOP.)

Nationalization alone was relatively unimportant to the Bank's post-war role, notwithstanding Dalton's confidence that 'power . . . has now moved from British private financiers and the City "establishment" to the Chancellor of the Exchequer', and notwithstanding the statutory provision that 'the Treasury may from time to time give such directions to the Bank as, after consultation with the Governor of the Bank, they think necessary in the public interest'. That remains a reserve power which has not been used. Instead the Bank's post-war leadership continued to secure its practical autonomy in a way which reflects interestingly on both institutions. The Bank, for instance, usually drew all the strength it needed by traditional top-level appointments from the City-bred *élite*, or – more rarely and less traditionally – from its own trained executives. Both were narrow sources of ability and, as far as leadership is concerned, 1946 saw no abrupt break with Montagu Norman's legacy. Certainly Lord Catto, succeeding Norman in 1944, was closer to the Treasury by virtue of his war-time service as adviser to the Chancellor than most Governors have been, but Lord Cobbold (Governor from 1949 to 1961) was a Norman protégé, and the post-war Bank continued to have the services of such veterans of the 1930s as H. A. Siepmann and Sir Otto Niemeyer.

The Treasury, on the other hand, appeared to make no attempt to alter the patterns of deference established between them. Indeed, Lord Bridges went out of his way to acknowledge the Treasury's submission to the Bank's superior expertise.

> The high officials of the Bank of England [he told the Radcliffe Committee in 1958], have long and intense training and experience in their particular field. They are specialists who have risen to the top through their skill and experience. . . . On the other hand, officers of the Treasury are laymen in the sense that most of them do not spend much of their lives in becoming experts in any particular subject.[43]

There was, therefore, no question of the Treasury telling the Bank how to run its affairs, nor was there any question of the Bank becoming another department of the Treasury. Communication between them tended to pass at a high and privileged level, an aloof relationship which both sides liked to rationalize as one between banker and customer.

But this begged a number of important questions. Where did power really lie? Which tail wagged which dog? As Lord Cobbold put it to the Radcliffe Committee (Q.260) 'I have found it very difficult to say just where any particular idea starts and finishes, or exactly where the initiative comes from', but he was emphatic that 'I am in a position to make suggestions to the Chancellor on any subject', and he left no doubt that, whatever might happen 'in the last resort', the Governor and the Court of the Bank of England enjoyed a considerable degree of independent initiative on Bank rate adjustments and all technical questions between the Bank and the City. The Governor regretted only that he didn't have more say on hire-purchase restrictions which were the most effective restraint on demand (QQ. 260–262).

During the active monetary policy of the 1950s this ill-defined relationship was severely tested – and found wanting, though for reasons which did not all fully appear at the time. But the picture gradually composed itself. In the foreground there was the abortive sensation of the Bank rate 'leak' inquiry of 1957. Successful in burying rumours of financial impropriety in dealings preceding the 7 per cent Bank rate of 19 September, the Tribunal of inquiry was to prove infinitely more interesting for revealing the way the whole financial 'Establishment' – City, Treasury, financial press – actually worked. It exposed the tolerant, perhaps lax, conventions of trust which made up their working relationship, and incidentally opened up a rich seam of sociological inquiry into *élites* which has been assiduously mined.[44]

Then, occupying the middle ground, there was the longer and more productive inquiry which kept the Radcliffe Committee on the Working of the Monetary System busy for two years from the middle of 1957. Appointed at a moment when years of inflationary pressures had defied all moderate restraints, it was to sit through months of always active, sometimes desperate, monetary measures, and although its findings can hardly be called conclusive it analysed the phenomena of the monetary system with a clarity which had its own influence on the system's institutions and conceptual framework.

Finally, very much in the background, there was a sharp but ostensibly secret struggle over the convertibility of sterling at a floating rate of exchange in 1952. Too important a dispute to be wholly concealed – one writer has compared it to the 'cavorting of an elephant under a dust sheet'[45] – the facts about the scheme, code-named 'Robot', have been gradually leaked to the public[46] and we now know it as a striking case history of departmental in-fighting which eventually spilled over into Cabinet dissensions. Indeed, some writers have gone a good deal further and represented the whole thing as an important instance – so unlike 1925 – of the way in which the massed powers of bureaucratic darkness can be sometimes routed by small forces of economic light. In fact, the parallels with 1925 are not too far-fetched. Here, it seems, was the same ruthless impatience on the part of the financial authorities to submit the British economy to the automatic disciplines of international monetary pressures.

Here also was the powerful alliance of the Bank of England and the Treasury's Finance divisions; and here too was the solitary crusader – not Keynes this time, but the Paymaster General, Lord Cherwell – determined to thwart what he regarded as a dishonourable and disastrous enterprise. Of course, there were some contrasts with 1925, and this was Lord Cherwell's case, for unlike the return to gold, which was at least publicly debated and internationally endorsed, the 'Robot' idea was a furtive scheme for abrupt, unilateral action which would have antagonized almost everyone – the United States, the sterling area countries and the members of the European Payments Union.

However, 'Robot' does compare with the return to gold for having stimulated a flow of vigorous dissent from the policies and the institutions of the financial establishment – and that is the immediately significant point. The 'Robot' project for floating exchange rates for the pound, which simmered on and off through 1952 and beyond, joined the Bank rate 'leak' inquiry and the Radcliffe Committee in undermining an apparently discredited system of economic management.

It is now becoming difficult to pick out individual voices from the Capitoline flock alerting Britain to her economic dangers. But Dr Thomas Balogh deserves pride of place for the trenchancy and range of an indictment which, in its 'pop' version, was published as 'The Apotheosis of the Dilettante' and in its classical form presented as a memorandum to the Radcliffe Committee in August 1958.[47] In both these analytical polemics he set out a clear prescription for structural reform at the Treasury as well as the Bank of England.

For the Bank, Balogh simply wanted to see the spirit of the 1946 Act properly fulfilled by its subjection to 'much more continuous Treasury Control'. This would have to stop well short of making the Bank a department of the Treasury, but it could be guaranteed by making certain senior Treasury officials – the Permanent Financial Secretary or his deputy, and perhaps the Economic Adviser – members of the Bank's governing body. This would meet the need, so alarmingly revealed by the Bank rate 'leak' Tribunal, for alternative (i.e. Treasury) policies to be aired before the Bank's settled views were presented authoritatively to the Chancellor of the Exchequer. Finally, there must be further reform of recruitment with a 'vigorous exchange of officials at all levels . . . of the hierarchy between the Treasury, the Board of Trade and the Bank of England. The Bank must be regarded as a part of the central government machinery.'

But what of the Treasury's place in that machinery? Balogh was not one of those who wanted to see the Treasury dismembered and abased, although he did see its influence since 1919 as almost wholly malign. The spurious title of 'Head of the Civil Service', the autocracy of Warren Fisher, the miscalculation of 1925, helped to feed Dr Balogh's powerful resentment against this complacent, self-perpetuating *élite*. Since the war little had changed, nothing had been learned. The Economic Section, both before and after its absorption in the Treasury, had been outmanoeuvred or ignored by the established Finance divisions of the Treasury – and the five severe exchange crises since the war pointed the moral.

At this point there are others available to endorse Balogh's case. In a second bout of autobiography Lord Salter has recently drawn attention to *his* role in squashing the 1952 'Robot' scheme. As Churchill's Minister of State for Economic Affairs he had had no illusions about the Treasury's power to neutralize any contenders for influence – hence his decision to hold his post within the Treasury rather than in some new department of Economic Affairs outside.[48] But even within the Treasury, where at least he knew what was in the wind, Salter found it difficult to mobilize support against the hasty implementation of 'Robot'. He turned for assistance to the Economic Adviser, Sir Robert Hall, and to Sir Edwin Plowden, both significantly outside the circle of Treasury men who were pressing the scheme. Eventually, the eloquent combination of Cherwell and Salter convinced Churchill that there must be something in their objections and 'Robot' was shelved, temporarily in spring and then decisively in summer 1952.[49]

For Salter, as for Cherwell, the objectionable aspects of 'Robot' had included its implicit bad faith towards overseas holders of sterling balances who would pay the price for a devaluation which went against the spirit of international monetary agreements. Even as a practical measure it failed to treat the root cause of the pound's difficulties in 1952 – a worldwide dollar shortage. But other commentators, for whom a floating exchange rate for the pound has since become a respectable notion, have stressed the alarming institutional breakdown that could permit a project like this to get so far without the influence of the Economic Section being properly brought to bear upon it. It was not the only breakdown of its kind. The evidence given to the Bank rate Tribunal made it possible to deduce that the Economic Adviser, inside the Treasury since 1953, had not been called into the crucial discussions on the 7 per cent decision.

Altogether, there was too much evidence that the transfer of the Economic Section from the Cabinet Office to the Treasury in November 1953 had made no significant impact on the routes of policy initiatives in the Treasury. As for 'planning', the existing machinery had been weakened by the departure of Sir Edwin

Plowden from his posts as Chief Planning Officer and Chairman of the Economic Planning Board in October 1953. No new Planning Officer had been appointed. The chairmanship of the Board was taken over by Sir Bernard Gilbert, then Second Secretary in charge of the Treasury's Home Finance and Supply Divisions. He was now to act as the Permanent Secretary's adviser on all financial and economic policy, for which nearly forty years' service in the Treasury was his major qualification.

Writing in the *Economic Journal* in December 1954 Mr Robin Marris gave some useful clues to the prevailing balance of economic planning power within the Treasury at that time. On the one hand, the Economic Section (which he had just left) numbered between twelve and fifteen – viz. a Director, Sir Robert Hall, a Deputy, Mr Ian Little, two Senior Economic Advisers at Assistant Secretary level, six to eight Economic Advisers and two or three juniors. Compared with the professional economist staffs of some governments, for example the Dutch, it was a very modest establishment which had no computer or professional statisticians of its own. In contrast, there was the large and well-equipped Overseas Finance Division of the Treasury which at its post-war zenith had between thirty and forty Administrative grade officials including two or three economists. It had a substantial statistics section. It had the ear of the Cabinet. The Bank of England and the Board of Trade were among its executive arms. It was, in other words, a most powerful and self-sufficient unit which dominated the all-important field of balance-of-payments policy.

Given all this, and given the administrative attitude which meant that 'if an aspect of economic policy requires for its rational implementation that some substantial piece of economic research be carried out, the normal procedure, by and large, is to drop the policy or to implement it irrationally', then it is not surprising that the Economic Adviser and his Section found difficulty in making headway against the lay administrative establishment. That establishment remained depressingly attached to its amateur status, convinced that 'adequate results can be obtained by the selection of suitable officials from the administrative class for training "on the job", coupled with the safeguard of constant advice from the sidelines from the small group of full-time professional economists'.[50] This seemed indeed the 'apotheosis of the dilettante' and it helped to make Balogh's case for 'the relevance of Civil Service reform in the economic policy making sphere'.

At this point it is worth noting that the current of criticism was not free of political colour. Dr Balogh made no bones about that.[51] Indeed, at a time when Conservative Chancellors were, in Mr

Brittan's phrase, 'highly non-expert', it was inevitable that their permanent advisers should be so heavily implicated in policy decisions. It was in the tradition of the service that they should adapt themselves with enthusiasm and imagination to the inferences of the governing party's policies, and in fact both parties have had reason to be grateful to them for doing so. But the case against the Treasury's official leadership in the 1950s seems to be that it showed too much enthusiasm, too much imagination. Andrew Shonfield has noted the tendency[52] and Samuel Brittan has recorded the results.[53] The advice given to Mr Butler, for example, by officials apparently 'too preoccupied with Mr Butler's political difficulties on the eve of an election', was bad advice which did lasting damage to his political reputation. Writing of the extraordinary 1955 sequence of pre-election 'Go' – the *6d.* off income tax give-away budget of April – and the post-election 'Stop' – monetary restrictions and education cuts in July – even a dispassionate academic textbook has had to explain the tax concession as 'an exclusively political move'[54] which in political terms proved a disastrous contribution to the sterling crisis 'trauma' of that year.

It was not the last such crisis. The 'trauma' of 1955 was followed by the Suez crisis 'trauma' of 1956 and the sterling crisis 'trauma' of 1957. The continued postponement of the pound's official convertibility had left it vulnerable to purely speculative attacks quite unrelated to the underlying economic situation. However, there seems to be some further degree of administrative culpability here in the deterioration of relations between the Treasury and the Bank of England. Already 'very bad' (Shonfield, p. 211) in 1955 they were sufficiently poor to jeopardize the safety of the reserves in 1957. At least, the failure to close the 'Kuwait gap' (through which loophole in the exchange controls British owners of sterling could speculate against the pound) has been attributed to the Bank's prolonged opposition – and the cost to the reserves has been estimated at some £70 million in the first half of 1957.[55]

PERIOD III: THE CONSERVATIVE GOVERNMENT, 1958–64

These are some of the issues which helped to build up the negative case against the administration of post-war economic policy up to 1958. But the next few years saw the formulation of remedial proposals, and in the process economic 'planning' with all its attendant apparatus acquired a new and positive attraction upon which both governing parties were prepared to converge.

Unlike the planning of the immediate post-war period, with its direct controls over limited supply and insatiable consumption, this was to be 'indicative' planning – the setting up of national targets and the creation of the social and economic framework in which those targets could be achieved by the relatively free play of supply and demand. The emphasis would not be on containment and restriction but on balanced growth – growth because nothing less would preserve, let alone increase, Britain's share in world trade and prosperity, and balance for any or all of a number of reasons. For example, by the mid-1950s the unique post-war experience of full employment had revealed its danger to lie in an apparently irresistible pressure for wage increases – increases which events had also shown to be almost invariably in excess of the growth of productivity. Paid for by price increases, and thus a higher cost of living, the consequent wage–price spiral had told disastrously on Britain's balance-of-payments position and was thus a major factor in the Stop-Go cycle. For this problem balance therefore meant a consistent policy for wages and incomes which would somehow combine full employment with price stability. Unfortunately, even in these conditions 'full employment' might be a statistical illusion. Post-war prosperity had not eliminated the tragic legacies of the 1930s – special areas of permanent depression in which the demand for labour fell far short of the supply. There was therefore a problem of regional balance which could only be solved in socially acceptable terms by programmes of regional development far more penetrating than the piecemeal measures which had been pursued since before the War. And the pattern of these programmes, with their comprehensive attention to the social and economic infrastructure of community life would share in the larger pattern of national development. Here too there would have to be a controlled balance within sections of the economy – a coherent transport policy, for example, or a planned balance between the competing fuel industries. There would have to be planned investment in the new technologies – from atomic energy to computers. Above all, there would have to be a planned balance of government investment and expenditure projected well into the future.

This is the point where the relatively marginal questions of Treasury control and Treasury organization fit in. This is the point where the Plowden Report of 1961 finds its place in the larger context of economic management. Because Plowden, taking its point of departure from the dominant presence of the state in the national economy, had absorbed the lessons of the last few years of economic history. Touching carefully on a politically controversial theme, it unmistakably condemned the sort of Stop-Go cycles that had been induced recently by the crude use of fiscal and monetary measures. For one thing, the measures themselves were unsuited to the effects desired (para. 23). It was now quite evident that hasty applications of the Bank rate brake and the tax-concession accelerator were, in the short term, totally ineffective because it took much longer than expected for the effects to work through, and in the long term manifestly harmful to the future of the British economy. They wasted resources. They demoralized policy. They were 'damaging to the real effectiveness of control of public expenditure' (para. 18).

Plowden therefore called for stability of expenditure policy 'so that long-term economy and efficiency throughout the public sector have the best possible opportunity to develop' (para. 12). This meant planning, and planning which would have to bear a quite unprecedented burden of responsibility for the long-term progress of the economy. With government investment running at so high a percentage of the total the decisions of the public sector were of immense significance for the whole.

In a context like this it is not surprising that disputes over the extent of Treasury control and departmental independence looked rather parochial. The real issue was one of maintaining the right balance and differentiation of function between departments which were working together in a common and rather massive enterprise. The Treasury's special dominance only made sense here because it was best placed to assess that balance and co-ordinate those functions. As for the Treasury's traditional tasks of restraining public expenditure, particularly in periods of stringency, Plowden poured scorn on the practice of making equal percentage subtractions all round as if one area of public expenditure was of the same social or economic value as any other. That some such crude notion was still current seemed to be suggested by the resignation of the three Treasury ministers in January 1958 in defence of a fixed ceiling of public expenditure. Indeed, the whole idea of varying the global total of public expenditure as a tool of economic management needed reappraisal, respectably Keynesian though it was. The new emphasis would have to be on the use of small, selected and timely variations in public investment as an influence on balanced growth – a shift, in other words, from macro-economic to micro-economic adjustments.

CALENDAR OF EVENTS: THE CONSERVATIVE GOVERNMENT, 1958–64

1958	6 January	Resignation of Thorneycroft, Powell and Birch. *Amory* Chancellor of the Exchequer; Mr Maudling (Paymaster General) to assist on economic affairs.
	20 March	Bank rate reduced to 6 per cent.
	15 April	*Budget:* (–£108m.) company tax reliefs; purchase tax reductions.
	22 May	Bank rate reduced to 5½ per cent. (GO.)
	19 June	Bank rate reduced to 5 per cent.
	28 July	Select Committee on Estimates reports on *Treasury Control of Expenditure.*
		End of credit restraints.
	14 August	Bank rate reduced to 4½ per cent.
	October	Hire-purchase restrictions abolished.
	20 November	Bank rate reduced to 4 per cent.
	December	Devaluation of the franc.
		Convertibility of £ announced.
1959	5 February	Relaxation of capital issues control.
	8 April	*Budget:* (–£359m.) 9*d.* off income tax. (GO.)
	30 July	Appointment of Plowden Committee on Public Expenditure.
	20 August	Report of Radcliffe Committee on the *Working of the Monetary System.*
	8 October	*General Election:* Overall majority of 100 for Conservative Party.
1960	21 January	Bank rate raised to 5 per cent. (STOP.)
	4 April	*Budget:* (+£72m.) profits tax, tobacco duties raised.
	28 April	Hire-purchase restrictions reintroduced, special deposits called in.
	23 June	Bank rate raised to 6 per cent.
	27 July	Amory resigns; *Lloyd* Chancellor of the Exchequer.
	27 October	Bank rate reduced to 5½ per cent.
	8 December	Bank rate reduced to 5 per cent.
1961	5 March	Revaluation of the mark.
	17 April	*Budget:* (+£58m.) surtax concessions; profits tax increased. Introduction of the 'Regulator'.
	20 July	Report of Plowden Committee on Public Expenditure.
	25 July	Bank rate raised to 7 per cent; emergency economy measures; cuts in public expenditure; 'Regulator' used; pay pause inaugurated.

	4 August	I.M.F. grants support for £.
	10 August	U.K. application to join E.E.C.
	5 October	Bank rate reduced to 6½ per cent.
	9 October	Post of Chief Secretary to Treasury created; Henry Brooke appointed.
	2 November	Bank rate reduced to 6 per cent.
1962	1 February	White Paper on Incomes Policy sets 2½ per cent norm.
	7 March	First meeting of the National Economic Development Council (N.E.D.C.).
	8 March	Bank rate reduced to 5½ per cent.
	22 March	Bank rate reduced to 5 per cent.
	1 April	End of pay pause.
	9 April	*Budget:* (+£9m.).
	26 April	Bank rate reduced to 4½ per cent.
	4 June	Hire-purchase restrictions eased.
	13 June	*Maudling* Chancellor of the Exchequer.
	26 July	National Incomes Commission announced.
	30 July	Major reorganization of the Treasury inaugurated.
	1 October	Sir Laurence Helsby and Sir William Armstrong succeed Sir Norman Brook and Sir Frank Lee as Joint Permanent Secretaries of the Treasury.
	3 October	Chancellor's Mansion House Speech; end of credit squeeze.
	5 November	Purchase tax reductions; investment allowances raised.
1963	3 January	Bank rate reduced to 4 per cent.
	14 January	De Gaulle opposes Britain's application to join E.E.C.
	6 February	N.E.D.C. approved 4 per cent per annum growth rate target. National Plan, *Growth of the United Kingdom Economy to 1966*, published.
	3 April	*Budget:* (−£618m.) income tax allowances increased; abolition of Schedule A; stamp duties reduced; investment incentives.
	18 April	N.E.D.C. approved report on *Conditions Favourable to Faster Growth*.
	19 October	Douglas-Home Prime Minister.
1964	March	N.E.D.C. report *The Growth of the Economy*.
	14 April	*Budget:* (+£115m.) tobacco and drink duties increased.
	September	Prospect of £700–800m. balance-of-payments deficit.

But what were the implications for the Treasury of this new conception of economic planning? It was no business of the Plowden committee to work out an economic strategy for sterling and the balance of payments – although it would not be unreasonable to deduce that an incomes policy was inseparable from Plowden's vision of balanced growth. On these points the Report of June 1961 was necessarily an incomplete prescription for the Treasury's future role, and other events were required to shape it. But in this respect, too, 1961 was a climacteric year. Producing its mid-summer sterling crisis, it also produced its official avowal of Conservative 'planning'. 'I am not frightened of the word,' said the Chancellor of the Exchequer stoutly, introducing his emergency budget of 25 July.

I believe that the time has come to establish new and more effective machinery for the co-ordination of plans and forecasts for the main sectors of our economy. There is a need to study centrally the plans and prospects of our main industries, to correlate them with each other and with the Government's plans for the public sector, and to see how in aggregate they contribute to, and fit in with, the prospects of the economy as a whole, including the vital external balance of payments.

This heralded the creation of the National Economic Development Council (N.E.D.C.), headed by the Chancellor of the Exchequer and two other ministers but essentially an independent body drawing its strength from the T.U.C., the employers' associations and the nationalized industries. Its objectives were to plan the strategies of growth for the public and private sectors of the economy alike, and although its powers were solely advisory the Chancellor of the Exchequer soon made it clear that he wanted it to have a real impact on the formation of government policy.

However, the appointment of N.E.D.C. did not raise the same kind of public speculation about the Treasury's position that was to be excited when the Department of Economic Affairs emerged in November 1964. Headed by the Chancellor, appointed by him and reporting to him, N.E.D.C. scarcely seemed a significant rival to the Treasury's managerial authority. Indeed, that authority was reinforced by two innovations in the course of 1961. Firstly the April budget had equipped the Chancellor with an important new fiscal device called 'the Regulator' – a discretionary power to vary taxes on consumption by up to ten per cent at any time in the fiscal year. It was a symptom of the tendency to displace the spring budget from its solitary dominance of the year, and it equipped the Treasury with a useful means of operating flexibly on consumer demand, whenever it chose. Secondly, in October the ministerial hierarchy of the Treasury was further strengthened by the creation of a Chief Secretaryship with senior Cabinet rank. The step was taken in the light of the heavy and increasing burdens falling on the Chancellor – burdens arising particularly from the long-term planning of public expenditure in relation to national resources. The new division of responsibility therefore allotted to the Chief Secretary (who was the former Minister of Housing, Mr Henry Brooke) 'the whole range of public expenditure both current and prospective, including the scrutiny of departmental Estimates and the framing of forward surveys'.[56] This was, in effect, the Supply and Establishments side of the Treasury's work and it left the Chancellor and the two other Parliamentary Secretaries free to concentrate on the management of economic and financial policy.

In this way any speculation about the Treasury's relations with the new agency of economic planning seemed effectively offset. Yet, it has been pointed out that 'the constitution of N.E.D.C. cannot be understood in isolation from the mood of profound distrust which had gathered round the Treasury by the time of the 1961 sterling crisis',[57] and this point is interesting. In both the Cabinet and the Treasury there appear to have been fears that 'Neddy', with its professional staff of economists standing outside the Whitehall Establishment, would be an embarrassing contradiction of the Treasury's sovereignty – and some members of the N.E.D.C. Office were happy to see it in that light. Under its Director General, Sir Robert Shone, and with its economic section run by Sir Donald MacDougall, the Office was rather well equipped to cut out an independent path.

This situation throws a slightly different light on the Treasury reorganization of 1962. In its construction of the powerful 'National Economy' and 'Public Sector' Groups of divisions it was a timely readjustment of the balance of power in economic management – and the adjustment, it need hardly be said, was in the Treasury's favour. The new National Economy Group, integrated as it was with the professional economists of the Economic Section, was now a much more formidable agency for economic planning than anything the Treasury had had before. Its National Economy Division 1 dealt with long-term as well as short-term forecasting of economic trends, and National Economy Division 2 co-ordinated policies for national economic growth – including problems of prices, incomes and manpower. It handled relations with N.E.D.C.

But what were those relations? Brittan has revealed that they got off to a rather acrimonious start early in 1962, and the provocation appears to have come from N.E.D.C.[58] Setting personalities aside, even dispassionate commentators were at a loss to predict how things would work out. Lord Bridges, writing concluding reflections for *The Treasury* some time in 1963, speculated whether Neddy could go on functioning as an effective body if its advice diverged from the Treasury's,[59] and Professor Daalder, in the same year, pointed gloomily to the fate of the Economic Advisory Council in the 1930s.[60] Overshadowed by a reinvigorated Treasury, Neddy seemed in danger of withering in a void.

Yet, says Mr Brittan, 'in the course of 1963–4, the centre of gravity of economic policy began to shift slightly away from the Treasury' as new sources of initiative made their impact on government. The Beeching Report on the railways, the Trend Report on scientific manpower, the Buchanan Report on traffic in towns and the Robbins Report on higher education were independent surveys which drew attention to wide problems of social reconstruction – and there was some measure of administrative response. In this congenial climate N.E.D.C. began to make its mark. Its first major report, 'Growth of the U.K. Economy to 1966', published in 1963, projected possible developments over a five-year period on the basis of a 4-per-cent growth rate in G.N.P. – and by some curious process of auto-suggestion this hypothetical figure, 'selected as a reasonably ambitious figure likely to bring out problems that have to be solved',[61] acquired the authority of a target, if not a prediction. Its success in capturing attention made up in some degree for the government's failure to launch a National Incomes Commission with trade-union support, and the Chancellor wisely turned to Neddy for help in restraining the pressures of pay claims and profits. On the other hand, notes Brittan, 'he did not consult the N.E.D.C. Office about his Budget judgement, and the Office was excluded from the Treasury's work on the short-term control of the economy'.[62] Even in 1964, it would seem that Neddy was not in the confidence of Whitehall.

This mattered in itself; it mirrored a wholly dangerous divorce between the new style of long-term planning and the short-term manoeuvres with which the Treasury was traditionally involved. And it also mattered in election year to a public which had been thoroughly alerted to the deficiencies of the British machinery of government. 1963–4 saw the 'What's-wrong-with-Britain' literary genre reach its height, and even if this cannot be credited with any dramatic impact on public administration it certainly influenced the climate in which its functions were being assessed. Andrew Shonfield, in his *British Economic Policy Since the War*, had long since exposed the fallibility of the administrative machinery responsible for economic management, and the implications of Thomas Balogh's indictment have already been noted. To these widely-read polemics might be added others, such as Michael Shanks's home-thoughts from Bulgaria, *The Stagnant Society* (1961), Norman Macrae's

Sunshades in October (1963) and Professor Brian Chapman's *British Government Observed* (1963). Finally, late in 1964, came Mr Samuel Brittan's *The Treasury under the Tories, 1951–1964*, the most cogent and informed diagnosis of the developments with which these pages are concerned. Each of these was a highly idiosyncratic work, but running through their often passionate criticism of recent economic management there were two consistent themes which have become the commonplaces of current interpretation.

The first directly related the poor performance of the British economy to the quality of British institutions – a diagnosis which gained in plausibility when the institutions and the performance were set beside those of our European competitors; the second can be summed up in what the Fabian pamphlet *The Administrators* (1964) apologetically described as a 'truism' – that the policies associated with recent economic disasters 'would have been different in most of these instances if officials had been different'.

This comprehensive indictment of men as well as measures reintroduces the themes with which the first half of this chapter was concerned. Although it has been convenient to treat the evolution of economic management apart from the general administrative evolution of the Treasury, the separation is highly artificial – and of no time is this more true than 1964. Following closely upon the rejection of Britain's first application to join the Common Market, a sharp reaction against our poor economic performance gave a cutting edge to criticisms of British institutions and, above all, of the Treasury and its personnel.

This last point is worth stressing. When *The Administrators* said that policies would have been different 'if officials had been different' it had added – 'if they had possessed, or obtained more expert knowledge and if they had looked farther ahead . . .'. But this hopeful qualification was not always offered by the more forceful critics of Treasury management. Criticism *ad hominem*, criticism which inferred the dire and irremediable culpability of identifiable Treasury officials was a special characteristic of the 'What's-wrong-with-Britain' style, and perhaps this was inevitable. It did not require great penetration to establish that responsibility, in the real sense of the professional judgements on which policies are founded, rested on relatively few, distinguished shoulders. The credibility, rather than the novelty of Brittan's book lay precisely in the informed way in which it distributed praise and blame for distinct policies upon those shoulders – which were not always anonymous. The 'Treasury Knights' had more than a walking-on part in his drama of the Tory years.

One would have to go back to the late nineteenth century for a comparable challenge to the anonymity of Treasury officials. But there is an important qualification to add. The criticisms of the 1960s had their constructive aspect. If one fights one's way through the arguments for and against official anonymity one can emerge with an apparently logical answer to this special situation in which official actions are being submitted to unprecedented scrutiny. That is, to ensure that those carrying real responsibility are in fact capable of answering for it publicly. This need not subvert the traditional character of the permanent Civil Service. It could be achieved, some have suggested, by the appointment of a new class of ministerial advisers, widely recruited from industry or the professions and all essentially expert. Chosen by the minister, trusted by him and giving him uninhibited advice, they might – it has been argued – bridge the gap between the minister's notional responsibility for everything which happens in his department and the reality. More important, they would satisfy the administrative reformers' aspiration for mobility and professionalism in the top echelons of the Civil Service, as well as the fashionable academic argument for an imitation of French methods.

On the eve of a predictable change in government these proposals were unusually pertinent. The Labour party had successfully identified itself with a programme of reform in the machinery of government, and since many would occur in the sphere of economic management there were special reasons for speculating about the future of the Treasury Knights. Could they still hope to take prisoner a socialist Chancellor of the Exchequer? Could they, in alliance with the Bank of England, still hope to outwit a long-term strategy for economic growth? Or would they be eclipsed by new sources of influence, by the bands of private advisers with first-class minds and thrusting personalities who were just waiting to surge into the corridors of power? The press, which had conditioned its reflexes to link 'Treasury' with 'fuddy-duddy', 'mandarin' and other modish pejoratives, made a special contribution to this highly-coloured speculation. In the confused early months of the Labour administration at least one Sunday newspaper thought it worthwhile to appoint a special 'Whitehall correspondent' to probe the personal conflicts behind the new balance of power in the Treasury. Permanent Secretaries, Second Secretaries and Economic Advisers suddenly became newsworthy.

And yet Mr Wilson had thrown his weight against such speculation. In the B.B.C. discussion already cited, he had, as a former civil servant, expressed himself with great caution about the notion of temporary advisers and ministerial *cabinets*. If outsiders were to be drawn into government departments they would come at a modest level in the hierarchy, and as for the French practice of appointing *cabinets* of personal advisers from outside the Civil Service, experience as a minister had taught him 'that I did far better when I relied on loyal civil servants who knew what I wanted. . . . I'm rather against the idea of bringing in a series of *éminences grises* or Rasputins or court favourites to advise a Prime Minister.' Later, in setting up the Fulton Committee, he was to stress that 'Civil servants, however eminent, remain the confidential advisers of Ministers, who alone are responsible to Parliament for policy; and we do not envisage any change in this fundamental feature of our Parliamentary system of democracy'.

Nevertheless, it was not difficult to infer that the advent of a Labour government would mean a major adjustment of the Treasury's special position in the machinery of government. Responsibility for economic planning, Mr Wilson had indicated, would be taken out of the Treasury, which was not only overloaded but had an unfortunate tendency to hold down production in the face of balance-of-payments difficulties. With the new emphasis on balanced growth it was clear that this would mean much more than a shift of administrative responsibility. It meant a change in the order of priorities with which the Treasury was traditionally associated – sterling and the balance of payments first, growth and full employment later. It could be anticipated that even within the sphere left to it the Treasury might have to bear subordination to the priorities of some new Ministry, of Production or Planning. Furthermore, there would be a challenge to its sovereignty in Civil Service questions. The case for the separation of Pay and Establishments from its Public Sector and Finance control was strongly argued, inside and outside the Labour party. No wonder the future course of Treasury development was of peculiar interest in October 1964.

CALENDAR OF EVENTS: THE LABOUR GOVERNMENT, 1964–8

1964	15 October	*General Election:* overall majority of 5 for Labour Party.
	16 October	Wilson forms government: *Callaghan* Chancellor of the Exchequer; creation of the Department of Economic Affairs under Mr Brown as First Secretary of State.
	26 October	White Paper, *The Economic Situation*, announces emergency economy measures including 15 per cent surcharge on manufactured imports.
	3 November	Parliament opens.
	8 November	'Paris Club' bankers arrange $400m. credit for Britain at I.M.F.
	11 November	*Budget:* (+£215m.) petrol duty up 6*d.*; income tax up 6*d.*; National Insurance contributions and retirement pensions increased; corporation tax announced for April 1965.
	18 November	Draft 'statement of intent' on voluntary incomes and prices policy circulated.
	23 November	Bank rate raised from 5 to 7 per cent.
	25 November	Bank of England announces $3,000m. credits from Central Banks.
	8 December	Bank of England instructs clearing banks on selective loans curb.
	16 December	Agreement between government, T.U.C. and employers' associations on incomes and prices 'statement of intent'.
1965	31 January	Government aids for exporters announced.
	1 February	National Health charges end.
	2 February	Aircraft cancellations; review of TSR-2 and F-111 ordered.
	10 February	Bank of England announces renewal of November $3,000m. support.
	11 February	White Paper on *Machinery of Prices and Incomes Policy*.
	15 February	Governor of Bank of England criticizes public expenditure in speech at Edinburgh.
	22 February	Chancellor announces 4¼ per cent per annum growth rate for public expenditure over next five years.

	17 March	Aubrey Jones appointed Chairman of Prices and Incomes Board.
	6 April	Cancellation of TSR-2.
		Budget: (+£217m.) capital gains tax; increased duties on tobacco and drink; entertainment allowances cut; controls on foreign investment; plan for corporation tax announced.
	27 April	Import surcharge reduced to 10 per cent.
	29 April	Bank of England calls in special deposits.
	5 May	Governor of Bank of England requests 5 per cent limit to increase in bank advances, exporters excepted.
	12 May	I.M.F. authorizes $1,400m. drawing by Britain.
	29 May	British and American banks renew 'swap' arrangement for $750m.
	3 June	Bank rate cut to 6 per cent; hire-purchase deposits increased.
	15 June	Government promises defence spending reduction to £2,000m. by 1970 at 1964 prices.
	27 July	Economy cuts: Chancellor announces £200m. cuts in local authorities and government investment; further exchange controls; further stiffening of hire-purchase terms; building licences.
	August	Sterling weakens but exports reach record level.
	10 September	Bank of England announces new support for £ from ten countries (excluding France).
	16 September	Department of Economic Affairs publishes *National Plan* for 25 per cent growth by 1970.
	22 December	Cabinet changes: Castle Minister of Transport; Jenkins Home Office, etc.
1966	17 January	White Paper on investment incentives.
	25 January	White Paper on Industrial Reorganization Corporation.
	1 February	Further request for 5 per cent limit to increase in bank advances.
	8 February	Further hire-purchase deposit and payment restrictions. Fulton Committee on Civil Service appointed.
	23 February	White Paper on *Public Expenditure: Planning and Control*.
	31 March	*General Election:* overall majority of 97 for Labour Party.
	3 May	*Budget:* (+£386m.) 40 per cent corporation tax; no change in income tax, supertax, purchase tax

		or duties; selective employment tax from 5 September; betting and gaming tax; restraint in overseas investment.
	15 May	Seamen's strike begins.
	13 June	Bank for International Settlements arranges $2,000m. credits for Britain.
	31 June	Seamen's strike ends.
	1 July	O'Brien succeeds Cromer as Governor of the Bank of England.
	3 July	Cousins resigns from Ministry of Technology.
	4 July	Prices and Incomes Bill published.
	13 July	June trade-gap of £55m. revealed.
	14 July	Bank rate raised to 7 per cent; special deposits doubled.
	20 July	Emergency economy measures: 10 per cent purchase tax 'regulator' used; travel allowances cut; 10 per cent on surtax; overseas spending cut; hire-purchase restrictions; voluntary incomes and prices freeze; Mr Brown offers resignation.
	25 July	Details of £150m. cuts in public expenditure: local authorities, nationalized industries investment cut.
	8 August	Bank of England extends restraint on bank advances.
	9 August	George Brown leaves D.E.A. for Foreign Office; Mr Stewart to D.E.A.
	11 August	Treasury announces restraint on dividends.
	12 August	Prices and Incomes Bill passed.
	23 August	First report of Prices and Incomes Board.
	13 September	New 'swap' facilities for $1,350m. announced.
	27 September	First National Productivity Conference.
	30 November	10 per cent surcharge removed.
	1 December	Investment grants increased.
		Record trade surplus in November.
1967	6 January	Ministerial changes: Mr Lee responsible for Prices and Incomes policy at D.E.A.
	20 January	Finance ministers meet at Chequers.
	26 January	Bank rate cut to 6½ per cent.
	13 March	Bank for International Settlements renews $1,000m. loan.
	16 March	Bank rate cut to 6 per cent.
	21 March	White Paper on Prices and Incomes Policy under voluntary restraint.

11 April	*Budget:* (−£12m.) No major changes; restraint on bank advances lifted.
2 May	Prime Minister announces application to join Common Market.
4 May	Bank rate cut to 5½ per cent.
5 June	Arab–Israel War.
7 June	Egypt closes Suez Canal.
9 June	White Paper on Regional Employment premiums.
13 June	White Paper on Productivity Agreements.
	Second National Productivity Conference.
21 June	£230m. increase in National Insurance Benefits; contributions raised.
30 June	End of period of 'severe restraint' in incomes policy.
24 July	Chancellor announces cutback of public expenditure to 3 per cent per annum rate of increase over three years.
28 August	Cabinet changes: Jay, Bottomley resign; Stewart leaves D.E.A.; Shore becomes Secretary for Economic Affairs under direct supervision of Prime Minister.
29 August	Relaxation of hire-purchase restrictions.
1 September	Resumption of oil supplies.
11 September	I.M.F. conference agrees on special drawing rights scheme.
	Dock strike.
3 October	E.E.C. critical of British monetary system in report on application to join Common Market.
10 October	Swiss banks lend Britain £37½m.
19 October	Bank rate raised to 6 per cent.
2 November	White Paper on *Economic and Financial Objectives of Nationalized Industries*.
9 November	Bank rate up to 6½ per cent.
12 November	Further credits arranged with Bank for International Settlements. France leaves the gold pool.
13 November	Prime Minister outlines scheme for technological collaboration with E.E.C. countries.
14 November	£107m. trade deficit announced.
16 November	Rumours on $1,000m. loan to support sterling; £ slumps.
18 November	£ devalued from $2.80 to $2.40 (14.3 per cent). Bank rate raised to 8 per cent; credit restrictions; hire-purchase terms stiffened; £100m. defence cuts; £100m. cuts in public expenditure; S.E.T.

		premiums withdrawn; export rebates cut; \$3,000m. stand-by credits arranged.
	27 November	De Gaulle announces opposition to British entry to E.E.C.
	29 November	Callaghan resigns; *Jenkins* Chancellor of the Exchequer.
	30 November	Chancellor publishes 'letter of intent' to I.M.F. promising policies of severe restraint.
	19 December	France formally vetoes British application to E.E.C.
	21 December	Chancellor warns of £600m. cuts in public expenditure.
1968	4 January	Sir William Armstrong's appointment as Head of Home Civil Service (from 1 April) announced. Sir Douglas Allen to succeed Armstrong as Joint Permanent Secretary of the Treasury on the Financial and Economic Side.
	16 January	Prime Minister announces cuts in public expenditure: estimated to save £325m. in 1968–9, £441m. in 1969–70. 'East-of-Suez' withdrawal accelerated; cancellation of F-111; raising of school-leaving age postponed; end of free school milk; cuts in university and road investment; Civil Service to be held at 1967–8 level.
	12 February	Renewal of stand-by facilities with Central Banks.
	22 February	Vote-on-Account reveals 6.6 per cent rise in public expenditure Estimates for 1968–9; £ weakens.
	March	Crisis in international gold dealings.
	15 March	London gold market closed; emergency Bank holiday proclaimed; George Brown resigns from government.
	16 March	Emergency meeting at Washington of gold pool countries; 'swap' arrangements enlarged; support for £ increased to \$4,000m.
	19 March	*Budget:* (+£923m.) purchase tax raised; duties on tobacco, drink, petrol increased; special levy on investment income; S.E.T. and betting tax increased; marriage rebate and children's allowance adjusted.
	21 March	Bank rate cut to 7½ per cent.
	3 April	White Paper on *Productivity, Prices and Incomes Policy in 1969 and 1968* published.
	5 April	Cabinet changes: Mrs Castle Minister for Employ-

	ment and Productivity. Taverne appointed to new post of Minister of State at the Treasury.
11 April	Prime Minister announces relinquishment of overall responsibility for D.E.A.
26 June	Fulton Report on the Civil Service; government accepts its main recommendations; Lord Shackleton named to supervise creation of Civil Service Department.

PERIOD IV: THE LABOUR GOVERNMENT, 1964–8

The Treasury since October 1964

In the event, not all these expectations have been fulfilled. The years since October 1964 have so far allowed the Treasury to exhibit just those qualities which its critics have attributed to it – resilience in the face of change, the despotic authority which economic stringency confers on those who hold the purse, the peculiar weight which attaches – in the Cabinet and in the public mind – to the Chancellor of the Exchequer and the department of the Premier. Expectations have not simply remained unfulfilled, they have been reversed. In October 1964 the mood in which the country would acclaim the ruthless surgery of the 1968 budget could have been foreseen with much less assurance than the decision to devalue the pound. Few of those commentators who now discern the Treasury's future at the centre of some huge, new department of economic management could have anticipated this at the birth of George Brown's Department of Economic Affairs.

The Department of Economic Affairs, set up in October 1964, was the principal embodiment of the Labour government's broad economic strategy for increasing investment, expanding exports and replacing inessential imports. As First Secretary of State for Economic Affairs, Mr Brown was responsible 'for framing and supervising the plan for economic development and for the general co-ordination of action to implement the plan, and of all economic policy related to industrial expansion, allocation of physical resources and regional implications of the expansion programme'. He was to supplant the Chancellor of the Exchequer as chairman of the N.E.D.C.

Indicted recently as a pre-Keynesian 'economic howler'[63], the latter decision was explained away at the time as recognition of a basic distinction between, on the one hand, the novel problems of shaping the physical foundations of economic growth, and, on the other, the traditional techniques of financial management which were the province of the Chancellor. Cooperation between the two was cheerfully expected to be 'a matter of continuous and perfect harmony'.

Commentators were less sanguine. Contradictions of personality as well as policy were implicit in the new arrangements, and the stage seemed set for a classic struggle, not only between leading figures in the Cabinet but between rival hierarchies of Whitehall. After all, the new D.E.A. had stripped the Treasury of its two National Economy Divisions, and had taken over most of the economic planning staff of the N.E.D.C. office. It had recruited skilfully in Fleet Street, acquiring, among others, such vigorous scourges of Treasury policies as Samuel Brittan and Michael Shanks. In the new Economic Adviser to the Cabinet, Dr Thomas (now Lord) Balogh, they could count on another ally hostile to the Treasury's traditional influence on economic management. These were formidable forces with which to confront the Financial and Economic Side of the Treasury headed by Sir William Armstrong and 'the last Gladstonian fiscal apostle remaining in the British Civil Service', Sir Richard Clarke.[64]

And yet, so the story goes, the Treasury 'won'.

It would be easier to reject this rather sensational view of relations between the two departments if it had not been endorsed, to some extent, by Mr Brown himself. Reviewing his experiences at the D.E.A. he has willingly presented its relations with the Treasury as a 'struggle' – and a struggle of personalities which the D.E.A. lost partly, he admits, because of the superior 'strength of the Treasury Knights in Whitehall jousting'.[65] Indeed, he deplores his failure to recruit a 'very, very distinguished Treasury official' to head his department at the outset. As it was, his irregular recruits from outside the Civil Service proved, with a few exceptions, 'quite unable to match the professionals when it came to discussion and decision-making'. To that extent the department's failure to hold its own was rooted in its men, not its measures.

But this is only part of the story, and a minor part which obscures the real issues between the departments. The crucial aspect of their relationship was surely the degree to which it was founded on an untried and questionable division of labour. Admittedly, it was possible for Sir Eric Roll, the first Permanent Secretary of the D.E.A., to define its functions in 1966 in exactly the same words used by Sir Richard Clarke of the Treasury in 1964 – viz.

(i) to relate each department's activities and requirements to the general objective of national economic policy, to the prospective availability of economic resources, and to the total of claims upon them;
(ii) to provide informed advice to departments, as partners in a joint enterprise, on all aspects of economic policy, and to help them to fulfil their departmental responsibilities efficiently and economically.[66]

This was not a transformation, but a transfer, of duties which still called for a very close working relationship with the Treasury. Both Sir Eric Roll and Sir Richard Clarke were to insist that this relationship existed and worked well.[67] At the same time, however, along this rather dubious line which defined 'physical' from 'financial' areas of economic policy there existed the possibilities of a fissure – which ultimately opened. It was, essentially, the fissure which in any emergency must yawn between the immediate and the long-term priorities of policy, and in the monetary crises of 1964 to 1968 it has been these short-term financial priorities – the defence of the pound, the balance of payments, the restraint of demand – which have inevitably carried the day.

It was slightly less inevitable that this should mean the eclipse of the D.E.A. and the abandonment of its *National Plan* of September 1965. Mr Brown has argued that devaluation in 1966 would have been the right opportunity to break out of piecemeal deflation into export-led expansion, and thus to preserve an approximation of the Plan's main objective, a 25-per-cent growth by 1970. But, as he also admits, failure was implicit in his initial 'Concordat' with the Treasury. This left the Treasury possessed not only of general short-term control, and of its traditional mastery of public expenditure, but in particular of those public investment plans which are an intrinsic part of any long-term economic strategy. 'In fact,' it has been argued, 'the real power of the Treasury was hardly touched by the institution of the D.E.A.'[68]

So much, one might say, for the government's attempt to administer a new economic strategy. The impression should be resisted. It is quite wrong that the personalized difficulties of the D.E.A. should dominate the picture of economic management – just as it is wrong to set up Treasury policies as the antithesis of a novel strategy for growth. The truth is that the management of agreed economic policies has been shared by the whole range of economic departments and agencies – and to their objectives the Treasury has made its own distinctive contribution.

From the outset, the Chancellor of the Exchequer registered his allegiance to the overall objective of growth. In his budget of April 1965 Mr Callaghan expounded the government's view that 'a Budget conceived and operated as the most immediate instrument of long-term objectives can and should make a great positive contribution to them. They are the counterpart of my Budget strategy and coupled with them the Budget itself can give the economy an aggressive forward thrust.' The major fiscal measure of this budget, the Corporation Tax, was designed to have a direct impact on the investment and growth of British industry. Less direct, the Capital Gains Tax was held to make a necessary contribution to the climate of an incomes policy. On the public expenditure side of the account the Chancellor promised contributions to the regional employment policies of the D.E.A. and the Board of Trade by way of more generous loan assistance to Local Authorities in less prosperous areas. In the specific field of the computer industry he could already boast Treasury support. The whole question of investment incentives was under a review which culminated in the scheme for cash investment grants announced in January 1966. In the same month the Industrial Reorganization Corporation was launched with its £150 million Treasury endowment. The budget of 1966, with its Selective Employment Tax and the regional employment premiums, attempted an even more dramatic transfer of resources to industrial growth points. The Treasury's White Paper of May 1967 – *Public Purchasing and Industrial Efficiency*[69] – outlined further means by which the government's huge spending power as a customer might be used to stimulate industrial development. As for nationalized industries, the Treasury's White Paper of November 1967 – *Nationalized Industries: A Review of the Economic and Financial Objectives*[70] – superseded criteria for performance last set out in 1961 and marked an important advance towards rational investment and pricing policies in this vital sector.

In the management of public expenditure, equally significant progress was embodied in the February 1966 White Paper on *Public Expenditure: Planning and Control*.[71] The end-product of a review, initiated in November 1964, it set out estimates for public expenditure over the next five years at the agreed *National Plan* average growth rate of 4¼ per cent per annum. There was nothing original about planning a norm; Mr Maudling had done so in 1963 in the wake of the Plowden Report. 'The essential and novel element,' claimed the White Paper, 'was the procedure of deciding first how much the country could afford; then deciding how this could best be deployed; and finally requiring each spending Minister to arrange his expenditure within his agreed allocations' (para. 14). The survey was, in fact, inseparable from the projections of the *National Plan*, and its figures – unlike those for the private sector, which could only produce forecasts – represented relatively firm commitments to the allocation of resources. Affecting, as they did, such a substantial proportion of the Gross National Product, these decisions on 'a rational pattern of priorities and a realistic view of the implications for the national economy' created a stable basis for developing efficiency in the public sector and gave the private sector something like a framework of certainty within which to make its own planning decisions. In other words, the Treasury's was one of the most concrete contributions to the *National Plan*. It was also a major contribution to a coherent prices and incomes policy and to the management of the balance of payments. 'Wages and salaries,' the White Paper pointed out, 'represent a relatively larger part of the total cost of public services than of industry generally,' and while the public sector's expenditure draws in a much smaller proportion of imports than the private sector's, its defence and overseas components were a significant burden on the balance of payments. A comprehensive public expenditure plan, accurately related to resources, was therefore a major contribution to a steady rate of economic growth.

Within Whitehall, the new approach had important implications for the administration of 'Treasury control'. The emphasis had now shifted decisively from the pettifogging requirements of detailed 'prior sanction' to broad allocations of programmes. Within these totals the departments were now on their mettle to make an effective distribution of their resources against proper criteria of cost/effectiveness. Furthermore, their Estimates had to be set within the context of the five-year plan, rolling forward each year. This was healthy exercise which eliminated much of the traditional bickering and uncertainty about totals and made for a more harmonious and responsible relationship between the Treasury and the departments.

But the man in the street, bemused by an alternation of savage, deflationary packages and an ever-rising scale of public expenditure, might well remain unimpressed. Indeed, the Vote-on-Account of February 1968, following so soon after the huge cuts of 16 January, revealed an apparent rise of ten per cent in central government expenditure which administered a shock to the foreign exchange market. It was no use explaining that the picture was incomplete, that the true rate of increase was 6·6 per cent, or that the figures included large items, such as the Selective Employment Tax, which were simply a transfer of revenue from one set of private pockets to another. The heavy selling of sterling was a sharp lesson in the price still to be paid for outdated parliamentary accounting procedures.

Yet, since 1963, the Treasury had taken several steps towards a more meaningful presentation of expenditure figures. In the April budget of 1965 Mr Callaghan had set out government transactions under functional categories which showed more clearly how they were related to the economy as a whole. 'Re-arranging figures will not solve our budgetary problems,' he said, 'but the new arrangement puts the problems into a more realistic framework, with much less chance of making them appear worse than they are.' The aggregate of Exchequer borrowing, traditionally placed 'below the line' – a confusing and archaic convention, dating from 1875 – was made to appear much healthier by distinguishing the categories of investment for which it was raised. Late in 1967, the National Loans Fund Bill (enacted in 1968) sought to give statutory form to this distinction by transferring the Exchequer's borrowing and lending transactions to an account separate from the main revenue and expenditure figures. The demands of the nationalized industries were thus divorced from central government expenditure in much the same way, and for much the same reasons, that Goschen divorced local government loans in 1887.

The historical point is unlikely to have appealed to Mr Callaghan. Early in his tenure he had made some deliberate gestures, symbolic of a new departure. Showing better taste than Mr Dalton, who had removed Gladstone's portrait because he couldn't stand its piercing eyes, he had had Disraeli turned out of his room. At the same time he broke with tradition by retiring Gladstone's battered budget-box to a museum showcase. His new, functional budget-box was a symptom of what was intended to be a forward-looking reign at the Treasury – and the list of measures outlined above shows that he didn't stop short at gestures. Neither the bitter circumstances of Callaghan's retirement under the shadow of devaluation nor the sterile sequence of deflationary measures which he had to present should obscure his constructive achievement. Facing the most consistently difficult circumstances of modern times, he combined an enforced orthodoxy of policy with an originality of outlook which should earn him a respectable place among twentieth-century Chancellors. He was a sturdy guarantor of the political and administrative authority of the Treasury.

The last point is not to be taken for granted. The concept of economic management with which the government started out did not accord a dominant role to the Treasury, and in some quarters there was a strong desire to see it humbled. Officially, of course, the strategy of growth was seen as a collaborative task for all the economic departments, under the effective chairmanship of the Prime Minister. By mid-1967, however, elements of this equilibrium were missing – not just because the Treasury had captured the short-term initiative with its monetary restraints but because much of the vigour had gone out of the D.E.A.'s drive for positive action on the economy. The neutral character of the 1967 budget stressed the limitation of that agency, and the National Productivity Conference in June illuminated some of the enormous potential for change. The solution was a new strategy, outlined by the Prime Minister on 20 June. Direct intervention in industry was to be spear-headed by the Industrial Reorganization Corporation backed up by a reinvigorated D.E.A. The new emphasis would be on the structural reform of industry at the grass-roots rather than on the overall management of demand. Rationalization, modernization and a greater drive for export productivity were the main objectives to be attained by selective policies of merger, investment incentives and discriminatory taxation. The ministerial reshuffle of 28 August marked the new departure with Mr Peter Shore's appointment to a reshaped D.E.A. under the direct supervision of the Prime Minister.

As an interesting experiment in the machinery of government this move raised questions which are almost more difficult to frame than to answer. After all, no peace-time Prime Minister since Ramsay MacDonald had taken direct charge of a department – and the precedent was hardly reassuring. How deep, then, was Mr Wilson's commitment, and in what guise was he making it? Was this the First Lord of the Treasury asserting himself as an overlord across the whole field of economic management, or were the Premier and the Cabinet Office throwing themselves behind an isolated departmental role? From the outset, a distinctive feature of the Labour government had been Mr Wilson's intention and capacity to superintend economic policy from his chairmanship of the appropriate committees. Supported by an enlarged and singularly competent Cabinet Office he already had much better access to the formative stages of policy than any of his predecessors. How meaningful, then, was the new departure, and what was its significance for the Treasury?

Mr Wilson's intention to take the chair at meetings of the N.E.D.C. appears to hold the clue to what proved a relatively modest and short-lived shift of emphasis.* He was putting his weight behind those aspects of the D.E.A. which had most to contribute to the structural reform of the economy – its Industrial Policy Division, which co-ordinated through N.E.D.C. the work of the 'little Neddies' for groups of industries, and its Regional Policy Division, which co-ordinated Whitehall's provincial planning policies and the work of the Regional Economic Planning Councils and Boards.[72] Pacemakers set close to the heart of industry, these agencies were of vital importance in a precarious economic context which precluded large-scale manipulation of demand. Wages and incomes were still locked under restraint. The cautious reflation measures of late August and early October 1967 demonstrated by their timidity just how small was the Treasury's room for manoeuvre. The immediate future clearly lay with micro-economic and not macro-economic operations.

In making this personal commitment the Prime Minister instituted no serious diminution of the Treasury's role. It is true that Cabinet Office advisers tended to replace Treasury men in key committees, and before long William Neild moved from the Cabinet Office to become Permanent Under-Secretary of the D.E.A. His predecessor, Sir Douglas Allen, became Joint Permanent Secretary of the Treasury on the Economic and Financial Side. But, interchange of personnel apart, Mr Wilson courted the closest possible liaison with the Treasury. The Chancellor of the Exchequer took over the

*In answer to a parliamentary question, Mr Wilson announced on 11 April 1968 that he had relinquished overall responsibility for the D.E.A., but 'I retain my present and previous responsibility for co-ordination, not only of industrial matters but of economic matters in general'

chairmanship of the Cabinet's Prices and Incomes policy committee and was expected to deputize for the Premier on the N.E.D.C. The Treasury's new Economic Adviser, Mr Michael Posner, was well known for his commitment to the kind of detailed intervention in industry now under discussion. There was little to stop the Treasury remaining part of a working relationship with the D.E.A. which would be quite faithful to the original blueprints of Labour policy.

This new balance of power, together with much else, was shattered by the devaluation of the pound on 18 November 1967. In the most painful way possible the initiative passed again to an axe-wielding Chancellor. The situation could do nothing to enhance the position of the Prime Minister, nor could it hold much comfort for Mr Callaghan. But it did wonders for his successor, Mr Jenkins. Little in the Treasury's recent history could be more remarkable than the feeling with which his appointment was greeted, for – not to belittle Mr Jenkins's substantial merits – the sentiment seemed directed in a high degree at the refurbished charisma of the Chancellorship. In the, apparently fallacious, belief that devaluation had at last given the Chancellor room to manoeuvre towards reflation and growth it was widely felt that the Treasury had again become a post worth having. To a greater degree than at any time since the war the future of the economy seemed to hang on sound budgetary judgement and severe fiscal management. The rewards for success were glittering, and no longer so remote.

As a skilled historian, with a first-class degree in Economics, Mr Jenkins was well fitted to resume the traditional authority of his office, and he soon showed himself sensitive to it. Gladstone's budget-box made its reappearance and the budget of 1968 acquired a portentousness which had been missing in some of its predecessors. By the end of March, when Cabinet changes were pending, Mr Jenkins was plausibly rumoured to feel strong enough to challenge the survival of a separate D.E.A. Its overseas planning functions had already gone to the Board of Trade; its responsibility for prices and incomes policy and a large section of its staff were soon to move to Mrs Castle's new Department of Employment and Productivity. The N.E.D.C. office was reclaiming its old independence as a planning organization. The time seemed ripe for the Treasury to recover such long-term planning jurisdiction it had lost with the departure of the National Economy Divisions in 1964.

The campaign (if there really was one) was thwarted and Mr Shore's position at the D.E.A. reinforced by the ministerial changes of 5 April 1968. Nevertheless, the wind was still in the sails of those who argued that a major reorganization of the machinery of government should produce a few super-ministries from the existing proliferation of agencies. A 'Ministry of Communications' was mooted which could absorb responsibilities now shared between the Ministries of Transport, Technology and the Board of Trade. A 'Ministry of Nationalized Industries' was strongly sponsored by the appropriate Select Committee of the House of Commons. Above all, it was argued, the time had come for the Treasury to take over effective control of long-, as well as short-term economic planning as a unitary Ministry of Economic Affairs. With the pledges given to the International Monetary Fund in the 'letter of intent' of November 1967, the pursuit of strictly controlled budgetary policies could no longer be jeopardized by a divided command.

Ironically, this kind of speculation was occurring at just the moment when the Treasury's managerial role in the Civil Service was coming up for dissection. The report of the Fulton Committee on the Civil Service, long awaited, emerged from a drizzle of press leaks on 26 June 1968.[73]

THE FULTON REPORT

The scope of the Committee's inquiry was the Home Civil Service as a whole, and there can be no question of reviewing the vast range of its findings here. But so far as its terms of reference included 'the structure, recruitment and management' of the Civil Service it necessarily bore heavily on the Treasury whose responsibilities these were. For this institution, before all others, its recommendations were most dramatic and most critical.

Analysing the deficiencies of the Civil Service in its mid-twentieth-century context – amateurism, rigidity, inefficiency, unimaginativeness – it concluded 'For these and other defects the central management of the Service, the Treasury, must accept its share of responsibility. . .'. Despite the recent improvement in its management services the Treasury has failed to keep the service up to date.'[74]

It recommended, therefore, the creation of a new Civil Service Department, absorbing both the existing Civil Service Commission and the functions of the Pay and Management Side of the Treasury. In its staffing 'The new departments should not in our view be predominantly staffed by officers who have spent most of their careers in the Treasury, and can thus have little experience of direct responsibility for management'. It 'will have to play a larger part than the Treasury does today and must have more ultimate authority'. For example, on questions of staffing in the departments it would have the last word. 'If the Treasury took the view that the total expenditure should be reduced, it would be free to challenge the policies of the spending departments, but not the assessment of staff costs approved by the Civil Service Department.' Above all, the new department 'should be in a position to fight, and to be seen fighting, the Treasury on behalf of the Service'.[75] Presumably these were among the recommendations which the government accepted in announcing the setting up of the new department under its minister, Lord Shackleton, and its Permanent Secretary and Head of the Home Civil Service, Sir William Armstrong.

There were few surprises in all this. The context of the debate from which the Fulton Committee arose has already been sketched and running through it was a consistent theme of unease with the Treasury's role. Long before the Fulton Committee set to work the dispossession of the Treasury's Pay and Management Side had become a cliché of reform from which serious thought and logic were rapidly draining. There were to be signs of this impoverishment in the Report itself.

In the event, however, it was the Report's broad indictment of Civil Service 'amateurism' which alerted readers to its conceptual prejudices. Quite apart from exciting resentment among the rank and file of civil servants, the use of this questionable pejorative term seemed to convict the Committee of sensationalism and unfairness. That was the view put, with 'shame and anger', by Lord Robbins when the House of Lords debated the Report on 24 July 1968, and the opinion was widely shared. Relatively few, however, were prepared to observe that the Treasury was the particular victim of these prejudices. Understandably, it was Lord Helsby, the retiring head of the Home Civil Service, who put the case with most force. 'The Treasury,' he wrote in *The Listener* on 18 July, 'is a traditional butt for criticism, a focal point for dissatisfaction with the ways of bureaucracy and the natural target of those with whom vituperation passes for reasoning. There may well be advantage in creating a new department with a brighter public image – so long as this is not expected to work wonders by itself.'

The point was worth making and it is worth amplifying. The Fulton Committee's prescription for the Treasury is arguably the weakest part of its whole case.

This betrays itself in several ways. There is, for a start, the rather tendentious historical argument on which the whole Report is founded, namely, that the modern British Civil Service stands condemned as a creation of the nineteenth-century philosophy of the Northcote–Trevelyan Report. It was Dr Eric Hobsbawm who pointed out the superficiality of this inference. No one, he said, has held it against the much admired French Civil Service that it was the product of ideas elaborated in the 1790s and institutionalized under Napoleon I.[76] As it is, the Report skated lightly over the Civil Service reviews which have taken place at regular intervals since the 1860s, relegating them to a note in the, initially unpublished, third volume of evidence. Yet, as an earlier chapter in this book has shown, the Civil Service, and the Treasury in particular, have been subject, in this century, to inquiries which could hardly have been more critically pre-disposed. Both the Haldane Committee in 1919 and the Select Committee on National Expenditure in 1942 had examined the Treasury's function in a climate far more hostile to its authority than that of the 1960s. Yet both had concluded that the Treasury's financial and managerial functions were inseparable and should be reinforced.

Of course, this in no way argues the relevance of their findings in 1968, but the Fulton Report's statement that 'The Treasury's concern for public expenditure led to its development as the central managerial authority for the Service as a whole'[77] is neutral to the point of evasion. It might have been possible to acknowledge that the Treasury's concern for public expenditure led to its *explicit designation* by Parliament, the Cabinet and public opinion as the central managerial authority. There can be no justification for the inference, commonly made, that in some dark way associated with Warren Fisher the Treasury had usurped its central role. This had been allotted to it, and, in its current form, allotted so recently as to be relatively untested. The Treasury's organizational adjustment to the specialized job of managing the Civil Service dates, at the very earliest, from the Joint Permanent Secretaryships of 1956, effectively from the upheaval of 1962. To abandon the enterprise in 1968 is going to look, in posterity's long view, more like fidget than reform.

By the same token one might ask – how old are the managerial techniques in which the Civil Service is found wanting? In what comparable areas are they better developed? The Report admits, a little grudgingly, that 'the Civil Service has played a major part in the development of organization and methods in this country'.[78] It could have gone further. In the use of automatic data-processing the Civil Service has been the pioneer. And at this point one wonders, what inhibited the Committee from acknowledging the work of the Treasury's O. & M. Divisions? They receive oblique reference, but the general remarks on O. & M. in the Civil Service damn with faint praise.[79] It emerges in Volume II, however, that the Management Consultancy Group on whose findings much of the Report is based 'did not visit Treasury O. & M. Divisions, but we understand that they have a special responsibility for automatic data-processing (A.D.P.) studies, for providing an O. & M. service for the smaller Departments and for the Service-wide development of O. & M.

techniques and O. & M. training.'[80] To neglect them in this way is puzzling, to say the least.

However, the prejudices of the Committee are bared most effectively by the Report's aspiration that the new Civil Service Department 'should be in a position to fight, and to be seen fighting, the Treasury on behalf of the Service'. Why this pugnacious metaphor? What moved the Committee to build into their ideal of Civil Service institutions a relationship of conflict when its objective was the removal of barriers and the alleviation of stress? There can be little doubt that this phrase was calculated to gratify many, found well beyond the ranks of the Civil Service, who at some time or other have had to depend on the Treasury's judgement in a material issue. No one doubts, least of all its officials, that the Treasury is an unpopular institution. But does one have to appeal to King James I to point out, in twentieth-century terms, that any Treasury which does its job must be generally disliked? To exploit this unthinking resentment in a serious appraisal of the machinery of government suggests alarming immaturity in the face of the facts of life.

And the specific proposal for the break-up of the Treasury's dual responsibility argues a dangerous optimism in the face of the facts of financial management. A time when public and political opinion is moving sharply against the size and cost of the public service is an odd moment to divorce the concept of managerial efficiency from the normal criteria of economy. For the Report to say 'the precise allocation of functions between the two departments will have to be worked out' confesses the Committee's uncertainty on this intractable problem. As it is, the Report conceded that 'The Treasury should retain responsibility for developing and disseminating techniques of financial analysis and systems of financial control, and this will give it an interest in certain aspects of departmental organisation as well as in interdepartmental procedures'.[81] This is valuable, but it strengthens the suspicion that the Fulton Committee's recommendations for the Treasury are a well-intentioned confidence trick which marks the confluence of certain fallacies.

There is 'the Finance Ministry fallacy' – the belief, that is, that even in the modern economy one can isolate the administration of monetary problems in some Ministry of Finance or Department of the Budget, quite divorced from broad economic policies and the management of personnel.[82] This would be retrograde, notwithstanding the example set by some other countries. The distinctive feature of recent evolution in the Treasury has been the way in which its organization studies, systems analysis and cost/effectiveness appraisals have enriched the criteria of expenditure control. As already pointed out, this cross-fertilization has been going on for a relatively short period, and to inhibit it now would be to fulfil the fallacy and turn the Finance rump of the Treasury into a case-hardened bastion of penny-pinching.

Closely linked with this is the 'Treasury-men-are-different' fallacy, which holds that tenure in the department permanently disqualifies its members for useful service elsewhere. The Report is quite explicit about this. The Civil Service Department is not to be staffed predominantly by Treasury men who can have 'little experience of direct responsibility for management'. The fact that there is constant interchange between the two Sides of the Treasury doesn't reassure the Committee either. It 'impedes the development of a full professionalism in each'. The other material fact, that the Treasury is constantly fed by secondments from other departments is not noted, although Lord Helsby pointed out in his evidence that 'of the nine Under Secretaries and above on the Establishment side of the Treasury, four have spent more of their careers outside the Treasury than in it'. Apparently one is to believe that the clean-limbed Principals who pass into (and out of) the Treasury in a steady flow are subtly tainted by some miasma lurking in the corridors of the New Public Buildings.

The nature of this taint is explained by the 'original sin' fallacy – which argues that the historic legacy of the Treasury's traditions condemns it irrevocably: it cannot be trusted. The Committee is convinced of the sentiment and sees no reason for questioning its source. Indeed, one can only guess at the lingering folk-memory of Lingen, Welby, Warren Fisher and others which may haunt Whitehall to this day. Whatever its foundations, the sentiment is irrational and is not going to be explained away. Against that hard fact opposition to the Fulton recommendation is wise to recoil.

Nevertheless it should be possible to express these reservations without seeming to reject the rest of the Fulton diagnosis. That has been, unquestionably, an immensely fruitful exercise and the Committee are to be congratulated on transcending the quality of some of the representations made to them. The Management Consultancy Group's share in this credit is large and one must hope that their findings will quicken and re-shape the Civil Service in the manner intended. Indeed, the prospect of a real improvement in its homogeneity, effectiveness and morale is something which has reconciled critics to the more questionable aspects of the Report. In this spirit Lord Helsby, Lord Bridges and Lord Sherfield, as former heads of the Treasury, have bleakly conceded that the mutilation of their former department may be inevitable, given the strength of feeling on the subject. This concession, and the official acceptance of the Report's recommendation, therefore marks an interesting victory for the principle of change for change's sake – ('A change is necessary for other sufficient reasons but also to demonstrate that a fresh start is being made') and for a particular view of Treasury history – ('There is today among civil servants a lack of confidence in the Treasury'). Time's comment on all this will prove more interesting than any historian's.

In fact, an historian can have less of value to say at this point in the Treasury's evolution than at any time in its past. He would certainly be wrong to argue that nine hundred years of institutional history should weigh heavily on its shoulders. He may take an antiquarian interest in the quainter survivals of its past; he would be mischievous to urge their preservation. He would do better to recall that the Treasury has been a plastic institution, always capable of being shaped to new tasks: and if he has any perception he will admit that the modern Treasury is better fitted to respond than it has ever been. It will need this flexibility. Challenged, on the one hand, as a department of economic management and, on the other, as a guardian of the public purse, it has a turbulent time ahead of it. One must hope the official was right who argued that the Treasury exists 'in order to curtail the natural consequences of human nature'. If so, its future is assured.

SOURCE NOTES

1. S. H. Beer, *Treasury Control* (1957), footnote, pp. 51–2.
2. This subject has been widely debated, notably by P. Einzig, *Control of the Purse* (1959); B. Crick, *The Reform of Parliament* (1964); G. Reid, *The Politics of Financial Control* (1966) and R. Butt, *The Power of Parliament* (1967).
3. J. Veverka, 'The Growth of Government Expenditure in the U.K. since 1790', in *Public Expenditure – Appraisal and Control* (1963), ed. A. T. Peacock and D. J. Robertson, Table III, p. 119.
4. A. T. Peacock and J. Wiseman, *The Growth of Public Expenditure in the United Kingdom* (1961), p. 107, Table 13. Cf. U. K. Hicks, *British Public Finance 1880–1952* (1954), p. 17; Veverka, *op cit.,* Table III.
5. Veverka, *op. cit.,* Table I, p. 114.
6. *Sixth Report from the Select Committee on Estimates* (1957–8), p. 53. Page references given in these source notes indicate written evidence or appendices attached to the *Report*. Oral evidence is cited in the text by the appropriate question number.
7. *ibid.*, p. xxxvi; cf. p.v.
8. *ibid.,* pp. 48–54.
9. *ibid.,* p. vii.
10. *ibid.,* pp. 48–9.
11. This point was commented on in the Treasury's *Observations* on the Select Committee's *Report – Seventh Special Report from the Select Committee on Estimates* (1958–9), p. 5.

12. Another of the Treasury's complaints in its *Observations,* p. 13, this point seems borne out by QQ. 359, 365 and 1674–5.
13. *Sixth Report from the Select Committee on Estimates, op. cit.,* pp. 236–7.
14. *ibid.,* p. 383.
15. *ibid.,* p. xxviii.
16. *ibid.,* p. xxxvii.
17. *ibid.,* p. xx.
18. *ibid.,* p. xxv.
19. *Observations of the Treasury,* p. 6, para. 14.
20. *Control of Public Expenditure* (1961), Cmd 1432.
21. *Public Administration,* vol. 41, spring 1963, pp. 5, 6.
22. *Control of Public Expenditure, op. cit.,* p. 13, para. 33. Further references will be given to the appropriate paragraph, in the text.
23. 'The Reorganization of H.M. Treasury', *O & M Bulletin,* February 1963, p. 26. For other accounts of the 1962 reorganization see, *Public Administration,* spring 1963, and Lord Bridges, *The Treasury* (1964), Chapter XIV.
24. Sir R. Clarke, *The Management of the Public Sector of the National Economy* (1964), p. 12.
25. *ibid.,* p. 21.
26. *ibid.,* p. 14. For a guide to the jargon see the Treasury's *Glossary of Management Techniques* (1967).
27. For studies in this problem see: R. N. McKean, 'Cost Benefit Analysis and British Defence Expenditure', in *Public Expenditure: Appraisal and Control,* (1963), ed. A. T. Peacock and D. J. Robertson pp. 36–60; and M. S. Feldstein, 'Cost-Benefit Analysis and Investment in the Public Sector', in *Public Administration,* winter 1964.
28. 'The Treasury Centre for Administrative Studies', in *Public Administration,* winter 1963, pp. 388–92; C. D. E. Keeling, 'The Treasury Centre for Administrative Studies', in *Public Administration,* summer 1965, p. 191.
29. Supplement to *O & M Bulletin,* May 1965. For other appraisals of modern developments see Sir J. Pitman, 'How it all began', in *O & M Bulletin,* August 1966; and J. N. Archer, 'Developments in Treasury Management Services', *O & M Bulletin,* May 1966 (reprinted in *Public Administration,* autumn 1966). A useful technical guide to current practices is A. Williams's *Output Budgeting and the contribution of micro-economics to efficiency in government* (1967), (C.A.S. Occasional Paper, No. 4).
30. *Sixth Report from the Estimates Committee* (1964–5), Memorandum submitted by the Acton Society Trust on 'Attitudes of Civic University Students towards an Administrative Career in the Civil Service'. The findings of the Estimates Committee can be usefully compared with an elaborate analysis of 'Recruitment to the Administrative Class, 1960–64' by C. H. Dodd and J. F. Pickering in *Public Administration,* spring and summer 1967. An earlier social and educational analysis is R. K. Kelsall's *Higher Civil Servants in Britain* (1955).
31. *Fifth Report from the Estimates Committee* (1963–4), Report, para. 51.
32. *Third Report of the Public Accounts Committee* (1958–9), Q. 3507 (4 June 1959).
33. *Second Report of the Estimates Committee* (1963–4), para. 88.
34. From *The Listener,* 5 March 1964, p. 380; later reprinted with other contributions from Mr Jo Grimond, Mr Enoch Powell and Lord Bridges, in *Whitehall and Beyond* (1964).
35. *Sixth Report from the Estimates Committee* (1964–5), Evidence.
36. Three of the more important commentaries which I have in mind are: *The Management of the British Economy 1945–60* (1965), by J. C. R. Dow, a former

member of the Treasury's Economic Section; *British Economic Policy Since the War* (1958), by A. Shonfield; and *The Treasury under the Tories, 1951–1964* (1964), by S. Brittan.

37. H. Dalton, *High Tide and After: Memoirs 1945–1960* (1962), p. 257. There is an alternative conspiracy theory, 'that Ministers, by doing nothing to make the balance of payments balance in 1947, deliberately promoted the failure of sterling convertibility forced on them by the Americans': A. J. Youngson, *The British Economy 1920–1957* (1960), p. 168.
38. H. Daalder, *Cabinet Reform in Britain, 1914–1963* (1964), p. 223.
39. The quality of economic planning under the first post-war Labour government is often belittled – see Brittan, *op. cit.*, pp. 156–7, or Youngson, *op. cit.*, 166–73 – but for a vigorous defence see *Economic Planning in the United Kingdom: Some Lessons* (1967), by Professor E. A. G. Robinson, a former member of the C.E.P.S. 'What I am anxious to bring out is that down to 1950, when there was the bonfire of controls, it was possible not only to plan but also to achieve a structural readjustment of the British economy' (pp. 29–30).
40. Dow, *op. cit.*, pp. 53–4.
41. Colin Cooke, *Life of Sir Stafford Cripps* (1957), p. 357.
42. Dow, *op. cit.*, p. 227.
43. *Committee on the Working of the Monetary System* (1959), Evidence, vol. 3, p. 47. Memorandum dated 30 December 1958.
44. See, for example, the special issue of the *Manchester School*, vol. 27, No. 1, September 1959. Also, R. A. Chapman in *Public Administration,* summer 1965.
45. Dow, *op. cit.*, p. 80.
46. The principal sources of information on this nominally secret debate are, in order of publication: Shonfield, *op. cit.*; Lord Birkenhead, *The Prof. in Two Worlds* (1961); Brittan, *op. cit.*, and Lord Salter, *Slave of the Lamp* (1967).
47. 'The Apotheosis of the Dilettante' was a contribution to *The Establishment* (1959), ed. H. Thomas; the memorandum appears in the Radcliffe Committee *Memoranda of Evidence,* vol. III, pp. 31–47. The two works have some passages in common.
48. Lord Salter, *Memoirs of a Public Servant* (1961), p. 339. Cf. the same author's *Slave of the Lamp, op. cit.*
49. Salter, *Slave of the Lamp,* pp. 215–24.
50. These quotations come from R.Marris, 'The position of economics and economists in the government machine: a comparative critique of the United Kingdom and the Netherlands', *The Economic Journal,* December 1954.
51. Radcliffe Committee *Memorandum*, paras. 1–4.
52. Shonfield, *op. cit.,* p. 215.
53. Brittan, *op. cit.*, pp. 178–9.
54. G. D. N. Worswick and P. H. Ady (eds.), *The British Economy in the 1950s* (1962), p. 34.
55. *ibid.,* p. 323.
56. Bridges, *The Treasury*, p. 163.
57. Brittan, *op. cit.,* p. 221.
58. *ibid.,* p. 240.
59. *ibid.,* p. 202.
60. Daalder, *op. cit.,* p. 238.
61. G. Polanyi, *Planning in Britain: the Experience of the 1960s* (1967) (Institute of Economic Affairs Research Monograph), p. 31.
62. Brittan, *op. cit.,* p. 332.
63. S. Brittan, 'Inquest on Planning in Britain', *Planning*, vol. XXXIII, No. 499,

January 1967, p. 6. This is a useful review of the planning experiment of the D.E.A. under Mr George Brown.

64. The phrase is Anthony Howard's, in his article 'A Clash Has Been Arranged', *Sunday Times*, 21 February 1965.
65. Mr George Brown, 'Why the D.E.A. lost to the Treasury Knights', *Sunday Times*, 31 March 1968.
66. Sir E. Roll, 'The Department of Economic Affairs', *Public Administration*, spring 1966, p. 4.
67. Sir R. Clarke, 'The Public Sector', *Public Administration*, spring 1966. This issue contains a valuable symposium on 'The Machinery for Economic Planning' under the new Labour government.
68. M. Shanks, 'DEA: fact, fiction and the future', *The Times*, 8 April 1968.
69. Cmd. 3291 (1967).
70. Cmd 3437 (1967).
71. Cmd 2915 (1966).
72. For a detailed explanation of this labyrinth see 'The Machinery for Economic Planning', *Public Administration*, spring 1966.
73. *The Civil Service* (1968) (5 vols), Cmd 3638.
74. *ibid.*, Report (vol. I), para. 21.
75. *ibid.*, paras. 255, 263, 268, 252
76. *The Listener*, 18 July 1968, 'The Fulton Report: a further view'. The article as a whole is a most effective chastisement of the Report's flabbier generalizations.
77. *The Civil Service*, Report (vol. I), para. 252.
78. *ibid.*, para. 164.
79. *ibid.*
80. *ibid.*, vol. 2. *Report of a Management Consultancy Group*, para. 282.
81. *ibid.*, vol. 1. para. 267 (c).
82. The dangers of this fallacy were effectively exposed by Peter Jay, 'Don't Split the Treasury', *The Times*, 1 July 1968.

Further Reading

This is not an exhaustive list of sources; the manuscript records of Treasury history are omitted. But I have selected a generous range of printed works which throw light on aspects of Treasury development.

Chapter 1
THE MEDIEVAL ORIGINS: 1066–1554

Few books attempt to deal with the whole of the five hundred years covered in this chapter, and there is no modern work devoted to a synthesis of administrative, fiscal and economic history. As I have good reason to appreciate, the ambiguities of medieval financial administration lend themselves better to tentative, scholarly monographs than to broadly generalized narratives. Consequently, the list of 'further reading' below contains many specialist studies in learned journals which will repay the trouble taken in finding them by the integrity of their treatment of detail. There are no short cuts.

Fortunately, Professor S. B. Chrimes has provided an introduction to the whole course of medieval administrative history which could serve the general reader as a point of departure. There is nothing comparable on fiscal or revenue history and the works by Ramsay and Dowell fall below the standards set more recently by Mitchell and Steele. General textbooks of medieval history, such as the volumes of the Oxford History of England by A. L. Poole, F. M. Powicke, M. McKisack and E. F. Jacob, deal intermittently with these topics but tend to treat finance as a marginal, rather than central, concern of government. Sir Goronwy Edwards, in his David Murray Lecture, has complained of a similar imbalance among historians of medieval Parliaments. Underlying this reticence is the lack of any work on the Treasurer comparable to Professor Tout's studies in the organs of household government.

Adams, G. B., *The Origins of the English Constitution* (Yale, 1920).
Barlow, F., *The Feudal Kingdom of England, 1042–1216* (London, 1955).
Broome, D., 'The Auditors of the Foreign Accounts of the Exchequer, 1310–27', *English Historical Review*, vol. 38, 1923.

Brown, R. A., 'The Treasury of the Later Twelfth Century', in *Studies presented to Sir Hilary Jenkinson*, ed. J. C. Davies (London, 1957).

Clarke, M. V., *Medieval Representation and Consent* (London, 1936).

Chrimes, S. B., *An Introduction to the Administrative History of Mediaeval England* (Oxford, 1966), 2nd edn.

Davies, J. Conway, *The Baronial Opposition to Edward II: Its Character and Policy* (Cambridge, 1918).

Dietz, F. C., *English Government Finance, 1485–1558* (Illinois, 1920).

Dowell, S. E., *A History of Taxation and Taxes in England from the Earliest Times to the Year 1885*, vol. 1 (London, 1888).

Edwards, J. G., 'The *Plena Potestas* of English Parliamentary Representatives', in *Oxford Essays in Medieval History, presented to H. E. Slater* (Oxford, 1934).

Edwards, J. G., *The Commons in Medieval English Parliaments* (Creighton Lecture) (London, 1958).

Edwards, J. G., *Historians and the Medieval English Parliament* (David Murray Lecture) (Glasgow, 1960).

Elton, G. R., *The Tudor Revolution in Government* (Cambridge, 1953).

Fryde, E. B. and M. M. 'Public Credit, with Special Reference to North-Western Europe', in *The Cambridge Economic History*, ed. M. M. Postan, E. E. Rich and E. Miller, vol. III (Cambridge, 1963).

Fryde, E. B., 'Materials for the Study of Edward III's Credit Operations, 1327–48', *Bulletin of the Institute of Historical Research*, vol. XXII, 1949.

Fryde, E. B., 'Loans to the English Crown, 1328–1331', *English Historical Review*, vol. 70, 1955.

Galbraith, V. H., *The Making of the Domesday Book* (Oxford, 1961).

George, Mrs Dorothy, 'Note on the Origin of the Declared Account', *English Historical Review*, vol. 31, 1916.

Gray, H. L., *The Influence of the Commons on Early Legislation* (Cambridge, 1932).

Hall, Hubert, *The Antiquities and Curiosities of the Exchequer* (London, 1891).

Harris, B. E., 'King John and the Sheriffs' Farm', *English Historical Review*, vol. 79, 1964.

Harriss, G. L., 'Fictitious Loans', *Economic History Review*, 1955–6.

Harriss, G. L., 'Aids, Loans and Benevolences', *Historical Journal*, vol. VI, 1963.

Holdsworth, Sir William, *History of the English Law*, vol. I (1922).

Holmes, G. A., *The Later Middle Ages, 1272–1485* (Edinburgh, 1962).

Holt, J. C., *Magna Carta* (Cambridge, 1965).

Hoyt, R. S., *The Royal Demesne in English Constitutional History, 1066–1272* (New York, 1950).

Hoyt, R. S., 'Royal Taxation and the Growth of the Realm in Mediaeval England', *Speculum*, vol. XXV, 1950.

Jacob, E. F., *The Fifteenth Century, 1399–1485* (Oxford, 1961).

Jenkinson, H., 'Medieval Tallies', *Archaeologia*, vol. LXXI, 1925.

Jenkinson, H., 'William Cade, a Financier of the Twelfth Century', *English Historical Review*, vol. 28, 1913.

Johnson, C. (ed.), *Dialogus de Scaccario* (London, 1950).

Jolliffe, J. E. A., *The Constitutional History of Medieval England* (London, 1937).

Jolliffe, J. E. A., 'The *Camera Regis* under Henry II', *English Historical Review*, vol. 68, 1953.

Jolliffe, J. E. A., 'The Chamber and the Castle Treasuries under King John', in *Studies in Medieval History presented to Sir F. M. Powicke*, ed. R. W. Hunt, W. A. Pantin and R. W. Southern (Oxford, 1948).

Johnson, C. (ed.), 'The Pipe Roll of 2 Richard I', *Pipe Roll Society*, 1925.

Kirby, J. L., 'The Rise of the Under-Treasurer to the Exchequer', *English Historical Review*, vol. 72, 1957.

Macfarlane, K. B., 'Loans to Lancastrian Kings: the Problem of Inducement , *Cambridge Historical Journal*, 1947–9.

McKisack, M., *The Fourteenth Century, 1307–1399* (Oxford, 1959).

Madox, Thomas, *The History and Antiquities of the Exchequer of England*, (London, 1711).

Maitland, F. W., *The Constitutional History of England* (Cambridge, various edns).

Mills, M. H., 'Exchequer Agenda and an Estimate of Revenue, Easter Term, 1284', *English Historical Review*, vol. 40, 1925.

Mills, M. H., 'Experiments in Exchequer Procedure (1200–1232)', *Transactions of the Royal Historical Society*, 4th Series, vol. 8, 1925.

Mills, M. H., 'The Reforms at the Exchequer (1232–1242)', *Transactions of the Royal Historical Society*, 4th Series, vol. 10, 1927.

Mitchell, S. K., *Studies in Taxation under John and Henry III* (Yale, 1914).

Mitchell, S. K., *Taxation in Medieval England*, ed. S. Painter (Yale, 1951).

Outhwaite, R. B., 'The Trials of Foreign Borrowing: the English Crown and the Antwerp Money Market in the Mid-Sixteenth Century', *Economic History Review*, 1966.

Poole, A. L., *Obligations of Society in the Twelfth and Thirteenth Centuries* (Oxford, 1946).

Poole, A. L., *From Domesday Book to Magna Carta, 1087–1216* (Oxford, 1955).

Poole, R. L., *The Exchequer in the Twelfth Century* (Oxford, 1912).

Powicke, F. M., *King Henry III and the Lord Edward* (Oxford, 1947).

Powicke, F. M., *The Thirteenth Century, 1216–1307* (Oxford, 1953).

Prestwich, J. O., 'War and Finance in the Anglo-Norman State', *Transactions of the Royal Historical Society*, 5th Series, vol. 4, 1954.

Ramsay, J. H., *The Revenues of the Kings of England, 1066–1399* (Oxford, 1925).

Richardson, H. G. and Sayles, G. O., *The Governance of Mediaeval England from the Conquest to Magna Carta* (Edinburgh, 1963).

Richardson, H. G., 'The Exchequer Year', *Transactions of the Royal Historical Society*, 4th Series, vol. 8, 1925.

Richardson, H. G., 'The Chamber under Henry II', *English Historical Review*, vol. 69, 1954.

Richardson, H. G., 'Richard fitz Neal and the Dialogus de Scaccario', *English Historical Review*, vol. 43, 1928.

Richardson, W. C., *Tudor Chamber Administration, 1485–1547* (Baton Rouge, 1952).

Round, J. H., 'The Origin of the Exchequer', in *Commune of London* (London, 1899).

Sainty, J. C., 'The Tenure of Offices in the Exchequer', *English Historical Review*, vol. 80, 1965.

Sayles, G. O., *The Medieval Foundations of England* (London, 1948 and later edns).

Schofield, R. S., 'The Geographical Distribution of Wealth in England, 1334–1649', *Economic History Review*, 1965.

Steele, A., *The Receipt of the Exchequer, 1377–1485* (Cambridge, 1954).

Stubbs, W., *The Constitutional History of England* (numerous edns).

Tout, T. F., *Chapters in the Administrative History of Medieval England* (Manchester, 1920–32).

Tout, T. F., *The Place of the Reign of Edward II in English History* (Manchester, 1936) revised edn.

Tout, T. F., 'The Civil Service in the Fourteenth Century', in *Collected Papers*, vol. III (1934).

Tout, T. F. and Broome, D. M., 'A National Balance Sheet for 1362–3', *English Historical Review*, vol. 39, 1924.

Treharne, R. F., *The Baronial Plan of Reform, 1258–63* (Manchester, 1932).

Turner, G. J., 'The Sheriffs' Farm', *Transactions of the Royal Historical Society*, New Series, vol. 12, 1898.

White, G. H., 'Financial Administration under Henry I', *Transactions of the Royal Historical Society*, 4th Series, vol. 8, 1925.

White, G. H., 'The Household of the Norman Kings', *Transactions of the Royal Historical Society*, 4th Series, vol. 30, 1948.

Wilkinson, B., *Constitutional History of Medieval England, 1216–1399*, 3 vols (London, 1948, 1952, 1958).

Wilkinson, B., *Constitutional History of the Fifteenth Century, 1399–1485* (London, 1964).

Willard, J. F., *Parliamentary Taxes on Personal Property, 1290–1334* (Cambridge, Mass., 1934).

Wolffe, B. P., 'The Management of English Royal Estates under the Yorkist Kings', *English Historical Review*, vol. 71, 1956.

Wolffe, B. P., 'Acts of Resumption in the Lancastrian Parliaments, 1399–1456', *English Historical Review*, vol. 73, 1958.

Wolffe, B. P., 'Henry VII's Land Revenues and Chamber Finance', *English Historical Review*, vol. 79, 1964.

Chapter 2
THE LORD TREASURER: 1554–1667

Further reading for this chapter is readily accessible, compact and apparently comprehensive, but it should not conceal the fact that no comparative study of the Treasurership has yet been made. The biographers of the Cecils, for example, have generally skirted the technical problems of their financial administration, and it is only Cranfield whose work has received detailed attention. However, F. C. Dietz and Maurice Ashley provide useful narratives of revenue history, Brian Outhwaite and Robert Ashton illumine the problems of government borrowing and Gerald Aylmer and Joel Hurstfield give valuable portraits of the public service as a whole. The role of financial business in Parliament may be assessed in Sir John Neale's classic studies of the Elizabethan House of Commons.

Ashley, Maurice, *Financial and Commercial Policy under the Cromwellian Protectorate* (London, 1934).

Ashton, Robert, *The Crown and the Money Market, 1603–1640* (Oxford, 1960).

Ashton, Robert, 'Charles I and the City', in Fisher, F. J., *Essays* (as below).

Aylmer, G. E., *The King's Servants: The Civil Service of Charles I, 1625–1642* (London, 1961).

Aylmer, G. E., 'The Officers of the Exchequer, 1625–42', in Fisher, F. J., *Essays* (as below).

Dietz, F. C., *English Government Finance, 1485–1558* (Illinois, 1920).

Dietz, F. C., *English Public Finance, 1558–1641* (American Historical Association, 1932).

Dietz, F. C., 'The Exchequer in Elizabeth's Reign', *Smith College Studies in History* (Northampton, Mass., 1923).

Elton, G. R., 'The Elizabethan Exchequer: War in the Receipt', in *Elizabethan Government and Society: Essays presented to Sir John Neale*, ed. S. T. Bindoff, J. Hurstfield and C. H. Williams (London, 1961).

Fisher, F. J. (ed.), *Essays in the Economic and Social History of Tudor and Stuart England, in Honour of* R. H. *Tawney* (Cambridge, 1961).

Hurstfield, J., *The Queen's Wards: Wardship and Marriage under Elizabeth I* (London, 1958).

Hughes, Edward, *Studies in Administration and Finance, 1558–1825* (Manchester, 1934).

Maccaffery, W. T., 'Place and Patronage in Elizabethan Politics', in *Elizabethan Government and Society* (as above).

Neale, Sir John E., *Elizabeth I and her Parliaments, 1559–81* (London, 1953).

Neale, Sir John E., *Elizabeth I and her Parliaments, 1584–1601* (London, 1957).

Neale, Sir John E., *Essays in Elizabethan History* (London, 1958).

Newton, A. P., 'The Establishment of the Great Farm of the Customs', in *Transactions of the Royal Historical Society*, 4th Series, 1918.

Outhwaite, R. B., 'The Trials of Foreign Borrowing: The English Crown and the Antwerp Money Market in the Mid-Sixteenth Century', in *Economic History Review*, 1966.

Pennington, D. H., 'The Accounts of the Kingdom, 1642–49', in Fisher, F. J., *Essays* (as above).

Prestwich, Menna, *Cranfield, Politics and Profits under the Early Stuarts* (Oxford, 1966).

Scott, W. R., *The Constitution and Finance of English, Scottish and Irish Joint Stock Companies* (1910–12).

Stone, L., 'The Fruits of Office: The Case of Robert Cecil, First Earl of Salisbury, 1596–1612', in Fisher, F. J., *Essays* (as above).

Tawney, R. H., *Business and Politics under James I: Lionel Cranfield as Merchant and Minister* (Cambridge, 1958).

Chapter 3
THE RISE OF THE TREASURY: 1667–1714

It is a pity to recommend secondary works when anyone with access to a large public, or university, library can consult the full text of Treasury Minute Books and the substance of Treasury correspondence in the *Calendar of Treasury Books*, published by H.M.S.O. (1904–61) for the period 1660 to 1718. The editorial introductions by W. A. Shaw should be read with caution: his judgements are often as inaccurate as his arithmetic. But Professor S. B. Baxter has condensed much of this material to produce what is, so far, the only detailed study of the Treasury establishment at any period. Unhappily for the general reader, *The Development of the Treasury, 1660–1702* is written in a vacuum from which political, economic and even fiscal history are deliberately excluded. However, an authoritative history of the public revenue, 1660–88, may soon be published by Professor C. D. Chandaman, and there are useful studies of fiscal administration by Hoon, Hughes and Ward. Numerous books on the Bank of England exist, each with something of value to contribute, and a comprehensive account of the 'financial revolution' has been published recently by P. G. Dickson. The Treasury's role is also set in the broad context of English economic, and political, history by Professors Charles Wilson and J. H. Plumb respectively, and their books provide excellent points of departure for 'further reading'.

I have made extensive use of manuscript sources at the Public Record Office, the British Museum and the Bodleian Library, Oxford, particularly for the career of Sir George Downing, whose biographer skips his Treasury work. For Parliamentary proceedings the most convenient source is W. Cobbett's *Parliamentary History of England*, volumes 4 and 5.

Acres, W. M., *The Bank of England from within*, 2 vols (London, 1931).

Aylmer, G. E., 'Place Bills and the Separation of Powers: Some Seventeenth Century Origins of the Non-Political Civil Service', in *Transactions of the Royal Historical Society*, 5th Series, 1965.

Baxter, S. B., *The Development of the Treasury, 1660–1702* (London, 1957).

Beresford, John, *The Godfather of Downing Street: Sir George Downing, 1623–84* (London, 1925).

Browning, Andrew, *Thomas Osborne, Earl of Danby and Duke of Leeds, 1632–1712*, 3 vols. (1944–51).

Clapham, Sir John, *The Bank of England: A History*, 2 vols (Cambridge, 1944).

Coleman, D. C., *Sir John Banks: A study of business, politics and society in later Stuart England* (Oxford, 1963).

Dickson, P. G. M., *The Financial Revolution in England: A Study in the Development of Public Credit, 1688–1756* (London, 1967).

Hargreaves, E. L., *The National Debt* (London, 1930).

Hoon, E. E., *The Organization of the English Customs System, 1696–1786* (Newton Abbot, 1968), 2nd edn with an introduction by R. C. Jarvis.

Horsefield, J. K., *British Monetary Experiments, 1650–1710* (London, 1960).

Hughes, Edward, *Studies in Administration and Finance, 1558–1825* (Manchester, 1934).

Jacobsen, G. A., *William Blathwayt: a late-seventeenth-century administrator* (New Haven, 1932).

Kennedy, W. C., *English Taxation, 1640–1799: An Essay in Policy and Opinion* (London, 1913).

Leadam, I. S., 'The Finance of Lord Treasurer Godolphin', in *Transactions of the Royal Historical Society*, 3rd Series, 1910.

Letwin, William, *The Origins of Scientific Economics* (London, 1963).

Plumb, J. H., *The Growth of Political Stability in England, 1675–1725* (London, 1967).

Richards, R. D., *The Early History of Banking in England* (London, 1929).

Rogers, J. E. T., *The First Nine Years of the Bank of England* (London, 1887).

Shaw, W. A., 'The Beginnings of the National Debt', in *Historical Essays*, ed. T. F. Tout and J. Tait (1907).

Waddell, D., 'Charles Davenant, 1656–1714: a Biographical Sketch', in *Economic History Review*, 1958–9.

Ward, W. R., *The English Land Tax in the Eighteenth Century* (Oxford, 1953).

Ward, W. R., 'The Office for Taxes, 1665–1798' in *English Historical Review*, vol. 70, 1955.

Wilson, Charles H., *England's Apprenticeship: A Social and Economic History of England, 1603–1763* (London, 1965).

Chapter 4
THE EIGHTEENTH-CENTURY TREASURY: 1714–80

With the work of Sir Lewis Namier and other modern scholars the eighteenth-century Treasury has become best known in its political role, as executed by the Lords of the Treasury and their Secretaries. This has meant the relative neglect of the permanent officials and they have yet to be rescued from their so-called 'facelessness', but the compilation of an authoritative list of all Treasury personnel, 1660–1870, by the Institute of Historical Research (to be published in 1969) should provide useful encouragement. My own account has been based on the manuscript records of the Treasury in the Public Record Office, scattered materials in the British Museum, obituaries in the *Gentleman's Magazine* and other genealogical reference books. The history of the Treasury site can be found illustrated in detail in the *Survey of London, Vol. XIV – Parish of St Margaret's Westminster*, Part 3 (1931). For further reading there are enough books to make it worthwhile listing them separately under the political, administrative and financial aspects of the Treasury's work.

Political Studies:

Brooke, John, *The Chatham Administration, 1766–68* (London, 1956).

Christie, I. R., *The End of the North's Ministry, 1780–82* (London, 1958).

Christie, I. R., 'Economical Reform and "The Influence of the Crown", 1780', in *Cambridge Historical Journal*, vol. 12, 1956.

Foord, A. S., *His Majesty's Opposition, 1714–1830* (Oxford, 1964).

Jucker, N. S. (ed.), *The Jenkinson Papers, 1760–1766* (London, 1949).

Kemp, B., *Sir Francis Dashwood: An Eighteenth-Century Independent* (London, 1967).

Namier, L. B., *The Structure of Politics at the Accession of George III* (London, 1957), 2nd edn.

Namier, L. B., *England in the Age of the American Revolution* (London, 1961), 2nd edn.

Namier, L. B., *Crossroads of Power: Essays on Eighteenth-Century England* (London, 1962).

Namier, L. B. and Brooke, J., *The History of Parliament: The Commons, 1754–90*, 3 vols. (London, 1964).

Namier, L. B. and Brooke, J., *Charles Townshend* (London, 1964).

Owen, J. B., *The Rise of the Pelhams* (London, 1957).

Pares, Richard, *King George III and the Politicians* (Oxford, 1953).

Plumb, J. H., *Sir Robert Walpole: The Making of a Statesman* (London, 1956).

Plumb, J. H., *Sir Robert Walpole: The King's Minister* (London, 1960).

Reitan, E. A., 'The Civil List in Eighteenth-Century British Politics', in *Historical Journal*, 1966.

Riley, P. W. J., *The English Ministers and Scotland, 1707–1727* (London, 1964).

Sutherland, L. S., *The East India Company in Eighteenth-Century Politics* (Oxford, 1952).

Administrative Studies:

Basye, A. H., *Lords Commissioners of Trade and Plantations, 1748–1782* (New Haven, 1925).

Baugh, D. A., *British Naval Administration in the Age of Walpole* (Princeton, 1965).

Binney, J. E. D., *British Public Finance and Administration, 1774–92* (Oxford, 1958).

Clark, D. M., *The Rise of the British Treasury: Colonial Administration in the Eighteenth Century* (Yale, 1960).

Clark, D. M., 'The Office of Secretary to the Treasury in the Eighteenth Century', *American Historical Review*, 1936–7.

Dickerson, O. M., *American Colonial Government, 1696–1765* (Cleveland, 1912).

Ellis, K., *The Post Office in the Eighteenth Century: A study in administrative history* (Oxford, 1958).

Hoon, E. E. (as for Chapter 3).

Hughes, Edward (as for Chapter 3).

Mackesy, P., *The War in America, 1775–1783* (London, 1964).

Pool, B., *Navy Board Contracts, 1660–1832: Contract administration under the Navy Board* (London, 1966).

Spector, M. M., *The American Department of the British Government, 1768–1782* (New York, 1942).

Thomson, M. A., *The Secretaries of State, 1681–1782* (Oxford, 1932).

Ward, W. R., *The English Land Tax in the Eighteenth Century* (Oxford, 1953).

Ward, W. R., 'Some Eighteenth-Century Civil Servants: The English Revenue Commissioners, 1754–98', in *English Historical Review*, 1955.

Economic and Financial Studies:

Ashton, T. S., *Economic Fluctuations in England, 1700–1800* (Oxford, 1959).

Andreades, A., *History of the Bank of England, 1640–1903* (London, 1924).

Dickson, P. G. M., *The Financial Revolution in England . . . 1688–1756* (London, 1967).

Hargreaves, E. L., *The National Debt* (London, 1930).

John, A. H., 'Insurance Investment and the London Money Market of the Eighteenth Century', in *Economica*, New Series, vol. 20, 1953.

Joslin, D. M., 'London Private Bankers, 1720–1785', *Economic History Review*, 1954.

Joslin, D. M., 'London Bankers in Wartime, 1739–84', in *Studies in the Industrial Revolution: Essays presented to T. S. Ashton*, ed. L. S. Pressnell (London, 1960).

Pressnell, L. S., 'The Rate of Interest in the Eighteenth Century', in *Studies in the Industrial Revolution: Essays presented to T. S. Ashton*, ed. L. S. Pressnell (London, 1960).

Sutherland, L. S., 'Samson Gideon and the Reduction of Interest, 1749–50', *Economic History Review*, 1946.

Sutherland, L. S., 'The City of London and the Devonshire–Pitt Administration, 1756–7' (Raleigh Lecture), *Proceedings of the British Academy*, 1960.

Turner, E. R., 'The Excise Scheme of 1733', *English Historical Review*, vol. 42, 1927.

Wilson, C. H., *Anglo-Dutch Commerce and Finance in the Eighteenth Century* (Cambridge, 1941).

Chapter 5
ECONOMICAL AND ADMINISTRATIVE REFORM: 1780–1866

Few readers will share the Victorian passion for Blue Books, but the parliamentary reports of commissions and committees are the most important source for this chapter and I have listed a selection of them first. Secondary works tracing aspects of 'Economical' and administrative reform follow, and I have added a few studies which suggest the bearing of economic theory and financial practice on 'Treasury control', although the Treasury scarcely figures in any of them.

Parliamentary Papers:

House of Commons Journals, vols. 38–42; *Reports from the Commissioners for Examining, Taking and Stating the Public Accounts* (1780–86).

P.P. *Reports from Committees*, First Series, vol. XII (1797–1803), *Select Committee on Finance*, 36 Reports.

P.P. 1806, vol. VII, *Reports from Commissioners for Enquiring into Fees in Public Offices.*

P.P. 1807–12, vol. II; vol. III, *Select Committee on Finance*, 13 Reports.

P.P. 1817, vol. III; vol. IV, *Select Committee on Finance*, 11 Reports.

P.P. 1817, vol. XV, *Proceedings of the Treasury respecting Offices.*

P.P. 1819, vol. II, *Select Committee on Finance*, 5 Reports.

P.P. 1822, vol. XVII, *Treasury Minutes respecting reductions in Civil Offices.*

P.P. 1822, vol. IV, *Select Committee on Public Accounts annually laid before Parliament.*

P.P. 1828, vol. V, *Select Committee on Income and Expenditure*, 4 Reports.

P.P. 1829, vol. VI, *Report of Commissioners appointed to inquire into and state the mode of keeping the Official Accounts in the Principal Departments connected with the Receipts and Expenditure . . .*

P.P. 1831, vol. X, *Report of Commissioners of Public Accounts on the Exchequer.*

P.P. 1831, vol. XIV, *Papers relating to Public Accounts.*

P.P. 1833, vol. XXIII, *Returns relating to Public Offices.*

P.P. 1837, vol. XLIV, *Treasury Committee of Inquiry into Fees and Emoluments.*

P.P. 1844, vol. XXXII, *Treasury Minutes on Book-keeping in Public Departments.*

P.P. 1847–8, vol. XVIII, *Select Committee on Miscellaneous Expenditure.*

P.P. 1851 (Sess. 2) vol. XXIV, *Royal Commission on Civil Superannuation.*

P.P. 1854, vol. XXVII, *Reports of Commissioners of Inquiry into Public Offices.*

P.P. 1856, vol. XV, 1857 (Sess. 1); vol. II, 1857 (Sess. 2); vol. IX, *Select Committee on Public Monies.*

H.C. 154 (1938), *Epitome of the Reports from the Committees of Public Accounts 1857 to 1937.*

Secondary Works on 'Economical' and Administrative Reform:

Binney, J. E. D., *British Public Finance and Administration, 1774–92* (Oxford, 1958).

Christie, I. R., 'Economical Reform and "The Influence of the Crown", 1780', *Cambridge Historical Journal*, vol. XII, 1956.

Christie, I. R., *Wilkes, Wyvill and Reform* (London, 1962).

Chubb, B., *The Control of Public Expenditure* (Oxford, 1952).

Cohen, E. W., *The Growth of the British Civil Service, 1780–1939* (London, 1941).

Einzig, P., *The Control of the Purse* (London, 1959).

Finer, S. E., 'Patronage and the Public Service', *Public Administration*, vol. XXX, 1952.

Foord, A. S., 'The Waning of the Influence of the Crown', *English Historical Review*, vol. 62, 1947.

Keir, D. L., 'Economical Reform', *Law Quarterly Review*, vol. 50, 1934.

Norris, J., *Shelburne and Reform* (London, 1964)

Reid, G., *The Politics of Financial Control* (London, 1966).
Smellie, K. B., *A Hundred Years of English Government* (London, 1950).

Studies in Finance and Economic Theory:

Anderson, O., 'The Administrative Reform Association of 1855', *Victorian Studies*, vol. VIII, 1965.
Ashton, T. S. and Sayers, R. S., *Papers in English Monetary History* (London, 1953).
Brebner, J. B., 'Laissez-faire and State Intervention in Nineteenth Century Britain', *Journal of Economic History*, Supplement, 1948.
Brown, L., *The Board of Trade and the Free Trade Movement, 1830–42* (Oxford, 1958).
Calkins, W. N., 'A Victorian Free Trade Lobby', *Economic History Review*, 1960.
Cannan, E., 'Ricardo in Parliament', *Economic Journal*, 1894.
Checkland, S. G., 'The Birmingham Economists, 1815–50', *Economic History Review*, 1948.
Coates, W. H., 'Benthamism, Laissez-faire and Collectivism', *Journal of the History of Ideas*, 1950.
Corry, B. A., *Money, Saving and Investment in English Economics, 1800–1850* (London, 1962).
Corry, B. A., 'Theory of the Economic Effects of Government Expenditure in Classical Political Economy', *Economica*, 1958.
Cramp, A. B., *Opinion on Bank Rate, 1822–60* (London, 1962).
Fetter, F. W., *Development of British Monetary Orthodoxy, 1797–1875* (Harvard, 1965).
Gordon, S., 'The London *Economist* and the High Tide of Laissez-Faire', *Journal of Political Economy*, 1955.
Grampp, W. D., *The Manchester School of Economics* (Oxford, 1960).
Grampp, W. D., 'On the Politics of the Classical Economists', *Quarterly Journal of Economics*, 1948.
Hawtrey, R. G., *A Century of Bank Rate* (London, 1962), revised edn.
Jarvis, R. C., 'Official Trade and Revenue Statistics', *Economic History Review*, 1964.
Link, R. G., *English Theories of Economic Fluctuations, 1815–48* (Oxford, 1959).
MacDonagh, O., 'The Nineteenth-century Revolution in Government: A Reappraisal', *Historical Journal*, 1958.
Parris, H., 'The Nineteenth-century Revolution in Government: A Reappraisal Reappraised', *Historical Journal*, 1960.
Roberts, D., 'Jeremy Bentham and the Victorian Administrative State', *Victorian Studies*, 1958–9.
Robbins, L., *The Theory of Economic Policy in English Classical Political Economy* (London, 1952).

Chapter 6
THE EVOLUTION OF AN *ÉLITE:* 1805–1914

The account of the Treasury's internal development and of the careers of individual officials is based on the manuscript records of the department – the Minutes, Fee Books, miscellaneous memoranda – at the Public Record Office and the Treasury. This has been supplemented from the usual biographical and genealogical reference works, school and university registers, and from the printed memoirs listed below. Among other manuscript sources the major ones are the Peel and Gladstone papers at the British Museum and the Trevelyan Letter Books at the Bodleian Library, Oxford.

Printed Primary Sources on Treasury and Civil Service Reform include these Parliamentary Papers:

House of Commons Journals, vols. 38–42; *Reports from the Commissioners for Examining . . . the Public Accounts* (1780–86).

P.P. Reports from Committees, First Series, vol. XII (1797–1803), *Select Committee on Finance*, Fifteenth Report.

P.P. *1822*, vol. XVII, *Treasury Minutes respecting Reductions in Civil Offices.*

P.P. *1847–8*, vol. XVIII, *Select Committee on Miscellaneous Expenditure.*

P.P. *1854*, vol. XXVII, *Report on the Organization of the Permanent Civil Service. Reports of Commissioners of Inquiry into Public Offices.*

P.P. *1854–5*, vol. XX, *Reports and Papers relating to the Reorganization of the Civil Service.*

P.P. *1860*, vol. IX, *Select Committee on Civil Service Appointments.*

P.P. *1873*, vol. VII, *Select Committee on Civil Service Expenditure.*

P.P. *1875*, vol. XXIII, *Civil Service Inquiry Commission Reports.*

P.P. *1887*, vol. XIX; *1888*, vol. XXVII; *1889*, vol. XXI; *1890*, vol. XXVII, *Royal Commission on Civil Establishments.*

P.P. *1912–13*, vol. XV; *1914*, vol. XVI, *Royal Commission on the Civil Service.*

Biographies:

A fuller list of biographical material relating to nineteenth-century Treasury officials and ministers is appended to Chapter 7, but those most relevant to this chapter are:

Officials:

Blackwood, Sir Stevenson Arthur, Some Records of the Life of, compiled by a friend and edited by his widow (London, 1896).

Guillemard, Sir Laurence, *Trivial Fond Records* (London, 1937).

Kempe, Sir John Arrow, *Reminiscences of an Old Civil Servant, 1846–1927* (London, 1928).

Kilbracken, Lord, *Reminiscences of Lord Kilbracken* (London, 1931).
Winnifrith, Sir John, 'The Rt. Hon. Sir Alexander Spearman, Bart. (1793–1874)', in *Public Administration*, vol. XXXVIII, 1960.
West, Sir Algernon, *Recollections, 1832 to 1886* (London, 1899).
West, Sir Algernon, *Contemporary Portraits* (London, 1920).
Wilson, Sir Charles Rivers, *Chapters from my Official Life*, ed. Everilda MacAlister (London, 1916).

Ministers:
Baring, Sir Francis (Baron Northbrook), *Journals and Correspondence from 1808 to 1852*, ed. Earl of Northbrook and Hon. Francis Baring, privately printed (Winchester, 1902, 1905).
Barrington, E. I., *The Servant of All. Pages from the Life of . . . James Wilson. Twenty Years of Mid-Victorian Life* (London, 1927).
Childers, E. S. E., *The Life and Correspondence of the Rt Hon. Hugh C. E. Childers, 1827–1896* (London, 1901).
Herries, E., *Memoir of the public life of the Rt Hon J. C. Herries* (London, 1880).
Hammond, J. L. B. and Hammond, L. B., *James Stansfeld* (London, 1932).

Secondary Works Dealing with Phases of Treasury History:
Gray, Denis, *Spencer Perceval: The Evangelical Prime Minister, 1767–1812* (Manchester, 1963).
Hart, Jenifer, 'Sir Charles Trevelyan at the Treasury', *English Historica Review*, vol. 75, 1960.
Hughes, E., 'Civil Service Reform, 1853–5', *History*, June 1942.
Hughes, E., 'Sir Charles Trevelyan and Civil Service Reform, 1853–5', *English Historical Review*, vol. 64, 1949.
Torrance, J. R., 'Sir George Harrison and the growth of bureaucracy in the early nineteenth century', *English Historical Review*, vol. 83, 1968.

In addition to the general accounts of nineteenth-century developments in government by E. W. Cohen and K. B. Smellie (above, Chapter 5) there are som e instructive studies of individual departments:
R. B. Pugh, 'The Colonial Office, 1801–1925', *Cambridge History of the British Empire*, vol. III, Chapter 19.
R. T. Nightingale, 'The Personnel of the British Foreign Office and Diplomatic Service, 1851–1929', *The Realist*, December 1929.
Young, D. M., *The Colonial Office in the Early Nineteenth Century* (London, 1961).

The Colonial Office also produced the most illuminating contemporary treatise on the internal management of a government department – *The*

Statesman, by Sir Henry Taylor, published in 1836. A modern edition has been edited by Professor C. Northcote Parkinson.

Chapter 7
THE VICTORIAN TREASURY AND ITS MASTERS

As a compromise with the vast range of potential 'further reading' on nineteenth-century government and the economy, I am listing here only the biographical material on Treasury officials and ministers, together with a selection of works on finance. For the general reader, S. G. Checkland's *The Rise of Industrial Society in England, 1815–1885* (1964) and W. Ashworth's *An Economic History of England, 1870–1939* (1961) provide excellent introductions to the social and economic context. At the time of writing, no secondary study has paid any special attention to the Treasury in the nineteenth century, but forthcoming publications by Roy MacLeod on the Local Government Board, Maurice Wright on the Civil Service and Henry Parris on central government since 1780 promise to redress the balance. The manuscript sources used include the general body of Treasury papers at the Public Record Office and ministerial collections at the British Museum, notably Gladstone's. Of particular importance are the diaries of Sir Edward Hamilton (54 volumes) at the British Museum and over fifty volumes of his official papers at the Public Record Office. The parliamentary papers are essentially the same as those listed for Chapter 6.

Biographies

Treasury Officials and Private Secretaries:

Blackwood, Sir Stevenson Arthur, Some Records of the Life of, compiled by a friend and edited by his widow (London, 1896).

Braithwaite, W. J., *Lloyd George's Ambulance Waggon; the Memoirs of W. J. Braithwaite, 1911–12*, ed. Sir H. N. Bunbury (London, 1957).

Gower, Sir George Granville Leveson, *Years of Content, 1858–1886* (London, 1940).

Guillemard, Sir Laurence, *Trivial Fond Records* (London, 1937).

Hamilton, Sir Edward, *Mr Gladstone: a monograph* (London, 1898).

Headlam, M. F., *A Holiday Fisherman* (London, 1949).

Headlam, M. F., *Irish Reminiscences* (London, 1947).

Headlam, M. F., 'Sir Thomas Little Heath', *Proceedings of the British Academy*, vol. XXVI, 1941.

Kempe, Sir John Arrow, *Reminiscences of an Old Civil Servant, 1846–1927* (London, 1928).

Kilbracken, Lord, *Reminiscences of Lord Kilbracken* (London, 1931).

Matheson, P. E., 'Lord Chalmers, 1858–1938', *Proceedings of the British Academy*, vol. XXV, 1940.
West, Sir Algernon, *Recollections, 1832 to 1886* (London, 1899).
West, Sir Algernon, *Contemporary Portraits* (London, 1920).
West, Sir Algernon, *Private Diaries*, ed. H. G. Hutchinson (London, 1922).
Wilson, Sir Charles Rivers, *Chapters from my Official Life*, ed. Everilda MacAlister (London 1916).
Wrench, Sir Evelyn, *Alfred Milner: The Man of No Illusions, 1854–1925* (London, 1958).

Treasury Ministers:
Asquith, H. H., Earl of Oxford, *Memories and Reflections* (London, 1928).
Baring, Sir Francis (Baron Northbrook), *Journals and Correspondence, 1808 to 1852*, ed. Earl of Northbrook and Hon. Francis Baring, privately printed (Winchester, 1902, 1905).
Barrington, E. I., *Servant of All. Pages from the Life of . . . James Wilson. Twenty Years of Mid-Victorian Life* (London, 1927).
Blake, Robert, *Disraeli* (London, 1966).
Cecil, Lady Gwendolen, *Life of Robert, Marquis of Salisbury* (London, 1921).
Childers, E. S. E., *The Life and Correspondenc' of the Rt Hon. Hugh C. E. Childers, 1827–1896* (London, 1901).
Chilston, E. A. Akers-Douglas, 3rd Viscoun *Chief Whip: The Political Life and Times of Aretas Akers-Douglas, 1st Viscount Chilston* (London, 1961).
Chilston, E. A. Akers-Douglas, 3rd Viscount, *W. H. Smith* (London, 1965).
Churchill, Winston S., *Lord Randolph Churchill* (London, 1906).
Elliot, Hon. A. R. D., *The Life of George Joachim Goschen* (London, 1911).
Erickson, A. B., 'Edward T. Cardwell: Peelite', *Transactions of the American Philosophical Society*, New Series, vol. 49, Part 2, 1959.
Gardiner, A. G., *The Life of Sir William Harcourt*, 2 vols. (London, 1923).
Gollin, A. M., *Balfour's Burden. Arthur Balfour and Imperial Preference* (London, 1965).
Gooch, G. P., *The Later Correspondence of Lord John Russell, 1840–78* (London, 1925).
Gooch, G. P., *The Life of Lord Courtney* (London, 1920).
Hammond, J. L. B. and Hammond, L. B., *James Stansfeld* (London, 1932).
Hicks-Beach, Victoria A. H., *Life of Sir Michael Hicks-Beach, Earl St Aldwyn* (London, 1932).
James, Robert Rhodes, *Lord Randolph Churchill* (London, 1959).
James, Robert Rhodes, *Rosebery, A Biography of Archibald Philip, Fifth Earl of Rosebery* (London, 1963).
Jenkins, Roy, *Asquith* (London, 1964).

Jones, Tom, *Lloyd George* (London, 1951).

Kennedy, A. L., *Salisbury, 1830–1903: portrait of a statesman* (London, 1953).

Lang, Andrew, *Life, Letters and Diaries of Sir Stafford Northcote, First Earl of Iddesleigh* (London, 1890).

Le Marchant, Sir D., *Memoir of John Charles, Viscount Althorp, Third Earl Spencer* (London, 1876).

Lewis, G. C., *Letters of the Rt Hon. Sir G. C. Lewis*, ed. Sir G. F. Lewis (London, 1870).

Martin, A. P., *Life and Letters of Robert Lowe, Viscount Sherbrooke* (London, 1893).

McKenna, S., *Reginald McKenna, 1863–1943: A Memoir* (London, 1948).

Morley, John, *Life of William Ewart Gladstone* (London, 1905).

Owen, F., *Tempestuous Journey: Lloyd George, His Life and Times* (London, 1954).

Parker, C. S., *Sir Robert Peel from his Private Papers* (London, 1899).

Russell, Lord John, *Recollections and Suggestions, 1813–73* (London, 1875).

Stansky, Peter, *Ambitions and Strategies: The Struggle for the leadership of the Liberal Party in the 1890s* (Oxford, 1964).

Studies in Nineteenth-Century Finance:

Anderson, O., 'Loans versus Taxes: British Financial Policy in the Crimean War', *Economic History Review*, 1963.

Ashton, T. S. and Sayers, R. S., *Papers in English Monetary History* (London, 1953).

Bagehot, Walter, *Lombard Street* (1873).

Bastable, C. F., *Public Finance* (London, 1892).

Brown, L., *The Board of Trade and the Free Trade Movement, 1830–42* (Oxford, 1958).

Bruce, M., *The Coming of the Welfare State* (London, 1961).

Buxton, S. C., *Finance and Politics: An Historical Study, 1783–1885* (London, 1888).

Checkland, S. G., 'The Mind of the City, 1870–1914', *Oxford Economic Papers*, 1957.

Chubb, Basil, *The Control of Public Expenditure* (Oxford, 1952).

Clapham, Sir John, *The Bank of England: A History, 1694–1914*, vol. 2 (Cambridge, 1944).

Corlett, J., *A Survey of the Financial Aspects of Elementary Education* (London, 1929).

Durell, A. J. V., *The Principles and Practice of the System of Control over Parliamentary Grants* (Portsmouth and London, 1917).

Eaglesham, E., *From School Board to Local Authority* (London, 1956).

Feavearyear, Sir A. E., *The Pound Sterling. A History of English Money* (Oxford, 1931).

Fetter, F. W., *Development of British Monetary Orthodoxy, 1797–1875* (Harvard, 1965).

Finer, S. E. and Maud, Sir John, *Local Government in England and Wales* (London, 1952).

Fisk, H. E., *English Public Finance from 1688* (London, 1921).

Giffen, Sir Robert, *Essays in Finance* (London, 1880, 1886).

Grice, J. W., *National and Local Finance* (London, 1896).

Hargreaves, E. L., *The National Debt* (London, 1930).

Hawtrey, R. G., *A Century of Bank Rate* (London, 1962).

Hennock, E. P., 'Finance and Politics in Urban Local Government, 1835–1900', *Historical Journal*, 1963.

Hicks, U. K., *British Public Finances, 1880–1952* (Oxford, 1954).

Hirst, F. W., *Gladstone as Financier and Economist* (London, 1931).

Horne, H. O., *A History of Savings Banks* (Oxford, 1947).

Hughes, J. R. T., *Fluctuations in Trade, Industry and Finance: A Study in British Economic Development, 1850–1860* (Oxford, 1960).

Hyde, F. E., *Mr Gladstone at the Board of Trade* (London, 1934).

Jevons, W. S., *Investigations in Currency and Finance* (London, 1909).

King, W. T. C., *A History of the London Discount Market* (London, 1936).

Mallet, Sir Bernard, *British Budgets, 1887–8 to 1912–13* (London, 1913).

Morgan, E. V., *The Theory and Practice of Central Banking, 1797–1913* (Cambridge, 1943).

Northcote, Sir Stafford, *Twenty Years of Financial Policy* (London, 1862).

Palgrave, R. H. I., *Bank Rate and the Money Market, 1844–1900* (London, 1903).

Parnell, Sir Henry, *On Financial Reform* (London, 1830).

Peacock, A. T. and Wiseman, J., *The Growth of Public Expenditure in the United Kingdom* (London, 1961).

Porter, G. R., *The Progress of the Nation* (1836, 1838, 1847, 1851, 1912 edns).

Rees, Sir James F., *A Short Fiscal and Financial History of England, 1815–1918* (London, 1921).

Robinson, H., *The British Post Office. A History* (Princeton, 1948).

Rostow, W. W., *The British Economy of the Nineteenth Century* (Oxford, 1948).

Sabine, B. E. V., *A History of Income Tax* (London, 1966).

Sayers, R. S. (ed.), *The Economic Writings of James Pennington* (London, 1963).

Shehab, F., *Progressive Taxation. A Study in the Development of the Progressive Principle in the British Income Tax* (Oxford, 1953).

Chapter 8
THE TREASURY IN WAR AND PEACE: 1914–47

Memoirs, biographies and other studies which shed light on the Treasury, its ministers and officials:

Beaverbrook, Lord, *Politicians and the War, 1914–1916* (London, 1928).

Beaverbrook, Lord, *Men and Power, 1917–1918* (London, 1956).

Blake, R., *The Unknown Prime Minister: The Life and Times of Andrew Bonar Law, 1858–1923* (London, 1955).

Boyle, A., *Montagu Norman. A Biography* (London, 1967).

Bridges, Lord, *The Treasury* (London, 1964), 2nd edn 1966.

Chamberlain, Austen, *Down the Years* (London, 1935).

Clay, Sir Henry, *Lord Norman* (London, 1957).

Cooke, C., *The Life of Sir Richard Stafford Cripps* (London, 1957).

Cross, C. *Philip Snowden* (London, 1966).

Dalton, Hugh, *High Tide and After. Memoirs 1945–1960* (London, 1962).

Grigg, P. J., *Prejudice and Judgment* (London, 1948).

Hamilton, Sir H. P., 'Sir Warren Fisher and the Public Service', *Public Administration*, vol. XXIX, spring 1951.

Harrod, R. F., *The Life of John Maynard Keynes* (London, 1951).

Heath, Sir Thomas L., *The Treasury* (London, 1927).

Jones, Tom, *A Diary with Letters, 1931–1950* (London, 1954).

Leith-Ross, Sir Frederick, *Money Talks* (London, 1968).

MacFadyean, Sir Andrew, *Recollected in Tranquillity* (London, 1964).

McKenna, S., *Reginald McKenna, 1863–1943. A Memoir* (London, 1948).

Raymond, J. (ed.), *The Baldwin Age* (London, 1960).

Snowden, Philip (Viscount Snowden), *An Autobiography*, 2 vols. (London, 1934).

Watt, D. C., 'Sir Warren Fisher and Rearmament', *Personalities and Policies* (London, 1965).

The following works provide general surveys of the economic and administrative developments covered in this chapter:

Ashworth, W., *An Economic History of England, 1870–1939* (Oxford, 1960).

Chester, D. N. (ed.) and Willson, F. M. G., *The Organization of British Central Government, 1914–1956* (London, 1957).

Daalder, Hans, *Cabinet Reform in Britain, 1914–1963* (London, 1964).

Hicks, U. K., *British Public Finances: their structure and development, 1880–1952* (Oxford, 1954).

Hicks, U. K., *The Finance of British Government, 1920–1936* (London, 1938).

Mowat, C. L., *Britain Between the Wars, 1918–1940* (London, 1956).

Pollard, S., *The Development of the British Economy, 1914–1950* (London, 1962).

Taylor, A. J. P., *English History, 1914–1945* (Oxford, 1965).
Youngson, A. J., *The British Economy, 1920–1957* (London, 1960).

Other monographs on aspects of economic and administrative policy:
Anderson, Sir John, *The Organization of Economic Studies in Relation to the Problems of Government* (Stamp Memorial Lecture) (London, 1947).
Anderson, Sir John, *Administrative Techniques in the Public Service* (Haldane Memorial Lecture) (London, 1949).
Blackett, Sir Basil P., 'The Era of Planning', in G. R. S. Taylor (ed.), *Great Events in History* (London, 1934).
Chester, D. N., 'The Central Machinery for Economic Policy', *Lessons of the British War Economy* (Cambridge, 1951).
Chubb, B., *The Control of Public Expenditure* (Oxford, 1952).
Colvin, I., *Vansittart in Office* (London, 1965).
Dale, H. E., *The Higher Civil Service of Great Britain* (London, 1941).
Dodwell, D. W., *Treasuries and Central Banks, especially in England and the United States* (London, 1934).
Einzig, P., *The Control of the Purse* (London, 1959).
Einzig, P., *In the Centre of Things. Autobiography* (London, 1960).
Franks, O., *Central Planning and Control in War and Peace* (London, 1947).
Gardner, R. N., *Sterling-Dollar Diplomacy* (Oxford, 1956).
Gilbert, M. J. and Gott, R. W., *The Appeasers* (London, 1963).
Hall, Sir Noel F., *The Exchange Equalisation Account* (London, 1935).
Hancock, K. J., 'The Reduction of Unemployment as a Problem of Public Policy, 1920–29', *Economic History Review*, Second Series, vol. XV, 1962.
Hancock, K. J., 'Unemployment and the Economists in the 1920's', *Economica*, vol. XXXVII, 1960.
Hancock, Sir W. K. and Gowing, M. M., *British War Economy* (History of the Second World War: United Kingdom Civil Series) (London, 1949).
Harris, S. E., *Monetary Problems of the British Empire* (New York, 1931).
Hawtrey, R. G., *Currency and Credit* (London, 1919).
Hawtrey, R. G., *The Exchequer and the Control of Expenditure* (London, 1921).
Hawtrey, R. G., *Monetary Reconstruction* (London, 1923).
Hawtrey, R. G., *The Gold Standard in Theory and Practice* (London, 1927).
Hawtrey, R. G., *Trade and Credit* (London, 1928).
Hawtrey, R. G., *Trade Depression and the Way Out* (London, 1931).
Henderson, Sir Hubert, *The Inter-War Years and other papers*, ed. Sir Henry Clay (Oxford, 1955).
Higgs, H., *The Financial System of the United Kingdom* (London, 1914).
Higgs, H., *Financial Reform* (London, 1924).
Hodson, H. V., *Slump and Recovery, 1929–1937* (London, 1938).

Humphreys, B. V., *Clerical Unions in the Civil Service* (Oxford, 1958).
Hurwitz, S. J., *State Intervention in Great Britain . . . 1914–1919* (New York, 1949).
Jones, J. H., *Josiah Stamp, Public Servant* (London, 1964).
Kelsall, R. K., *Higher Civil Servants in Britain, 1870 to the present day* (London, 1955).
Keynes, J. M., *The Economic Consequences of the Peace* (London, 1919).
Keynes, J. M., *A Tract on Monetary Reform* (London, 1923).
Keynes, J. M., *The Economic Consequences of Mr Churchill* (London, 1925).
Keynes, J. M., *A Treatise on Money* (London, 1930).
Keynes, J. M., *Essays in Persuasion* (London, 1931, 1951).
Keynes, J. M., *Essays in Biography* (London, 1933).
Keynes, J. M., *The General Theory of Employment, Interest and Money* (London, 1936).
Lewis, W. A., *Economic Survey, 1919–1939* (London, 1949).
Lloyd George, D., *War Memoirs* (London, 1933–6).
Lloyd, E. M. H., *Experiments in State Control* (Oxford, 1924).
MacFadyean, Sir A., *Reparation Reviewed* (London, 1930).
Mackintosh, J. P., *The British Cabinet* (London, 1962).
Mallet, Sir B. and George, C. O., *British Budgets, Second Series, 1913–14 to 1920–21* (London, 1929).
Mallet, Sir B. and George, C. O., *British Budgets, Third Series, 1921–22 to 1932–33* (London, 1933).
Marwick, A., 'Middle Opinion in the "Thirties": Planning, Progress and Political "Agreement",' *English Historical Review*, 1964.
Morgan, E. V., *Studies in British Financial Policy, 1914–25* (London, 1952).
Morrison, H., *Government and Parliament. A Survey from the Inside* (London, 1954).
Morton, W. A., *British Finance, 1930–1940* (Madison, 1943).
Nevin, E. T., *The Mechanism of Cheap Money. A Study of British Monetary Policy, 1931–1939* (Cardiff, 1955).
Pigou, A. C., *Aspects of British Economic History, 1918–25* (London, 1947).
Richardson, H. W., 'The Basis of Economic Recovery in the Nineteen Thirties. A Review and New Interpretation', *Economic History Review*, 1962.
Richardson, H. W., *Economic Recovery in Britain, 1932–9* (London, 1967).
Salter, Lord, *Memoirs of a Public Servant* (London, 1961).
Sayers, R. S., *Financial Policy, 1939–45* (History of the Second World War, United Kingdom Civil Series) (London, 1956).
Sayers, R. S., 'The Return to Gold, 1925', in *Studies in the Industrial Revolution*, ed. L. S. Pressnell (London, 1960).
Scott, J. D. and Hughes, R., *The Administration of War Production* (London, 1955).

Skidelsky, R., *Politicians and the Slump. The Labour Government of 1929–1931* (London, 1967).

Waight, L., *The History and Mechanism of the Exchange Equalisation Account* (Cambridge, 1939).

Wheeler-Bennett, J., *John Anderson, Viscount Waverly* (London, 1962).

Chapter 9
THE TREASURY AND THE POST-WAR ECONOMY: 1947–68

I could not hope in this chapter to give a detailed account, at one and the same time, of the internal organization of the Treasury, the working of the financial system, the development of the modern British economy and the political context in which it has been managed. For that reason, a handful of books – by Bridges, Brittain, Brittan and Dow – is not simply desirable 'further reading' but essential *preliminary* reading for anyone anxious to master the administrative and economic context within which the Treasury has recently evolved. Fortunately, the last twenty years have been remarkably well served by commentators, and there is no need to draw the line with these four. I have disposed a selection of books, articles and official reports under fairly arbitrary categories to reflect the main themes of my chapter, and have added material which has appeared since the time of writing.

The Treasury and the Civil Service:

Armstrong, Sir William, 'The Tasks of the Civil Service', *Public Administration*, vol. 47, spring 1969.

Beer, S. H., *Treasury Control. The co-ordination of financial and economic policy in Great Britain* (Oxford, 1956).

Bridges, Lord, *The Treasury* (London, 1966) 2nd edn.

Brittan, Samuel, *The Treasury under the Tories, 1951–1964* (Harmondsworth, 1964).

Brown, R. G. S., 'Organization Theory and Civil Service Reform', *Public Administration*, vol. 43, autumn 1965.

Chester, D. N., 'The Treasury, 1962', *Public Administration*, vol. 40, winter 1962.

Civil Service, Committee on the ('Fulton') 1968 Cmnd 3638. vol. 1, Report; vol. 2, Report of a Management Consultancy Group; vol. 3, Surveys and investigations; vol. 4, Factual, statistical and explanatory papers; vol. 5, Proposals and opinions.

Dodd, C. H. 'Recruitment to the Administrative Class, 1960–64', *Public Administration*, vol. 45, spring 1967.

Estimates Committee, Sixth Report, Session 1957–8, 'Treasury Control of Expenditure'.

Estimates Committee, Fifth Report, Session 1963–4, 'Treasury Control of Establishments'.

Estimates Committee, Sixth Report, Session 1964–5, 'Recruitment to the Civil Service'.

Fabian Group, *The Administrators: The Reform of the Civil Service*, Fabian Tract 355, (London, 1964).

Gunn, L. A., 'Ministers and Civil Servants: Changes in Whitehall', *Public Administration: Journal of the Australian Regional Groups of the R.I.P.A.*, vol. 26, March 1967.

Keeling, C. D. E., 'The Treasury Centre for Administrative Studies', *Public Administration*, vol. 43, summer 1965.

Mallaby, Sir George, 'The Civil Service Commission', *Public Administration*, vol. 42, spring 1964.

Morton, W. W., 'The Management Functions of the Treasury', *Public Administration*, vol. 41, spring 1963.

Nairne, P. D., 'Management in the Administrative Class', *Public Administration*, vol. 42, summer 1964.

Pickering, J. F., 'Recruitment to the Administrative Class, 1960–64', *Public Administration*, vol. 45, summer 1967.

Public Administration, (special issues):

vol. 41, spring 1963, 'The Plowden Report'.

vol. 43, autumn 1965, 'Who are the Policy Makers?'.

vol. 44, spring 1966, 'The Machinery for Economic Planning'.

vol. 47, spring 1969, 'The Fulton Report'.

Recruitment to the Administrative Class, 1957, Cmnd 232.

Woods, Sir John, 'Treasury Control', in *The Civil Service in Britain and France*, ed. W. A. Robson (London, 1956).

Finance and Public Expenditure:

Abramovitz, M. and Eliasberg, V. F., *The Growth of Public Employment in Great Britain* (London, 1957).

Artis, M. J., *Foundations of British Monetary Policy* (Oxford, 1965).

Brandon, Henry, *In the Red: the struggle for Sterling, 1964–66* (London, 1966).

Bridges, Sir Edward, 'Treasury Control', Stamp Memorial Lecture, 1950 (London, 1950).

Brittain, Sir Herbert, *The British Budgetary System* (London, 1959).

Caulcott, T. H. 'The Control of Public Expenditure', *Public Administration*, vol. 40, autumn 1962.

Chapman, R. A., 'The Bank Rate Decision of 19th September 1957', *Public Administration*, vol. 43, summer 1965.

Clarke, Sir Richard, 'The Management of the Public Sector of the National Economy', Stamp Memorial Lecture, 1964 (London, 1964).

Clarke, Sir Richard, 'The Public Sector', *Public Administration*, vol. 44, spring 1966.

Collins, E. A. 'The Price of Financial Control', *Public Administration*, vol. 40, autumn 1962.

Collins, E. A. 'Inflation and Public Expenditure', *Public Administration*, vol. 46, winter 1968.

Einzig, Paul, *Control of the Purse* (London, 1959).

Feldstein, M. S., 'Cost-Benefit Analysis and Investment in the Public Sector', *Public Administration*, vol. 42, winter 1964.

Monetary System, Committee on the Working of ('Radcliffe') 1959, Cmnd 827. Report (1 vol.); Minutes (1 vol.); Principal Memoranda (3 vols.).

Normanton, E. L., *The Accountability and Audit of Governments: A comparative study* (Manchester, 1966).

O & M Bulletin, H.M. Treasury, 'A Quantitative Assessment of O & M Work', Supplement, May 1965; 'A Second Quantitative Assessment of O & M Work', Supplement, May 1967; 'Progress in Treasury O & M', February 1968; 'History of O & M in the United Kingdom', August 1968.

Peston, M., 'On the Nature and Extent of the Public Sector', *Three Banks Review*, No. 67, September 1965.

Peacock, A. T. and Robertson, D. J., *Public Expenditure – Appraisal and Control* (London, 1963).

Peacock, A. T. and Wiseman, J., *The Growth of Public Expenditure in the United Kingdom* (London, 1967), 2nd edn.

Public Expenditure, Control of, 1961, Cmnd 1432 (London, 1961).

Public Expenditure: Planning and Control, 1966, Cmnd 2915 (London, 1966).

Public Expenditure: A New Presentation, 1969, Cmnd 4017 (London, 1969).

Reid, Gordon, *The Politics of Financial Control* (London, 1966).

The Management of the Economy:

Armstrong, Sir William, 'Some Practical Problems in Demand Management', Stamp Memorial Lecture, 1968 (London, 1969).

Blackaby, F., 'Economic Policy in the United Kingdom, 1949 to 1961', in *Economic Policy in Our Time*, vol. 2 (Amsterdam, 1964).

Brittan, S., 'Inquest on Planning in Britain', *Planning*, vol. 33, January 1967.

Cairncross, Sir A., 'The Work of an Economic Adviser', *Public Administration*, vol. 46, spring 1968.

Caves, R. and associates, *Britain's Economic Prospects*, (London, 1968).

Clarke, R. W. B., 'The Formulation of Economic Policy', *Public Administration*, vol. 41, spring 1963.

Dow, J. C. R., *The Management of the British Economy, 1945–60* (Cambridge, 1965).

Harrod, Sir Roy, 'Problems of Planning for Economic Growth in a Mixed Economy', *Economic Journal*, March 1965.
Macrae, N., *Sunshades in October* (London, 1963).
Polanyi, G., *Planning in Britain: the Experience of the 1960s* (London, 1967).
Pollard, S., *The Development of the British Economy, 1914–68* (London, 1969).
Postan, M. M., 'A Plague of Economists?', *Encounter*, vol. 30, January 1968.
Robinson, E. A. G., *Economic Planning in the United Kingdom: Some Lessons* (Cambridge, 1967).
Shanks, M., *The Stagnant Society* (London, 1961).
Shonfield, A., *British Economic Policy Since the War* (London, 1958).
Worswick, G. D. N. and Ady, P. H., *The British Economy in the 1950s* (Oxford, 1962).
Youngson, A. J., *Britain's Economic Growth, 1920–1966* (London, 1967).

Parliament and the Machinery of Government:
Butt, R., *The Power of Parliament* (London, 1967).
Chapman, Brian, *British Government Observed* (London, 1963).
Chester, D. N. and Willson, F. M. G., *The Organization of British Central Government, 1914–64* (London, 1968).
Daalder, Hans, *Cabinet Reform in Britain 1914–63* (London, 1964).
Johnson, Nevil, *Parliament and Administration: the Estimates Committee, 1945–65* (London, 1966).
Mackintosh, J. P., *The British Cabinet* (London, 1968), 2nd edn.
Nicholson, Max, *The System* (London, 1967).
Sampson, A., *The Anatomy of Britain* (London, 1967), 2nd edn.
Shore, Peter, *Entitled to Know* (London, 1966).
Stankiewicz, W. J. (ed.), *Crisis in British Government: The Need for Reform* (London, 1967).
Thomas, Hugh (ed.), *The Establishment* (London, 1959).
Thomas, Hugh (ed.), *Crisis in the Civil Service* (London, 1969).
Whitehall and Beyond, B.B.C. Publications (London, 1964).

Index